WENDELL PHILLIPS, SOCIAL JUSTICE, AND THE POWER OF THE PAST

ANTISLAVERY, ABOLITION, AND THE ATLANTIC WORLD

R. J. M. Blackett and James Brewer Stewart, Series Editors

WENDELL PHILLIPS SOCIAL JUSTICE AND THE POWER OF THE PAST

EDITED BY A J AISÉIRITHE AND DONALD YACOVONE

LOUISIANA STATE UNIVERSITY PRESS
BATON ROUGE

Published by Louisiana State University Press

Manufactured in the United States of America
First printing

Cover illustration. Wendell Phillips (1811–1884), likely by Edwin Tryon Billings, oil on canvas, 75.2 x 62.3 cm., ca. 1880. Originally owned by Oliver Wendell Holmes, Jr., and given to the Massachusetts Historical Society by his will. Collection of the Massachusetts Historical Society.

Frontispiece: Wendell Phillips by Mathew Brady, 1853–1860. Courtesy of the Library of Congress.

DESIGNER: Michelle A. Neustrom
TYPEFACE: Whitman
PRINTER AND BINDER: Maple Press (Digital)

LIBRARY OF CONGRESS CATALOGING-IN-PUBLICATION DATA

Names: Aiséirithe, A J, editor. | Yacovone, Donald, editor.
Title: Wendell Phillips, social justice, and the power of the past / edited by A J Aiséirithe and Donald Yacovone.
Description: Baton Rouge : Louisiana State University Press, 2016. | Series: Antislavery, abolition, and the Atlantic world | Includes bibliographical references and index.
Identifiers: LCCN 2016012818| ISBN 978-0-8071-6403-7 (cloth : alk. paper) | ISBN 978-0-8071-6404-4 (pdf) | ISBN 978-0-8071-6405-1 (epub) | ISBN 978-0-8071-6406-8 (mobi)
Subjects: LCSH: Phillips, Wendell, 1811–1884. | Abolitionists—Massachusetts—Biography. | Antislavery movements—United States.
Classification: LCC E449.P56 W46 2016 | DDC 326/.8092—dc23
LC record available at http://lccn.loc.gov/2016012818

The paper in this book meets the guidelines for permanence and durability of the Committee on Production Guidelines for Book Longevity of the Council on Library Resources. ♾

FOR

Joe and Peggy

AND

Mary E. Yacovone

CONTENTS

ACKNOWLEDGMENTS

Perry Miller once described the work of a historian as akin to that of a "lone wolf" who grinds away in a solitary study excavating the past. He imagined that the great ones, if they caught sight of one another on campus, acted like battleships of separate sovereigns with nothing in common exchanging distant salutes in mid-ocean. We cannot imagine inhabiting that world. As historians we spend enormous time alone with our thoughts and the evidence of things past, but artful scholarship would remain elusive without the assistance and guidance of our colleagues and so many librarians, archivists, and other professionals. In this kind of an enterprise we owe the greatest debt to our fellow contributors who showed remarkable patience and resilience in what must have seemed like an interminable process. We could not be more grateful. Their excavations of the life of Wendell Phillips are as inspiring as they are insightful. We also owe an enormous debt to series editors Richard Blackett and James Brewer Stewart, especially to Jim. His experience, wisdom, dedication, and unequaled knowledge of Wendell Phillips and the antislavery movement shaped every aspect of our work. There is good reason why Jim's colleagues refer to him as the "dean of antislavery studies" and without him our book would have been impossible.

Coeditor A J Aiséirithe first conceived and led the effort to reinvigorate Wendell Phillips's place in history and memory. In 2011, she organized the three-day Wendell Phillips Bicentennial Commemoration, which took place at the Harvard Law School and brought together an international group of scholars and speakers to explore Phillips's indispensable role in the abolition of slavery, the promotion of women's and immigrant rights, his foray into electoral politics during the Civil War, his much forgotten work on behalf of workers—male and female, white and black—his campaign against unrestrained and unregulated capitalism, and the influence he exerted long after his death. For their help in making the Phillips Commemoration happen, we are both deeply indebted to James Brewer Stewart, emeritus of Macalester College, Harvard

University's John Stauffer, Dan McKanan at the Harvard Divinity School, and particularly David Harris, Managing Director of the Harvard Law School's Charles Hamilton Houston Institute for Race and Justice. He is a leader and a terrific colleague. We also could not have staged that event without the indispensable contributions of Rev. Dr. Terasa Cooley, Rev. Dorothy Emerson, Dean Grodzins, Paul Marcus of Community Change, Horace Seldon of the National Park Service in Boston, Peter Accardo of the Houghton Library, Robin De Blosi at Old South Meeting House, Deborah Cunningham at Primary Source, Pleun Bouricius at Mass Humanities, and the generous support of Harvard University's Faculty of Arts and Sciences, Harvard Divinity School, the Houghton Library, and Mass Humanities. Without them all no conference would have happened and no book could have been imagined.

Many of our academic colleagues also provided indispensable knowledge, advice, and support for this book, and we are so very appreciative, especially to Mary Ann Calo; Carol Faulkner; Roy Finkenbine; Paul Finkelman; Henry Louis Gates, Jr.; Lori Ginzberg; Allen Guelzo; David Harris; Stephen Kantrowitz; Roger Nichols; Marilyn Richardson; John Stauffer; and Elizabeth Varon. We also owe a debt of thanks to Oona Beauchard, Hobson Woodward, and Mary E. Yacovone of the Massachusetts Historical Society; Khadijah J. Brown, Director, Facilities Management, and Barbara Connolly, Special Assistant to the Superintendent, Boston Public Schools; Sheldon Cheek, Pablo Gonzales, and Tom Wolejko of Harvard's Hutchins Center; Joice Himawan, director of Abington's Dyer Memorial Library; Bruce Kirby, Manuscript Division, Library of Congress; Ryan McNabb of the Boston African American National Historic Site; AnnaLee Pauls, Rare Books and Special Collections, Princeton University Library; and Kim Tenney, Fine Arts Reference Librarian, Boston Public Library. In Minneapolis, Susan Weir and Jonathan Miller provided crucial assistance.

WENDELL PHILLIPS, SOCIAL JUSTICE, AND THE POWER OF THE PAST

INTRODUCTION

Tribune of the People

DONALD YACOVONE

> Nothing but Freedom, Justice, and Truth is of any permanent advantage to the mass of mankind.
>
> —WENDELL PHILLIPS, "Public Opinion" (1852)

> I confess that the only fear I have in regard to republican institutions is whether, in our day, any adequate remedy will be found for this incoming flood of the power of incorporated wealth.
>
> —WENDELL PHILLIPS, "The Foundation of the Labor Movement" (1871)

> Although the conventions of popular government are still preserved, capital is at least as absolute as under the Caesars, and, among capitalists, the money-lenders form an aristocracy.
>
> —BROOKS ADAMS, *The Law of Civilization and Decay* (1896)

The 1915 installation of the Wendell Phillips statue in Boston's grand Public Garden inspired a local commentator to observe that, "When all is said, it is the last part of his life that is the most remarkable. Most men's minds freeze at 40. Most fighters tire at 50. The rest are glad to call it off at 60. But at 70 Phillips was still going strong, and just as unacceptable to the foes of human liberty as he had been at 25."[1] Phillips had become more than just the nation's leading "public man," with "his name, his utterances, [and] his acts . . . constantly recorded in the newspapers," as his early biographers wrote. He seemed providential, sent by the future into the past as an indispensable model.[2] But, Janus-like, Phillips also proved an imminent figure—even envisioning modern email: "If I live forty years I expect to see a telegraph that will send messages without wires and both ways at the same time." More to the point, his support for civil rights and denunciations of corporate wealth made him, as Louis Filler wrote fifty years ago, "an arrow to the future which extends its flight into our very own era."[3]

Wendell Phillips matters. While other activists achieved renown, none equaled his nor did they exert so profound an influence for so long. Born in 1811 to the bluest of Boston blue bloods, he traced his lineage to Massachusetts's founding families. His father, John Phillips, the city's first mayor, ensconced his family in a home designed by Charles Bulfinch on Beacon Street, where it still stands with the city's famed Common as its front yard. He graduated from Harvard College and the Law School, and imagined himself as destined to become a man of consequence, perhaps one of the powerful aristocrats who ruled the commonwealth from their perch on Beacon Hill. He was, according to Thomas Wentworth Higginson, "placed by birth in the most favored worldly position."[4] Phillips's perceptive biographer James Brewer Stewart observed in this book's lead essay that his parents had made their son "a morally exacting young man who was anxious not only to learn well in order to live correctly, but also to become someone whom others might someday look to as a powerful leader, just as they did to his father and had to his illustrious forebears." The phrase "gentleman of property and standing" might have defined him well.

Yet in an astonishing turn of events, he rejected his social class and even his own wealth—giving most of it away by the time of his death in 1884. Beginning in 1837, he stunned friends and family by taking up the most incendiary causes of his era, becoming a blazing white-hot supernova of abolitionism and postwar radicalism. Phillips's unpredictable turn to abolitionism so shocked his family that they considered committing him to an insane asylum.[5] Only William Lloyd Garrison rivaled Phillips in importance to the antislavery movement, and no other reformer equaled his eloquence or intellectual depth. Dominating the lecture circuit—the liveliest "social media" of the era—he became a celebrity on both sides of the Atlantic. Amazingly, he delivered his famed "Lost Arts" oration over two thousand times, earning $150,000—about $2 million in current value—from a public that clamored for it. His primary memorialist, George William Curtis, would justifiably assert that the orator's address at Faneuil Hall in defense of the martyred Elijah P. Lovejoy and free speech stood in national importance alongside Patrick Henry's at Williamsburg and Abraham Lincoln's at Gettysburg.[6]

Everyone in nineteenth-century America—North and South—knew of Wendell Phillips, inspiring heart-felt praise but mostly irate attacks. He earned the reputation as abolitionism's "Golden Trumpet," and the phrase "eloquence of abuse" was coined to capture the aura he cast from the lecture platform. Once, when traveling between New York and Boston, Phillips met an unnamed proslavery clergyman. Painfully aware of Phillips's fame (or notoriety), the man asked, "'if you are so opposed to slavery, Mr. Phillips, why don't you go down South and preach to the rebels?' 'For the same reason, sir,' was the reply, 'that you do not go to hell to preach religion to sinners.'" Such was his acerbic wit. Even his enemies recognized the power Phillips wielded, and the Richmond, Virginia, *Inquirer* damned him as "an infernal machine set to music."[7]

Phillips was white, rich, aristocratic, and famous. While enjoying unquestionable power and privilege, his choices and self-fashioning disrupted presumed categories of identity. In religion, as Dan McKanan's "A Puritan Radical: Wendell Phillips's New England Religion" so eloquently explores, he was no ordinary puritan but occupied the crossroads of Orthodox and Liberal faiths. In abolitionism, he allied with pacifists and nonresistants, but as Dean Grodzins's "Wendell Phillips, the Rule of Law, and Antislavery Violence" carefully shows, Phillips never became either himself, although his commitment to the rule of law both restrained his enthusiasm for revolution and moved him to urge runaways to resist re-enslavement with force.[8] Phillips often claimed that the "age of the reading man has come" and that the "age of bullets is over." But he also made an international hero of Haiti's Toussaint L'Ouverture (even keeping a portrait of him in his parlor) and Boston's Crispus Attucks. When the eve of civil war spawned countless threats against his life, Phillips carried a concealed pistol, and bodyguards—black and white—protected him and his home with revolvers and John Brown's pikes.[9]

James Brewer Stewart emphasizes in "Comfortable in His Own Skin: Wendell Phillips and Racial Egalitarianism" that Boston could not have produced a person less likely to become one of the country's leading exponents of racial equality. Thoroughly self-possessed and manifestly confident in himself and his abilities, he seamlessly glided between personal elitism and public egalitarianism. Indeed, the upbringing that made most others of his ilk seep arrogance and racial hate made him generously democratic and immune to imagined racial threat. Even among New England abolitionists and reformers, Phillips stood out for his commitment to equality. Ralph Waldo Emerson, Higginson observed, "always confessed to feeling a slight instinctive aversion to negroes," and Theodore Parker never could get over his "dislike of the Irish." Phillips, however, became the "tribune of the people."[10] At both personal and intellectual levels, as Stewart explains, Phillips bonded with African Americans. Garrison notwithstanding, Phillips became the nation's most important white advocate of racial equality.

Although born to rule, he nevertheless gave up his right to vote until after the Civil War and, late in life, only reluctantly allowed others to promote him for elected office—mostly for tactical or symbolic purposes. Before the war, he would not vote (although he advanced black enfranchisement), refused to take any oath of allegiance to a nation committed to slavery, rejecting politics as a prop to tyranny, and joined Garrison in damning the Constitution as a "covenant with death and an agreement with hell." As the constitutional historian Michael Les Benedict reminds us, when the South threatened secession, "Rather than preserve the Union through another compromise with Southerners," Phillips thundered that the North should build them "a bridge of gold" out of it "and pay their toll over it." Although driven by ardent patriotism and fetishizing the Founding Fathers, he nonetheless became the North's most articulate disunionist and sought to crush the Constitution as the instrument that held four millions in perpetual bondage. Phillips, as Benedict carefully details in "Wendell Phillips, the Constitution, and Constitutional Politics before the Civil War," did not simply express antislavery purity, wishing to avoid complicity in the perpetuation of slavery. He "engaged in a certain kind of politics that present observers tend not to see although it is all around us—what analysts in other countries readily see as *constitutional politics*."

Ironically, few could match Phillips's political intensity, and he worked closely with antislavery politicians to shape policy and events. After the Civil War, Republican Radicals in Congress looked to Phillips for guidance. Even his ardent enemy President Andrew Johnson understood Phillips's influence: "where Mr. Phillips stood a few months ago, the Radicals stand to-day; where he stands to-day, they will doubtless be a few months hence."[11] He had become, as one of his early biographers recorded, "the most prominent figure in unofficial life. Every word he spoke or wrote had the weight of an oracle." His insistence on full equality for all African Americans, compensation for the theft of their freedom, and land to insure their futures, embodied the highest democratic ideals of the era. As he wrote in 1870, "Freedom is only an installment of the debt we owe the Negro."[12] When former colleagues like Garrison abandoned the field, thinking their work complete, Phillips pressed on with fierce determination to reconstruct the South *and* the North. In 1866, Charles Sumner urged Phillips to keep up his agitation. You are, he exclaimed, "doing indispensable work, in this I express the conviction of every Senator and every Representative on our side of pending questions."[13] Throughout his career, he had sought political influence, not political power. As Lincoln's secretary of state, William H. Seward, once told the Massachusetts radical, "Yes, you make opinion, and we use it." But the black activist Archibald H. Grimké observed more accurately: "The public sentiment which Lincoln obeyed, Phillips created."[14]

Recent trends in the scholarship of abolitionism and the contentious 1850s, however, are increasingly refocusing on traditional political history to comprehend the advent of the Civil War and the demise of slavery. In our era, riven by irreconcilable and toxic political schisms not too unlike those of the 1850s, this shift is understandable. Certainly, antislavery scholarship remains overwhelmingly committed to the sympathetic trends initiated over forty years ago, especially regarding African Americans and women. But one can also perceive a sidelining drift that disturbingly questions antislavery and reform motivation and refocuses attention away from the abolitionist movement and toward traditional political figures, especially Abraham Lincoln and Republican Party leaders, as if political trends alone can account for sectional strife and the death of slavery.[15] Wendell Phillips reminds us, however, that antislavery agitation created the constituencies that empowered the politicians, "gave them their votes, got them their offices, furnished them their facts, and gave them their audience." In short, as Phillips avowed, "Garrison [and the abolitionist movement] made Lincoln possible."[16]

The abolitionists, however, did far more than create opportunities for politicians. To Phillips, the antislavery movement represented the beginning of a moral and social revolution—one that he would expand to include restraint of corporate power, justice for workingmen and women and the poor, rights of Native Americans and emigrants, temperance, an end to capital punishment, and countless other causes. More than an abolitionist and a reformer, Phillips filled a vital role in the structure of the nation's political culture. He sought the revitalization of democracy and the fulfillment of its promise, and saw agitators like himself as an essential element of the political system. Fully grasping the dangers posed by Tocqueville's "tyranny of the majority," the "slave power," the "money power," and the ruinous excesses of the capitalist labor system, he understood that no formal institutional mechanism existed to correct the system's power imbalances. The agitator, especially an independent one like Phillips, filled that role.

W. Caleb McDaniel's elegant "The Transatlantic Mind of Wendell Phillips and the Problem of Democracy in America" not only details the transatlantic intellectual world that Phillips occupied, but how it shaped his understanding of democratic society—especially its shortcomings. It also gave him essential insight into how it might be redirected. As McDaniel writes:

> In an aphorism that circulated widely in modern books about the ancients, the Athenian ruler Solon was reported to have "compared the people to the sea, and orators and counsellors to the winds; for that the sea would be calm and quiet, if the winds did not trouble it." Phillips believed a similar class of orators and counselors, ready to agitate the majority opinion, was precisely what American democracy needed in order to deal with the weaknesses that abolitionists had exposed. "If the Alps, piled in cold and still sublimity, be the emblem of Despotism," Phillips said in more than one speech, "the ever-restless ocean is ours," an "ocean of unchained democracy" that would remain pure so long as it was stirred constantly by agitators and orators like himself.

As a Harvard undergraduate, Phillips had made a study of heroism and governance, about how great leaders shaped events. He focused especially on English leadership and the role of the statesman, determining that the successful ones combined the powers of the scholar and the visionary. To Phillips, a republic could survive only with patriot-statesmen of great virtue and learning, willing to dedicate themselves to inspire and represent the interests of the citizenry. These individuals would play the critical role of resisting the instinctive inclination of society and government toward apathy and tyranny. Such leaders, prophets really, bore responsibility for reawakening "the people to great ideas that are constantly fading from their minds." Phillips concluded that in a democratic republic the only force that could vigilantly monitor government and remind the citizenry of the values they must cherish would be the "agitator."[17]

In his 1852 essay "Public Opinion," Phillips held that republics required constant agitation—what he considered to be an essential component of the machinery of state. He saw that Americans could become dangerously complacent about government, seeing it as a mechanism that would go of itself.

"The republic which sinks to sleep, trusting to constitution and machinery, to politicians and statesmen for the safety of its liberties," he maintained, "never will have any." With his reading of Tocqueville, he understood the central flaw in the nation's political system: that it could democratically settle on tyranny—indeed, *already had settled* on the worst of tyrannies. Thus, the "people are to be waked to a new effort, just as the Church has to be regenerated, in each age. The antislavery agitation is a necessity of each age," he counseled, "to keep ever on the alert this faithful vigilance, so constantly in danger of sleep."[18]

"The people never err," he liked to say, "'Vox populi, vox Dei.'" The people were the voice of God, not on any single subject, he explained, but rather over time. The people mean right, he believed, and in the end "will have the right," but only when informed by the truth. The agitator filled that essential role, dispensing right values through a free press. For Phillips, the press represented the great equalizer, key to the agitator's success and survival of the republic. "The day was," he wrote, "before gunpowder, when the noble, clad in steel, was a match for a thousand. Gunpowder levelled peasant and prince. The printing press had done the same." Napoleon, Phillips contended, rightly feared "three newspapers more than a thousand bayonets." Only with a free press could the agitator guide opinion and force change. Newspapers—or in today's world, the electronic media—form public opinion and determine the fate of nations. As Daniel Webster once declared, "There is not a monarch on earth whose throne is not liable to be shaken by the progress of opinion and the sentiment of the just and intelligent part of the people." Just as surely as if one placed a keg of gunpowder under the Senate chamber, Phillips asserted, the man "who launches a sound argument, who sets on two feet a startling fact . . . is just as certain that in the end he will change the government."[19]

For good reason we think of Wendell Phillips first and foremost as an abolitionist. It became a cause that occupied him for the majority of his adult life. As Stewart documented so thoroughly in his biography, Phillips became the driving force behind the Massachusetts Anti-Slavery Society and the American Anti-Slavery Society, setting agendas, managing the bureaucracies, drafting almost two-thirds of the resolutions introduced at the organizations' meetings, and orchestrating the editing of the *National Anti-Slavery Standard.*[20]

Yet his speeches—delivered from the antislavery platform or published in the press—had the greatest impact on the public and on himself. No one rivaled Phillips as an orator, and by the time of the Civil War he had become one of the most popular lecturers on either side of the Atlantic. He nearly always spoke without notes and, untethered from a podium, he could range around a platform like a ship-of the-line with cannon loaded to the lips, firing in all directions at once. He spoke seemingly without effort, "all melody and grace and magic, all wit and paradox and power," as George William Curtis remembered. "It was consummate art."[21] As Stewart wrote in this book's opening essay, "Wendell Phillips Is the Subtlest, Stubbornest Fact of the Times: Abolition's Golden Trumpet and the Fall of the Slaveholders' Republic," Phillips's 1837 maiden speech at Faneuil Hall on the murder of Elijah P. Lovejoy proved critical to Phillips's career—and to the course of American history: "For the rest of his life, Phillips believed that this was the moment when he first understood what actually lay behind the chaos overcoming Faneuil Hall, the violence that had overtaken far away Alton, and the anti-abolitionist thuggery he had silently witnessed in his hometown. It was a republican nightmare, the unopposed power of a perverted system of human relations founded in tyranny—slavery—that was spreading devastation and turmoil across the nation and within his own community. He felt, as he remembered, that he was 'recognizing for the first time the death grapple' into which he 'had unthinkingly been drawn.'"

At that famous meeting called to consider the tragic events in Alton, Illinois, Phillips became enraged by James T. Austin, attorney general of the commonwealth. Austin had praised the murderers of Lovejoy—an abolitionist publisher—as defenders of order and equal in greatness to the Founding Fathers. Pointing to the portraits of Otis, Hancock, Quincy, and Adams that hung on the walls of Faneuil Hall, Phillips exclaimed, "I thought those pictured lips would have broken into voice to rebuke the recreant American,—the slanderer of the dead." Rather than defend abolitionism, Phillips indicted Lovejoy's murderers as a mob intent on destroying free speech and liberty. Lovejoy, not his killers, had "'planted himself on his constitutional rights,'—appealed to the laws,—claimed the protection of the civil authority,—taken refuge under 'the broad shield of the Constitution.' . . . He took refuge under the banner of liberty,—amid its folds; and when he fell, its glorious stars and stripes, the emblem of free institutions, around which cluster so many heart-stirring memories, were blotted out in the martyr's blood."[22]

With his spontaneous speech, Phillips changed the tenor of that meeting and influenced a generation of Americans. Thus, the movement against slavery, which Phillips did so much to guide, in effect became his training ground for the development of a broad conception of reform—especially for the role of the agitator. He had witnessed the power and perverted interests that could control government leaders and the public, endangering the most elementary rights guaranteed by a republic. Moreover, in publically opposing the state—in the form of its attorney general—and with success, he had grasped for the first time how an ardent, learned, and dedicated agitator could change opinion and alter the course of history. As he would later write of the abolitionist movement, "Our aim is to alter public opinion. . . . The press, the pulpit, the wealth, the literature, the prejudices, the political arrangements, the present self-interest of the country, are all against us." As Phillips recalled, in 1831 there "was the most entire ignorance and apathy on the slave question. . . . No one preached, no one talked, no one wrote about it." But by the mid-1850s, no American could travel anywhere "in the world but [that] men will throw this troublesome question in his face." The abolitionist movement had awakened the nation to its real state, as Phillips asserted, and made it "the question of this generation." His understanding of the role and power of the agitator/prophet was complete.[23]

It took an astounding level of courage to face down the crowds that called for his head—and keep speaking. Threats on his life became almost a daily occurrence, and in 1861 after rioters broke up an antislavery meeting, Phillips even asked newly elected Governor John A. Andrew to call out the militia, which he refused to do. Abolitionists went to the city's mayor for protection, but in response he instead closed Tremont Temple so that the Massachusetts Anti-Slavery Society could not meet there. But Phillips would not be silenced and in a typical move even taunted his enemies. In January 1861, with civil war looming, Phillips declared in Boston's Music Hall: "Take your distorted Union, our nightmare monster, out of the light and range of these laws of trade and competition; then, without any sacrifice on your part, slavery will go to pieces! God made it a law of his universe, that villainy should always be loss. . . . All hail, then, Disunion!" His audience, half filled with his enemies, shrieked in disgust. Why an assassin's bullet didn't end his days is difficult to comprehend.[24]

Boston had been the epicenter of uncompromising immediate abolitionism, renowned—and reviled—for its interracial activism. We often forget, however, that because of its abolitionism the Boston of Phillips's day, *especially* during the Civil War, also proved most inhospitable for abolitionists, if not plainly dangerous. As had been the case since the day in 1835 when rioters dragged Garrison through the city's streets with a rope around his neck, the broadcloth class, the gentlemen of property and standing, had led the effort to suppress the abolitionists. When Phillips and his colleagues sought to commemorate the execution of John Brown in December 1860, merchants, traders, brokers, and lawyers led the mob to oust them. Men like Rufus Choate, Jr.; B. F. Russell; Oliver Stevens; Thomas L. Perkins; Thomas Jefferson Coolidge; William Aspinwall; and Amos A. Lawrence, who saw their financial destinies tied to the South, ejected Phillips and his colleagues from Tremont Temple. As the Worcester *Spy* observed, Boston was "choked with cotton and cankered with gold."[25]

Once the war commenced, opposition to abolitionism only increased. In July 1862, the Boston *Post* complained that, when "treasonable abolitionism is exterminated secession will cease, the war [will] stop and the Union [will] be restored." Even in Newburyport, Garrison's birthplace, the *Herald* joined in the chorus of opposition, complaining that the more "the government gets mixed up with the slavery question the worse it will be for all of us. The war has nothing to do with slavery." Caspar Crowninshield, from one of Boston's most distinguished families, could not even tolerate the moderate course of Lincoln. He complained bitterly to Charles Francis Adams, Jr., that the "whole government and form of government is rotten. . . . It can not be denied that most of our leading men are vulgar disgusting brutes. Look at Abe Lincoln. Is it not enough to disgust any one to think that such a poor miserable whelp of an Illinois lawyer should hold the fate of 30,000,000 people in his hands?" Even John Murray Forbes, who in 1863 would prove essential to the organization of the famed Fifty-fourth Massachusetts Regiment, not much earlier had believed that emancipation was "only another name for murder, fire and rape."[26]

The "threat" of emancipation sparked creation of the "People's Party," which dedicated itself to the defeat of Senator Charles Sumner. Even *before* Lincoln issued the Preliminary Emancipation Proclamation, anti-Sumner forces and other conservatives rallied to promote colonization, an effort guaranteed to raise the ire of nearly all abolitionists. On February 28, 1862, the legislature passed an act of incorporation for the Massachusetts Colonization Society, embodying the state of opinion in the commonwealth. Perhaps no one symbolized Boston and its history more than Robert C. Winthrop, the former Speaker of the U.S. House of Representatives, Webster's replacement in the Senate, direct descendent of the puritan colonial governor, and the longest-serving president of the Massachusetts Historical Society. In May 1862, fearing that Boston and the North would have unwanted blacks thrust upon them, Winthrop asserted that "there is now an emergency to which no one can be altogether insensible." Colonization, thus, would prove essential to rid the North of those "destined to a reluctant and wretched existence upon our own shores." He made it abundantly clear that he opposed all "Wholesale projects of emancipation,—whether under color of confiscation, or upon any pretense of imaginary necessities of martial law." Emancipation in the District of Columbia, Winthrop asserted, would prove a colossal mistake and a threat to the Border States, a move that would in the end not benefit "blacks or whites."[27]

The January 1, 1863, Emancipation Proclamation may have sparked great joy among abolitionists and reformers, but it also incited vitriolic attacks. The Boston *Post* thundered that the "President has no authority to free slaves *en mass*, either by constitutional law or by the war power." The city's Catholic *Pilot* wanted no part of black freedom, called for the suppression of abolitionists, and proclaimed that soldiers had enlisted for the "vindication of the constitution" and for nothing else. The former diplomat and congressman from Newburyport, Caleb Cushing, proclaimed the end of white government and the rise from the "infernal depths of a black, red or yellow consolidated Republic." It is also telling that the reelection of Lincoln in 1864 drew only 40 percent of the vote in Boston, with 60 percent either voting for McClellan or not voting at all.[28]

In this hostile environment, Phillips could see both an opportunity and the necessity to further the cause of freedom. With the future at stake, especially with so much opposition to black freedom, and with unprecedented energy and daring—at times, perhaps, too much—Phillips immersed himself in politics and political strategy. His political experience during the war would prove essential to promotion of his antislavery and civil rights agenda—even though marked by failure. As we now can see, it also provided an invaluable lesson for his postwar alliance with the former Civil War general, Democrat, and master of controversy Benjamin F. Butler. In both cases, Phillips would face harsh criticism.

The old abolitionist Franklin B. Sanborn had praised Phillips in 1915 for a rare ability among Boston patricians: "he could change his mind." He observed that in 1861 the country's leading disunionist had become, much to his credit, an ardent defender of the Union and war against the South. But had Phillips changed his mind, or had circumstances become completely transformed by the cannon in Charleston, South Carolina? For nine days after the attack on Fort Sumter, Phillips remained silent. He agonized over what to say, feeling that support for the government would "renounce my past . . . disavow every profession of faith, bless those that I have cursed, start afresh with a new set of political principles, and admit my life has been a mistake." Then, in a typical Phillips move, he appeared in the city's Music Hall on April 21, surrounded by American flags, and exclaimed that he was not taking back one word: "No, not one of them! I need them all,—every word I have spoken this winter,—every act of twenty-five years of my life, to make the welcome I give this war hearty and hot."[29]

Phillips changed to meet changed circumstances: "so far as the slavery clauses of the Constitution of '89 are concerned, it is dead," he exclaimed in December 1861. Disunionism no longer made sense. No loggerheaded ideologue, he recognized that the war offered an unprecedented opportunity and that he would be recreant to his principles if he failed to seize the moment. Never a nonresistant, Phillips had not tied his abolitionism to Liberal theology, but instead bonded it directly to law and political ideology. He did not have to overcome a wrenching dilemma over whether to adhere to the Sermon on the Mount or resort to violence. Instead, he had practiced constitutional politics and adhered to a form of republicanism that placed liberty above property. In his mind, disunionism, like war, was more a strategy to destroy slavery than an effort to maintain personal purity. Thus, once the South fired on the flag, allowing it to slip away unchallenged would be both an act of constitutional suicide and the loss of the first real opportunity to transform the whole nation and extinguish slavery. He imagined old John Quincy Adams stirring from his coffin, crying out: "The hour has struck! Seize the thunderbolt God has forged for you, and annihilate the system which has troubled your peace for seventy years!" His endorsement of the war propelled Phillips into prominence, turned enemies into admirers, and gave him enormous new authority. It also allowed him to assert his agitator's role in the treacherous arena of politics.[30]

In March 1862, Phillips journeyed to Washington, D.C., to deliver two antislavery lectures, meet President Lincoln, and lobby as many representatives and senators as he could reach. Sumner escorted him to the floor of the Senate where he met with antislavery New Englanders Henry Wilson and John P.

Hale—who sometimes felt the sting of a Phillips speech—and the even more conservative Republican Lyman Trumbull of Illinois. One evening at the home of Pennsylvania's long-serving congressman and Speaker of the House Galusha Grow, he shared dinner with Gen. John C. Frémont, who captivated the Bostonian. Ignoring his wife Ann's warnings about falling in league with politicians and abandoning his moral high ground, Phillips almost instantly saw in Frémont, the Republican Party's first presidential candidate, the Cromwell he sought who would at long last drive a stake in the heart of slavery. Not long afterward, he began declaring publically that "Abraham Lincoln simply rules; John C. Fremont governs."[31]

Phillips became fixated on Frémont—as he later would on Butler—as the strongest lever he could find to move the Republican Party toward immediate and unconditional abolition and full equality. Phillips and other abolitionists who had previously eschewed politics backed Frémont over the disappointing Lincoln, either as an independent candidate or as the party's 1864 standard bearer. As early as February, even the crusty editorial powerhouse Horace Greeley had proclaimed Lincoln a failure and considered Frémont as one of his possible replacements.[32] As 1864 progressed, however, support for the "Pathfinder" dwindled, especially among abolitionists who disdained Frémont's dalliance with Democrats and his failure to back full equality. Additionally, the threat of electing McClellan if Frémont drew off too much support from Lincoln proved sufficient during the summer of 1864 to convince most of Phillips's fellow abolitionists to abandon the fight against the president. Phillips unwisely remained committed until Frémont finally withdrew on September 22, compelled by Lincoln's revived strength after Gen. Sherman delivered Atlanta to the Union. Phillips then found himself facing hostile crowds and damage to his reputation and influence.[33]

Yet, Phillips's error may have been more timing than strategy. Lincoln and the Republicans consistently had failed to measure up to antislavery goals and showed little indication that they ever would. In light of the racism manifested by the party—especially Lincoln, who had been a lifelong advocate of colonization—and the policies thus far enacted, Phillips had every reason to doubt the existence of any commitment by the administration to full freedom. Even the Emancipation Proclamation, which freed no slaves directly and seemed implemented out of fear and desperation rather than principle, and Lincoln's policies in occupied Louisiana only reinforced his view. Phillips's aim had been to move the party and the North toward abolitionism and equality, and prior to the 1864 election he had done so powerfully and effectively.

For instance, at the 1862 August First celebration—the annual commemoration of West Indian emancipation—at Island Grove in Abington, Massachusetts, Phillips flexed his muscle. He understood that his hard-won fame had made him a force in public events. In fact, the issue of the *Liberator* that carried his Abington remarks sold out in a flash.[34] At Island Grove, he meant to move Lincoln and the North to adopt emancipation as a war aim. Up until that point, the North had waged a war solely for the Union, even obeying the Fugitive Slave Law and returning runaways to their masters. Fugitives that ran into Union lines for their safety could be, and often were, forced out at bayonet point, even after Congress dropped enforcement of the Fugitive Slave Law. The nation was tearing itself apart over slavery, and the North would do nothing about the war's cause—and if a rumored negotiated peace was made, slavery would remain. What then was the point? Phillips did his part to recast northern thinking on slavery, the Union, and the aim of the war: "I do not think that anything which we can call the *Government*, so far has any *purpose* to get rid of slavery. On the contrary, I think the present purpose of the government, so far as it has now a purpose, is to end the war and save slavery. I believe Mr. Lincoln is conducting this war at present, with the purpose of saving slavery." As Lincoln himself had made clear, he would do whatever served the interests of the Union, and as he said in his famous letter to the New York editor Horace Greeley, "If I could save the Union without freeing any slave, I would do it, and if I could save it by feeing some and leaving others alone I would also do that. What I do about slavery, and the colored race, I do because I believe it helps to save the Union."[35]

Phillips would have none of that. Even though he knew that Lincoln had already decided to issue the preliminary Emancipation Proclamation, perhaps *because* he knew of Lincoln's intended move, he meant to stay one step ahead and help insure it, and more.[36] He sought to transform northern opinion—have it comprehend that there could be no peace, no nation, and no union with slavery. Thus, Phillips asserted that Lincoln was

> waging a war which he dare not describe, in the service of a political idea that he does not shape into words. He is not fighting vigorously and heartily enough even to get good terms in case of a treaty,—not to talk of victory. All savages call

> clemency cowardice; they respect nothing but force. The Southern barbarians mistake clemency for cowardice; and every act of Lincoln, which he thinks is conciliation, they take for evidence of his cowardice, or his distrust. I do not say that McClellan is a traitor, but I say this, that if he had been traitor from the crown of his head to the sole of his foot, he could not have served the South better than he has done since he was commander-in-chief (applause); he could not have carried on the war in more exact deference to the politics of that side of the Union.

Either misunderstood or deliberately misconstrued by the northern press, Phillips was condemned as a traitor who encouraged men not to enlist. Headlines screamed "Phillips Spouting Foul Treason." The New York *Herald* called for Phillips to be incarcerated at Fort Warren in Boston Harbor. Others cried out that Phillips was "an enemy; a political nuisance, a traitor, and a pernicious man." It is a speech, another paper exclaimed, "which, in treason and sedition, has outstripped anything he has yet uttered. Surely, if any man can commit treason by words spoken or written, this is the blackest hue and if any man ought to have been arrested since the beginning of this war, Wendell Phillips is that man."[37]

In fact, Wendell Phillips supported war, but not as it was then fought, and opposed northern opinion as it then existed:

> Now, I think, and if I were in the Senate I should have said to the government, that every man who under the present policy loses his life in the swamps of the South, and every dollar sent there to be wasted, only prolongs a murderous and wasteful war, waged for no purpose whatever. This is my meaning. In this war, mere victory on a battlefield amounts to nothing, contributes little or nothing toward ending the war. . . . The war can only be ended by annihilating that oligarchy which formed and rules the South and makes the war,—by annihilating a state of society. . . . Our present policy neither aims to annihilate that state of things we call "the South," made up of pride, idleness, ignorance, barbarism, theft, and murder, nor to replace it with a substitute. Such an aimless war I call wasteful and murderous. . . .
>
> It is not the South we have got to conquer; it is the Egypt of the Southern half of Illinois; it is the Devil in the editor's chair of the Boston Courier (merriment); it is the lump of unbaked dough, with no vitality except hatred of Charles

> Sumner, which sits in the editorial chair of the Daily Advertiser (applause); it is the man who goes down to Virginia with the army, and thinks he goes there to watch the house of General Lee, and make the slaves work for him, while the master has gone to Corinth or to Richmond. These are the real enemies of the republic. . . .
>
> It is the proslavery North that is her own greatest enemy. Lincoln would act, if he believed the North wanted him to. . . . He is not a genius; he is not a man like [General John C.] Fremont, to stamp the lava mass of the nation with an idea; he is not a man like [General David] Hunter, to coin his experience into ideas. I will tell you what he is. He is a first-rate *second-rate* man. (Laughter.) He is one of the best specimens of a second-rate man, and he is honestly waiting, like any other servant, for the people to come and send him on any errand they wish. In ordinary times, when the seas are calm, you can sail without a pilot,—almost anyone can avoid a sunken ledge that the sun shows him on his right hand, and the reef that juts out on his left; but it is when the waves smite heaven, and the thunder-cloud makes the waters ink, that you need a pilot: and to-day the nation's bark scuds, under the tempest, lee-shore and mælstrom on each side—needing no holiday captain, but a pilot, to weather the storm.

Just like his 1862 address, Phillips's support for Frémont in 1864—while somewhat naive and ineptly applied—reflected his conception of the agitator's role. As he wrote in July 1864, "Remember, I am not a politician, but mainly an agitator—my special work being to make *party progress possible.* I shall never succeed by doing, as you are now doing, filing down my protests against their shortcomings, and joining in their support. If Lincoln is re-elected, and repeats for another four years the indecision, heartlessness, and infamous pandering to negrophobia and the slave power which have marked his last four," he would be justified in concluding that "'Have I not gone on to do, during my second term, just what you praised me for in my first?'"[38]

On the eve of the 1864 election, at least one anonymous correspondent to the *Liberator* from New Bedford, Massachusetts, readily grasped Phillips's strategy.

> However, as the persistent refusal of the Abolitionists in times past to compromise their principles with any political party has unquestionably . . . [been] productive of the best results, I am by no means sure but that their adherence even

> now to their old policy, and thereby sustaining Mr. *Phillips*, would not in the end be the wisest course to pursue. Mr. P. is undoubtedly right in theory according to the established custom of all true reformers; and I still hold to the opinion that with the growth of the public mind upon the great subject of human rights and real civilization, this noble philanthropist will be duly esteemed as one who possessed unwavering courage in the times of the country's sternest trial, as a true patriot and friend of mankind.[39]

Phillips's well-known agitation for racial equality after the Civil War continued the antislavery struggle. But for him "the Anti-Slavery cause was only a portion of the great struggle between Capital and Labor. Capital undertook to own the laborer. We have broken that up."[40] Historians of the post–Civil War period, if they mention him at all, have understandably emphasized his efforts to promote versions of the Fourteenth and Fifteenth amendments to the Constitution and his other postwar civil rights work. But in doing so they largely overlooked his support for labor rights and his critique of corporate capitalism and have failed to see the continuity of his career as an agitator. Moreover, the failure to seriously scrutinize the later portion of his career has prevented us from appreciating his enduring influence, something that two generations of Americans after his death thoroughly understood. Through the resourceful essays of Peter Wirzbicki and Millington W. Bergeson-Lockwood, however, we can better see both the importance of Phillips's later career and his continued significance.[41]

Wirzbicki's "Wendell Phillips and Transatlantic Radicalism: Democracy, Capitalism, and the American Labor Movement" places "Phillips in the context of transatlantic discourses of radical democracy, working-class empowerment, and hostility to entrenched privilege." Phillips's journey to Europe in 1841, where he saw immense wealth juxtaposed with grinding poverty, revealed to him what awaited the United States if democracy failed to flourish and the moneyed class remained unchecked. He supported the Chartists and other European radicals, but before the Civil War he had not yet developed the sophisticated and far more searching critique of capitalism and labor rights that dominated his later years. Even though many fellow abolitionists, utopians, and reformers did eloquently and passionately critique the condition of northern free labor throughout the 1840s and 1850s, Phillips did not focus on it until 1865.[42] As Wirzbicki emphasizes, Phillips, Garrison, and other prominent abolitionists did not believe that American workers suffered as badly as those in Europe and opposed efforts that distracted attention away from the plight of the slave. But Phillips, because of his prominence in so fecund an area as Boston, became increasingly concerned over the larger American social structure and, as Wirzbicki reminds us, as early as 1853 charged that "Capitalists are our feudal barons."[43]

Phillips's emergence as a labor leader and critic of capitalism—clearly tied to his antebellum career as an agitator—occurred quickly and vehemently after the Civil War. Before the close of 1865, he came out aggressively for the eight-hour workday and the next year attempted to rally feminists to back the movement. They found it a distraction from female suffrage, but for him it was the only way to insure that "every child born in America must have an equal chance in life."[44] Soon, as Wirzbicki asserts, Phillips would discover that the "combined power of capitalists, especially the railroad barons, had become the new enemies of democracy in the 1870s, comparable, he thought, to the power of antebellum slave holders." Enormously popular books like Henry George's *Progress and Poverty* confirmed that stark economic inequality had become an inescapable and dangerous fact. By 1880, massive corporate consolidation had taken place on an unprecedented scale, especially in the railroad, steel, and coal industries. By 1900 the wealth of one man, Andrew Carnegie, equaled 0.5 percent of the country's entire gross national product, the greatest fortune ever amassed by a single American. Coming at a time when unskilled labor could expect to earn no more than $1.50 a day, Phillips justifiably warned that law would not be made in state legislatures, but "in Vanderbilt's count-room."[45]

In the fall of 1871, Phillips issued one of his most dire warnings in the familiar surroundings of Boston's Music Hall. As Boston's most vexatious prophet, Phillips explained the new threat posed by the "great money power" that "looms over the horizon." Previous generations thought they had guaranteed public safety and democracy through entail and distribution of estates. But, Phillips admonished, they "forgot that money could combine; that a moneyed corporation was like the papacy, a succession of persons with a unity of purpose, that it never died. . . . The corporations of America mean to rule it the same way, and, unless some power more radical than that of ordinary politics is found, will rule it inevitably. I confess that the only fear I have in regard to republican institutions is whether, in our day, any adequate remedy will be found for this incoming flood of the power of incorporated wealth. No statesman, no public man yet, has dared to defy it . . . , and the only hope of any effectual grapple with it is by rousing the actual masses . . . to grapple with this great force."[46]

Phillips had come to see political activism as the best means short of revolution to secure his goals. Millington W. Bergeson-Lockwood's "The People Coming to Power! Wendell Phillips, Benjamin Butler, and the Politics of Labor Reform" sees the continuity of Phillips's later career, its innovations—especially regarding the political process—and the route the great agitator had chosen to defend republicanism and fulfill the democratic promise. As he had done as an abolitionist, Phillips awakened the public to political and economic corruption by employing his extraordinary oratorical skills to move "audiences with utopian visions of political justice and economic equality where everyday people, not political leaders or bosses, shaped the destiny of the nation." But he did far more. As Bergeson-Lockwood details, Phillips "intertwined his dedication to labor reform, hatred of financial corruption in politics, and faith in the electoral process" and invested it all in a political movement, especially the campaigns of Benjamin F. Butler for governor of Massachusetts, just as he staked his hope for emancipation in the 1864 campaign of John C. Frémont.

For legions of historians who have denigrated Butler as a corrupt demagogue, the alliance of the prophet and the politico may seem perverse. Phillips, however, had known Butler since he was a youth, and once the Civil War began they found common ground on nearly every important issue. Butler even supported the right of his black soldiers to vote in Pennsylvania, ignoring the state's ban on black suffrage—and much later, while Massachusetts's governor, would make pioneering black judicial and patronage appointments. Phillips, who remained in touch with Butler during the war, proposed that Lincoln make him general in chief of the Union army. Afterward, they united in support of the labor, woman suffrage, and prohibition movements. Even after Phillips's death, Butler proudly claimed the mantle of the great agitator's quest for African American civil rights.[47] Moreover, in the context of Gilded Age America, torn by gross inequities of wealth, industrial and rural exploitation, and the rise of labor unions, populists, and socialists of every hue, their alliance helped spotlight many of the most grievous injustices of the era. At his most audacious, Phillips starkly defined the issues at the September 1871 labor reform convention in Worcester, Massachusetts: "We affirm, as a fundamental principle, that labor, the creator of wealth, is entitled to all it creates." He insisted on the "overthrow of the whole profit-making system, the extinction of all monopolies, the abolition of privileged classes, universal education and . . . the poverty of the masses." His campaigns with old Ben Butler made the last fourteen years of his life some of his most consequential and helped make Wendell Phillips one of the most influential social critics of his era—and for generations after.[48]

Hélène Quanquin's "The Rights of Others: Wendell Phillips and Women's Rights" and Angela F. Murphy's "Wendell Phillips and the American Indian" focus on aspects of Phillips's career that have largely gone unanalyzed, displaying the breadth of Phillips's role as agitator—and its limitations. Phillips was remembered and honored for generations after his death as an important supporter of woman's rights and female suffrage. Yet his rhetoric proved surprisingly condescending, adopting a tone he never used with other groups, holding women largely culpable for their own plight. In 1866, he confessed to not sensing much public interest in the subject and held that neither law nor men represented the greatest obstacle to the advancement of woman's rights. "Let woman know that nobody stops her but herself. She ties her own limbs; she corrupts her own sisters; she demoralizes civilization." He did not doubt that women could do anything that men do, but contended that adherence to traditional social fashion prevented them from trying. Quanquin rightly focuses on the uniqueness of the problem facing feminists, that personal intimacy with men, particularly as husbands, warped male perception and limited their grasp of the issue. "Let woman go to the ballot-box, and the rudest man will in time be ashamed not to carry there his good manners," as Phillips once croaked. In relying on tired traditional notions of the influence of woman, Phillips may have hampered the movement and damaged his effectiveness.[49]

Similar limitations attended his efforts on behalf of Native Americans. Phillips had become a prominent national defender of Indian rights, especially against the interests of the railroads (which he also condemned as corporate predators) that fully intended to push through Native Americans lands. Thus, when state and federal authorities clashed with California's Modoc Indians, Phillips wasted no time in appealing directly to President Grant—whom he largely supported—protesting the execution of the Modocs. "Such an act will be *murder* on the part of the National Government," he protested. "The Indians owe this Government no *allegiance* for they have never had any *protection* from it in any of their rights."[50]

Clearly, as Murphy explains, the plight of Indians bore a resemblance to that of African Americans and other suppressed groups, thus attracting Phillips's passionate agitation. Yet ideas of individual land ownership, education, suffrage, and assimilation, central to African Americans, proved unattractive to Native Americans, who wished to preserve their culture and independence. Despite all their good intentions, Phillips and most of his fellow reformers, as Murphy perceptively relates, "could not recognize fundamental differences between Native and African American populations, which blinded him to the unique cultural and political requirements of American Indians."

Combative, eloquent, brilliant, and relentless, Wendell Phillips dominated the central social issues of his time—and during the half-century after his death he became one of the most influential and ubiquitous figures in popular memory. As Donald Yacovone's "Race, Radicalism, and Remembering Wendell Phillips" documents with surprising detail, hardly a day passed without his popular quotations or discussions of him appearing in the country's newspapers, even in the South. Although forgotten today, even in his native Boston, Phillips had been a vital influence for African Americans, populists, socialists, communists, labor leaders, reformers, progressives, feminists, literary figures, biographers, and social commentators—even high-school graduation orators—who celebrated his name and drew inspiration and guidance from his example.

Phillips's legacy counted. It played a central role in the conflict over the changing meaning of the Civil War, the struggle for racial equality, the defense of labor, and in the radical critique of American capitalism that stretched from the Gilded Age to the end of the Progressive Era and beyond. Phillips lived long enough to exert enormous influence on the next generation of radicals—men like Eugene Debs, Ezra Heywood, Henry George and his disciple the author Hamlin Garland, Henry Demarest Lloyd, and even the Presbyterian socialist Norman Thomas. As his legacy began disappearing from popular culture in the mid-1920s, however, it increased among academics and cultural critics who found in him the ideas and principles that would help propel the civil rights and labor movements. As Oswald Garrison Villard remarked in 1935, "It has been one of the misfortunes of the American labor movement that it has had no other spokesman as trained and gifted or as eloquent" as Phillips.[51] His near total absence from contemporary popular culture represents a stark contrast to his previous centrality and tells us much about the place of social and economic justice in modern political discourse.

The little-known Phillips Community in Minneapolis is a striking example of how historical memory of Wendell Phillips once worked and how it continues to shape one small part of our world today. Activists and volunteer journalists David Moore, Harvey M. Winje, and Susan Ann Gust in "The Phillips Community of Minneapolis: Historical Memory and the Quest for Social Justice" provide an extraordinary story of a multiethnic community—with a significant Native American population—that combated larger governmental and private interests to better the lives of its residents and build community unity.

In March 1868, Wendell Phillips lectured in Minneapolis and toured the city. Could he ever have imagined what impact such a visit would have? As they proudly relate, Moore, Winje, and Gust, who for decades have lived in Minneapolis's Wendell Phillips Community, see in Phillips a local champion, "our condemner of corruption, our denouncer of economic exploitation, our opponent of racism and sexism, our educator, and speaker of truth to power." For them, Phillips's legacy "challenges our thoughts, deepens our resolve, and enriches our political imaginations as we engage a neighborhood that is Minneapolis's poorest, most multiethnic, least well-educated, most politically ill-served, most transient, and most heavily exploited by outside interests." In the early 1970s when they discovered Oscar Sherwin's 1958 biography, *Wendell Phillips: Prophet of Liberty*, "it revolutionized our understanding of our own community, inspiring us with the name of history's most distinguished advocate of racial and gender equality and working peoples' rights." For the first time, they "felt the weight of history shifting in our favor. We found ourselves directly connected to a formidable hero of yesteryear, who, over a lifetime, had devoted his enormous talents to causes much like those with which our neighborhood has always contended." In his speeches and in his career as an agitator they discovered the wisdom and ideals that seemed to reach out from the past, and like the unfailing flight of an arrow, point them toward a future they could shape.

This book is not the last word on Wendell Phillips. As opposed to standard biography, our format allows specialists to delve far deeper into aspects of Phillips's career than is otherwise possible. Yet, more, much more, could—and should—be written on his seemingly endless pursuits and influence. Delving even deeper into his role as an agitator and into the freighted question of Garrisonian disunionism and the Civil War should attract the attention of scholars.

Phillips's role as a political activist, his postwar civil rights work, efforts on behalf of the Irish and other immigrant groups, his condemnation of capital punishment, support for temperance, and especially his labor agitation and role as a critic of corporate wealth and power cry out for further reconsideration. As the Rev. Henry Ward Beecher remarked after witnessing Phillips's massive public funeral in February 1884, clearly "He has taught some lessons." Some of those should be applicable today.

NOTES

1. Uncle Dudley, "Wendell Phillips Today," *Boston Globe*, July 5, 1915.

2. George Lowell Austin, *The Life and Times of Wendell Phillips* (Boston: B. B. Russell & Co., 1884), 5; Carlos Martyn, *Wendell Phillips: The Agitator* (New York: Funk and Wagnalls Co., 1890), iii.

3. Wendell Phillips Stafford, *Wendell Phillips: A Centennial Oration* (New York: NAACP, 1911), 29; Louis Filler, ed., *Wendell Phillips on Civil Rights and Freedom* (New York: Hill and Wang, 1965), xvi.

4. Thomas Wentworth Higginson, *Wendell Phillips* (Boston: Lee & Shepard, 1884), v–vii, xvi.

5. Martyn, *Wendell Phillips*, 427.

6. Ibid., 115; Curtis's address at the memorial service took place on April 18, 1884. *A Memorial of Wendell Phillips, from the City of Boston* (Boston: City of Boston, 1884), 44–45. As late as 1910, Americans still recognized the anniversary of Phillips's 1837 Faneuil Hall speech; see the Trenton (NJ) *Evening Times*, November 6, 1910.

7. "Wendell Phillips and His Times," unidentified newspaper clipping, Livermore Collection, box 5, PU#23, Princeton University; E. M. Irish, *Abraham Lincoln—Wendell Phillips: Addresses* (Kalamazoo, Mich.: privately printed, 1910), 43.

8. Harry S. Stout, *Upon the Altar of the Nation: A Moral History of the Civil War* (New York: Viking, 2006), 61, as often happens, incorrectly labeled Phillips an abolitionist pacifist.

9. James Brewer Stewart, *Wendell Phillips: Liberty's Hero* (Baton Rouge: Louisiana State University Press, 1986), 104, 156–59, 184, 199; *Christian Recorder*, June 16, 1866, in which James Redpath reported that he had seen the L'Ouverture portrait in Phillips's home. Although scholars now use "Louverture" as the correct rendering of the Haitian's name, to avoid competing spellings in the text we are employing the form used in Phillips's lifetime. Richard J. Hinton, "Wendell Phillips: A Character Study," *The Arena* 13 (1895): 237, revealed that when sensing danger Phillips packed a "six-inch Colt." George W. Smalley, "Memories of Wendell Phillips," *Harper's Magazine* 89 (June 1894): 134. Smalley, who married Phillips's adopted daughter, served as one of the bodyguards.

10. Higginson, *Wendell Phillips*, xv.

11. Stewart, *Liberty's Hero*, quoted, 278–79.

12. Martyn, *Wendell Phillips*, 352–53; Roy E. Finkenbine, "Wendell Phillips and 'The Negro's Claim,' A Neglected Reparations Document," *Massachusetts Historical Review* 7 (2005): 105, 116.

13. Charles Sumner to Wendell Phillips, March 17, 1866, quoted in Martyn, *Wendell Phillips*, 352–53.

14. Stewart, *Liberty's Hero*, 134, 137–39; Wendell Phillips, "Garrison," *North American Review* 129 (August 1879): 144–45; Archibald H. Grimké, *A Eulogy on Wendell Phillips* (Boston: Rockwell and Church, 1884), 33.

15. This trend is especially evident in Andrew Delbanco's dismaying *The Abolitionist Imagination* (Cambridge: Harvard University Press, 2012), 42–43, which in our age of terrorism, as Robert Penn Warren once had done, casts a man like John Brown in the mold of a dangerous fanatic. Additionally, in response to Beverly Gage's "Terrorism and the American Experience: A State of the Field," *Journal of American History* 98 (June 2011): 73–94, D. J. Mulloy makes John Brown into "a religious fanatic, someone who believed he had been specially chosen by God to be an avenging warrior in the antislavery cause" in "Is There a 'Field?' And if There Isn't, Should We Be Worried about It?" *Journal of American History* 98, no. 1 (2011): 111–14. For the redirection toward political history, see James Oakes, *The Scorpion's Sting: Antislavery and the Coming of the Civil War* (New York: W. W. Norton, 2014), and his *Freedom National: The Destruction of Slavery in the United States, 1861–1865* (New York: W. W. Norton, 2013). Brenda Wineapple's *Ecstatic Nation: Confidence, Crisis, and Compromise, 1848–1877* (New York: HarperCollins, 2013) is a wonderful exception. Also see Thomas G. Mitchell, *Antislavery Politics in Antebellum and Civil War America* (Westport, Conn.: Praeger, 2007).

16. Phillips, "Garrison," 144–45; Phillips, "The Philosophy of the Abolition Movement," in *Speeches, Lectures, and Letters, First Series* (Boston: Lee and Shepard, 1894), 136.

17. Stewart, *Liberty's Hero*, 28–30, 161.

18. Phillips, "Public Opinion," in *Speeches, Lectures, and Letters, First Series*, 53–54.

19. Ibid., 41, 44–46.

20. Stewart, *Liberty's Hero*, 128.

21. George William Curtis, "Editor's Easy Chair," *Harper's New Monthly Magazine*, April 1887, 625.

22. Phillips, "The Murder of Lovejoy," in *Speeches, Lectures, and Letters, First Series*, 6, 8.

23. Phillips, "Philosophy of the Abolition Movement," 106, 110, 148, 150–51, 153.

24. Stewart, *Liberty's Hero*, 213; Phillips, "Disunion," in *Speeches, Lectures, and Letters, First Series*, 369–70.

25. Edith Ellen Ware, *Political Opinion in Massachusetts during the Civil War and Reconstruction* (New York: Columbia University, 1916), 85–87, 89.

26. Ibid., 91, 100–101; Edward C. Ware, "Boston during the Civil War," *Proceedings of the Massachusetts Historical Society* 71 (1953–57): 199.

27. Ware, *Political Opinion*, 97, 102–3; Thomas H. O'Connor, *The Boston Irish: A Political History* (Boston: Northeastern University Press, 1995), 88–89; Robert C. Winthrop, "African Colonization," in *Addresses and Speeches on Various Occasions*, 4 vols. (Boston: Little, Brown, and Co., 1895), vol. 2: 526–29; Robert C. Winthrop to John Pendleton Kennedy, April 14, December 30, 1862, John Pendleton Kennedy Papers, Enoch Pratt Free Public Library, Baltimore.

28. Ware, *Political Opinion*, 103–4, 126; Dale Baum, *The Civil War Party System: The Case of Massachusetts, 1848–1876* (Chapel Hill: University of North Carolina Press, 1984), 60–61, 76–77.

29. Stewart, *Liberty's Hero*, 218–220; "Under the Flag," and "The War for the Union," in Phillips, *Speeches, Lectures, and Letters, First Series*, 396–414, 418.

30. Donald Yacovone, *Samuel Joseph May and the Dilemmas of the Liberal Persuasion, 1797–1871* (Philadelphia: Temple University Press, 1991); "Under the Flag," and "War for the Union," in Phillips, *Speeches, Lectures, and Letters, First Series*, 396–414, 418. For an alternate interpretation, see A J Aiséirithe, "Piloting the Car of Human Freedom: Abolitionism, Woman Suffrage, and the Problem of Radical Reform, 1860–1870," PhD diss., University of Chicago, 2007.

31. Stewart, *Liberty's Hero*, 232–34, 235 quoted.

32. Harold Holzer, *Lincoln and the Power of the Press* (New York: Simon & Schuster, 2014), 497–98. Greeley also considered generals Grant and Butler as possible Lincoln replacements. Garrison also abandoned his disunionism, but came out squarely for Lincoln.

33. James M. McPherson, *The Struggle for Equality: Abolitionists and the Negro in the Civil War and Reconstruction* (Princeton: Princeton University Press, 1964), 268–86; Wineapple, *Ecstatic Nation*, 307–11.

34. *Liberator*, August 22, 1862.

35. Henry Louis Gates, Jr., and Donald Yacovone, eds., *Lincoln on Race and Slavery* (Princeton: Princeton University Press, 2009), 243. Phillips's remarks are taken from "The Cabinet," in Phillips, *Speeches, Lectures, and Letters, First Series*, 448–63.

36. Holzer, *Lincoln and the Power of the Press*, 403.

37. *Liberator*, August 15, 29, 1862.

38. Ibid., July 15, 1864.

39. Ibid., November 4, 1864.

40. Phillips letter in Boston *Daily Advertiser*, August 10, 1872, reprinted in Martyn, *Wendell Phillips*, 402.

41. Timothy Messer-Kruse, *The Yankee International: Marxism and the American Reform Tradition, 1848–1876* (Chapel Hill: University of North Carolina Press, 1998), is an exception; Stewart, *Liberty's Hero*, 259–62.

42. See Phillips's 1865 address: "The Eight Hour Movement," in *Speeches, Lectures, and Letters, Second Series* (Boston: Lee and Shepard, 1894), 139–44.

43. The reformer and utopian George Ripley similarly rejected the wage system as "Commercial Feudalism," and Albert Brisbane rejected it as false. James L. Huston, *Securing the Fruits of Labor: The American Concept of Wealth Distribution, 1765–1900* (Baton Rouge: Louisiana State University Press, 1998), 275, 345, 348–49.

44. Phillips, "The Eight Hour Movement," 139; Messer-Kruse, *The Yankee International*, 29–33.

45. Huston, *Securing the Fruits of Labor*, 355–56; Thomas C. Cochran and William Miller, *The Age of Enterprise: A Social History of Industrial America* (New York: Harper & Row, 1961), 234; Wendell Phillips, *The People Coming to Power! Speech of Wendell Phillips, Esq., at the Salisbury Beach Gathering, September 13, 1871* (Boston: Lee and Shepard, 1871), 13.

46. Phillips, "Foundation of the Labor Movement," in Wendell Phillips, *The Labor Question* (Boston: Lee and Shepard, 1884), 13.

47. Jonathan W. White, *Emancipation: The Union Army and the Reelection of Abraham Lincoln*

(Baton Rouge: Louisiana State University Press, 2014), 129–30; Howard P. Nash, Jr., *Stormy Petrel: The Life and Times of General Benjamin F. Butler, 1818–1893* (Rutherford, N.J.: Fairleigh Dickinson University Press, 1969), 183; Hans L. Trefousse, *Ben Butler: The South Called Him Beast!* (New York: Twayne, 1957), 223. See Donald Yacovone, "Race, Radicalism, and Remembering Wendell Phillips," in the present volume.

48. Phillips, "The Foundation of the Labor Movement," 152.

49. Phillips, "Woman's Rights and Woman's Duties" and "Suffrage for Woman," in *Speeches, Lectures, and Letters, Second Series*, 117, 128–38.

50. Wendell Phillips to Ulysses S. Grant, September 11, 1873, in John Y. Simon et al., eds., *The Papers of Ulysses S. Grant*, 32 vols. (Carbondale: Southern Illinois University Press, 2000), vol. 24: 204.

51. Oswald Garrison Villard, "Wendell Phillips, After Fifty Years," *American Mercury* 34 (January 1935): 98.

1

WENDELL PHILLIPS IS THE SUBTLEST, STUBBORNEST FACT OF THE TIMES

Abolition's Golden Trumpet and the Fall of the Slaveholders' Republic

JAMES BREWER STEWART

INQUIRY

Wendell Phillips persistently demanded what the vast majority of pre–Civil War Americans could never condone. He condemned the U.S. Constitution as slavery's guarantor and insisted that the North secede from the Union. In his eyes, to cast a ballot was to vote for slavery, so he called for boycotting elections. He extolled as heroes those who equated slave insurrection with black liberation, hot-blooded warriors like John Brown and Toussaint L'Ouverture. Racial bigots provoked his unremitting scorn, and so did those who denied that women were equal with men. He assailed politicians of all persuasions with undiluted venom, and rejoiced at the infamy he called down upon himself.[1]

But for all the unpopularity of Phillips's positions, civically engaged Americans at the time quickly acknowledged that he exerted an enormous force on the nation's politics as events moved the country ever closer to civil war. Although the abolitionist movement he spoke for was minuscule and marginalized, Phillips himself was anything but. Instead, as universally acknowledged, his gifts for oratory were incomparable, and he enjoyed unmatched access to audiences all over the free states.

For this, slaveholders feared him deeply. Delivered with such rare rhetorical mastery, his attacks on them made him, they complained, "an infernal machine set to music." "Solomon Sizzle"—a certain Bostonian satirist—mocked proslavery politicians in Phillips's hometown by putting the following words into the mouth of an unhappy cotton merchant: "Wendell Phillips—I shudder in horror. . . . He has bruised us. He has made us sore. . . . The very people who hear us talk go straight from us to him, to hear what he says about us, and laugh at the fun he makes of us." And even in the war's immediate aftermath in 1866, when a radical like Phillips began calling for black equality through a massive reconstruction of the defeated South, conservatives acknowledged that "abolition's golden trumpet" wielded serious political power: "Mister [Thurlow] Weed lags in the rear; Mr. [Henry] Raymond is only six months behind Mr. [Horace] Greeley and Mr. Greeley is only six months behind Thad Stevens and Thad Stevens is only six days behind Wendell Phillips, and Wendell Phillips is no more than six inches from the tail and the shining pitchfork of the master of them all."[2]

How, contemporaries wondered, did Wendell Phillips develop so deep and sustained a resonance with northern political culture? In 1860, a writer for the moderate Republican *Ohio State Journal* registered a warning about him that begins to address this question and to open for us the inner world of this extraordinary public figure. The columnist observed that "For the present generation Wendell Phillips is the subtlest, stubbornest fact of the times." Reflecting upon his encounter with Phillips's oratory, this commentator concluded that the key to Phillips's rhetorical mastery was his "unmatched ability to take premises which we all grant to be true" and to "weave them into an enchantment of logic from which there is no escape." No matter how extreme his doctrines, in other words, Phillips invariably anchored them in political values in which his listeners deeply believed. When he propounded northern disunion, for example, Phillips pictured the idea as the essence of democratic freedom, which, as the critic put it, left "God's natural laws to work out their solution. . . . You are hurried along by reasoning like this," he complained, "and cannot make a ready answer. The more you consider it, the more mercilessly logical it appears. It strikes deep and pervades the ideas you have cherished." Another thoughtful critic added the observation that Phillips "appealed to men on the basis of old and established principles. . . . His position accordingly supposes in his audience a pre-existing community of faith, a pre-existing wealth of affection for certain ideas and institutions."[3]

This, according to these firsthand witnesses, is why people found themselves so drawn to Wendell Phillips: instead of assailing or scoffing at their most deep-seated values and loyalties, he evoked and convincingly played upon them. He called forth his listeners' reverence for tradition and their faith in the value of applying the lessons of the past. And somehow, by so doing, he literally became in the eyes of his listeners "an infernal machine set to music" or, if one prefers, "abolition's golden trumpet." With either descriptor, Phillips's immense charisma is impossible to deny.

But something seems amiss here. For better than four decades historians have rightly emphasized just how contemptuous Garrisonian abolitionists were of the very historical precedents and institutions to which Phillips is reported to have appealed. Despite their many other disagreements, scholars of abolitionism persuasively picture their subjects as immersing themselves in radical individualism, not in affection for "*old and established principles*" and a "*preexisting community of faith.*" Garrisonians indulged their romanticism by embracing the moment, valuing iconoclastic spontaneity and rarely appealing to a "*preexisting wealth of affection for certain ideas and institutions.*" Though every bit as iconoclastic in doctrine as his Garrisonian comrades, Phillips nevertheless expressed reverence for precisely what his fellow reformers so eagerly cast aside, that is, precedents and analogies drawn from the past.[4]

This variance between contemporaries' analyses of Phillips's rhetoric and the prevailing judgments of historians invites us to inquire: Why did people so deeply in disagreement with him still gather in throngs to thrill to his oratory? How, more broadly, did his embrace of "old and established principles"—his sense of history—inspire and sustain his abolitionist commitment? And, most broadly of all, what was it in Phillips's biography that allowed him to master mainstream antebellum politics while providing such powerful leadership for some of the nation's most unruly activists? Addressing such questions allows us better to assess, and to appreciate, Wendell Phillips's eminence as a champion of racial democracy and his vitality in bringing on an emancipatory civil war.

HISTORY

Wendell Phillips's attachments to the past began in the spectacular Beacon Hill home where he was born in 1811. Designed by Charles Bulfinch, overlooking Boston's Common and completed in 1806, this five-story Georgian residence registered the political and social eminence of Wendell's father, John Phillips—millionaire attorney, legendary philanthropist, gifted orator, Speaker of the Massachusetts Assembly, and first mayor of incorporated Boston. Just as important, this new home bespoke the uncommon achievements of John Phillips's lineage, an unbroken genealogy of eminent puritans stretching back to the founding of John Winthrop's colony and further yet to Cromwell's England.[5]

As Wendell learned early, his forebears left their enduring impress on the history of the commonwealth and on Boston's Revolution of 1776. Their founding of Phillips Exeter and Phillips Andover academies well exemplified their rich contributions to the public good and stood as a challenge to their descendents to match them, which is precisely what John Phillips did. For him, family imperatives dictated distinguished leadership of both city and commonwealth, which in turn meant a heavy involvement in Federalist politics. That provided opportunities aplenty for young Wendell to take the measure of family friends like Harrison Gray Otis, Nathaniel Appleton, Samuel Sewall, and Josiah Quincy. Wendell certainly observed closely when these commanding figures, but particularly his father, presided over significant civic occasions. Then, too, Wendell could vault the fence across the street whenever militia musters, Fourth of July celebrations, or election-day festivities took over the Common and orators held forth on patriotic themes.[6]

Evidence suggests that this stimulating political environment fired this young "Brahmin's" imagination and kindled his ambitions. Many years later, a friend passed on an anecdote that Phillips had recounted of himself that, as a five-year-old, he used to arrange parlor chairs in rows, stand before them with a Bible propped in front of him, and address an imaginary audience. The story suggests that Wendell, early on, was already imagining himself as someone able to command others through the force of his personality, as someone whose words could alter the course of events.[7]

The Bible featured in the story also confirms that Wendell's early upbringing was suffused with religious injunctions that he develop a life of self-discipline and Christian service. As the youngest of five children, Wendell became the family's sustained focus of religious attention. In the intimacy of the family setting he received loving, concentrated instruction from two quite powerful women, his mother, Sarah Walley Phillips, and his zealously Calvinistic grandmother, Margaret Phillips, and at age thirteen he declared himself to have been saved by Christ's atonement.[8]

Parental preachments and Phillips's personal conversion endured. Years later, he tellingly revealed that he felt "best satisfied" with himself "when I see anything in me that reminds me of my mother." She presented him with a Bible which he read every day while in college and in which, decades later, he marked the passages he wished to have read at his funeral. Phillips once explained that the sum of his mother's injunction to him was: "Be good and do good: this is my whole desire for you. Add other things if you may—these are central." Careful nurture by John, Sarah, and Margaret Phillips were making Wendell into a morally exacting young man who was anxious not only to learn well in order to live correctly, but also to become someone whom others might someday look to as a powerful leader, just as they did to his father and had to his illustrious forebears.[9]

As he set off to pursue these high ambitions at Harvard in 1827, everything seemed to work in Phillips's favor. Tall, athletic, and startlingly good looking, he had an impact on his classmates that was truly profound. "Though I had never seen him before, I was drawn to him by an irresistible attraction," one recalled. Added another, "Phillips was really handsome, in figure and feature a young Apollo." One can only speculate about Phillips's reactions when his friends insisted that he allow them to measure his body to "see how nearly his proportions came to that Grecian example of manly beauty." Although he embodied "elegant manners and social position," his classmates discovered that this aristocratic young man also possessed a uniquely powerful and appealing personality.[10]

Phillips's honesty, his openness, and above all his high moral character seemed invariably to capture his classmates' admiration and elicit their trust. His "love of all that is honest" meant that he "always detested a mean action," observed one. He was "perfectly transparent . . . no subterfuge, no pretense about him. He was known to be just what he seemed." In the final analysis, Phillips possessed what his classmates called "character," which referred to "his kindly, generous manner, his brightness of mind, his perfect purity and whiteness of soul," as one classmate put it. He became a "sincere, conscientious, devoted friend" to all who sought him out, with a "love of all that is honest and without even a word or a thought that the purest might not know or listen to."[11]

By internalizing his parents' injunction to embrace self-discipline, Phillips now had developed an instinctive self-confidence that opened him to others yet made him able to project himself as an inspirational figure. And by the grace of his immense rhetorical abilities, Phillips turned self-projection into a high art. By the time he reached college he had discovered his genius at forensics. The gifts that belonged to Harrison Gray Otis and Josiah Quincy and to his own father also belonged to him, only even more abundantly. "What first led me to observe him and to fix him in my memory," one classmate remembered, "was his elocution and I began to look forward to declamation day with interest mainly on his account." He possessed "the same remarkable eloquence whether in extempore debate or in declamations," another recalled.[12]

Phillips made no surviving comments upon realizing the potency of his talent, but once it revealed itself, he began exploring its implications in his college writings. In these analytical papers and expository essays he set forth attitudes, beliefs, and assumptions of a rising conservative "aristocrat" that were one day to inspire him to reshape the nation as an abolitionist. And since, as Harvard Library borrowing records attest, Phillips made history into his passion, he felt confident about turning his thoughts to the past when assigned to write on topics such as the properties of eloquence, the traits of a great leader, ancient versus modern civilizations, or the British peerage as compared with the French aristocracy.[13]

Throughout these essays he elaborated on all-embracing assumptions first learned at home: unfettered passion led inevitably to personal ruin, social destruction, and collective degradation. Deep emotion channeled by historical precedent and personal restraint, however, were powerful agents that promoted the public good. In times of great crisis, moreover, Phillips believed that boldly heroic figures who embraced tradition (such as his puritan and Revolutionary forebears) had come forward at the crucial moment, acting decisively to banish tyranny and revive the people's liberty.

When asked to analyze the most directly personal of all the topics he was assigned, the properties of eloquence, Phillips worked through all these themes, writing that eloquence addresses men "in whom feelings are centered with burning interest. . . . The more powerful the speaker's language, the stronger the *passion* inspiring it." Yet the passionate orator should never be allowed to devolve into demagoguery, enflaming his listeners' feelings in order to make them "tools for his schemes of aggrandizement." Eloquence must instead be restricted to the legislative chamber, Phillips insisted, and directed to "*deliberative*, sensible men" whose respect for historical precedent made them custodians of the people's highest "interests"—figures strikingly reminiscent of his father. The eloquent speaker himself, Phillips continued, must "view his subject in every light and form his conclusions in an instant." Yet this moment of pure spontaneity did not alone spark true eloquence, which could be achieved only when the speaker added "the most essential requisite of all," his capacity for self-control through the "regulating of his own thoughts." In this paean to the liberating counterpoint between primal impulse and iron-fisted restraint, Phillips came as close as he ever would to writing his autobiography.[14]

Extending this analysis in an essay comparing the history of the French and the British aristocracy, Phillips predictably indicted a "licentious" and "artificial" French nobility for having provoked the "mad enthusiasts" of revolution in 1789, the tragic results of which demonstrated to his satisfaction why people must submit "to the wisdom of those who have gone before" or "bind posterity in chains which we think it degrading to wear." Nor was it a surprise that he embraced the British peerage, "knit with the very vitals of the constitution" and enmeshed in its nation's history while thwarting the tyrants Charles II in 1649 and James II in 1688, and while facing down "atheism and anarchy" when crushing Revolutionary France in 1815. Phillips imagined Edmund Burke's responses to England's deepest moment of crisis to be the fullest embodiment of the eloquence described in the earlier essay: "He arose in all his might. . . . A giant among pigmies he exposed their arrogant pretensions with all the energy and fire of his mind. He thundered," Phillips concluded, "and a tumultuous nation was stilled."[15]

Phillips was now discovering his heroes, powerful figures of action from the past who struck spontaneously with dramatic power to enforce their passion for orderly freedom—Burke, Pitt, Cromwell, Wellington, the signers of the Magna Carta and the leaders of the Glorious Revolution. Before too long, Phillips was to make dramatic gestures of his own, seeking to crush the moral anarchy he feared was spreading across the nation because of slavery. To his list of patriot heroes he was to add Elijah Lovejoy, Crispus Attucks, William Lloyd Garrison, Toussaint L'Ouverture, and John Brown. Soon enough he would find himself compelled to act dramatically on his panoramic vision of history, not just study and write about it.

AGENCY

Phillips stayed on at Harvard, obtained his law degree in 1834, set up his practice, and lapsed into deep disquiet. Pursuing clients and litigating disputes was a terrible comedown for someone who had been lionized by his peers, spoke like Cicero, identified deeply with the heroes of British history, and yearned to match the accomplishments of his forebears. What he desperately lacked was a sense of his life's true purpose and moral direction, not to mention any confidence in his ability to discover them. While building his practice half-heartedly he began retreating by immersing himself in the history of his family, the expectations of which also bore heavily upon him. In happier times, images of

Pitt and Burke had fired his ambitions, but now he immersed himself in genealogies of his own heroic Phillips ancestors, digging out the minutiae that often gives family history its most personal meaning.[16]

Absorbed in the challenges of reconstructing his family tree and deciphering heraldic insignia, he corrected minor factual errors. Samuel Phillips of Rowley (the son of the first John Phillips) had graduated from Harvard in 1650 (not 1651!). He inscribed on the huge folio into which he recorded his research the revealing motto "PENTENS EXEMPLA SUCORUM," a phrase from Cicero (who else?) meaning "redeem the examples of inspiration." He solicited help from other genealogists, assuring one expert candidly "that as a young attorney not much employed *professionally*" he had time aplenty for such projects. Seeking background information, he read histories of New England towns and diaries of early puritans. He discovered and noted with pride that the first John Phillips had been lent the cost of his passage to Massachusetts by John Winthrop and that this founding patriarch had once defended "a man who had been fined for having an Anabaptist book." Phillips was living deep within the past, searching fruitlessly in directions where once he had found self-assurance and promise.[17]

As Phillips researched, conflict over slavery exploded in Boston. He hardly noticed. On October 21, 1835, he watched silently as a mob of noisy anti-abolitionists dashed past him looking to lay violent hands on the most controversial of the local abolitionists, William Lloyd Garrison. This first exposure to the cause that would soon transform his life had no discernable impact on him. Yet the incident did represent a step in that direction, giving him something of substance to discuss after meeting Ann Terry Greene, a vivacious, dedicated member of Boston's Female Anti-Slavery Society, the only surviving member of an opulent merchant family and arguably the wealthiest woman in Massachusetts. Soon enough, she introduced him to Garrison, and Phillips began mixing on the fringes of Boston's Garrisonian circle.[18]

It is not too much to say that Ann Terry Greene liberated Wendell Phillips. His sudden, overwhelming love for her was what finally drove him to reenact, to his own best understanding, the courageous behavior he ascribed to his historical heroes. By undertaking a daring gesture that expressed his passionate commitment to Ann, he quelled in a moment his inner turmoil and opened a future that seemed promising beyond measure.

This familiar story centers on Ann's always fragile health, which dangerously collapsed after she and Phillips began courting, raising alarm that she was about to die. The choices facing Phillips were either to stand by in silent agony or to act on impulse to arrest the compounding crisis. For as long as he could remember he had aspired to achieve the power and distinction that his upbringing, religion, ambition, education, and family honor all demanded. Yet his gifts of eloquence and personal leadership had not saved him from impending obscurity. He knew, moreover, that Ann Greene offered love and understanding in a world that otherwise baffled him. In early December 1836, he "fell into great distress" when informed of her prognosis, confronted her caretakers, and demanded that he be allowed to speak to her privately. Though fearing herself too weak to survive the audience, Ann finally relented, heard his pleas, and accepted his proposal of marriage.[19]

Phillips had acted with impulsive passion in hopes of creating a future restored to order and filled with promise, and this is precisely what happened—a lifetime replete with challenge and fulfillment that touched his deepest emotions, accorded with his most cherished values, and marshaled every one of his many talents. In historians' parlance, Phillips, through Ann, had discovered personal "agency." He now began finding creative ways to draw empowerment, not baffled frustration, from his high expectations, his family's history, his historical imaginings, his vast wealth, and his rich assortment of talents.

The ever-sustaining source of Phillips's agency became his fifty-five years married to Ann. After several frustrating years of seeking cures for her crippling debilities they had accepted her condition as permanent and all but sealed themselves from the outside world when, in 1841, they moved to a nondescript townhouse far from the family mansion on Beacon Hill. Wendell became Ann's vigilant nurse, her emotional therapist, and her conduit to the outside world. She offered him his richest intellectual challenges and his most generative sources of inspiration and renewal. In an environment that both referred to as "the hospital" they nevertheless shared a relationship in which both flourished.[20]

Since a full account of their highly unusual marriage is available elsewhere, it will not be attempted here.[21] Suffice it to observe that Wendell defined his role as husband by predictably relying on the same dynamics with which he was now building the rest of his life—spontaneity (the rich, often exuberant emotional and intellectual life they shared) vouchsafed by the exercise of vigilant control (his imperative to serve as Ann's protector and custodian). As confidence in their relationship strengthened, Ann provided Wendell with the fullest possible expansion of agency—permission for him to leave her for extended periods to undertake speaking tours first across New England and later throughout the Midwest. Thanks to Ann and to no one else, Phillips embraced the one vocation truly suited to his gifts and began presenting himself to the public much as he believed Burke had done in England a generation earlier, as a heroic apostle for liberty.

SPEECH

Phillip's dramatic seizure of abolitionist leadership during his famous November 1837 speech in Faneuil Hall decrying the murder of abolitionist editor Elijah P. Lovejoy is a familiar story. Still, it deserves careful examination since it allows us finally to begin addressing directly the questions: Why did people so deeply in disagreement with Phillips still gather in throngs when he spoke? How did his sense of history sustain his abolitionism? How did he manage to master antebellum politics while leading such unruly and marginalized Garrisonian abolitionists?

An endlessly stubborn abolitionist editor, Lovejoy had stood firm against several attacks while living in Alton, Illinois. But when the mob put a torch to his office he emerged gun in hand, only to crumple dead as the bullets hit him. For Phillips, it was a profoundly transforming event: "the gun that was aimed at the breast of Lovejoy brought me to my feet," he recalled. "I can never forget the agony of that moment." Ann had introduced him to Boston's abolitionists, but Lovejoy's murder now moved him to unite with them as he sat in Faneuil Hall at a heavily attended protest meeting.[22]

Phillips had no thought of speaking until he took in the remarks of James T. Austin, Massachusetts's attorney general, who angrily asserted that the mob had been perfectly within its rights to kill Lovejoy. Lovejoy's abolitionism had posed dangerous threats to domestic safety, so he deserved removal by any means necessary. The Alton mob had behaved similarly to Boston's Revolutionary generation, Austin contended. If Lovejoy had the right to publish, then George III had enjoyed an equal right to tax the colonies. As with Sons of Liberty like John Hancock and Sam Adams, Lovejoy's killers had been left no choice but to act as an "orderly mob" to purge their city of "the disgusting instruments of their degradation."

Amid chaotic shouting and ineffectual cries for "order," Phillips pushed his way, unannounced, to the platform. Though he would later maintain that "events rather than my own will" had led him to this moment, we have seen that he had actually been preparing for it for years, albeit unwittingly, and that it was thanks to Ann that he was now about to introduce himself as liberty's foremost rhetorical champion.[23]

For the rest of his life, Phillips believed that this was the moment when he first understood what actually lay behind the chaos overcoming Faneuil Hall, the violence that had overtaken faraway Alton, and the anti-abolitionist thuggery he had silently witnessed in his hometown. It was a republican nightmare, the unopposed power of a perverted system of human relations founded in tyranny—slavery—that was spreading devastation and turmoil across the nation and within his own community. He felt, as he remembered, that he was "recognizing for the first time the death grapple" into which he "had unthinkingly been drawn."

As he mounted the podium, he looked directly across the hall at the portraits of John Hancock, James Otis, and Sam Adams, whose gravestones crowd in next to that of Phillips's father, John Phillips, in the Old Granary burial ground. He always claimed that it was to those portraits, not to the audience, that he really was speaking as he laid claim to the highest purpose for his eloquence. Just as he had written in his Harvard essay, he had "formed his thoughts in an instant" and now, entirely self-controlled, he began retracing them one by one as he tore into Austin's contentions. With a compelling synthesis of iron self-possession, deepest passion, and an abiding devotion to the past, Phillips structured his speech on the selfsame designs he had been developing ever since childhood.[24]

He was surprised, Phillips began, to hear the commonwealth's voice of law and order—Austin—endorse mob violence. He was even more disturbed by the applause Austin had received "within these walls," dedicated as they were to patriotism and liberty. To compare the actions "of the drunken murderers of Lovejoy" with the inspired resistance of the "patriot fathers" was a perversion of truth and an "insult to their memory." The "glorious mantle of Revolutionary precedent could never be thrown over the mobs of our day," Phillips insisted, because "the men of the revolution went for rights as secured by law. The rioters of today go for their own wills, right or wrong." Pointing to the portraits of Adams, Hancock, and Otis and instantaneously collapsing the moment deep into the past, he described his initial reaction to hearing Austin compare Lovejoy's killers to these supreme heroes: "I thought the pictured lips would have broken into voice to rebuke the recreant American—the slanderer of the dead. . . . In the sentiments he has uttered on soil consecrated by the prayers of Puritans and the blood of patriots, the earth should have yawned and swallowed him up." As the audience exploded with cheers and angry cries, Phillips stood aloof and relaxed on the platform, the picture of gentlemanly ease and self-possession and starkly in contrast to the ranting Austin.

Lovejoy himself deserved recognition for patriotism every bit as heroic as Hancock's and Sam Adams's, Phillips concluded. His action had revealed that he, like them, was a man of supreme will who had sought to liberate not only Alton but also the nation from the tyranny of enslavement. "The crisis had come," said Phillips; "it was time to assert the laws." Someone had to take bold steps to show the people "the priceless value of the freedom of the press and set right their confused ideas." Lovejoy had "looked out over the community, staggering like a drunken man, and had rightly concluded that the people had become "deaf to argument." So he raised his revolver, hoping desperately "that they might be stunned into sobriety. Insulted laws called for it," Phillips declared, for Lovejoy had seen the "necessity of resistance." Had the year been 1776 instead of 1837, none would have charged the Revolutionary martyr, Joseph Warren, with "imprudence" as Austin had charged Lovejoy; no one would have said of him that "he died as a fool dieth." Once Phillips finished, the meeting quickly adjourned since no one dared follow him to the podium. Little wonder that commentators on Phillips's oratory marveled at his "*unmatched ability to take premises which we all grant to be true*" and to "*weave them into an enchantment of logic for which there is no escape.*"[25]

Phillips elicited such powerful responses by making of himself a most uncommon Garrisonian. For all his personal piety, he almost never spoke against slavery in the prophetic language of Jesus or Jeremiah. In starkest contrast to Garrison, his closest collaborator, he was not much for quoting scripture, condemning sinners, demanding repentance, prophesying retribution, or praying for "moral revolution"—not in the Lovejoy speech and rarely thereafter. Instead, he challenged slavery on fundamental political grounds by communicating in an ideological idiom that nearly all Americans instinctively accepted no matter how deep and many their partisan differences—the language of republicanism. No matter how extreme his doctrines or grating his personal attacks, it was impossible to confuse Phillips's content with the religious zealotry and supposed "infidelity" that turned so many against the abolitionists.

Whatever their views on his specific positions, the premises underlying Phillip's oratory struck listeners as axiomatic because he directly touched their republican sensibilities. Though historians make clear that there were many conflicting varieties of antebellum "republicanism," certain broad assumptions underlay this political persuasion that were in harmony with Phillips's understanding of history. A republican outlook meant inquiring of the past for reasons that would explain why corrupting power in whatever perceived form was threatening the people's precious liberty. It likewise meant invoking the past's great patriots when calling for mobilization in defense of democratic freedom. These were the axioms to which Phillips appealed in his Lovejoy speech. And it was those same assumptions that a commentator quoted earlier had in mind when observing that Phillips's power over his audiences derived from his challenging them "*on the basis of old and established principles.*"[26]

For these reasons, Phillips's criticisms of slavery invariably stressed its destructive moral impact on all of American political culture. He most certainly regarded the actual enslavement of black humanity as a gross perversion of every Christian ethic, but beyond this he feared that the power of slavery was running rampant through all the nation's institutions and was increasing its strength by spreading violence, degradation, and tyranny. It was an "abnormal element which nobody had counted in" that "sends out poisonous branches over this fair land and corrupts the very air we breathe." In Phillips's view, slavery must be abolished because, by heinously exploiting black people, the southern planters were orchestrating the no less monstrous enslavement of all Americans everywhere, in their churches, their politics, and their personal moral choices. Slavery "saps our strength and blinds our foresight," and Americans were "no longer aware of its deadly influence on the body politic," Phillips warned.[27]

To combat this juggernaut he challenged the people to rise up against the "tyranny of this many-headed monster" by completing the unfinished tasks of their nation's republican history: "In order to establish the rights of the slave, we must first establish our own," he insisted. "The patriot as well as the abolitionist" must become energetically "concerned in this struggle" to finish "what our fathers left unfinished when they declared all men free and equal." The abolitionist mission, he declared, was "to enlarge the canvass of law till it covers all men, both black and white." Phillips's republican vision foresaw powerful laws that would one day erase all distinctions of color. Only then would civil liberty, political freedom, and economic self-determination reign in Massachusetts as well as in South Carolina. Fully grounded in the political culture of his age, Phillips's formulations gave him much common ground with his audiences. They no less than he distrusted "corrupting" power and had been mobilizing in elections against a variety of unrelated enemies—the "tyranny" of Andrew Jackson, the "money power" of bankers, the "secret influence" of Masonry, the "unnatural hierarchy" of Catholicism, the conspiracies of labor "bosses," and so on. Deeply conscious of these affinities, Phillips now offered himself to the public as a Burkean patriot-hero.[28]

PRESENTATION

For orators, the 1840s and 1850s were fortunate times. As the population grew by millions, so did literacy and the sophistication of readers and audiences. The North contained a hive of reading rooms, libraries, debating societies, and civic-minded voluntary associations founded, staffed, and attended by rapidly developing business and professional classes. Expanding networks of roadways, railroads, and telegraph lines meant cheaper, swifter, and wider distribution of information. Lecturers could now venture into places unreachable before. A huge reading public now formed an orator's second audience. Up-to-date printing presses and new stenographic techniques could turn out twenty thousand newspaper impressions an hour and circulate a speaker's remarks just as they had been delivered. Every forward-thinking community sponsored a lyceum that presented in one season any number of "elevating" subjects, and a rich mixture of politicians, authors, and reformers took to the lecture circuit. Moving far beyond the narrow confines of the Boston Garrisonians, Wendell Phillips joined them to offer sectional confrontation as well as edification.[29]

Phillips developed a popular repertoire of "elevating" speeches on "Chartism," "Water," "Geology," "Street Life in Europe" and—his most popular—"The Lost Arts." He repeated them hundreds of times, adding ten to fifteen thousand dollars annually to his very considerable fortune.[30] But by inviting Phillips, local lyceums automatically multiplied opportunities for him to speak as an abolitionist. One critic's complaint illustrated this point perfectly. Phillips's reputation as a master of forensics rested on his abolitionism, this analyst wrote, not as a commentator on street life in Europe: "Beautiful and golden as the speaker's oratory was, the audience, we think, was not satisfied." Listeners wanted Phillips's "latest research and thoughts lit up by the light of the latest events. . . . If a man who has devoted his life to the negro question is to lecture, by all means let him lecture on the negro, or some subject akin to that." To this Phillips responded with the standing offer to lecture on the problem of slavery for no fee *if* lyceum boards would pay him for speaking on non-controversial topics. When exactly this came to pass in Lee, Massachusetts, Phillips exulted to Ann that "So the walls fall down and prejudice melts year by year—I see more and more the wide influence of the Lyceum movement in smoothing the way to other things."[31]

Phillips possessed the license to behave so independently because he had achieved "stardom." Following foreigners Jenny Lind and Fanny Kemble, he was among the first of his generation to achieve national visibility as a popular figure whom people would pay to see. Thanks to heavy newspaper promotion, the public was well aware of his reputation and wanted to find out what Wendell Phillips looked like, how he behaved, and what he "really" sounded like. As Phillips himself shrewdly observed, people did not attend his lectures out of a sense of obligation to become "edified" but because they desired vicarious participation in the controversies associated with his name. People did not say "If I don't go, my neighbors won't do their duty. I'm sorry to waste an hour but I must set a good example for my children." Rather, the listener hastened to the lecture hall "because his heart is there half an hour before he is. . . . He goes because he can't stay away, . . . to share in the great struggle and glow in the electric conflict." Before and after his speeches people hounded him for autographs testifying to their encounters with the famous man. The casual researcher can stumble on Phillips's "mark" in practically every northern historical society's autograph file, his signature commonly scrawled below his favorite slogan—"Peace if Possible, Justice at Any Rate!"[32]

So as people entered the lecture hall they did not simply expect to hear a speaker give a talk about slavery; instead, they were well prepared and eager to participate in a significant dramatic event orchestrated by the genius of Wendell Phillips. In no sense did he disappoint them. His platform style was by all accounts arresting, his impact unforgettable.

People often expressed surprise at their first sight of Phillips, for his appearance contradicted their expectations. He seemed not a flinty extremist but an open, relaxed, humble, friendly man: "Can this be the fiery reformer . . . ? Can this be the rank agitator . . . ? Could this easy, effortless man be Wendell Phillips?" Such exclamations echo through the contemporary descriptions. He projected great physical authority for he was full framed, athletic looking with a profile that grew more rugged with age. Yet there was an "absence of vindictiveness or even severity, though not of firmness in his appearance." He carried no notes and stood directly before his audience with no podium to set him apart from them. Then, suddenly but quietly, he leaped "at a single bound into the middle of his subject." The "keynote to Phillips's oratory," wrote Thomas Wentworth Higginson perceptively, "was its conversational power, raised to the highest power." No other orator, in his opinion, "ever began so entirely on the plain of his average hearer. It was as if he simply repeated, in a slightly louder tone, what he had been saying to a familiar friend at his elbow." The moment Phillips began to lecture, the psychological distance between himself and his audience vanished. He "held them by his quietness," observed Higginson, establishing a powerful intimacy with audiences of hundreds.[33]

As Phillips warmed to his subject, none could doubt that a genuine extremist was bathing them in inflammatory rhetoric and aiming at their deep passions. Nevertheless, by every account, his delivery was absolutely calm, "like a marble statue, cool and white, while a stream of lava issued red hot from his lips." Another witness likened him to "a volcano, whose bosom nourishes inexhaustible fire . . . while all without is unruffled and unindicative of the power within." As he continued speaking, using simple democratic language, his voice would grow deeper and his sentences would begin flowing in "a long sonorous swell, still easy and graceful, but powerful as the soft stretching of a tiger's paw." A certain E. A. S. Smith, no prominent abolitionist or culture critic, offered this extremely revealing first reaction: "I have never been so absorbed by a speaker. . . . He had all the ease and manner of one who is the perfect master of his subject and is confident of its truth and all the grace of a graceful man. The topics he touched upon were all powerful, finely illustrated, and it appeared to me that they must convince everyone there that they must be up and doing. His manner was so informal that I thought we might [call it] a talk rather than address."[34]

These responses make clear why audiences found Phillips so captivating. He was the master of what sociologist Irving Goffman has termed "fresh talk," that is, the speaker's ability to appear immediately receptive to the feelings of his listeners even as he seems to be sharing his thoughts and emotions. The effect is one of self-revealing spontaneity, unencumbered by the distractions of a written script, memorized lines, superficial hyperbole, or stumbling diction which heighten the audience's distance from the speaker. "He opens his heart to you as the spring buds do theirs," wrote one observer. "You never think to ask from whom he learned to do so." Or, as Henry David Thoreau put it, Phillips's rhetoric was unique because he was "at the same time an eloquent speaker and a righteous man." All these observations repeat precisely what Phillips's college friends had once said of him, that he was transparent and wholly without guile.[35]

It all seemed arrestingly simple. Phillips calmly said what was on his mind, and the more he projected this impression of utter honesty the more he induced his listeners to settle in as his biting phrases carried them along. (Demagogues, Phillips had written decades before, inflamed mob passions. Orators elevated and instructed listeners' interests.) His words were "like oil on the billows of a chafed sea; he rebukes the winds of strife and the waves of faction. . . . The severe front of the tyrant or turncoat present begins to relax. . . . He is the mobber of mobs." The point is crucial. Phillips's extremism has always unnerved and inspired modern readers, and his listeners undoubtedly responded in similar ways. But unless intent on harassing him, audiences never felt that Phillips was trying to intimidate them or goad them to abandon their self-control: "No waste of power. No 'bursts of eloquence.' Everything is subdued, strong and telling. He steals upon the audience and surprises them into enthusiasm. . . . He has exactly the manner of an agitator, [but] it was entirely without agitation."[36]

In forensics there is a point at which style unites with content to achieve aesthetic unity. What Phillips actually said, therefore, was just as important as his way of expressing himself, creating a single artistic creation to which audiences responded as one might to a provocative painting or sculpture. One commentator suggested that Phillips's artistry evoked images of "a beautiful damsel *en dishabille*. . . . His quotations, then, are ringlets rolled up in papers, and the main part of his lecture like a loose gown which now and then reveals a neck of pearl and a voluptuous breast of snowy whiteness and beautiful proportions." Another chose a military metaphor: "Those simple, brief sentences of which his speeches are made up, form a coat of mail so cunningly and closely wrought that no lance can pierce it." Phillips's son-in-law resorted to a classical parallel: "There was much of the Greek in him in the sense of ordered beauty and art. . . . They were much more evident when you heard him. . . . The symmetrical quality of mind and speech which is almost the rarest in modern oratory." A sensual woman, chain mail, Grecian symmetry—the diversity of the imagery reveals the deeper reasons why people flocked to hear him. By opening his rhetorical imagination to others, he stimulated his listeners to fire their imaginations as well.[37]

"He had many surprises in thought and diction," one contemporary recalled.[38] The level of understatement achieved here will depress anyone who has carefully read Phillips's speeches. Epigrams, analogies, parables, tall tales, teeth-grinding sarcasm, one-liners, vignettes, historical reflections, and grand patriotic themes greet the reader from every direction. One blending of many of these elements appeared so repeatedly in Phillips's speeches that it is worth experiencing more deeply, an endlessly flexible formulation fusing into a single evocative vision of the nation's history, geography, and economy. It elaborates what might be called the "moral terrain" of the national past, present, and future while invoking the compelling value of the republican ideology that gave Phillips and his audiences such powerful rapport. Rather than attempting extended analysis of this entire trope, it is sufficient, one hopes, to offer readers a firsthand exposure to a representative example. It is transcribed stenographically from Phillips's Fourth of July oration delivered in Framingham, Massachusetts, in 1859. Please read it carefully:

> It is a glorious country that God has given us, fit in every respect but one to look upon, this holiday of the Union, and seem worthy of the sun and the sky that look down upon us; for it is the people taking possession by right, by inheritance, by worth, of the wealth, the culture, the happiness, and the achievements of the age. Show me such another! In the rotten, shiftless, poor, decrepit, bankrupt South, can you find the material that can erect a barrier against the onward and outward pressure of a people such as ours? Yes,—when the dream of the girl dams up Niagara, when the bulrush says to the Mississippi, "Stop!" then will Carolina or Mississippi say to the potency of New England, with her three million educated, earnest, governing hearts,—say to her, in the tone of this worn-out, effete, rotten Whiggery of Harvard College, "Stop here!" [great enthusiasm] Why, by the vigor of such a civilization as ours, we shall take the State of Mississippi by the nape of its neck, and shake every decrepit white man out of it and give it into the hands of the slave that now tills it, and make America to represent the ideal to which our fathers consecrated it. Be worthy of this day! Create a sympathy among those toiling millions for liberty. What is it that makes us powerless? It is that your Church teaches us to look down on the black

man; it is that your State teaches us, with this letter of Winthrop (the Massachusetts Whig Senator Robert C. Winthrop, supporter of the 1850 Fugitive Slave Law) that we have no duty outside the narrow circle of Massachusetts law. Here, under the blue sky of New England, we teach the doctrine, that wherever you find a man down-trodden, he is your brother; wherever you find an unjust law, you are bound to be its enemy; that Massachusetts was planted as the furnace of perpetual insurrection against tyrants [loud applause]; that this is a bastard who has stolen the name of Winthrop [tremendous cheering]—been foisted into the cradle while the mother was out [loud laughter and applause]; that the true blood of the Bradfords, the Carvers, the Endicotts and the Winthrops crops out in some fanatical abolitionist, whom the Church disowns, whom the State tramples under foot, but who will yet model both, by the potency of that truth which the elder Winthrop gave into our hands, and which we hold to-day as an example for the nation. [Prolonged applause.] This is my speech for the Fourth of July.[39]

INVITATION

Now reread that passage, please. Keep in mind as you do so this essay's attempts to explain the enormous potency of Phillips's oratory by referencing his biography. Next, imagine yourself in 1859 listening to Phillips while sitting in a large attentive audience made up of commercial and business leaders as well as of politically engaged farmers, artisans, and shopkeepers. As a well-informed historian, you know that people like these believed as fervently as Phillips did in extending the "wealth, culture, happiness and achievements" of their northern free-labor society. You are likewise aware that, as sectional conflict deepened, voters such as these concluded in ever greater numbers that, "by right, by inheritance and by worth," their republican North and not the slave-holding overlords of a "rotten, shiftless, poor, decrepit, bankrupt South" must determine the national destiny. Imagine all this as you reread the passage, and perhaps you'll sense on some tangibly personal level the beauty and power of Phillips's oratory. You might likewise gain an insight as to why someone felt moved to describe him as "the subtlest, stubbornest fact of the times." Perhaps you'll also better understand how Phillips inspired such an enormous number of people to anticipate a post-emancipation America that was rooted in puritan history, upheld by the rule of law, and dedicated to biracial egalitarianism.

EPILOGUE

In 1912, the distinguished black poet and activist James Weldon Johnson recalled the ceremony that had marked his graduation from his Jacksonville, Florida, elementary school in 1887:

> The real enthusiasm was aroused by "Shiny." He was the principal speaker of the day, and well did he measure up to the honour. He made a striking picture, that thin little black boy standing on the platform, dressed in clothes that did not fit him any too well, his eyes burning with excitement, his shrill, musical voice vibrating with such great intelligence and earnestness as to be positively handsome. What were his thoughts as he stepped forward and looked into that crowd of faces, all white with the exception of a score or so lost to view? I do not know, but I fancy he felt loneliness. I think there must have rushed over him a feeling akin to that of a gladiator tossed into the arena and bade to fight for his life. I think that solitary little black figure standing there felt that for the particular time and place he bore the weight and responsibility of his race: that for him to fail meant general defeat; but he won, and nobly. His oration was Wendell Phillips's "Toussaint L'Ouverture," a speech that may be classed as rhetorical, or even bombastic; but when the words fell from "Shiny's" lips the effect was magical. How a young orator could stir so great enthusiasm was to be wondered at. When, in the famous peroration, his voice, trembling with suppressed emotion rose higher and higher and then rested on the name "Toussaint L'Ouverture," it was like touching an electric button which loosed the pent-up feelings of his listeners. They actually rose up to him.[40]

NOTES

1. For modern biographies of Phillips, consult Irving Bartlett, *Wendell Phillips: Brahmin Radical* (Boston: Beacon Press, 1961), and James Brewer Stewart, *Wendell Phillips: Liberty's Hero* (Baton Rouge: Louisiana State University Press, 1986).

2. *New York World* quoted in the *National Anti-Slavery Standard*, November 24, 1866.

3. *Ohio State Journal*, reprinted in *Liberator*, April 5, 1861; *Christian Examiner* reprinted in *Liberator*, December 4, 1861.

4. Lewis Perry, *Radical Abolitionism: Anarchy and the Government of God in Antislavery Thought* (Ithaca: Cornell University Press, 1973); Lawrence J. Friedman, *Gregarious Saints: Self and Community in American Abolitionism, 1830–1860* (New York: Cambridge University Press, 1982); Ron-

ald Walters, *The Antislavery Appeal: Abolitionism after 1831* (Baltimore: Johns Hopkins University Press, 1976); Andrew Delbanco, *The Abolitionist Imagination* (Cambridge: Harvard University Press, 2012); Stewart, *Wendell Phillips*, 190, emphasis added.

5. For a photograph of the Phillips mansion, see Stewart, *Wendell Phillips*, 2.

6. Stewart, *Wendell Phillips*, 1–17; "Memoir of John Phillips," *Boston Monthly Magazine*, November 1825.

7. Mary C. Crawford, *Romantic Days in Old Boston* (Boston: Little, Brown and Co., 1922), 152; Carlos Martyn, *Wendell Phillips: The Agitator* (New York: Funk & Wagnalls, 1890), 27.

8. Stewart, *Wendell Phillips*, 8–9.

9. Ibid., 8–10; Wendell Phillips to Elizabeth Pease, January 11, 1846, Antislavery Collection, Boston Public Library.

10. Roscoe Conkling Bruce, "The College Career of Wendell Phillips," *Harvard Illustrated Magazine* 17 (April 1901): 184: Bartlett, *Wendell Phillips*, 20–21; Phillips classmate John Tappan Pierce quoted in Martyn, *Wendell Phillips*, 45–48; Phillips classmate Edgar Buckingham quoted from the Edward Buckingham Papers, Harvard University Archives.

11. Buckingham Papers; John Tappan Pierce quoted in Martyn, *Wendell Phillips*, 43–47.

12. Buckingham Papers.

13. Library Records, Harvard University Archives, document that Phillips borrowed all eight volumes of Gibbon's *Decline and Fall of the Roman Empire*; eight volumes of Hume's *History of England*; the writings of Edmund Burke, Machiavelli, Locke, and Montesquieu; and the histories of the Stuart Kings, Cromwellian England, and France in the seventeenth and eighteenth centuries. By no means were all these titles required as assignments.

14. Wendell Phillips, "On Forming Habits of Extemporary Speaking" (1831); "Your Idea of What Makes Writing to Be Poetical, Prose or Eloquent" (November 1830); "Whether Eloquence Is Diminished by the Gradual Progress of Literature and Science" (undated); "Whether Attachment to Ancient Usages Be a Greater Evil than a Fondness for Innovation—A Speech" (1831); "Whether the Proposed Parliamentary Reform Will Endanger the Monarchic and Aristocratic Portion of the Constitution?" (1831) Wendell Phillips Composition Books, Harvard University Archives, emphasis in original.

15. "A Comparison of Burke and Sir Joshua Reynolds" (1831), Phillips Composition Books, Harvard University Archives.

16. Stewart, *Wendell Phillips*, 36–42.

17. Wendell Phillips genealogical file, Crawford Blagden Papers, Houghton Library, Harvard University, emphasis in original.

18. Stewart, *Wendell Phillips* 42–45.

19. Ibid., 45–48.

20. There has been much speculation about the nature of Ann Phillips's illness. Contemporary definitions included "morbidity" and "neurasthenia" while recent speculations center on rheumatoid arthritis, rheumatic fever, and fibromyalgia. Whatever the cause, the effect was blinding headaches, painful sensitivity to light, persistent indigestion, chronic joint and muscle pain, and eventually skeletal deformation as a result of being bedridden. See Stewart, *Wendell Phillips*, 46–48, 82–86, 164–65, 311–13. Close family friend Edmund Quincy offered a diagnosis

that many others must have accepted at the time: "It is one of those mysterious complaints in which the organic . . . is mixed up with a good deal that is imaginary. But that is a dead secret for neither of them would forgive such a suggestion. The end of it," he predicted in 1846, "will be long life." On this last point, Quincy was correct. Ann Phillips died three years after her husband, in 1887 at age seventy-six (Edmund Quincy to Richard Webb, July 14, 1846, Antislavery Collection, Boston Public Library).

21. For substantial treatments of the Phillipses' marital relationship and their shared approaches to facing the outside world, consult Irving Bartlett, *Wendell and Ann Phillips and the Community of Reform, 1840–1880* (New York: W. W. Norton, 1979), and Stewart, *Wendell Phillips*, 42–51, 88–96, 174–75.

22. Phillips's recollections in *National Anti-Slavery Standard*, April 27, May 25, 1867.

23. Stewart, *Wendell Phillips*, 59–65.

24. Ibid., 59–65; George W. Smalley, "Memoir of Wendell Phillips," *Harper's Magazine*, June 1894, 133–41.

25. Wendell Phillips, "The Murder of Lovejoy," in Phillips, *Speeches, Lectures, and Letters* (Boston: James Redpath, 1863), 2–10; Stewart, *Wendell Phillips*, 189, emphasis added.

26. For an extended discussion of Phillips and republican ideology see Stewart, *Wendell Phillips*, 69–72, 97–98, 162–63, 323–24, emphasis added.

27. Phillips's recollection in *National Anti-Slavery Standard*, May 25, 1867.

28. "The Right of Petition" and "The Murder of Lovejoy," in Phillips, *Speeches, Lectures, and Letters*.

29. Angela Ray, *The Lyceum and Public Culture in the Nineteenth-Century United States* (East Lansing: Michigan State University Press, 2005); Alvin W. Gouldner, *The Dialectics of Ideology and Technology* (New York: Seabury Press, 1976).

30. By today's valuations, the Phillipses' inherited wealth made them billionaires, to which Wendell's speaking fees added a comfortable annual income. Unlike the other great abolitionist philanthropists, Gerrit Smith and Lewis Tappan, Wendell and Ann never underwrote highly visible enterprises but instead seem to have given away much of their wealth very quietly and without explanation, mostly to private individuals in need. Paying tuition at Harvard for namesake Wendell Phillips Garrison and raising an adopted daughter, Phoebe Garnaut, could have made only minimal demands on their resources. Evidence for their having disbursed their assets to individuals in need is found in the many private appeals and Phillips's responses, found in the Crawford Blagden Papers. In truth, however, no one knows what happened to the Phillips fortune, which could as easily have been lost in ill-advised investments as in support of worthy endeavors. When Ann Phillips died in 1887, she left no significant estate.

31. Wendell Phillips to Ann Phillips, February 25, 1855, Crawford Blagden Papers, Houghton Library, Harvard University.

32. Wendell Phillips, "The Pulpit," in *Speeches, Letters, and Lectures, Second Series* (Boston: Lee & Shepard, 1891), 252–75.

33. Thomas Wentworth Higginson, *Wendell Phillips* (Boston: Lee and Shepard, 1884), 265–67: Andover *Advertiser* reprinted in *Liberator*, March 20, 1857; *New Englander Magazine*, reprinted in *Liberator*, November 15, 1850.

34. E. A. S. Smith to Caroline Weston (no date), Antislavery Collection, Boston Public Library; Lillie Buffum Chace Wyman, "Reminiscences of Wendell Phillips," *New England Magazine*, February 1903, 715–36; *Liberator*, August 6, 1852; Martyn, *Wendell Phillips*, 193–94.

35. Irving Goffman, *Forms of Talk* (Philadelphia: University of Pennsylvania Press, 1981); *Liberator*, March 30, 1857; December 4, 1863; March 25, 1845.

36. Testimony reprinted in *Liberator*, December 15, 1850; February 19, 1855. Martyn, *Wendell Phillips*, 493.

37. *New Englander Magazine*, reprinted in *Liberator*, November 15, 1850; *Ohio State Journal*, reprinted in *Liberator*, April 5, 1861; Smalley, "Memoir of Wendell Phillips," 133–41.

38. Martyn, *Wendell Phillips*, 494.

39. *Liberator*, July 18, 1859.

40. James Weldon Johnson, *The Autobiography of an Ex-Coloured Man*, reprinted in John Hope Franklin, ed., *Three Negro Classics* (New York: Discus Book, 1965).

2

THE TRANSATLANTIC MIND OF WENDELL PHILLIPS AND THE PROBLEM OF DEMOCRACY IN AMERICA

W. CALEB McDANIEL

Wendell Phillips believed that every thinking American in the antebellum period had to confront two questions. The first was why slavery survived in the South. The second was why the North allowed it and refused to listen to abolitionists like him. For Phillips, the first question was always the easier. He viewed the South as a region that time had passed by, a place ruled by an aristocratic class whose ideals were more suited to a feudal age. Slaveholders "believed with the Englishman, that one man is born, booted and spurred, and another saddled and bridled ready for the first one to ride," Phillips recalled in 1866. They also "disbelieved in common schools" and free presses, which might disseminate dissenting views. In such a benighted region it was no wonder to Phillips that barbaric practices like slavery survived.[1]

Phillips believed his own region was different, more democratic and enlightened. "The North *thinks*," he often said; it was a land of "free speech, free printing, free labor, and free institutions." But this raised a painful problem that troubled Phillips throughout his career: how could this thinking, democratic society remain so deaf to abolitionist appeals or, even worse, actively try to silence them?[2]

In dealing with that question, Phillips was a rigorous and creative theorist of democracy. His best biographers, including Irving Bartlett, Oscar Sherwin, and James Brewer Stewart, have always known this. Sherwin called Phillips a "philosopher of agitation," while Bartlett found in his writings "a carefully articulated theory of American institution[s]." My own discussion, however, will identify two underappreciated sources of Phillips's political thought—one transatlantic, and the other ancient in origin.[3]

First, Phillips was informed by the writings of European liberals like Alexis de Tocqueville and John Stuart Mill, revealing the transatlantic dimensions of his thought. Second, Phillips's fascination with ancient Athens, another interest he shared with European liberals, illuminates his philosophy of agitation. In short, the mind of Wendell Phillips ranged widely across space and time, though many of his key insights emerged from reflection on the problems of democracy in his own backyard.

Phillips's initial conversion to abolitionism was powered above all by his perceptions of decline and danger in the supposedly democratic North. In the 1830s, he was outraged that leading New Englanders—men who had benefited from "all that republican education ought to have secured"—openly defended anti-abolitionist mobs. Over the next two decades Phillips witnessed more of the same: more mobs tried to stifle abolitionist speech, more elites spoke in favor of compromise with the "Slave Power," and even New England's greatest statesman, Daniel Webster, approved of a Fugitive Slave Law that allowed aristocratic planters to extend their iron grasp across the Mason-Dixon Line. For Phillips, it was easy to understand why the South, weighed down by nearly medieval institutions, remained "one great brothel" and prison; it was harder to explain why, in the North, "the press says, 'It is all right'; and the pulpit cries, 'Amen.'"[4]

Widespread indifference to slavery in the North posed a challenge to Phillips's fundamental beliefs about the nature of democracy. Put simply, the challenge concerned what to do when a democratic majority was illiberal, apathetic, or morally wrong. Part of the reason for northern indifference, Phillips knew, was that "the heart of the common people [was] chilled by a bitter prejudice against the black race." But the fact that the people's hearts *could* be frozen by such prejudices also raised larger questions about the legitimacy of majority rule itself.[5]

On the one hand, the "age of democratic equality"—with its idea that the many should rule—distinguished the North from the aristocratic South. Yet democratic equality also allowed the masses, when wrong, to stamp out dissent with nearly as much impunity as aristocrats. In Phillips's mind, the schoolhouses, newspapers, and common education of the North were supposed to prevent unjust prejudices from taking root, but when they did not, the same democratic principles that justified popular education allowed the prejudices of the majority to overwhelm dissenting minorities, both by legal and extralegal means. After the murder of abolitionist editor Elijah P. Lovejoy by a mob in Alton, Illinois, Phillips watched, aghast, as some northerners argued that it was wrong for citizens even "to publish opinions disagreeable to the community"—a principle that seemed to give the majority even more power to regulate speech than "the despotism of the Sultan." Yet, the reaction to Lovejoy's murder, he soon learned, would not be an isolated incident. "Every statement we have laid down has been denied by overwhelming majorities against us," Phillips said of abolitionists in 1853, and that remained true for most of his life.[6]

Even more troubling than the majority's overwhelming power, however, was its imperviousness to change. For decades, Phillips and his fellow abolitionists tried to awaken the "slumbering conscience" and "dead hearts" of northerners. But they were met more often by yawns and shrugs than by mobs. Phillips found northerners too concerned with their own selfish interests, or too afraid to trouble the status quo, to listen to abolitionist appeals. On controversial topics, even northerners—presumably free to think whatever they chose—showed "all the timidity of the Old World," afraid to embrace their own democratic principles.[7]

That pervasive timidity in northern life—the lack of independent thinking, the "habitual caution which treads on eggs without breaking the shells"—was harder to understand, for Phillips, than the haughtiness of aristocrats in the South. It did help to explain why, as he put it, "the elements which control public opinion and mould the masses are against us. We can but pick off here and there a man from the triumphant majority." But these facts only deepened the challenges to Phillips's democratic faith. "It seems to me that, on all questions, we dread thought," Phillips said, echoing his fellow Bostonian Ralph Waldo Emerson. "We shrink behind something," refusing to "sail outside" of the mainstream or "attempt to reason outside of . . . [its] limited, cribbed, cabined" ideas. How was this possible in a society that prided itself on common schools, a flourishing press, and—nominally, at least—freedom of speech?[8]

Phillips shared that question not only with like-minded Americans, but also with many European thinkers who were his contemporaries, especially Alexis de Tocqueville and John Stuart Mill. Their writings proved critical in helping him to understand and describe what he knew from experience in the American North. First, Tocqueville, whom Phillips quoted often in his abolitionist speeches, offered a compelling analysis of how the principle of popular sovereignty gave the majority nearly tyrannical sway in every arena of American life.

Moreover, Tocqueville's masterwork, *Democracy in America*, identified timidity, conformity, and acquiescence to despotic abuses as dangers that always loomed in a democratic society. As Mill explained in a famous review of the book, Tocqueville feared that the danger of democracy, "both in government and in intellect and morals, is not of too great liberty, but of too ready submission . . . not of too rapid change, but of Chinese stationariness"—precisely the problems that Phillips had encountered as a radical in a conservative North.[9]

Today the affinities between Tocqueville and Mill are better known among scholars than Phillips's affinity with them, but these transatlantic liberals gave Phillips a language for articulating what he, too, saw as the greatest dangers confronting democracy: a loss of "moral courage and pride of independence," as Mill's review put it, a refusal to "deviate from the beaten path," and a culture that made the majority's opinions gradually "more difficult to change." Such insights comprised part of the reason why Phillips considered Mill one of Europe's "largest brains" and "profoundest thinkers," as well as why he once called Tocqueville "that most illustrious of all historical annalists, that profoundest of all statesmen."[10]

Phillips also shared with European liberals like Tocqueville and Mill a habit of reflecting on the past, particularly the ancient past, in order to understand or put into starker relief the problems of democracy in his own day. In fact, though most biographers have emphasized Phillips's interest in American and English history, Phillips took special inspiration from the history of ancient Athens—a society that he often cited as a model for American civilization.[11]

Phillips loved Athens for reasons directly related to the Tocquevillian problems he perceived in his northern surroundings. While American apathy toward slavery and hostility toward abolitionism suggested that democracy might be inimical to free discussion and courageous thinking, ancient Athens had a reputation as a democracy in which philosophers and powerful orators were able to sway the people from bad decisions and encourage new ideas. In an aphorism that circulated widely in modern books about the ancients, the Athenian ruler Solon was reported to have "compared the people to the sea, and orators and counsellors to the winds; for that the sea would be calm and quiet, if the winds did not trouble it." Phillips believed a similar class of orators, ready to agitate the majority opinion, was precisely what American democracy needed in order to deal with the weaknesses that abolitionists had exposed. "If the Alps, piled in cold and still sublimity, be the emblem of Despotism," Phillips said in more than one speech, "the ever-restless ocean is ours," an "ocean of unchained democracy" that would remain pure so long as it was stirred constantly by agitators and orators like himself.[12]

Even in his love for Athens and its ever-restless ocean, however, Phillips revealed the transatlantic ambit of his mind. Mill was fascinated and inspired by Athenian democracy for much the same reason as Phillips: because he believed it modeled democratic deliberation, dissent, and free discussion. In one respect, however, Phillips differed fundamentally from Tocqueville, Mill, and many other European liberals: he never suggested that the problems of democracy required limiting or chaining it in some way—a possibility his contemporaries were more willing to consider.

For some European liberals, for instance, the lesson of Athens was that direct democracy could not work, and that the best republic was one ruled by a clerisy or (in Mill's phrase) a "learned class" that could counteract the passions of the mob. Many others favored somehow restricting suffrage according to the "capacity" of different groups for self-government; Mill, for example, entertained the idea of educational tests for voting or the awarding of extra votes to the most qualified electors.[13]

Phillips knew of these proposals but rejected all of them. "Some object to universal suffrage," Phillips once scribbled in his commonplace book, but "more evils are entailed by refusing it than by granting it." Besides, he asked, "looking at the history of govts which have refused it, remembering also that power corrupts the holder, whence shall we expect anything *better*"? Even if one allowed "that people are ignorant & led by demagogues," the idea that it would be better to have them led by aristocrats was disproved, in Phillips's mind, by the dastardly reign of slaveholding aristocrats in the South. This made his challenge, as a thinker and an agitator, twofold: he not only had to counteract the problems of mass conformity, apathy, and majority tyranny he saw in democratic rule but also had to do so without abridging, even a little, the people's right to govern themselves.[14]

Phillips brought to that task an unlikely set of influences, for he was, as James Brewer Stewart put it, the "offspring of aristocrats." Born into a family of wealth and educated at elite schools like Boston Latin and Harvard College, Phillips was in many ways an improbable democrat. Yet even during his time at Harvard, Phillips jettisoned many of his classmates' assumptions about the superior education and privileges of their social class. In his senior essays, written in 1831, Phillips argued that print was demolishing traditional distinctions between elite leaders and "the rabble" who had once been thought to "know nothing." Now that "the works of the learned" were no longer "sent to be neglected on the shelves of academies," but instead were "scattered" abroad by the press, they were "read of all men" and improved "the Many" instead of only "the Few," Phillips wrote.[15]

Other members of Phillips's class tended to regret this democratization of knowledge, but as Stewart notes, the new era of popular education and discussion "gave him no fear." In another senior essay on "the popular forms in which so much of Modern literature is given to the world—Encyclopedias, Reviews, Annuals, Newspapers," Phillips wrote that "their advantages far outweigh their defects. They must be considered the creatures and the bulwarks of that spirit of free discussion that characterizes the age." Half a century later, when Phillips returned to Harvard to deliver his Phi Beta Kappa address, "The Scholar in a Republic," he still believed that "book-learning" and "book-men" were often too conservative, and favored "that free speech" and "keen debate" found in more popular literature.[16]

As a lifelong Anglophile, Phillips remained especially drawn to transatlantic journals like the *Edinburgh Review* and the *Westminster Review*. In 1846, he even confessed to fellow abolitionist Sidney Howard Gay that "there's nothing I like better than poring over English papers." He crammed his commonplace book with quotations from the *Edinburgh*, the *Westminster*, *Blackwood's Magazine*, and other transatlantic quarterlies, and then crammed his abolitionist speeches with anecdotes and illustrations drawn from their pages.[17]

English newspapers brought intellectual stimulation on many topics without immediate relevance to antislavery. A sample of articles in just two issues of the *Westminster Review* that Phillips read included a biography of the Danish historian Barthold Georg Niebuhr, an essay on Roman poets, a review by John Stuart Mill of William Whewall's moral philosophy, and others on American geology, the French Revolution, and wood engravings by female artists. To be sure, Phillips did read even these with an abolitionist's eye; for instance, he made special note of the article on Niebuhr, which concluded that scholars were too easily corrupted by politics. Still, his extensive notes—which included quotes from Coleridge and Novalis, discussions of theology, and diagrams of Corinthian and Ionic columns copied from the *Encyclopædia Britannica*—suggest the impressive breadth of his reading.[18]

That reading gave Phillips a mantle of erudition that he wore most visibly in popular lectures like "Street Life in Europe" and "The Lost Arts"—talks that usually garnered him invitations to return to a town and present more controversial material. More significantly, however, British quarterlies reinforced Phillips's longstanding view that the press was ushering in a new age in which education would be distributed to the many instead of the few. For example, one *Westminster Review* article on "The Ancient Egyptians: Their Arts and Manufactures" argued that most of the skills and inventions of the modern world had been anticipated by past civilizations, only to be forgotten because there was no press to record and spread news of scientific discoveries—the exact same point that Phillips made in "The Lost Arts." "The past had knowledge," Phillips concluded in that speech. But unlike in the modern world, "it was the knowledge of the classes, not of the masses." Although "the science of Egypt was amazing," it had been "the privilege of the king and the priest. . . . Our distinction lies in the liberty of intellect and the diffusion of knowledge."[19]

Despite his belief in the democratic power of the press, however, Phillips had a difficult time reconciling this belief in Americans' distinctive "liberty of intellect" with the facts he encountered as an abolitionist, which suggested that northern intellects and hearts were far from free. But in confronting that paradox, Phillips was far from alone. Alexis de Tocqueville had observed a similar lack of free thought during his tour of the United States, and sometime in the 1840s or 1850s Phillips began to turn more and more frequently to Tocqueville's writings to understand his experience as an agitator in a democracy.

Phillips may well have learned about Tocqueville's book from his beloved "English papers"; a note in his commonplace book indicates that he read the October 1840 issue of the *Edinburgh Review*, which opened with a lengthy review of *Democracy in America* by John Stuart Mill. Nevertheless, however Phillips may have first learned of Tocqueville, he quickly came to consider the Frenchman a kindred thinker. As Phillips's friend and first biographer, Thomas Wentworth Higginson, remembered, Phillips "read newspapers enormously" but "drew habitually from but few books." Of the "few books" that did influence Phillips, Higginson mentioned "Tocqueville's 'Democracy in America' [as] being among the chief."[20]

Tocqueville's work held obvious attractions. In the first place, Tocqueville, like Phillips, believed that the press was a democratizing force in modern society. "When I compare the Greek and Roman Republics with these American

States," Tocqueville said after visiting New England, "the manuscript libraries of the former, and their rude population, with the innumerable journals and the enlightened people of the latter . . . I am tempted to burn my books, in order to apply none but novel ideas to so novel a condition of society." Tocqueville was doubly gratifying to Phillips because he believed that the United States was the country, to date, where the leveling impulses of the age were farthest advanced. "Tocqueville tells us that all nations and all ages tend with inevitable certainty" toward self-government and democracy, Phillips told one of his audiences during the Civil War, "but he points out, as history does, this land as the normal school of the nations, set by God to try the experiment . . . to remove the obstacles, point out the dangers, find the best way, encourage the timid, and hasten the world's progress."[21]

Yet Tocqueville was also attractive to Phillips because he recognized weaknesses in American democracy that abolitionists already knew well. First, Tocqueville's analysis of the potential tyranny of the majority in America helped Phillips understand why abolitionists were so despised and assaulted, and why the response of elected officials to mob violence was often so tepid. In one speech after a Boston mob in 1860, Phillips noted, "as Tocqueville has hinted," that majority rule often led to the election of poor statesmen and the suppression of minority views. Here, "the majority rules, and law rests on numbers, not on intellect or virtue," Phillips said, calling this "a sound rule." "But the harm is, that, while theoretically holding that no vote of the majority can authorize injustice, we practically consider public opinion the real test of what is true. . . . and hence, as a result, the fact which Tocqueville has noticed, that practically our institutions protect, not the interests of the whole community, but the interests of the majority."[22]

In these lines Phillips more or less summarized Tocqueville's first volume of *Democracy in America*, but the second volume also resonated with Phillips's experiences in the North. In it Tocqueville turned from his mostly positive impressions of the United States to darker musings about where democracy might lead. One real possibility, he thought, was that, in the absence of aristocracy, the equalizing of condition would lead many citizens to concern themselves solely with money and the pursuit of selfish interests—a problem Tocqueville called "individualism." The result would be a future in which "the interest of man is confined to those in close propinquity to himself," and in which even neighbors "became indifferent and as strangers to one another."[23]

In the worst-case scenario, Tocqueville feared that democratic citizens would become so mired in selfish pursuits that they would lose interest both in non-material goods and in anyone other than themselves—a danger that Tocqueville summarized again in his book on pre-revolutionary France, which Phillips also seems to have read. Inhabitants of democratic countries were "too easily inclined to think of nothing but their private interests," he wrote, "ever too ready to consider themselves only, and to sink into the narrow precincts of self, in which all public virtue is extinguished." Such people might believe themselves free, and might actually be well-off in a material sense. But Tocqueville warned that this society of isolated, industrious individualists was actually ripe for exploitation by benevolent despots. So long as they maintained formally democratic procedures and did not disturb commercial pursuits, such despots would be able to gradually consolidate the state's power. When they did, democrats would simultaneously be too atomized to challenge it and too accustomed to ignoring dissenting views to notice what was happening around them.[24]

For the moment, Tocqueville managed to believe that Americans had avoided this fate by creating institutions to ward off such a dystopian future. Phillips, on the other hand, thought that these bleak possibilities had already arrived. He often noted individual self-interest as the primary obstacle that abolitionists had to overcome, both in the North and the South. In the South, he once declared, "the slave question halts and lingers because it cannot get the selfishness of men on its side." But the same, he feared, was true of the North, where most men's thoughts were too "absorbed in pricing calico and adding up columns of figures" to feel concern for the rights of the oppressed. Northerners did not know the "distinction between duties and dollars," and seemed to confirm Tocqueville's observation that democracy made people industrious yet isolated and uninterested in the plight of their neighbors.[25]

In the antebellum North, Phillips also found ample confirmation for another of Tocqueville's fears: that majority rule and selfish individualism would, paradoxically, make democratic citizens reluctant to think or speak for themselves. After visiting the United States, Tocqueville claimed that he "[knew] of no country in which there is so little true independence of mind and freedom of discussion." "As long as the majority is still undecided," Tocqueville claimed, "discussion is carried on; but as soon as its decision is irrevocably pronounced, a submissive silence is observed." Fearing the loss of social capital, Americans also feared thinking independently or discussing new ideas freely, even when the empire of newspapers gave them the means to do so.[26]

Phillips agreed with that distressing analysis, and no antebellum American confirmed the point more vividly for him than Daniel Webster, a politician who seemed to foreshadow Tocqueville's direst warnings. After Webster's fall from grace in an infamous speech on the Fugitive Slave Law, Phillips often charged him with never having "had an original idea," only "borrowed" ones. But Phillips also suspected, like Tocqueville, that in this failing Webster merely represented a larger tendency in American democracy to borrow ideas from others. "In the country once," Phillips told one audience, "I lived with a Democrat who never had an opinion on the day's news till he had read the Boston Post," a trait that struck Phillips as a dangerous perversion of his own habit of poring over the papers. Yet, among Webster Whigs and Democrats alike, the tendency to borrow ideas seemed rampant in the North. "I read in this [life] one of the dangers of our form of government," Phillips concluded of Webster in 1859, before adding a fitting paraphrase of *Democracy in America.* "As Tocqueville says so wisely, 'The weakness of a Democracy is that, unless guarded, it merges in despotism.' Such a life is the first step, and half a dozen are the Niagara carrying us over."[27]

Tocqueville encouraged Phillips to see compromising politicians and indifferent northern merchants not as isolated villains, but instead as emblems of "the dangers of our form of government"—dangers that had brought northern, as well as southern, society to a precipice. Within Tocqueville's description of the dangers, however, Phillips also found good reason to see his own vocation of agitator as part of the solution. In fact, appreciating Phillips's reading of Tocqueville helps to explain the thing about Phillips that many of his peers found hardest to understand: his close identification with William Lloyd Garrison.

Even in New England, most other members of Phillips's social class viewed Garrison as a vulgar fanatic whose views on religion, violence, women's rights, and slavery ranged from blasphemous to eccentric in the extreme. But Phillips, while he did not always agree with Garrison's views, welcomed the idiosyncratic editor as a breath of fresh air compared to the stifled intellectual climate represented by Webster, or the countless slavish followers of papers like the Boston *Post.* Indeed, his affinity with Tocqueville led Phillips to see Garrison as more than just an abolitionist focused on a specific goal. Simply by challenging received opinion and expressing dissent, agitators like Garrison provided a larger service to American democracy that would not end even once slavery did, Phillips believed. "Never, to our latest posterity, can we afford to do without prophets, like Garrison, to stir up the monotony of wealth, and reawake the people to the great ideas that are constantly fading out of their minds." Because he viewed manifestations of anti-abolitionism not just as temporary obstacles, but as "dangers of our form of government," Phillips also viewed "the antislavery agitation" as "an essential part of the machinery of the state."[28]

Phillips's Tocquevillian analysis of democracy's dangers also helps to explain his admiration for John Brown, a figure who was, at first glance, very different from Garrison. In Phillips's mind, however, both were heroic figures who helped counteract the ills that Tocqueville diagnosed in American culture. If Garrison's relentless agitation and eccentric views served to "stir up" settled opinion in the North, Brown showed Phillips that such efforts were not in vain. The raid on Harpers Ferry showed that his generation of Americans was not wholly "poisoned with printing ink or cotton dust," but that at least one man "still thinks for himself" and was able to act without "stop[ping] to ask what the majority thought." Whereas a dozen men like Webster were the Niagara threatening to carry Americans over the precipice, Brown's half-a-dozen raiders showed that an "insurrection of thought" was still possible—even in Tocqueville's America.[29]

In these and numerous other antebellum speeches, Phillips skillfully translated Tocqueville's warnings into the abolitionists' idiom, and in the process, he offered his fellow Garrisonians a way to understand themselves not only as abolitionists, but as "teachers of American Democracy" whose radical agitation was crucial to the health of popular government. Both from his experiences and from his reading of Tocqueville, Phillips concluded that "republics exist only on the tenure of being constantly agitated." That notion was obviously attractive to Garrisonian radicals, of course, but the idea that agitation was necessary to keep a republic free was itself a radical view in the antebellum United States. Many Americans in the early republic viewed the discussion of controversial ideas as a threat to the survival of the Union and, therefore, of American democracy itself. Supreme Court Justice Joseph Story spoke for many American thinkers in deploring "Ultraism" and the "restless spirit of innovation and change—a fretful desire to provoke discussions of all sorts."[30]

Phillips did, however, find an ally in a prominent non-American thinker who frequently contributed to the English reviews that Phillips loved: John

Stuart Mill. Mill, like Phillips, was deeply impressed by *Democracy in America* and especially its insight that the greatest weakness democracy faced was "not anarchy or love of change," but "stagnation and immobility." Like Phillips, too, Mill believed that to counteract these dangers, modern democrats needed both to educate people better about the rights of others and to create, "somewhere" in their society, a "support for opinions and sentiments different from those of the mass." That was one reason why, from at least 1850, Mill took notice of Phillips and his fellow abolitionists in the United States. As he intimated in one letter to Harriet Taylor, "the chief slavery abolitionists Garrison, Wendell Phillips, the negro Douglas &c." provided examples of the kind of "public meetings or agitation" needed in a modern democratic society.[31]

Indeed, for much of the next decade, Mill's philosophical and political writings dwelled on the problem of how to protect unpopular views in a democracy that tended to worship the opinion of the majority. His most famous work, *On Liberty*, was an explicit response to Tocqueville's warnings about the tyranny of the majority and argued that individuality had to be preserved, not just for the sake of the individual's liberty, but for the sake of free society as a whole. "In this age," he wrote, "the mere example of nonconformity, the mere refusal to bend the knee to custom, is itself a service" to the common good, "precisely because the tyranny of opinion is such as to make eccentricity a reproach."[32]

Mill was most concerned to ensure that nonconformist views found expression in the halls of power, and the political essays he wrote after *On Liberty* all dealt with proposals for parliamentary reform that he hoped would increase the likelihood of minority viewpoints' being heard in legislative assemblies. Among his more extreme proposals was to award multiple votes to members of educated minorities whose unpopular views might otherwise be left unrepresented in Parliament. But Mill also approved of another proposal, adapted from one suggested by parliamentary reformer Thomas Hare, to allow all voters to list a slate of preferred candidates, who would be elected upon reaching a certain quota of votes cast irrespective of electoral districts.

The point of this scheme of "personal" or "proportional" representation was, according to Mill, to ensure that iconoclasts had a more viable chance to receive direct representation in the House of Commons. "Hundreds of able men of independent thought" could provide, within the government, "a rallying point, for opinions and interests which the ascendant public opinion views with disfavour." Mill did not contest the right of the numerical majority to ultimately decide policy, but he hoped that double-voting or proportional representation might at least make political deliberations more wide-ranging and open to new ideas, thereby loosening the stranglehold of mainstream opinion on the minds of most politicians. His goal, as Nadia Urbinati and other historians have explained, was to recreate within the walls of Parliament something like the *agora* of ancient Athens—a marketplace of ideas in which orators could express multiple points of view, both popular and unpopular, before political decisions were made. Indeed, Mill's hope was that Hare's scheme would allow "modern democracy" to still "have its occasional Pericles," the powerful orator who could persuade the majority to change.[33]

As an orator himself, Phillips liked this idea. In fact, during the Civil War, Phillips delivered a lengthy speech endorsing the scheme of proportional representation that "Stuart Mill has been urging in England for twenty years." Phillips's detailed summary of Mill's views suggest that he had probably read widely on the subject in his English reviews or in Mill's *Considerations on Representative Government*, published in 1861. But however he learned of it, Phillips agreed with Mill's complaint that current electoral systems, which allowed voters only to cast ballots for those in a particular geographical district, made little sense in an age when newspapers made it possible to learn about candidates elsewhere. Meanwhile, existing procedures led to the election of "the most selfish and the most timid" men who refused to diverge from majority opinion out of fear that they would not be reelected.[34]

Mill's analysis further encouraged Phillips to see unoriginal politicians like Daniel Webster as symptoms of larger problems with American democracy: it was not realistic to think that current methods of voting by electoral districts would ever produce original thinkers as candidates. The result, however, was disastrous for the cause of democracy. If independent thinkers and members of minority groups could never enter Congress, they could never form that "point of resistance" to the majority "which is always needed in a Democracy to sustain an unpopular reform." "We need not say with De Tocqueville, 'Every Government is always just as rascally as the people will allow,'" Phillips said, returning to the writer whose reflections had inspired both him and Mill, "but we may ask what sort of a Government have we a right to expect" when only those politicians who held to conventional wisdom could hope to be elected.[35]

Phillips also shared Mill's broader vision of a "modern democracy" modeled on ancient Athens. In multiple speeches before and after the Civil War,

Phillips, too, cited the free discussion of the *agora* as a model for American democrats to follow. In an 1859 speech on "The Education of the People," for instance, Phillips contrasted the ancient civilization of Egypt, which "kept its knowledge for priests and nobles," with the "democratic" civilization of Greece, which "busied itself with every man in the market-place, day by day." In Athens, the "scholar," like Pericles, "thought life wasted if he did not hear, at the moment, the echo and the amen to his labors in the appreciation of the market-place. The Greek trusted the people," Phillips concluded, and "our civilization takes its shape from the Greek."[36]

In another speech that same year—which also saw the publication of *On Liberty*—Phillips recalled the ancient story of Anacharsis, who witnessed a debate in the forum of Athens and saw the vote that followed. Anacharsis concluded that, under Athenian liberty, "wise men argue causes, and fools decide them." Phillips implied that the same was often true in the United States. But he took reassurance from the fact that even "unruly Athens," where the "caprices of the mob" could overturn the wisdom of the wisest, "probably secured the greatest human happiness and nobleness of its era" because it allowed open discussion in the *agora*. "Now my idea of American civilization is," said Phillips, "that it is a second part, a repetition of that same sublime confidence in the public conscience and the public thought which made the groundwork of Grecian Democracy." "Every public meeting in Athens was opened with a curse on any one who should not speak what he really thought," Phillips thundered in another wartime speech, and he hoped to inspire the same courageous dissent in all of his audiences.[37]

In short, Phillips agreed with Mill that ancient Greece still provided instructive lessons for moderns striving to correct democracy's weaknesses. As late as his Phi Beta Kappa address, Phillips again identified Egypt as the "hunker conservative of antiquity" and again compared Athens with the better impulses of American democracy. Praise for Athens was itself a somewhat eccentric move, however, for Phillips as well as Mill. Both men lived at a time of extensive European debates over the politics of the ancient world, debates in which advocates for Athens still found themselves in the minority. Conservative historians like William Mitford and Charles Rollin, whose eight-volume *Ancient History* Phillips read as a student at Harvard, usually favored Sparta or Rome as ancient models for modern republics. French liberals like Benjamin Constant, on the other hand, believed that the modern and ancient worlds were too different to speak meaningfully to each other.[38]

Both sides of the political spectrum took a dim view of the Greeks' respect for individual liberty, and many pointed out that Athens was hardly democratic. Tocqueville, for one, depicted Athens as an oligarchic state which, despite "her universal suffrage, was after all merely an aristocratic republic in which all the nobles had an equal right to the government." But Mill and some other English radicals, most prominently George Grote, opposed these views, and Phillips's statements on ancient Greece accord most closely with theirs. Mill and Grote defended Athens over Sparta, presenting the Athenian *agora* as a dynamic political society in which disagreements were fully aired and all views were given a hearing. And while conservative historians focused on Sparta's longevity as a sign of its superiority, Millian liberals pointed to the cultural, philosophical, and artistic achievements of Athens as proof that it had more successfully balanced individual liberty with public-spiritedness.[39]

Phillips agreed: Athens had "the largest intellects" of the ancient world, and its art and philosophy lit "the torch that gilds yet the mountain peaks of the Old World." Still, defending Athens had additional liabilities for an American abolitionist. Conservative southern writers in the United States like John C. Calhoun and Thomas Dew learned a different lesson from the success of ancient Greece: that liberty was best preserved by a decentralized government and loose, federal relations among small states, a position they used to deflect challenges to slavery. The nature of Greek slavery and civilization was also a contentious matter in American writing on slavery and race from Thomas Jefferson to David Walker and beyond. Finally, ancient Athens was also the scene of a famous tragedy—the death of Socrates—that gave even its defenders pause. Abolitionists, including Phillips, often cited the persecution of Socrates as analogous to the treatment of abolitionists in the United States, and even for Mill, Socrates's death served as a powerful illustration of how numerical majorities could punish the eccentric genius.[40]

Phillips also conceded that Athens was far from a perfect model. In one of his last addresses he admitted that while "Greece had her republics . . . they were the republics of a few freemen and subjects and many slaves." Nonetheless, Phillips believed that Athens could withstand most charges brought against it by conservative writers. Unlike southern writers who viewed the political organization of Greece as its crowning glory and the main way to avoid the despotism of numerical majorities, Phillips highlighted the unsettled state of Athenian society and its reputation for constant discussion as the reasons for its success. Democrats could not trust "machinery" or institutions to make their liberties safe, Phillips said, citing Tocqueville's analysis of the French Revolution in support. Grecian civilization confirmed that only free discussion, agitation, and eternal vigilance could stave off the worst effects of majority rule.[41]

Like Mill, Phillips also believed that the exceptions to free discussion in Athens—like Socrates's death—were all the more reason why the ideals of the *agora* had to be preserved. Precisely because Athens showed that the dangers of majority tyranny could never be entirely erased, democrats had to continually reassert the importance of Socratic agitation. Noticing the similarities between the repression of Socrates and the repression of American abolitionists did not discourage Phillips from praising Athens, but only made clearer what writers like Constant rejected: that the democracy of the ancient world had lessons to teach democracy in America, both about the dangers of this form of government and about the ways to ward them off.[42]

All of these uses of Athens required Phillips, no less than Mill, to de-emphasize some aspects of Athenian history while highlighting others. But, as Urbinati notes, liberal historians—"like their rivals—belonged to an age in which the ancients conveyed a strong ideological meaning." Historiography about Greece at the time was always shot through with transparent political aims, and Phillips was less concerned by a lack of total objectivity in existing histories of Athens than by the fact that much scholarly history at the time was dominated by conservative writers.[43] Indeed, Phillips often worried that history in the United States, like American democracy itself, was plagued by a shortage of original thinking and dissenting interpretations. "I am amazed at what men call History," Phillips confessed to abolitionist John Jay in 1864. He feared that the field was too dominated by pedants "whose judgment on practical matters one would not give two cents for" but whose histories, packaged into "still volumes & decent, Beacon-street style" were fed to "the rising generation" as if it were their mothers' milk. He believed history needed to be written by "men disciplined by practical affairs."[44]

Such lines reveal some of Phillips's old suspicion of "book-learning" applied to the discipline of history. In his Phi Beta Kappa address, Phillips even confessed that, although his "favorite study was history" in college, his career as an agitator had given him a different perspective on its writing. "The world and affairs have shown me that one half of history is loose conjecture, and much of the rest is the writer's opinion," Phillips said, adding that "most men see facts not with their eyes, but with their prejudices." Most history written by bookmen betrayed mainly their prejudices against the people and their open hostility to agitations like abolitionism; it served mainly to confirm what conservative writers already wanted to see.[45]

Of course, a critic might justifiably have retorted that Phillips saw only what he wanted to see in Athenian democracy, too. But for Phillips, a biased history which encouraged new thoughts and discussion was at least preferable to "timid scholarship [which] either shrinks from sharing in these agitations, or denounces them as vulgar and dangerous interference by incompetent hands with matters above them." Mill most likely would have agreed. Three decades before, he made similar points in the review of William Whewall's moral philosophy that was published in one of the issues of the *Westminster Review* that Phillips read. Mill blasted Whewall as an example of the scholars produced by most "English universities [where] no thought can find place, except that which can reconcile itself with orthodoxy" and settled opinion. Far better to have scholarship, Mill thought, which challenged existing norms.[46]

Reading Tocqueville pushed both Phillips and Mill to emphasize the importance of agitation, both in scholarship and society. In the final analysis, however, Phillips distinguished himself from Mill, Tocqueville, and many other European liberals on one important point: he never suggested that the dangers of democracy should be met by limiting universal suffrage.

Mill also noted this difference between himself and Phillips in the only extant letter where he acknowledged the beliefs that he and the famous American abolitionist shared. At the end of the Civil War, American abolitionist Moncure D. Conway reported to Phillips, after "pass[ing] half a day with John Stuart Mill," by then a noted friend of the Union, that Mill had "made many inquiries about you, and was much gratified when I told him how you believed in his works." Mill asked Phillips, through Conway, for copies of his speeches, and when he received them, he had almost nothing but praise for what he found. Phillips's approval of Hare's scheme of proportional representation was especially gratifying to Mill, who said that "it is hardly possible to state the merits of the principle more forcibly . . . than Mr Phillips has done. It is indeed at once a direct corollary from the first principles of democracy, and a most powerful corrective of all evils liable to arise from the forms of democratic government hitherto in use." Mill added that he was pleased to receive "so strong a confirmation, from such authority, of my opinion concerning Tocqueville, which I shall now hold with increased confidence."[47]

On one point, however, Mill was unconvinced by Phillips's speeches. Whereas Phillips argued for universal suffrage, Mill remained open to some sort of "educational qualification" for voting. Mill did believe that any such qualification would have to be joined with a comprehensive system of public education that would help to assure that all could meet it. Yet he declared that "intelligence of public affairs, or the power of judging of public men," required—at a bare minimum—that a citizen be able to read.[48]

Having always tied the spread of newspapers with the spread of democracy, Phillips certainly understood the power of reading. But he viewed any suggestion that it serve as a qualification for voting as a sign of too little trust in popular rule. Unfortunately, from the end of the Civil War to the end of his life, Phillips felt himself increasingly surrounded by liberals willing to entertain the idea of voting restrictions. Some, like Mill, emphasized that it was unacceptable for white southerners to restrict the voting rights of the formerly enslaved during Reconstruction. Mill made an exception to his support for voting qualifications because of the unique circumstances of freedpeople in the United States. But many liberals nonetheless dreamed of a not-too-distant future when they could consider some amount of suffrage restriction. In his 1881 Phi Beta Kappa speech, Phillips noted "the growing dislike of universal suffrage" among "our easy classes" and once again noted, with dismay, the likeness between the South and his beloved North. "The white South hates universal suffrage; the so-called cultivated North distrusts it."[49]

Just as Phillips showed no fear for the democratization of knowledge, he never shared in that distrust of universal suffrage. On the contrary, he believed, for two reasons, that a democracy without universal suffrage was not worthy of the name. First, Phillips argued that simply having the right to vote—even if one did not use it—had an educative and elevating effect on the electorate. Because only those entrusted with power over the government would take genuine interest in government, the right to vote was a tool for acquiring the virtues—like disinterestedness, independent thinking, and participation in free discussion—that Phillips considered essential to the duties of citizenship. In 1859, Phillips even quipped that giving the ballot to the masses made "pulpits" and "colleges" superfluous: because "responsibility teaches as nothing else can."[50]

Educational qualifications for voting made little sense, for the franchise itself was a great "instrument . . . of education, both moral and intellectual." But Phillips often added a second argument against restricting suffrage, which was that general education was impossible without general enfranchisement.

Wealthy elites would only be compelled to help educate the "poor, ignorant" citizen once that citizen had the power to vote. Simply on the grounds of "the highest expediency," therefore, it made sense to enfranchise every woman and man first, instead of waiting until each could meet some educational test.[51]

Even in his insistence on suffrage for all, however, Phillips used arguments drawn from the transatlantic intellectual world in which he moved. The idea that civic participation itself gave people the education they needed to vote was also advanced in Mill's work and in Tocqueville's. Indeed, when arguing in the 1850s for women's right to vote, Phillips noted that "Tocqueville, after travelling in this country," concluded that the "jury trial" served as a "school of civil education open to all the people," and Mill made similar points.[52]

But whereas Mill and Tocqueville believed participation in civic practices short of voting could still serve an educative function, Phillips maintained that "the ballot-box" itself, no less than "the jury-box," was essential to educate the people, and he insisted that universal suffrage was the logical implication of American principles. "The humblest man and the feeblest has the same civil rights, according to the theory of our institutions, as the most gifted," Phillips noted. "Intellect . . . gets no tittle of additional civil right, no one single claim to any greater civil privilege than the humblest individual, who knows no more than the first elements of his alphabet."[53]

In sum, while Phillips justified universal suffrage partly on grounds that Mill and Tocqueville could appreciate, his refusal to entertain restrictions on democracy set him apart, both from them and from many other thinkers in the Anglo-American world he knew best. Living at a time when suffrage was still extremely limited in every country with representative institutions, Phillips was forced both by his reflection and his experience to an unusual position. Most advocates of universal suffrage overlooked or did not take very seriously the subtle criticisms of democracy made by Mill and Tocqueville while, on the other hand, Mill and Tocqueville saw democracy's weaknesses but remained reluctant to embrace universal suffrage at once. Wendell Phillips, however, embraced universal suffrage unequivocally while simultaneously reminding other antebellum northerners of the dangers that confronted even them, despite their presumably more democratic states.

His positions on suffrage, if anything, made the duty of agitation even more imperative in Phillips's theory of democracy, for it was the only recourse he allowed to an enlightened minority like the abolitionists who knew that the majority was wrong; even they would receive not "one tittle" of extra civil right just because they were right. All they could do, like Socrates, was to stir the waters, hoping thereby to ward off the stagnation and stationariness to which democracies were prone.

What they could not do, Phillips believed, was abandon democracy just because of its weaknesses, or just because it sometimes killed Socrates or mobbed Garrison. "I plant myself always on democratic principles," he said in 1865. "I am a democrat, ingrained, from top to toe." "Trust the people with the gravest questions," he advised, "and in the long run you educate the race; while, in the process, you secure, not perfect, but the best possible institutions." His legacy as a thinker was to call out both the imperfections and the possibilities of popular democracy and bequeath them to future democrats. To keep democracy safe, he believed, all of those who came after him would have to remain as vigilant and ever-restless as the agitators of Athens or antebellum America who had come before.[54]

NOTES

1. "Speech of Wendell Phillips, Esq., at the Brooklyn Academy of Music," *National Anti-Slavery Standard*, February 24, 1866. See also the similar ideas expressed in Wendell Phillips, *Speeches, Lectures, and Letters* (Boston: Lee and Shepard, 1870), 399, hereafter cited as *SLL*.

2. Phillips, "Under the Flag," *SLL*, 399; "Speech of Wendell Phillips, Esq." See also Susan-Mary Grant, *North over South: Northern Nationalism and American Identity in the Antebellum Era* (Lawrence: University Press of Kansas, 2000), 127.

3. Irving Bartlett, *Wendell Phillips: Brahmin Radical* (Boston: Beacon Press, 1961), 2; Oscar Sherwin, *Prophet of Liberty: The Life and Times of Wendell Phillips* (New York: Bookman Associates, 1958). See also Sherwin, "Philosopher of Agitation," *Phylon* 6, no. 3 (1945): 232–39; Sherwin, "'Ignoble Ease and Peaceful Sloth, Not Peace,'" *Phylon* 9, no. 4 (1948): 346–52; James Brewer Stewart, *Wendell Phillips: Liberty's Hero* (Baton Rouge: Louisiana State University Press, 1986); Richard Hofstadter, *The American Political Tradition and the Men Who Made It* (New York: Vintage Books, 1948). I regrettably came across Sherwin's early articles only after completing my own book about Phillips and the Garrisonian abolitionists, but my agreement with Sherwin's view of Phillips is clear here and in the book. See W. Caleb McDaniel, *The Problem of Democracy in the Age of Slavery: Garrisonian Abolitionists and Transatlantic Reform* (Baton Rouge: Louisiana State University Press, 2013).

4. Phillips, "The Boston Mob," *SLL*, 225; Phillips, "Philosophy of the Abolition Movement," *SLL*, 108, 109. See Stewart, *Wendell Phillips*, 54–75.

5. Phillips, "Philosophy of the Abolition Movement," *SLL*, 152. On broader antebellum strug-

gles over the dangers of majority rule, see *Moral Minorities and the Making of American Democracy* (New York: Oxford University Press, 2014).

6. Phillips, "Public Opinion," *SLL*, 44–45; Phillips, "The Murder of Lovejoy," *SLL*, 7, 8; Phillips, "Philosophy of the Abolition Movement," 110.

7. Phillips, "Philosophy of the Abolition Movement," 107, 109; Phillips, "Harper's Ferry," *SLL*, 264.

8. Wendell Phillips, "The Pulpit," *Speeches, Lectures, and Letters: Second Series* (Boston: Lee and Shepard, 1894), 271, hereafter cited as *SLL: Second Series*; Phillips, "Harper's Ferry," 265, 266. For Emerson's similar ideas, see Alex Zakaras, *Individuality and Mass Democracy: Mill, Emerson, and the Burdens of Citizenship* (New York: Oxford University Press, 2009).

9. For Mill's review, see *Edinburgh Review* 72 (October 1840), 35.

10. *Edinburgh Review* 72 (October 1840): 35; Phillips, "The Pulpit," *SLL: Second Series*, 272; "Speech of Wendell Phillips, Esq." On Tocqueville and Mill, see Alan S. Kahan, *Aristocratic Liberalism: The Social and Political Thought of Jacob Burckhardt, John Stuart Mill, and Alexis de Tocqueville* (New York: Oxford University Press, 1992); Nicholas Capaldi, *John Stuart Mill: A Biography* (New York: Cambridge University Press, 2004), 148–56; Zakaras, *Individuality and Mass Democracy*, 14–18; Alex Zakaras, "John Stuart Mill, Individuality, and Participatory Democracy," in *J. S. Mill's Political Thought: A Bicentennial Reassessment*, ed. Nadia Urbinati and Alex Zakaras (New York: Cambridge University Press, 2007), 200–220.

11. On Phillips's interest in history, see Stewart, *Wendell Phillips*; James Brewer Stewart, "Boston, Abolition, and the Atlantic World, 1820–1861," in *Courage and Conscience: Black & White Abolitionists in Boston*, ed. Donald M. Jacobs (Bloomington: Indiana University Press, 1993), 101–26.

12. Phillips, "Public Opinion," 54; Phillips, "Harper's Ferry," 265. Solon quoted in Francis Bacon's popular collection of apothegms from the ancient world; for an edition Phillips may well have seen, see Francis Bacon, *Essays, Moral, Economical, and Political* (Boston: Hilliard, 1835), 236. Phillips's speeches frequently cited quips from "Lord Bacon" and once explicitly cited James Spedding's life and works of Bacon, several volumes of which contained references to this same Solon quote.

13. For "learned class," see *Edinburgh Review* 72 (October 1840): 45. On European liberals' openness to limiting suffrage, see Kahan, *Aristocratic Liberalism*; Alan S. Kahan, *Liberalism in Nineteenth-Century Europe: The Political Culture of Limited Suffrage* (Houndmills, Basingstoke, Hampshire, U.K.: Palgrave Macmillan, 2003).

14. Wendell Phillips Commonplace Book, Antislavery Collection, Boston Public Library, archive.org/stream/commonplacebookuoophil#page/n227/mode/2up, emphasis in original.

15. Stewart, *Wendell Phillips*, 3; "The Boasted Superiority of the Present Age," in Wendell Phillips, "Student Themes and Dissertations, 1825–1831," HUC 8827.386.70, Harvard University Archives.

16. Stewart, *Wendell Phillips*, 32; "Of the popular forms in which so much of Modern Literature is given to the world," in Phillips, "Student Themes and Dissertations, 1825–1831"; Phillips, "The Scholar in a Republic," *SLL: Second Series*, 339, 343, 344.

17. Wendell Phillips to Sidney Howard Gay, July[?] 1846, Gay Papers, Columbia University.

18. See various entries in Phillips Commonplace Book, archive.org/details/commonplacebook uoophil. My list of articles is drawn from issues that Phillips cited there, even if he did not cite the

particular article. The wide range of Phillips's reading is also noted in Stewart, *Wendell Phillips*, 194. See also WP to Elizabeth Pease, August 12, 1842, Ms.A.1.2.12.2.77, Boston Public Library.

19. "The Ancient Egyptians: Their Arts and Manufactures," *Westminster Review* 36 (July 1841): 1–35; Wendell Phillips, "The Lost Arts," in Carlos Martyn, *Wendell Phillips: The Agitator* (New York: Funk and Wagnalls, 1890), 546. Compare "The Lost Arts" in *SLL: Second Series*, 382. The paragraph on Egypt in this version is much more confusing than Martyn's, which seems to better capture the idea Phillips had expressed elsewhere. See also "The Boasted Superiority of the Present Age."

20. Thomas Wentworth Higginson, *Wendell Phillips* (Boston: Lee and Shepard, 1884), xiii. For Phillips's citation of another article that appeared in the same issue as Mill's 1840 review, see Phillips Commonplace Book.

21. Tocqueville, *Democracy in America*, trans. Henry Reeve (1835; New York: George Adlard, 1838), 180, 182; Phillips, "War for the Union," *SLL*, 420.

22. Phillips, "Mobs and Education," *SLL*, 321, 333.

23. Alexis de Tocqueville, *Democracy in America, Part the Second: The Social Influence of Democracy* (New York: J. & H. G. Langley, 1840), 105. See also Alan S. Kahan, *Alexis de Tocqueville* (New York: Continuum, 2010), 45–46. On the more pessimistic dimensions of Tocqueville's work, see Arthur Kaledin, *Tocqueville and His America: A Darker Horizon* (New Haven: Yale University Press, 2011).

24. Alexis de Tocqueville, *On the State of Society in France before the Revolution of 1789*, trans. Henry Reeve (London: John Murray, 1856), xxi.

25. Phillips, "Sims Anniversary," *SLL*, 82; Phillips, "Mobs and Education," 333, 338.

26. Tocqueville, *Democracy in America*, 244, 245.

27. Phillips, "Idols," *SLL*, 248, 249. Phillips's critique echoed Ralph Waldo Emerson's own attack on Webster's "sterility of thought." *Emerson's Antislavery Writings*, ed. Len Gougeon and Joel Myerson (New Haven: Yale University Press, 1995), 77.

28. Phillips, "Public Opinion," 53.

29. Phillips, "Harper's Ferry," 264; Phillips, "The Puritan Principle and John Brown," *SLL: Second Series*, 297, 301.

30. Phillips, "Idols," 244; Phillips, "Public Opinion," 54. On fears of agitation in the early republic, see Mark G. Schmeller, "Imagining Public Opinion in Antebellum America: Fear, Credit, Law, and Honor," PhD diss., University of Chicago, 2001, chap. 5, Joseph Story quoted on 262. Also see Seth Cotlar's discussion of the early national backlash against participatory democracy and radical agitation in Cotlar, *Tom Paine's America: The Rise and Fall of Transatlantic Radicalism in the Early Republic* (Charlottesville: University of Virginia Press, 2011).

31. Mill quoted in Kahan, *Aristocratic Liberalism*, 47.

32. See the edition of *On Liberty* (1859) included in *The Collected Works of John Stuart Mill*, ed. John M. Robson, 33 vols. (Toronto: University of Toronto Press, 1977), vol. 18: 269.

33. Mill, "Considerations on Representative Government," in *Collected Works*, ed. Robson, vol. 18: 456, 459, 460. See Nadia Urbinati, *Mill on Democracy: From the Athenian Polis to Representative Government* (Chicago: University of Chicago Press, 2002).

34. "Address of Wendell Phillips," *Liberator*, July 11, 1862.

35. Ibid.

36. Phillips, "The Education of the People," *SLL*, 312, 313.

37. Phillips, "Harper's Ferry," 267, 268; Phillips, "Under the Flag," 398.

38. Phillips, "The Scholar in a Republic," 345. For Phillips's knowledge of Rollin, see Library Charging Lists, 1828–29, UAIII 50.15.60 (v. 83), p. 33, Harvard University Archives, pds.lib.harvard.edu/pds/view/14622420?n=234. On contemporary political debates about Athens and Mill's role in them, see Urbinati, *Mill on Democracy*, chap. 1; Jonathan Riley, "Mill's Neo-Athenian Model of Liberal Democracy," in *J. S. Mill's Political Thought*, ed. Urbinati and Zakaras, 221–49; Eugenio Biagini, "Liberalism and Direct Democracy: John Stuart Mill and the Model of Ancient Athens," in *Citizenship and Community: Liberals, Radicals, and Collective Identities in British Isles, 1865–1931*, ed. Biagini (Cambridge, U.K.: Cambridge University Press, 1996), 21–44; Frank M. Turner, *The Greek Heritage in Victorian Britain* (New Haven: Yale University Press, 1981), chap. 5.

39. Tocqueville, *Democracy in America: Part the Second*, 64.

40. Phillips, "The Scholar in a Republic," 345. On southern uses of ancient Greece, see Michael O'Brien, *Conjectures of Order: Intellectual Life and the American South, 1810–1860* (Chapel Hill: University of North Carolina Press, 2004), 591–623; *Speeches of John C. Calhoun: Delivered in the Congress of the United States from 1811 to the Present Time* (New York: Harper & Brothers, 1843), 86. On Greece's role in debates about ancient African civilization, see Stephen G. Hall, *A Faithful Account of the Race: African American Historical Writing in Nineteenth-Century America* (Chapel Hill: University of North Carolina Press, 2009), 33–35. On Socrates's experience as parallel to abolitionists, see Phillips, "The Pilgrims," *SLL*, 229, or search for "Socrates" in a digitized edition of the *Liberator*.

41. Phillips, "The Scholar in a Republic," 336; Phillips, "Harper's Ferry," 270.

42. See Urbinati, *Mill on Democracy*, 13.

43. Ibid., 18.

44. Wendell Phillips to John Jay, August 4, 1864, Jay Family Papers, Columbia University.

45. Phillips, "The Scholar in a Republic," 334–35.

46. Ibid., 344; "Whewall's Moral Philosophy," *Westminster Review* 58 (October 1852): 349. Evidence that Phillips read this issue of the *Review* can be found in Phillips Commonplace Book, archive.org/stream/commonplacebookuoophil#page/n271/mode/2up. Whether he also read the article by Mill on Whewall is unknown.

47. Moncure D. Conway to Wendell Phillips, August 2, [1865], bMS, Am 1953 (437/2), Houghton Library, Harvard University; John Stuart Mill to Moncure D. Conway, October 23, 1865, *Collected Works of John Stuart Mill*, ed. Robson, vol. 16: 1105, 1106. Mill would later cite Wendell Phillips's support for Hare's system when trying to convince English liberals to adopt it. See Mill to John Elliot Cairnes, September 1, 1867, *Collected Works*, ed. Robson, vol. 16: 1314.

48. Mill to Conway, October 23, 1865.

49. Phillips, "Scholar in a Republic," 346.

50. Phillips, "Idols," 246.

51. Phillips, "Woman's Rights," *SLL*, 27, 29.

52. Ibid., 28.

53. Ibid., 19.

54. "Massachusetts Anti-Slavery Society Annual Meeting," *Liberator*, February 17, 1865; Phillips, "Harper's Ferry," 267. Phillips made the first statements while arguing for voting rights for freedmen in the South.

3

A PURITAN RADICAL

Wendell Phillips's New England Religion

DAN MCKANAN

Wendell Phillips has sometimes been remembered as the stray Calvinist among the Garrisonians, the one "champion of Orthodoxy" to side with the Quakers, Unitarians, and come-outers who agitated for immediate abolition, women's rights, and national disunion. And it is true that he once began a sermon by declaring, "I thank God for John Calvin."[1] He also has been portrayed as religiously tone deaf, inclined to dismiss the theological speculations of his comrades as secondary to the abolitionist cause. And it is true that he began another address, in which he had been asked to speak on the relationship between Christianity and absolute religion, by confessing that "the subject is one not very familiar to my beaten path of thought."[2] Yet, such characterizations do not do justice to Phillips's active engagement in religious controversies and organizations. Like his friend Garrison, he condemned proslavery religion and criticized organized churches even after the Civil War. But he gladly visited the pulpits of abolitionist allies, speaking to both Theodore Parker's transcendentalist congregation in Boston and to Henry Ward Beecher's church in New York, which was closer to the Orthodox side of the Unitarian-Orthodox split. Religion mattered to Phillips—and the sort of religion that mattered was neither theologically Calvinist nor fully aligned with the heterodoxy of other radicals.

Phillips was, rather, a champion of what he saw as the true religion of New England—a puritan faith characterized by a preference for action over speculation and a refusal to accept any arbitrary authority in the church. These commitments, more than any system of doctrine, constituted what Phillips called "the central idea of New England." He relentlessly criticized both Orthodox and Unitarian churches for straying from the "Puritan principle," and relentlessly praised abolitionist societies, vigilance committees, and autonomous congregations for their fidelity.[3] As Phillips participated in these organizations, he continually strove to help his peers understand that their work had both deep historical roots and profound religious significance. He also warned them against the tendency of even liberal religion to devolve into speculation or elitism.

TWO ALTERNATIVE INTERPRETATIONS

I do not mean to deny the insights of scholars who have characterized Phillips as Orthodox or as theologically indifferent. He *did* admire the tradition of John Calvin, and he *was* wary of technical theology, and both of these attitudes were components of his New England religion.

Phillips's family of origin, unlike most of their Brahmin peers, belonged to a congregation that rejected the Unitarian movement. He played on this family loyalty throughout his career, citing a Calvinist belief in original sin as reason for not joining the Non-Resistance Society in 1838, and tweaking transcendentalist radicals for excessive optimism in the years after the Civil War.[4] Among his biographers, Oscar Sherwin may have placed greatest emphasis on Phillips's orthodoxy. Describing Phillips's involvement in the Radical Club hosted by the Unitarian minister John T. Sargent, Sherwin notes that Phillips's "friends observed how the radical instantly assumed, when religion was the topic under consideration, the garb of exemplary conservatism. Against iconoclasts and liberals, he was the champion of orthodoxy."[5]

Sherwin buttresses this view with many citations from Phillips's speeches, which taken together demonstrate that Phillips did indeed find much to value in orthodox Calvinism, and that he saw a clear distinction between his own religious views and those of his ultra-liberal Garrisonian comrades. One difference was in his respect for scripture. In an era when many liberals pitted the New Testament against the Old, and Jesus against Paul, Phillips affirmed that "I am Orthodox; I believe in the Bible; I reverence Saint Paul."[6] He admitted that Paul was "liable to mistake" and especially untrustworthy in his views on women—but, for Phillips, this was not reason to dispense altogether with Paul's wisdom. He agreed with Stephen Foster that "there is enough in mere humanity, without the Bible, to condemn slavery," but he still found it helpful to "claim it in behalf of justice and liberty" because "on every field where justice has triumphed, the Bible has led the van."[7] Phillips was able to affirm the whole Bible, despite its errors, because he regarded it as faithful to the complexity of human nature itself: "The Bible . . . is a record of the struggle, as all history seems to be, between the conservative and the progressive elements in society. . . . It has two sides,—the priesthood and the prophets."[8]

Sherwin's biography began as a 1940 doctoral thesis and was published in 1958. In that context, it is not surprising that Phillips's paradoxical view of biblical authority struck him as evidence of "orthodoxy." In the middle of the twentieth century, the preeminent American theologian was Reinhold Niebuhr, a scholar generally recognized as a paragon of "neo-orthodoxy." Like Niebuhr, Phillips had an affinity for the great themes of Calvinist Christianity, such as skepticism about human virtue and a willingness to grapple with the biblical witness in its entirety. Like Niebuhr, Phillips dissented from the cultural captivity of the mainstream clergy, but also repudiated the pacifist dreams of his radical comrades. Like Niebuhr, Phillips brought a historically critical sensibility to particular biblical texts. All of these things would have made him reasonably Orthodox (though not fundamentalist) in 1940, but *not* in 1843. In Phillips's own day, his casual embrace of historical criticism alone would have marked an enormous gulf between him and the orthodox clergy. Thus, it is no accident that he expressed his "orthodox" opinions in a debating club for free religionists rather than in an orthodox congregation.

An alternative view is especially prominent in James Brewer Stewart's biography—though Stewart also echoes Sherwin on many points. This view holds that Phillips thought primarily in the political categories of "republicanism" rather than in the theological categories of Orthodoxy and liberalism. While most abolitionists used "the prophetic language of Jeremiah and Jesus," writes Stewart, Phillips "spoke of slavery in the political language of republican ideology. . . . Phillips was far less immediately concerned than were most of his colleagues with redeeming souls for Christ and decrying the nation's standing in the sight of God. Instead, Phillips hated slavery as an institution that was preeminently social and political." When his allies went on the attack against sabbatarianism or biblical literalism, Stewart points out, "Phillips confessed that 'these *theological* reforms have but a secondary interest to me.'"[9] Stewart is surely right to suggest that Phillips cannot be understood apart from the republican vocabularies he gleaned from his study of classical history. But, writing in the wake of post-1960s secularization, he overestimated the degree to which Phillips separated, or indeed could have separated, "political" from "religious" categories. For Phillips, republican ideals implied a certain type of religion. That is why he commemorated the national centennial with a speech at the Old

South Meeting House, and why he praised the United States on that occasion for having "shown the world that a Church without a bishop, and a State without a king is an actual, real, every-day possibility."[10] Phillips espoused a republican civil religion that drew deeply from the wells of puritan religion, and that resulted in surprising alliances in both the religious and the political sphere.

THE CONTEXT FOR PHILLIPS'S NEW ENGLAND RELIGION

In declaring his devotion to "New England" religion, Phillips expressed a rough fidelity to the religious experiment launched two centuries earlier. The puritan or "Standing Order" churches of Massachusetts, Connecticut, and New Hampshire were a special case in the history of Christianity. As "established" state churches, they received tax funds and collaborated with civil authorities. But they were congregational in their polity: local congregations were not subordinate to any institutional structure larger than themselves. This set them apart from all the established churches of Europe, where monarchs shared ecclesial authority with bishops or national associations of clergy. The New England way generated a fruitful paradox. Like other established churches, the Standing Order churches were responsible not only to their own members but to the whole of society. But authority for exercising that responsibility could not be delegated to a higher authority, resting instead on the shoulders of the members themselves.

This was the paradox that Wendell Phillips inherited. But Phillips championed "the central idea of New England" at a time of profound crisis for the heirs of the puritans. By the 1830s, New England religion had become a minority faith in Massachusetts. Boston, especially, was home to a growing community of Catholic immigrants, while revivalist Baptist and Methodist congregations were growing far more rapidly than their competitors. Like the Baptists and Methodists, the anti-revivalist Universalists were organized on a sectarian basis that utterly repudiated the Standing Order—and in 1833 all these communions worked together to end tax support for churches in Massachusetts.

Outpaced and defunded by external competition, the Standing Order churches of Massachusetts also experienced a wrenching internal division during Phillips's childhood. When Harvard College appointed an avowed Unitarian to its most prestigious chair in 1805, conservative ministers organized a rival seminary at Andover and began breaking fellowship with their more liberal colleagues. Local congregations then began lining up on one side or the other, with more than a few splitting into two competing churches, sending many congregations into acrimony over the division of physical assets. The church attended by Phillips's family remained Orthodox, while most elite Boston congregations opted for Unitarianism. For a time, both Orthodox and Unitarian congregations retained tax support, but the 1833 dissolution of the Standing Order left them in an ambiguous situation. In principle, they wished to retain the "churchly" ideal of accountability to society as a whole, but they lacked institutional structures corresponding to that ideal.[11]

For most of Phillips's adulthood, the Standing Order churches remained in a state of institutional ambiguity. Only after the Civil War did they create denominational bureaucracies in the form of national bodies composed of member congregations: the Unitarians' National Conference of Unitarian Churches and the Orthodox National Council of Congregational Churches. Prior to this, there were myriad competing visions of what a New England religion for the future might look like. At least three alternatives were, in fact, more salient for Phillips than the two groups that would achieve denominational permanence as Unitarians and Congregationalists. The "come-outers"—including Phillips's friend William Lloyd Garrison—regarded themselves as faithful Christians but repudiated all institutional church structures, in part because the churches had failed to speak forthrightly against slavery. The so-called "Union Churches," most with Orthodox heritages, shared this repugnance for "proslavery" religion but not for institutional structures as such. Many also declared themselves neutral in the debate over the Trinity.[12] And the transcendentalists, occupying the left fringe of the Unitarian movement, repudiated biblical authority and thus translated their fathers' "liberal Christianity" into a post-Christian "religious liberalism."[13] These three traditions grew up alongside the abolitionist movement, and (with the Unitarians and Congregationalists) mirrored the schisms among abolitionists. Orthodox Congregationalists typically supported the Tappan brothers' American and Foreign Anti-Slavery Society; Union Churches were linked to the Liberty Party; and come-outers, Unitarians, and transcendentalists all found a warm welcome in Garrisonian organizations.[14]

Unlike the Unitarians and Orthodox Congregationalists, the come-outers, Union Churches, and transcendentalists never created enduring denominational structures. Instead, they cross-fertilized from the 1840s to the end of the century, with many individuals or congregations connected to them eventually gravitating to the Unitarian or Orthodox camp. Wendell Phillips was friendly to all three of these variations on the New England way, and regarded all of them as more faithful to the New England heritage than either the mainstream Unitarians or Orthodox Congregationalists.

This understanding of the New England religion also explains the link between Phillips's religious and political views: Just as Phillips was a classic republican who sided with anarchists, so he was also a Calvinist who sided with transcendentalists and come-outers—in both cases because his true commitment was to the blend of autonomy and accountability that he saw at the heart of New England. In his speeches, Phillips developed his understanding of the New England religion in two ways. On the one hand, he frequently talked directly about the Pilgrim and puritan founders, lifting up what he viewed as their most important work. On the other, he praised exemplary come-outers, Union Churchmen, and transcendentalists as the true heirs of the puritans in his own day.

PHILLIPS'S ACCOUNT OF THE PURITAN PRINCIPLE

In an 1855 speech for the "Pilgrim Society" of Plymouth, Phillips sounded his theme with particular clarity. The Pilgrims, he alleged, had "originated no new truth" and thus proved that "it is not truth which agitates the world!" Their preference for action led them across the Atlantic. And their love of freedom was expressed in their early vote that "each man build his own house"—a fact that prompted Phillips to comment that "I am for having each man build his own mental house now, without having too much uniformity in the architecture." Puritan action and puritan freedom both continued to unfold in the accomplishments of their children. The puritans' "stain of bigotry" could easily be forgiven, so long as their descendents stood firm for "a free altar, free lips . . . and a free family." Against antiquarian sentimentality, Phillips insisted that puritan faith was thoroughly progressive. Would Elder Brewster "be contented with the Congregational Church and the five points of Calvin?" he asked. "No, Sir; he would add to his creed the Maine Liquor Law, the Underground Railroad, and . . . Sharpe's Rifles" for Kansas. And he would exchange pulpits with the likes of Theodore Parker and Henry Ward Beecher—the former a transcendentalist and the latter then serving a congregation in the Union Church tradition.[15]

For Phillips, the puritan preference for free action explained why Massachusetts had been at the forefront of the American struggle for national independence. During the Revolution, he explained, Boston's "fit successors of

Knox and Hugh Peters" (that is, ministers faithful to the founders of puritanism) endorsed the cause of independence and thus "consecrated their pulpits to the defence of that doctrine of the freedom and sacredness of man which the State borrowed so directly from the Christian Church." Campaigning for the preservation of the Old South Church building after its congregation had erected a new edifice in the Back Bay, Phillips conceded that the "church has removed its altar" and relocated, but insisted that "these walls received as real a consecration when Adams and Otis dedicated them to liberty." Phillips consistently used religious terms like "consecration" and "worship," and invoked religious figures such as Martin Luther, when speaking on patriotic themes. For him, the holy cause of the Revolution was the crucial link between the puritans and the abolitionist faith of his own day.[16]

When Phillips spoke of the New England churches of his own day, it was most frequently to underscore their apostasy from the true puritan path. Preaching to Theodore Parker's congregation in 1859, he observed that "I have studied the history of the New England Church; I know what the world owes to Calvinism; to the pulpit; I have no wish to tear a leaf from its laurels . . . but God knows that, within the last thirty years, the ecclesiastical machinery of New England has manufactured hypocrisy just as really as Lowell manufactures cotton."[17] This judgment echoed a point Phillips had made repeatedly in the 1840s, when the Garrisonians were locked in an agitating battle with any churches that refused to join the abolitionist or women's rights causes. Recapping the argument in 1853, Phillips affirmed that "in nothing have the Abolitionists shown more sagacity or more thorough knowledge of their countrymen than in the course they have pursued in relation to the Church." Recognizing the "overwhelming" influence exercised by New England churches, Garrison and his allies saw early on that they had only "two paths": to "work through the Church" if it would work with them or to "join battle with it if it refused." Garrison's first outreach had been to Boston's religious leaders; he had turned against them only after they turned away from him.[18]

THREE EXEMPLARS OF NEW ENGLAND RELIGION

In keeping with his understanding of the true puritan as a free individual, Phillips typically contrasted the corrupt churches with heroic individuals. None were singled out as frequently as William Lloyd Garrison, Theodore Parker, and

John Brown. Implicit in this praise is an endorsement of the communities—come-outer, Unionist, and transcendentalist—that these individuals fostered.

Garrison was Phillips's first abolitionist hero and his closest ally until the Civil War, when Garrison's complacent optimism about the Republican Party slowly diverged from Phillips's commitment to continued agitation. At times, Phillips cast Garrison as the Luther of the nineteenth century, the first to say, "Here I stand; God help me; I can do nothing else!" on behalf of the slave. But Phillips also drew a distinction between Luther and Garrison: while the former had tried to "be Protestant" without fully "com[ing] out of Catholicism," the latter recognized the duty of coming out of a corrupt church.[19] In this sense, Garrison was no Lutheran, but a puritan. And so in his eulogy for Garrison, Phillips used his favorite quote for encapsulating the puritan ideal: Archimedes's "Give me a spot and I will move the world." He also praised his friend for the "plain, sober common-sense" that "underlay Cromwell" and "distinguishe[d] 1640 in England from 1790 in France."[20]

Through the 1840s, Phillips's loyalty to Garrison effectively insulated him from other strands of abolitionist sentiment. But the 1850 passage of the Fugitive Slave Law, and the rise of Vigilance Committees designed to block its implementation, blurred old ideological boundaries and created space for Phillips to form some new alliances. One of his closest friends in this period was Theodore Parker, the firebrand Unitarian preacher who had been shunned by his ministerial colleagues for his thoroughgoing commitment to transcendentalism.[21] The two were neighbors from 1847 on, and worked together on behalf of such fugitives as Anthony Burns. Gradually, Phillips came to see his friend—born just one year earlier—as an heir of the puritans on a par with Garrison. When illness and fear of arrest for his role in the Harpers Ferry raid forced Parker to leave the country in February 1859, Phillips began filling his pulpit on occasion, a practice he continued after his friend's death in May 1860. Phillips often used these occasions to present Parker as an object lesson in New England religion.[22]

For Phillips, Parker was another Archimedean individual who could move society by exercising his individual autonomy. "I stand in the place of one whose great offence was that he practiced what he preached," Phillips announced just a few months after Parker's departure. He explained that Parker had "differed but little, at the outset, from the faith of the Unitarians that he saw around him; but he pronounced the word 'Liberty'—and Unitarianism vanished with a shriek! He found himself alone, with God's sky above him, and the world for an audience."[23] The idea that one could simultaneously be alone and have the world as an audience epitomized the paradoxical wisdom of New England religion. Like his state-supported predecessors in the Unitarian ministry, Parker had a ministerial responsibility that extended to society as a whole—yet in order to exercise that responsibility he needed to be free from priestly hierarchy. Phillips made the same point a few months later, when contrasting Parker with his "Broad Church" Unitarian adversaries. "We have had a broad Church for fifteen years," he declared, "broad enough for all races and colors, all sects, creeds, and parties . . . ministered to by one whose broad diocese is bounded on the north by the limits of habitable land, runs west with civilization, and east with the English language, and on the south stretches to the line where men stop thinking and live only to breathe and to steal."[24]

Phillips also praised Parker's congregation for giving puritan individuality a communal form. Impressed by their choice to replace Parker not with one individual but with an array of speakers, he commended them for allowing their pulpit to be "occupied by men and by women, by black men and white men, by the clergy and by laymen." This was no idiosyncrasy, but an authentic way of honoring the fact that "New England was the vanguard of that Protestant protest against the idea of a priest." (Phillips invoked his own genealogy in support of this point, noting that his ancestor had told the Watertown congregation that he would not serve them as minister if they thought his ordination in England had given him any authority!) Phillips also praised the congregation for its anti-creedalism, which he observed was consistent with the practice of Boston's earliest churches. In all respects, this radical congregation was "not an abnormal monster but the normal growth of New England progress."[25]

The sermon I have just been quoting was entitled "The Pulpit," and in it Phillips actually made an interesting contribution to the theological discipline of ecclesiology. A "pulpit," he affirmed, was distinct from a "church" in the same way that a "prophet" was distinct from a "priest." "I believe in more of a church than most of you do," he reminded the congregants. Organizations for the cultivation of "religious sentiment and devotional feeling" could be a good thing, so long as they did not devolve into the "petty despotisms" so common in New England. But the pulpit was different. Its function was to "dictate earnest words to make our neighbor a better man and better citizen" and thus to "clear the clogged channels of life." As the example of the Hebrew prophets made clear, the true pulpit was obliged to "cover everything . . . politics, national manners, the thoughts, sins, and customs of the day." Its "diocese was as broad as conscience." Here we see the ideal of the state church transmuted into the democratic idiom of free speech, and the corollary was that the pulpit could not be monopolized by a professional clergy or by any distinct class of society. The diversity of life could be conveyed only by a diverse roster of speakers. Phillips affirmed that "a man cannot argue the Woman Question. . . . We know nothing of slavery; we never shall know it until God's hand sweeps the strings of four millions of broken hearts, and lets us hear from the plantations of the Southern half of this nation." (Since Phillips had frequently spoken on both women's rights and slavery, presumably his point was that neither topic could be *fully* understood without the voices of those most directly affected.) A further corollary of Phillips's view of the pulpit was that it could never be institutionalized. Like Amos or Jeremiah, a true pulpit would "spring into being whenever there is an earthquake in society."[26] No one exemplified this preacherly springing into being as fully as Theodore Parker.

Much as Phillips admired Parker, he saved his most fervent puritan rhetoric for John Brown. In some ways, this was a surprising choice. Brown was an ally of Gerrit Smith, whose view of the Constitution as an antislavery document had elicited mountains of scorn from Phillips in the 1840s. Like Smith, Brown participated in the Union Church movement by organizing his own nondenominational congregation; unlike Smith, he never gravitated toward theological liberalism. But theological and constitutional differences made little difference in the late 1850s, when the Kansas struggle commanded the attention of all abolitionists. Thus, Parker and other transcendentalists joined Smith in bankrolling the raid on Harpers Ferry. Phillips stood sympathetically aloof from the work of the Secret Six, only to emerge as Brown's rhetorical champion after the fact. Phillips eulogized Brown on at least three separate occasions: at Henry Ward Beecher's Plymouth Church on November 1, 1859; at Brown's graveside on December 8; and at Parker's church on the eighteenth of that month. He played the puritan theme on all three occasions.

Speaking at Beecher's church in the interval between the Harpers Ferry raid and Brown's execution, Phillips cast Brown as the first to realize the "idea" of American civilization. Too many Americans, he lamented, clung to the timidity of Europe, which believed "that man is created to be taken care of by somebody else." By acting out "the common sense of the masses," on the other hand,

Brown proved that "men do not need any guardian." Characterizing Brown as "a regular Cromwellian dug up from two centuries," Phillips suggested that only such a person had the power to help the nation distinguish right from wrong. "If in a world of sinners you were to put American Christianity, it would be calm as oil. But put one Christian, like John Brown of Osawatomie, and he makes the whole crystallize into right and wrong." Indeed, Brown's singularity made him the true government of Virginia, while the rest was only "a chronic insurrection."[27] Once again, here is the paradoxical wisdom of New England: broad social responsibility was possible only if individuals had the freedom to act.

Such rhetoric was perhaps inevitable at Beecher's Church, which was after all called the *Plymouth* Church. But Phillips made the same point even more emphatically for Parker's radical Unitarians, beginning his sermon there with "I thank God for John Calvin." After a perfunctory acknowledgment that Calvin had "burned Servetus," he launched into a celebration of Calvin and the puritans, scarcely touching on John Brown until he was half-finished. The puritan principle, he explained, had two aspects: "the republicanism of the Church" that rejected "priestcraft and power," and a preference for action over speculation. He illustrated this with a variation on the Archimedean image: anyone might *believe* that they can float in the ocean by simply holding their arms at their sides, but only the puritan could actually *do* it. Perhaps seeking to challenge his audience of radical transcendentalists, Phillips leaned more heavily on puritan history in this sermon than in the one for Beecher's church. But his ultimate point was that the puritans were better honored by free action than by rote imitation. On this point, he even echoed Emerson: "And ever again, in every generation, the living soul, like the bursting bud, throws up the incumbent soil and finds its way to the sunshine and to God." The puritans of every age were those "who hold their ears open for the message of the present hour." And so he imagined the puritan fathers saying to John Brown, "You are ours, though you have gone beyond us."[28]

NEW ENGLAND RELIGION AFTER THE CIVIL WAR

Neither John Brown nor Theodore Parker lived to see the fruit of their abolitionist efforts. William Lloyd Garrison, for his part, bitterly disappointed his old friend Phillips in the years after the war: while Garrison saw the work of the American Anti-Slavery Society as complete once emancipation was achieved,

Phillips strove to carry forward the antiracist impulse that had initially led Garrison to plant the *Liberator* in prejudiced Boston rather than slaveholding Baltimore. Deprived of old friends, Phillips turned to a new organization as the venue for his articulation of a postbellum religion for New England. This was the Free Religious Association (FRA), organized in 1867 by transcendentalists and other radical Unitarians as a venue for their dissent from cautious denominational leaders. Phillips spoke at the FRA's first anniversary gathering in 1868 and participated in its inaugural public lecture series in 1869. On both occasions he had a unique role to play: the other speakers were either radical transcendentalists or persons chosen to represent traditions clearly distinct from the New England heritage, such as Roman Catholicism or Reform Judaism. Only Phillips was prepared to put in a good word for the Orthodox side of the New England heritage.

Speaking on "The Relation of Religion to Philanthropy and to Social Science" in 1868, Phillips sounded the old, familiar note of Garrisonian comeouterism. He had begun life, he explained, "with a most profound faith in the honesty and in the efficiency of church organization," but was "bayoneted out of that conviction" by his experience as an abolitionist. Again and again, established churches had betrayed the cause of human rights, persuading Phillips that when ideas "crystallize" into organizations they become "millstones" preventing further progress. Church organizations might sometimes, like ice on a river, provide a useful bridge—but one can never expect them to move forward.[29]

Phillips then turned to a theme that anticipated the social gospel theologies of the rising generation. Distinguishing institutional religion from true Christianity (unlike the free religionists, Phillips saw Christianity as the highest form of religion), he argued that, while churches seek to alleviate evils, "social science and the religious philosophy of the New Testament seek, not relief, but cure." Developing a sharp contrast between what later activists would term "charity" and "justice," Phillips placed temperance, the eight-hour workday, economic cooperation, and full suffrage for women and African Americans in the latter category. "All Labor asks is *justice*, not charity; all woman asks is *justice*, not pity; all the negro asks is *justice*, not humanity." He also articulated a version of what would later be called social salvation, arguing that "Society is the body of which the religion of the age is the soul. . . . The reason why I maintain that the religion of this age is in a corrupt and hide-bound and marvelously decrepit state, is because society, which forms its body here, is a capital punishment, pro-slavery, fourteen-hours-a-day, woman-under-the-heel society." Somewhat paradoxically, he used the same principle to argue that Christianity was superior to other religions because its fruit in European and American society was superior to the societies of the East.[30]

Forty years later, when the social gospel was fully ascendant in American religion, a president of the FRA would remember this speech as "the most stirring and valuable speech to be found in the volumes of the Association's proceedings" precisely because of its "demand for social reconstruction."[31] But neither Phillips nor the other staunch abolitionists in the FRA were able to make it into a vehicle for socially engaged religion. Its radical Unitarian leaders preferred a debating society for religious liberals, confirming Phillips's fears that the transcendentalists and the orthodox were equally apostate from the activist spirit of the puritans. Frustration with the ethereal direction taken by the FRA probably motivated Phillips's comment, more than a decade later, that "It has been my lot to find more bigotry and narrowness among free religionists than among their opponents."[32]

Phillips gave vent to the same frustration in his 1869 lecture for the FRA, on the provocative theme of "Christianity a Battle Not a Dream." Challenging the free religionists' tendency to treat all religions as equal, Phillips insisted that Christianity "occupies an entirely . . . different level from any other of what are called . . . the religions of the world." But the superiority lay in its activism, not its doctrines. Christianity was the only religion that attempted to "reform the world by ideas"—making Jesus "the great AGITATOR of the centuries." Likewise, Christ rejected priestly authority by "*intrust[ing]* his gospel to the poor, to the common-sense of the race." He even worked in a dig at Unitarianism: Jesus's achievement was so much superior to that of "Shakespeare and Plato," and Europe's achievement was so much superior to that of India, that it was impossible to believe that Jesus was merely a man. Still, Phillips's goal was not to convert Unitarians into Trinitarians or transcendentalists into Calvinists, but to turn all of their attention from speculation to action. "A large proportion of the men who discuss radical religion, as well as Orthodox religionists, mistake the essence of Christianity for speculation." But "open the New Testament" and you will find a frontal attack on "the problems that make up the society of today." On this basis, he added, Voltaire and Paine had been better Christians than mitered bishops. He concluded by suggesting that most churches simply shut down their pulpits to allow more time for "laboring among the poor and depraved." In an age when liberal and orthodox religion alike revolved around the sermon, Phillips dared to suggest that the true heritage of the puritans was something else altogether.[33]

CONCLUSION

In my own work as a historian of the religious left, and of Unitarian Universalism, I have often been struck by a paradox. Throughout the main years of abolitionist struggle, the Unitarian and Orthodox heirs of New England puritanism were locked in theological battle—and yet both groups were significantly overrepresented in abolition, as compared to their Presbyterian, Methodist, and Baptist neighbors (though not in comparison to come-outers, Union Church members, and transcendentalists). After the Civil War, both traditions evolved in a leftward direction theologically, all the while maintaining a roughly constant distance from one another. Both remained at the forefront of religious activism in the social gospel and civil rights eras. After the Stonewall rebellion launched the gay liberation movement, their denominational descendents were quick to embrace the cause, even as other denominations fell into a generation-long debate over sexuality. Today, the rival seminaries that were born from the Unitarian Controversy—Andover and Harvard—educate large numbers of students from one another's traditions, and a popular joke says that "UCC" stands for "Unitarians Considering Christ" rather than "United Church of Christ."

Wendell Phillips's vision of a New England religion is the best explanation I've seen for why Unitarian Universalists and UCCers have so much in common. These churches have achieved impressive records of activism because they have remained faithful to the paradoxical balance of New England religion: broad concern for society as a whole, alongside fierce devotion to individual and local initiative. This is not to suggest that either tradition is everything that Phillips might have wished for. In both denominations, Phillipsian activism has always coexisted with doctrinaire metaphysics, sectarian narrowness, and bureaucratic timidity. Just as Phillips preferred the come-outers, Union Churchpeople, and transcendentalists at the fringes of Orthodoxy and Unitarianism, so in latter days he likely would have gravitated to the People's Churches, Community Churches, Black Humanist fellowships, and other freewheeling congregations that always populated the boundaries of New England religion. In all of these expressions, Wendell Phillips would say, the puritan spirit has lived on.

NOTES

1. Oscar Sherwin, *Prophet of Liberty: The Life and Times of Wendell Phillips* (New York: Bookman Associates, 1958), 640–43; Wendell Phillips, "The Puritan Principle and John Brown," December 18, 1859, in Wendell Phillips, *Speeches, Lectures, and Letters: Second Series* (Boston: Lee and Shepard, 1891), 294.

2. James Brewer Stewart, *Wendell Phillips: Liberty's Hero* (Baton Rouge: Louisiana State, 1986), 118; Wendell Phillips, "Christianity a Battle, Not a Dream," in *Speeches: Second Series*, 276.

3. Phillips, "The Puritan Principle and John Brown," 295–96; Phillips, "The Pulpit," in *Speeches: Second Series*, 252; and Phillips, "The Pilgrims," in Wendell Phillips, *Speeches, Lectures, and Letters* (Boston: James Redpath, 1863), 231.

4. Stewart, *Wendell Phillips*, 68, 161.

5. Sherwin, *Prophet of Liberty*, 640.

6. Phillips, "Suffrage for Women," in *Speeches: Second Series*, 125.

7. Phillips, "The Bible and the Church," 1850, in *Speeches: Second Series*, 245–46.

8. Phillips, "The Bible and the Church," 1859, in *Speeches: Second Series*, 248.

9. Stewart, *Wendell Phillips*, 69, 118.

10. Phillips, "Old South Church Meeting House," *Speeches: Second Series*, 231. The phrase "a Church without a bishop, and a State without a king" was also the title of a hymn on the Pilgrims written by Rev. Charles Hall in 1844. Though the hymn was premiered at an anti-Catholic lecture given by the orthodox clergyman George Barrell Cheever, it was subsequently embraced by both the orthodox and Unitarian communities. See George Barrell Cheever, *The Hierarchical Despotism* (New York: Saxton and Miles, 1844), 64.

11. On the Unitarian controversy, see David Robinson, *The Unitarians and the Universalists* (Westport, Conn.: Greenwood, 1985); Conrad Wright, *The Unitarian Controversy: Essays on American Unitarian History* (Boston: Skinner, 1994); Conrad Wright, ed., *A Stream of Light: A Sesquicentennial History of American Unitarianism* (Boston: Unitarian Universalist Association, 1975); Sydney E. Ahlstrom and Jonathan S. Carey, *An American Reformation: A Documentary History of Unitarian Christianity* (Middletown, Conn.: Wesleyan University Press, 1985).

12. The most complete study of the Union Churches is Douglas M. Strong, *Perfectionist Politics: Abolitionism and the Religious Tensions of American Democracy* (Syracuse, N.Y.: Syracuse University Press, 1999).

13. An excellent overview of Transcendentalism is Philip F. Gura, *American Transcendentalism: A History* (New York: Hill and Wang, 2007).

14. On religious differences among abolitionists, see Lawrence J. Friedman, *Gregarious Saints: Self and Community in American Abolitionism, 1830–1870* (New York: Cambridge University Press, 1982); John R. McKivigan, *The War Against Proslavery Religion: Abolitionism and the Northern*

Churches (Ithaca: Cornell University Press, 1984); and Lewis Perry, *Radical Abolitionism: Anarchy and the Government of God in Antislavery Thought* (Ithaca: Cornell University Press, 1973).

15. Phillips, "The Pilgrims," 228–36.

16. Phillips, "The Old South Meeting-House," *Speeches: Second Series*, 234, 237–41.

17. Phillips, "The Bible and the Church," 1859, 250.

18. Phillips, "The Philosophy of the Abolition Movement," *Speeches: First Series*, 122.

19. Ibid., 128, 122.

20. Phillips, "William Lloyd Garrison," *Speeches: Second Series*, 468.

21. Stewart, *Wendell Phillips*, 152.

22. Phillips, *Speeches: Second Series* contains three sermons given at Parker's congregation: "The Bible and the Church" (April 24, 1859), 248–51; "The Puritan Principle and John Brown," 294–308; and "The Pulpit" (November 18, 1860), 252–75; as well as Phillips's address at Parker's memorial service, June 17, 1860, 428–39. *Speeches* contains "Mobs and Education," delivered on December 16, 1860. The first two of these were preached during the period after Parker had left the country but before his death; Dean Grodzins's review of congregational records (in an email communication of May 27, 2011) reveals three additional sermons in this period, meaning that Phillips tied with Young Hegelian scholar Reinhold Solger as the second most popular substitute preacher. (Ralph Waldo Emerson was easily first.) Irving H. Bartlett, *Wendell Phillips: Brahmin Radical* (Boston: Beacon, 1961), 224–31, offers an extended analysis of "The Pulpit," "Mobs and Education," and "Disunion," given at Music Hall on January 20, but neglects the sermons given before Parker's death.

23. Phillips, "The Bible and the Church," 1859, 249.

24. Phillips, "Idols," *Speeches: First Series*, 250.

25. Phillips, "The Pulpit," 252–54.

26. Ibid., 254–64.

27. Phillips, "Harper's Ferry," *Speeches: First Series*, 264, 276, 272.

28. Phillips, "The Puritan Principle and John Brown," 294–308.

29. Phillips, "The Relation of Religion to Philanthropy and to Social Science," *Proceedings at the First Annual Meeting* (Boston: Free Religious Association, 1868), 90–91.

30. Ibid., 92–93, 103, 95.

31. Edwin D. Mead, "Opening Address of the President," *Proceedings at the Fortieth Annual Meeting* (Boston: Free Religious Association, 1907), 22.

32. Wendell Phillips, "Appendix," *Letters of Lydia Maria Child* (Boston: Houghton Mifflin, 1882), 265.

33. Phillips, "Christianity a Battle," 277, 280–86, emphasis in original.

4

WENDELL PHILLIPS, THE RULE OF LAW, AND ANTISLAVERY VIOLENCE

DEAN GRODZINS

On May 28, 1863, the famous African American regiment, the Fifty-fourth Massachusetts, paraded past Wendell Phillips's front door. The men marched through Boston to the ship that would take them south to battle the "slaveholders' rebellion," and their circuitous parade route seems to have been plotted in part to pass his house.[1] If so, it would have been a fitting tribute. Over the previous two years of Civil War, the great abolitionist orator had probably done more than any other person to persuade the northern public that the army should lift its ban against the recruitment of black troops. This proposal had become federal policy in January 1863, when President Abraham Lincoln issued the final Emancipation Proclamation.

On Phillips's second-floor balcony, watching the passing column of blue uniforms, stood his friend and antislavery mentor William Lloyd Garrison, who before the war had advocated the pacifist doctrine of "non-resistance" and had denounced all forms of force as illegitimate and unchristian, but who now endorsed the war against slavery. Garrison's hand rested on a bust of John Brown, apostle of armed resistance to the Slave Power, who had been hanged in 1859 for trying to start a slave revolt in Virginia.[2] Phillips had hailed Brown as a martyr.

The scene on the balcony represented a symbolic resolution of a long argument among antislavery advocates over whether to use violence to further their goals. Garrison and Brown had stood at opposing poles of this debate, while Phillips, who admired both men, had seemed balanced between them. In the 1850s, however, as the Civil War approached, he had found his balance increasingly difficult to maintain.

He had never been a pacifist. He had dissented at the Boston Peace Convention of 1838, where Garrison embraced nonresistant doctrine, and always acknowledged that individuals had the right to kill in defense not only of life, but of liberty.[3] Nonetheless, in the 1850s, even as a growing number of his antislavery associates endorsed political violence, Phillips could never quite bring himself to join them.

One of Brown's backers, Thomas Wentworth Higginson, puzzled over his reserve and concluded that the problem lay in Phillips's temperament: although "a man of personal courage," Phillips was not in "his very fibre, a man of action."[4] Yet many retiring and bookish thinkers—and Phillips was neither—have enthusiastically embraced the use of violent means to attain political ends. Phillips was constrained from doing so by a deep, if unconventional, commitment to the rule of law.

Phillips graduated from Harvard Law School in 1833. The following year, he was admitted to the state bar, which required him to take oaths to support the constitutions of Massachusetts and the United States, and he opened a law office in Boston.[5] Routine case work bored him, however, and by 1838, he had largely abandoned his practice to become a full-time reform agitator. His later decision to renounce allegiance to the U.S. Constitution cost him his bar membership. Yet he never ceased to think of himself as a lawyer. Throughout the antebellum period and beyond, he listed himself as a "counsellor" or "lawyer" in the *Boston Directory*, and he continued doing certain kinds of legal work, for example, giving legal advice to fugitive slaves. He apparently even maintained a law office, at 11 Court Street in Boston, as late as 1851.[6]

He always presented himself as a lawyer in his writings and speeches. Notable examples include his 1847 book attacking Lysander Spooner's claim that slavery was unconstitutional, and his 1855 testimony before the Committee on Federal Relations of the Massachusetts legislature, urging that state probate judge Edward G. Loring be removed from office as punishment for proslavery activity. (Judge Loring, who was also a federal court commissioner, had in that capacity ordered the rendition of the fugitive slave Anthony Burns.) In these instances, Phillips took on the role of a lawyer presenting a case. His arguments were closely reasoned from legal principles and full of citations to legal precedent and quotations from legal authorities.[7]

Phillips occasionally commented on the legal profession, making clear both what kind of legal career he disdained, and what kind he saw himself as pursuing. For example, in his Loring testimony, he expressed contempt for "*nisi prius* lawyers, bound by quiddling technicalities."[8] Several years later, in a lecture, he passed judgment on Rufus Choate, former U.S. senator from Massachusetts and celebrated defense attorney, who had just died. Choate had staunchly opposed abolitionism and three other reforms dear to Phillips's heart: temperance, women's rights, and abolition of the death penalty. Phillips noted that Choate's passing had elicited an outpouring of eulogy, which had pronounced him a "ripe scholar, a profound lawyer, a faithful servant of his client, a gentleman."[9] To Phillips, however, such tributes only proved that Choate had possessed none of the qualities of a truly great lawyer: "Not one high moral trait specified; not one patriotic act mentioned; not one patriotic service even claimed. . . . Not a word of one effort to lift the yoke of cruel or unequal legislation from the neck of its victim; not one attempt to make the code of his country wiser, purer, better; not one effort to bless his times or breathe a higher moral purpose into the community; not one blow struck for right or for liberty, while the battle of the giants was going on about him."[10]

Phillips contrasted Choate with lawyers worthy of eulogy: Papinian, who accepted death rather than justify, as commanded, an atrocious murder by the Roman Emperor Caracalla; or Coke, Selden, Mansfield, and Erskine, who defied the British monarchs in the name of liberty; or the late Boston attorney (also, briefly, U.S. senator), Robert Rantoul, Jr., who had battled for temperance, legal reform, and the slave.[11] Phillips clearly wished to model himself on great lawyers such as these.

Phillips's vision of the great lawyer was analogous, in the purposes it served for him, to the vision of the great preacher articulated by Ralph Waldo Emerson in his Divinity School Address (1838). Emerson, whom Phillips greatly admired, severely criticized conventional New England preaching, with its emphasis on doctrine and biblical exegesis, as spiritually dead. He declared that preachers must become "bards of the holy ghost" and even write their own scriptures. Emerson had followed his father and grandfather into the pulpit; now, he defined the work of ministry in a way that allowed him both to justify his decision to abandon his ministerial career and become a lecturer, essayist, and poet, and yet to see himself as pursuing the deepest goals of ministry by other means.[12] So Phillips, who had followed his father into the law, defined the work of the lawyer in such a way that he could both justify his decision to become an agitator and see himself as still pursuing a legal career of the noblest kind.

Phillips forcefully articulated the need to respect the law when he discussed anti-abolitionist riots and temperance legislation. His recurring theme in treating the former topic was that abolitionists, although often accused of spreading anarchy and disorder, in fact scrupulously obeyed the law, while their opponents flagrantly violated it.

He made this argument in the speech that first won him fame, on the "Murder of Lovejoy" (1837). Rev. Elijah P. Lovejoy, of Alton, Illinois, had been killed in a gun battle with a mob bent on destroying the press he used to print his antislavery newspaper. Phillips defended Lovejoy as a champion of law and order. He explained that Lovejoy had not fallen back on the "natural right of self-defence"; nor was his a case of a man protecting his property, nor of two gangs in a street fight. Lovejoy, Phillips pointed out, had been enrolled as part of the city watch. His case, therefore, was one of "the police of the city resisting rioters."[13] Later, in other speeches, Phillips placed the blame for the anti-abolitionist riots in Boston in 1835 and 1860 squarely on the city authorities, charging them with gross dereliction of duty for failing to disperse the mobs.[14] Similarly, whenever Phillips addressed the temperance question, he complained bitterly about the chronic failure of Boston authorities to enforce state temperance laws. By 1863, he had grown so frustrated that he demanded the city police force be placed under state control.[15]

Owing to these strong commitments to antislavery, temperance, and rule of law, Phillips never could develop a consistent stand regarding a major legal issue on which the antislavery and temperance causes came to work at cross-purposes: Should juries decide questions of law, as well as questions of fact, in criminal cases? They always had been allowed to do so, but this tradition was challenged in the mid-nineteenth century by those who argued that only judges could answer legal questions accurately, fairly, and above all consistently from jurisdiction to jurisdiction. Business interests drove this jury reform, because they believed that a national commercial system could not be established without uniform application of the laws.[16] They found allies in the temperance movement, who were frustrated that juries almost never convicted anyone for illegally selling liquor. In the 1840s, temperance advocates applauded when judges began screening out jurors who openly opposed temperance laws.

When courts began to try violations of the Fugitive Slave Law of 1850, however, some temperance advocates who, like Phillips, were also abolitionists, had second thoughts. They did not want judges to screen out jurors who considered the law unconstitutional. As one lawyer, a temperance man now defending fugitive slave rescuers, noted regretfully in 1854, "Everybody said it was a great thing to put down the rumsellers and shut up the rum shops. No matter if the trial by jury does go with them. . . . The conviction of the rumsellers . . . was purchased at too great a price, which, to obtain it, the right of jury trial was surrendered."[17]

Phillips seems to have been unwilling to acknowledge that this conflict between temperance and antislavery existed. He complained only that in all trials in Boston "that had antislavery or temperance in them, you might be certain of one thing,—you would never see an Abolitionist nor a temperance man on the jury. If he got there, it was an accident, and there were always enough to neutralize him."[18]

At the same time, he never endorsed the views of his friend and neighbor, the radical clergyman Theodore Parker, who in response to the Fugitive Slave Law began arguing that a juror could ignore both the law and facts of the case and vote according to the dictates of his individual conscience. Parker was endorsing, in unqualified terms, jury nullification.[19] Phillips supported the rule of law and legal institutions too strongly to do the same. Such support is even apparent in his refusal to recognize the authority of the U.S. Constitution.

In the 1840s, Phillips produced a series of writings to support the claim that the federal Constitution was proslavery. He argued that its provisions showed it to be such; that its framers intended it to be such; that the federal courts had always interpreted it to be such; that both Congress and state legislatures had always assumed it to be such when framing laws; and that the "uninterrupted practice by all parties" confirmed it. According to Phillips, American slavery was fully constitutional and fully legal, and any antislavery activists who argued otherwise, such as his disputant Lysander Spooner, were only deluding themselves. Phillips deduced from this analysis that abolitionists could not with any intellectual or moral consistency vote or hold government office and must agitate for the free states to secede from the Union.[20]

Some important abolitionists who took a disunionist stand, Garrison most conspicuously, linked it to a broad critique of all forms of government as unjust. Phillips, by contrast, denied that rejection of the U.S. Constitution led to "no-governmentism or anarchy."[21] In fact, even while refusing to acknowledge the authority of the national government, he always accepted the authority of the state and local governments of Massachusetts. Phillips never seems to have renounced his oath, on being admitted to the state bar, to uphold the constitution of the commonwealth. He had no qualms about giving testimony before the state legislature, as he did often, or a state constitutional convention, as he did in 1853, to urge action on issues that mattered to him. His demand for vigorous enforcement of local temperance laws was consistent with his overall position. So, too, was his strong support for campaigns to overturn Massachusetts laws and Boston ordinances he considered unjust, such as those that required racially segregated trains and schools, forbade interracial marriage, denied women the vote, and permitted the death penalty.

Phillips saw the governments of Boston and Massachusetts as products of the double heritage of puritanism and the Revolution that he cherished. If any one figure embodied these traditions for Phillips, it seems to have been the patriot leader and Massachusetts governor Samuel Adams—an interesting choice, as Adams had been half-forgotten by the mid-nineteenth century. Yet Phillips, in speeches and lectures, invoked Sam Adams's name again and again, praising him as "the ablest and ripest statesman God ever gave to the [Revolutionary] epoch," and numbering him among the handful of heroes "who make [American] history worth anything in the worlds [*sic*] annals." Phillips seems to have admired Adams in part because he identified with him. He referred to Adams in the context of his being, like Phillips himself, a Bostonian, a Calvinist, an alleged "fanatic," who "thought slavery a crime," and above all as one of those who, "without arms, by force of reason, have revolutionized their times."[22] Phillips probably also admired Adams for his major role in writing and winning approval for the Massachusetts Constitution, as well as for his refusal to endorse the federal Constitution without the addition of a bill of rights to protect the liberty of the people and state sovereignty—a stand Phillips surely appreciated.

Phillips remained hopeful that the governments of his city and commonwealth would become ever more powerful forces for the moral improvement of the people. In his view, governments with such potential were worthy of allegiance. The federal government, bound by its proslavery Constitution and anchored by a proslavery political consensus, was not.

Phillips's rejection of federal authority had practical consequences for his response to the Fugitive Slave Law of 1850. Yet in large measure, his disunionism amounted to a symbolic boycott. He would not hold any public office that required an oath to uphold the U.S. Constitution, which meant that he would not hold any public office, nor would he vote for anyone who, upon assuming public office, would have to take such an oath, which meant that he would not vote.

Significantly, however, Phillips rejected any suggestion that he not pay taxes, even federal taxes. The U.S. government in fact levied no direct taxes in the 1840s and 1850s, so he could have made a painless political point by announcing he would not pay them, but he never admitted this possibility, even hypothetically. Instead, he argued that we could acknowledge the *power* of government over us without acknowledging its *authority*, and that we could only be held responsible for our "voluntary acts." Therefore, if the government ever decided to trust taxpaying to "the voluntary good will of its subjects," then "I, for one, will refuse to pay."[23]

His position on voting and taxes can be usefully contrasted with that of Henry David Thoreau. In "Civil Disobedience," Thoreau describes being jailed in his hometown of Concord, Massachusetts, for protesting the proslavery U.S. war with Mexico by refusing to pay his poll tax. This was not, it should be noted, a federal tax, but a state one. Thoreau considered all American governments, including that of Massachusetts, implicated in the war, so he would no longer give money to support any of them. He grounded his stand in skepticism about the worth of government in general. As he famously asserted, "That government is best, which governs not at all," a view Phillips emphatically did not share.[24]

When Thoreau refused to pay his poll tax, he disenfranchised himself, but he did not mention this consequence in his essay, probably because he did not care.[25] He deprecated the moral significance of voting and seldom if ever bothered to vote. Phillips, by contrast, considered voting a civic duty of first importance, which is why he viewed nonvoting as a provocative act: "The position of a non-voter, in a land where the ballot is so much idolized, kindles in every beholder's bosom something of the warm sympathy which waits on the persecuted, carries with it all the weight of a disinterested testimony to truth, and pricks each voter's conscience with an uneasy doubt, whether after all voting *is* right."[26]

That Phillips limited his antigovernment protest primarily to nonvoting and non-officeholding meant that he in effect limited its scope to a small number of citizens like himself, white men of high social standing. Women and most African Americans could not vote or hold office anyway, so their protesting in this manner would have been meaningless, and even most white men would not have found the protest very politically effective. Thoreau's decision not to vote seems to have been dismissed by the townsfolk of Concord as just another of his many eccentricities. By contrast, the decision of Phillips not to vote made an impression, because as the rich, charismatic scion of the first mayor of Boston, and a brilliant orator, everyone assumed he was choosing to renounce a great public career. Such was the impression Phillips's protest made on Richard Henry Dana, Jr.: "When I hear of sacrifices made for the cause of freedom, of contributions to the relief of the oppressed, what, I ask, is the sacrifice of this or that office, or this or that preferment, the vulgar contributions of money, earned perhaps by compromises with slavery, to the sacrifice which [Phillips] has made, of the bright dreams of his youth, of professional and political distinction, of high station, and of reflection of new honors on an honored name he has inherited, and greater yet, of the consciousness of leading a life of intellectual contest in the professional arena, before the public eye! All this he has sacrificed . . . because he would not misconstrue the Constitution."[27]

Many abolitionists first publicly endorsed a form of antislavery violence when they began to argue that a runaway slave, or the rescuers of one, had the right to kill the slave catcher. The issue became pressing in September 1850, when Congress enacted a new Fugitive Slave Law.[28] Until this point, masters had been thwarted trying to claim their human property in Massachusetts, where the unpopularity of slave catching and state antislavery laws worked against them. The Fugitive Slave Law, however, established a national slave-catching bureaucracy, comprised of federal court commissioners; there were six of them operating in Boston alone. In response to the existential threat that the law posed to the Boston black community, its leaders urged blacks to take up arms to protect themselves. At a meeting of "colored citizens," shortly after the law took effect, the businessman Joshua B. Smith displayed his revolver and announced to thunderous applause that he would not be taken alive.[29]

The white abolitionist minister Theodore Parker, Phillips's friend and neighbor, endorsed the black position when he announced in a sermon that the "man who attacks me to reduce me to slavery, in that moment of attack alienates his right to life, and if I were the fugitive, and could escape in no other way, I would kill him with as little compunction as I would drive a mosquito from my face."[30] When, shortly afterwards, Parker hid a fugitive slave at his house for a week, he armed himself with a pistol and sword to protect her.

Even some advocates of nonresistance asserted that anyone who had not renounced all forms of violence would have to recognize killing slave catchers as a morally justifiable act. The prominent nonresistant Henry Wright declared in a resolution to a September 1850 meeting of the Western Anti-Slavery Society (WASS) "the right and duty of every fugitive slave, of every abolitionist, of every man and woman . . . to act on the principle of DEATH TO KIDNAPPERS, whether they come to us as voters, Presidents, Judges, Marshals, constables, *posse comitatus*, or slaveholders."[31] Wright may have intended this sanguinary resolution to be a *reductio ad absurdum* statement of the non-pacifist position, but the WASS meeting, possibly to his surprise, approved it.

Phillips cared deeply about the freedom of runaway slaves. One of the principal grounds for rejecting the authority of the U.S. Constitution was its "fugitive slave clause," which required that fugitives from "service or labor" who escaped to a free state be "delivered up" to their masters (IV:2:3). Phillips never accepted the legitimacy of the Fugitive Slave Law, which he (like African American leaders) usually referred to as a "bill," even years after its enactment.[32] He never had qualms about helping slaves escape to freedom. Yet, as he confessed in a speech in 1849, "I go against underground railroads": "I would not have a cellar or a garret for [the fugitive]. I would, at least, be at liberty to place him in my parlor, and set the door open, and bid the thousands passing in the street look in, if they chose. I would remind [supporters of the Fugitive Slave Law] that 'we are a law abiding people,' and ask [them] to try it. . . . I would pronounce that voice so decisively in the name of Massachusetts law, that the slave should never doubt his safety from the moment he touched the soil of the Bay State."[33] In other words, Phillips thought that the antislavery laws of Massachusetts trumped the proslavery laws of the United States, and he wanted to operate openly in the name of the former, rather than clandestinely—or, he might have added, violently—against the latter.

Because Phillips believed in abiding by the laws of Massachusetts, he could not easily endorse the right of runaway slaves in Boston to kill their hunters. Murder was, of course, a crime under Massachusetts law. Although he felt bound to admit the right of fugitives to resist capture by any means necessary, he could not ignore Massachusetts law.

Phillips seemed unable to resolve this dilemma. In 1850 and 1851, even as he excoriated the Fugitive Slave Law and its Massachusetts supporters and became a leader of the Boston Vigilance Committee, which was dedicated to protecting local blacks from the slave catcher, he said nothing on the issue of violent resistance. He may have hoped the question would not come up. Initially, most white Boston abolitionists, apparently including Phillips, persuaded themselves that, because public sentiment in their hometown was so broadly and strongly opposed to the return of runaway slaves, the Fugitive Slave Law could never be enforced there. In October 1850, the antislavery mass meeting that created the Boston Vigilance Committee even approved a resolution, with Phillips's support, urging blacks who had fled Boston after the new Fugitive Slave Law was enacted to return and "remain with us," because "we have no fear that anyone will be taken back to the land of bondage."[34]

Then in April 1851, federal authorities in Boston seized a fugitive from Georgia, Thomas Sims. Sims stabbed one of the arresting officers but failed to kill him and was jailed in the Boston Court House. Phillips helped lead protests against the arrest, and antislavery lawyers defended Sims vigorously, but to no avail. He was sent back to Savannah in chains. Even then, Phillips waited another year to clarify his position on forceful resistance. He finally took a stand in a speech to mark the anniversary of the Sims "surrender." His remarks reveal how much he still struggled with the issue.

Phillips now recommended that any fugitives still in Boston leave at once for the safety of Canada: "THIS IS THE COURSE I WOULD ADVISE EVERY MAN TO ADOPT. THIS, UNLESS THERE ARE, IN HIS PARTICULAR CASE, IMPERATIVE REASONS TO THE CONTRARY, IS HIS DUTY." Only if such "imperative reasons" prevented emigration should the fugitive arm himself. Phillips conceded that any fugitive was "entitled . . . to use every means he has or can get to resist arrest at the last resort"; as Phillips noted, authorities from "Grotius down to Lord Brougham" held that, "when government ceases to protect, the citizen ceases to owe allegiance." Yet Phillips insisted that a fugitive who exercised his natural right to self-protection by killing a slave catcher must not then defy the laws of Massachusetts by fleeing. Instead, he should allow himself to be arrested and tried for murder in a Massachusetts court. Phillips argued that a Yankee jury might not convict him and that, at any rate, if the fugitive was being held for murder in Massachusetts, he might not be able to be returned to his owner in the South. Phillips told fugitives: "It has now reached that pass when even the chance of a Boston gibbet may be no protection from a Georgia plantation; but if I were in your place, I would try!"[35] Not surprisingly, no fugitive seems to have taken Phillips's remarkable advice.

Two years after Phillips gave this speech, he found his commitments to lawful action again challenged when federal authorities in Boston seized another fugitive slave, this one from Virginia, Anthony Burns. Thomas Wentworth Higginson quickly organized a rescue attempt, which was to involve an armed assault on the Boston Court House, where Burns, like Sims before him, was being held. Higginson wanted the attack to occur while a thronged protest meeting was taking place at Faneuil Hall, a short distance from the Court House. He expected Phillips, who was the principal speaker, to help send a mob from the meeting to support the small rescue party as it broke down the Court House door. Phillips did not do it, however, and the rescue failed, merely producing a melee in which one of Burns's guards was killed.

Phillips later blamed the disaster on miscommunication with Higginson, but his own dislike of violent resistance to the laws and respect for legal institutions may well have affected his actions. The day after the "Burns riot," when rumors reached him that an anti-abolitionist mob might attack his house, his first response was to alert the city police. He only reluctantly, after much importuning, and for the sake of his invalid wife, allowed an informal posse of abolitionist men, armed with clubs, to guard his house overnight. The attack, however, never came.[36]

Several days later, Commissioner Loring "restored" Burns to his master. Soldiers marched Burns through streets thronged with angry protestors and onto a ship that sailed him back south. Outraged, a group of Massachusetts abolitionists, led by Henry Ingersoll Bowditch, founded the Anti–Man Hunting League. The league was a tightly organized, secretive organization, dedicated to using "all proper means for rendering difficult or impossible the coming or the remaining of the manhunter amongst us." Phillips was among the first to join. Soon, however, according the disgusted Bowditch, Phillips "retreated." Phillips never explained his resignation, but he seems to have withdrawn when league members decided that "proper means" encompassed taking slave catchers hostage. Phillips apparently would not participate in a kidnapping, even for a righteous cause.[37]

In the late 1850s, a growing number of abolitionists, among them Higginson, Parker, and most famously, John Brown, concluded that they must actively foment a slave uprising in the South. Before this time, most abolitionists had considered slave revolts justified but unwise. Phillips himself had shared this view. He had maintained that slaves in the South not only had good reason to rebel but the right to do so. One of his major objections to the U.S. Constitution, therefore, was that it authorized Congress to use military force to "suppress insurrections" (I:8). Although he considered this power "innocent" in itself (because the rule of law was a good thing), he noted that it had been given to Congress "with the fact directly in view that slavery exists among us," and so in effect represented a pledge to place "the whole national force against the unhappy slave if he imitate our fathers and resist oppression."[38] Because Phillips recognized that the federal government could intervene against slave rebellions, he had discouraged them as doomed to fail. In 1851, he had advised "the slave to be guided by a policy of peace . . . because he has no chance" to win his rights by force of arms.[39]

As the sectional crisis of the 1850s intensified, however, a growing number of abolitionists grew alarmed by what they saw as the success of the Slave Power in tightening its hold over the federal government, foisting slavery on the western territories, and forcing the North to acquiesce to proslavery laws. In this context, some abolitionists began to reconsider slave revolts, no longer viewing them primarily in terms of slave self-liberation, but rather as a way to frighten slaveholders and throw the South on the political defensive. Phillips came close to endorsing slave revolts on these terms in 1857–59, but his pronouncements were always qualified by his support for the rule of law and his faith in peaceful agitation as the best method to change bad laws.

Phillips began publicly reconsidering slave revolts in the winter of 1857–58, when he added to his regular lyceum repertory a lecture celebrating the life and achievements of Toussaint L'Ouverture, leader of the Haitian slave revolution.[40] The lecture was one of the first sympathetic accounts of L'Ouverture to receive widespread popular notice in the United States. Phillips's stated purpose in telling Toussaint's story was to persuade his mostly "Anglo-Saxon" audiences that the "Negro race," measured "either by its great men or its masses, either by its courage, its purpose, or its endurance" was their equal. Yet Phillips also implicitly prompted his listeners to reconsider their hostility toward slave revolts, not only in Haiti, but also in the U.S. South. As one newspaper report noted, "Without mentioning American slavery by name, [Phillips] so constantly kept it before his hearers that none could fail to see the moral of his lecture."[41]

Perhaps because the lecture was implicitly about the South, it was hardly an unqualified endorsement of revolutionary violence. According to Phillips, Toussaint always strove to uphold law and order and minimize bloodshed and was not to blame for the notorious atrocities of the revolution, which Phillips attributes to others, principally Haitian slaveowners and their allies. The only clear argument Phillips felt comfortable advancing to justify the uprising itself was that it began legally. The original black uprising, he claimed, occurred at the behest of the French royal governor of the island, who had lost authority in the turmoil following the onset of the 1789 revolution in France, and so had turned to the slaves for support, offering them freedom if they took up arms on his behalf. To Phillips, this so-called insurrection "bore for its motto on one side of its banner, 'Long Live the King'; and on the other, 'We Claim the Old Laws.' Singular mottoes for a rebellion! In fact it was the *posse comitatus*; it was the only French army on the island; it was the only force that had a right to bear arms."[42]

Not long after Phillips began lecturing on L'Ouverture, he helped to publish and distribute an incendiary broadside by Lysander Spooner, whose essay on the unconstitutionality of slavery he had rebutted a dozen years before. Spooner now urged abolitionists to organize "military companies," "land . . . (at numerous points at the same time) in the South," and "raise the standard of freedom."[43] "Short of actually picking up a gun," remarks Phillips biographer James Brewer Stewart of this episode, "Phillips clearly was trafficking with insurrectionary violence as heavily as he could."[44]

Spooner's "war" plan, however, which Phillips implicitly endorsed, was in its details surprisingly un-warlike. Spooner wanted preparations for the invasion of the South to be carried on openly, with maximum publicity. He recommended that supporters of his plan establish newspapers to advocate for it and make pledges "not to vote for any person for any civil or military office whatever, who is not publicly committed to the enterprise." Spooner made any invasion contingent, moreover, on winning the support of a substantial number of white southern non-slaveholders, who he argued could be induced to cooperate "by appeals to their safety, interest, honor, justice, and humanity"; Spooner helpfully provided an example of just such an appeal on the verso of his broadside. He blithely predicted that if "any considerable number of the American people will join us, the work will be an easy and bloodless one."[45]

Spooner, and evidently Phillips, intended the broadside to alarm the South, which eventually it seems to have done; it would be discovered by southern secessionists and quoted to justify their cause in the crisis of 1860–61. But it first alarmed John Brown and his coconspirators, among them Higginson. Higginson and Brown each met with Spooner in 1858–59 and together persuaded him temporarily to withdraw his proclamation from circulation.[46] They feared it might put southerners on guard against Brown's own, very different plan for a slave revolt, which was secretly to raise and train guerrillas to attack the federal arsenal at Harpers Ferry, Virginia, and distribute the weapons there to the slaves. Brown and Higginson never imagined the resulting conflict would be "bloodless."

Although Spooner, who was principally a political theorist, turned to Phillips for help, the soldierly Brown refused to do so. In early 1858, when he assembled Higginson, Parker, and others into a clandestine committee to supply his guerrilla force with money and weapons, he specifically rejected a recommendation that Phillips be asked to join. "I have noticed," Brown reportedly remarked, "that men so eloquent as Mr. Phillips are seldom men of action, and it is only men of action that I would have involved with me in the movement."[47]

Brown's somewhat cryptic remark probably referred to Phillips's well-known belief that the most effective instrument of social change was "talk." Phillips celebrated abolitionists as the "all-talk" party and argued that this was the real basis of their power, because ideas and public opinion had become the dominant forces in American political life.[48] Unlike some nonresistants at their most enthusiastic, he never thought that social change should be effected only by persuading individuals to act differently; in many cases, as with temperance, he thought that change could only be reliably effected through law.[49] Still, his ultimate faith was in the power of peaceful agitation, as was evident even in the praise he lavished on Brown in 1859.

Late that year, Brown and his guerrillas launched their long-planned Harpers Ferry raid, but state militia and federal troops quickly defeated them, and Brown himself was captured, jailed, tried, and hanged. Phillips delivered one of the first widely noticed speeches applauding the failed Harpers Ferry assault and, later, eulogized Brown at his funeral in upstate New York. Yet in these pronouncements, Phillips insisted that he still believed in "moral suasion" and that the "age of bullets is over. The age of ideas has come."[50] Brown, obviously, believed the age of bullets was still very much here.

Brown thought slaves could destroy slavery by taking up arms; Phillips voiced skepticism, even as he extolled Brown's acts. American slavery, he declared, would not in fact fall through insurrection, but through the outside "interference" of the North, "a wiser, higher, more advanced civilization," on the barbaric South.[51] He did not clearly state what this "interference" would look like, but he seemed to think of it largely in terms of political and economic pressure, not military assault.

Phillips published Spooner's plan not because he thought it practical—he warned Spooner that if anyone actually tried to put the plan into effect, the government would surely crush it—but to "spread the panic."[52] Spooner's plan may have appealed to him because it consisted almost entirely of agitation, with a few weapons thrown in for emphasis. Again, Phillips viewed Harpers Ferry as a natural outgrowth of the agitation that he and other abolitionists had long practiced and really just another form of it: "Insurrection of thought always precedes the insurrection of arms. The last twenty years have been an insurrection of thought."[53] Brown had done what abolitionists had long sought to do—make "the whole [issue] crystallize into right and wrong," and get the people to "marshal themselves on one side or the other."[54]

Although Phillips had once asserted that he shrank "from using human life as raw material for the production of any state of public opinion, however valuable," he made an exception for those who, like Brown, gave their "full consent" to use their lives this way.[55] Because Brown and his men had shown themselves willing to die for the slave, they would help the abolitionist cause. That they were willing to kill for the slave was, for Phillips, of more questionable propagandistic value, which may be why, in his speeches on Brown, he never mentions it.

In justifying Brown's attack, Phillips continued to claim the mantle of the rule of law, but he did so with difficulty. He had no problem denouncing the many legal irregularities of Brown's hasty "treason trial" in Virginia: "Wounded, fevered, lying half unconscious on his pallet, unable to stand on his feet, the trial half finished before his first request for aid had reached his friends,—no list of witnesses or knowledge of them till the crier, calling the name of some assassin of his comrades, wakes him to consciousness; the judge a tool, and the prosecutor seeking popularity by pandering to the mob; no decent form observed, and the essence of a fair trial wholly wanting, our history and law alike protest against degrading the honored name of *Jury Trial* by lending it to such an outrage as this."[56]

Phillips ran into complications, however, when he tried to prove that Brown was "a representative of law."[57] He could sustain this claim only by pronouncing unlawful the government of Virginia itself. As a slave state, he argued, Virginia did not exist on the necessary basis of the "willing submission of all its citizens," nor perform its necessary duty "of rendering equal justice between man and man." It was, therefore, little more than "a pirate ship, and John Brown sails the sea a Lord High Admiral of the Almighty, with his commission to sink every pirate he meets on God's ocean of the nineteenth century."[58]

The stand Phillips took seemed very similar to that held by the political abolitionists he had long criticized, who had argued that slavery was illegal and unconstitutional. Phillips remained a disunionist, however, for another year and a half, until the last chance for proslavery compromise had passed, and civil war had commenced. He had always claimed that proslavery forces flouted the law while antislavery forces upheld it. Such was obviously now the case, with the slave states up in arms against the government, which was led by Lincoln, an antislavery president. Under such circumstances, Phillips had no difficulty ending his long boycott of the Constitution and standing "under the flag."[59] He did not hesitate to repurpose his L'Ouverture lecture, turning what had been an endorsement of slave revolts in the South into a call for lifting the ban against black soldiers in the Union Army.[60]

The only unqualified endorsement of extralegal political violence Phillips ever made came years after the Civil War and had nothing to do with slavery. It sheds light, however, on his thinking in the 1840s and 1850s. On June 30, 1881,

Phillips delivered "The Scholar in a Republic," his last major address, on the occasion of the centennial celebration of Phi Beta Kappa at Harvard University. The grand old man swept the audience off its feet. Yet, according to Higginson, who was an eyewitness, "many a respectable lawyer or divine felt his blood run cold, the next day, when he found that the fascinating orator whom he had applauded to the echo had really made the assassination of an emperor seem as trivial as the doom of a mosquito."[61]

Higginson referred to the murder of Czar Alexander II of Russia by a suicide bomber, three months before Phillips spoke. The American press had identified the assassin as a "Nihilist," a term that Ivan Turgenev had popularized in his novel *Fathers and Sons* (1862). In Russia, it designated a distinct movement opposed to Christian belief and authoritarian rule, but Americans used as it a catch-all to designate any Russian faction advocating revolutionary violence.

Phillips, in his speech, did not mention Alexander's name nor utter the word "assassination," but he did praise the movement credited with instigating Alexander's murder. "Nihilism," he declared, "is a righteous and honorable resistance of a people crushed under an iron rule . . . [,] the last weapon of victims choked and manacled beyond all other resistance. It is crushed humanity's only means of making the oppressor tremble. . . . I honor Nihilism, since it redeems human nature from the suspicion of being utterly vile, made up only of heartless oppressors and contented slaves." Phillips denounced American criticism of Nihilism as the "most disgusting" kind of "cant." The Nihilists, he insisted, were the "spiritual descendants" of the great heroes of the American Revolution, such as Sam Adams, and of John Brown. Although Phillips admitted that we naturally "pity the suffering of any human being, however richly deserved" (meaning, that of the czar), yet "such pity must not confuse our moral sense. Humanity gains."[62]

If these remarks, as Higginson reports, shocked those who read them the day after they were delivered, the shock must have grown to panic the day after that, July 2, 1881, when an assassin shot the president of the United States, James Garfield. Although no one could prove that the shooter, when "loading his pistol, was rehearsing to himself the eloquence of Mr. Phillips," some linked the "reckless rhetoric" and the "bloody deed," seeing both as evidence of "Nihilism in America."[63] Phillips, characteristically, retracted nothing.[64]

He could endorse Nihilism without qualifications, unlike violent resistance to slavery, because Russia was a despotism while America was a democracy. True rule of law, he believed, required rule of the people. In America, the people made laws to govern themselves, and when they made bad laws, such as those protecting slavery, they could be persuaded by agitators like himself to unmake them. In Russia, there was only "the arbitrary law of the tyrant." Even if the czar proclaimed good laws—such as Alexander's 1861 decree abolishing serfdom, an act that had led some Americans to compare him to Abraham Lincoln as a "great emancipator"—the Russian people had no hand in them. Russians had no freedom of speech with which to debate an issue, and no vote with which to decide it. Under such circumstances, Phillips believed, there was no "ground for any hope of peaceful change" from below, because there was "no fulcrum upon which you can plant any possible lever." The method of agitation that he cherished, talk, could not work, and the agitator had no tools left but daggers and dynamite.[65]

NOTES

I would like to thank James Brewer Stewart, Donald Yacovone, and A J Aiséirithe for their valuable criticism of earlier drafts of this article.

1. Luis F. Emilio, *A Brave Black Regiment: History of the Fifty-Fourth Regiment of Massachusetts Volunteer Infantry*, 2nd ed. (Boston: Boston Book Co., 1894), 31–33. The obvious route for the parade would have been straight down Washington Street, through the heart of downtown Boston, yet the regiment detoured off Washington to Essex Street, passed Phillips's house, then immediately turned onto Chauncy, a side street, before taking a big loop, down Summer, High, Federal, and Franklin, back to Washington.

2. Ibid., 32.

3. For Phillips's dissent in 1838, see "Peace: Proceedings of the Peace Convention," *Liberator*, Sept. 28, 1838.

4. Thomas Wentworth Higginson, *Cheerful Yesterdays* (Cambridge: Riverside Press, 1900), 139–40; Higginson, *Contemporaries* (Boston: Houghton, Mifflin, 1900), 263.

5. Phillips was admitted to the Middlesex Bar Association in 1834, although he never practiced there, and later joined the Suffolk County Bar. See William Thomas Davis, *Bench and Bar of the Commonwealth of Massachusetts* ([Boston:] Boston History Company, 1895), vol. 1: 280; D. Hamilton Hurd, *History of Middlesex County, Massachusetts* (Philadelphia: D. Hurd, 1890), lxvi; George Lowell Austin, *The Life and Times of Wendell Phillips* (Boston: B. B. Russell, 1884), 44.

6. See the *Boston Directory* (George Adams) for 1851, 1855, 1857, 1867, and 1873. Phillips's wife would recall much later that he closed his Court Street office in 1837 or 1838, but it is still listed in the 1851 directory. See also James Brewer Stewart, *Wendell Phillips: Liberty's Hero* (Baton Rouge: Louisiana State University Press, 1986), 63.

7. Wendell Phillips, *Review of Lysander Spooner's Essay on the Unconstitutionality of Slavery*

(Boston: Andrews & Prentiss, 1847); Phillips, "Removal of Judge Loring," *Speeches, Lectures, and Letters* (Boston: James Redpath, 1863), 154–212.

8. Phillips, "Removal of Judge Loring," 181.

9. Phillips, "Idols," *Speeches*, 251.

10. Ibid., 251–52.

11. Ibid., 253–54.

12. See Conrad Wright, "Emerson, Barzillai Frost, and the Divinity School Address," in *The Liberal Christians* (Boston: Beacon Press, 1970), 41–61.

13. Phillips, "Murder of Lovejoy," *Speeches*, 5–6.

14. Phillips, "The Boston Mob," *Speeches*, 213–27; "Mobs and Education," *Speeches*, 319–42.

15. Phillips, "A Metropolitan Police," *Speeches*, 495–523.

16. Morton Horowitz, *The Transformation of American Law, 1780–1860* (Cambridge: Harvard University Press, 1977), 141–43.

17. John Parker Hale, "Trial by Jury," *Liberator*, December 22, 1854. Hale, presidential candidate of the Free Soil Party in 1852, had defended those accused of participating in the 1851 rescue of the fugitive slave Shadrach Minkins, and at the time he gave this lecture, in December 1854, was one of the lawyers defending Phillips himself, who was under federal indictment for his alleged role in the failed rescue of the fugitive slave Anthony Burns.

18. Phillips, "A Metropolitan Police," 513.

19. Dean Grodzins, "'Slave Law' versus 'Lynch Law' in Boston: Benjamin Robbins Curtis, Theodore Parker, and the Fugitive Slave Crisis, 1850–1855," *Massachusetts Historical Review* 12 (2010): 1–33.

20. Phillips, *The Constitution a Proslavery Compact, or Extracts from the Madison Papers* (New York: American Antislavery Society, 1845); Phillips, *Can Abolitionists Vote or Take Office Under the United States Constitution?* (New York: American Antislavery Society, 1845); Phillips, *Review of Lysander Spooner's Essay.*

21. See also Lewis Perry, *Radical Abolitionism: Anarchy and the Government of God in Antislavery Thought* (1973; rev. ed., Knoxville: University of Tennessee Press, 1995), 164–66.

22. Phillips, *Speeches*, 53, 81, 90, 218, 225, 297, 326, 358, 373, 541; *Speeches, Lectures, and Letters, Second Series* (Boston: Lee and Shepherd, 1894), 227, 233–34, 237, 240, 242, 243, 332, 337, 356, 357, 386; quotations from *Speeches: Second Series*, 234, 356, 227, 386, and *Speeches*, 541. For Samuel Adams's historical reputation in Phillips's day, see Pauline Maier, "Coming to Terms with Samuel Adams," *American Historical Review* 81 (1976): 12–17.

23. Phillips, *Can Abolitionists Vote*, 31–32.

24. Henry David Thoreau, "Civil Disobedience," in *Thoreau: Collected Essays and Poems*, ed. Elizabeth Hall Witherall (New York: Library of America, 2001), 203. See also John C. Broderick, "Thoreau, Alcott, and the Poll Tax," *Studies in Philology* 53 (1956): 612–26; Broderick finds that, despite what Thoreau indicates in his essay, he had actually stopped paying his poll tax in 1843, years before the Mexican War began.

25. Massachusetts had a tax requirement for voting from 1821 to 1891. See Alexander Keyssar, *The Right to Vote: The Contested History of Democracy in the United States* (2000; rev. ed., New York: Basic Books, 2009), 104–5, 334 (table A.10).

26. Phillips, *Can Abolitionists Vote*, 28.

27. Richard Henry Dana, *Remarks . . . before the Committee on Federal Relations on the Proposed Removal of Edward G. Loring, Esq. from the Position of Judge of Probate* (Boston: Alfred Mudge & Son, 1855), 13.

28. For more on the debates over rule of law and political violence among Boston abolitionists in the 1840s and 1850s, see Grodzins, "'Constitution or No Constitution, Law or No Law': The Boston Vigilance Committees of 1841, 1846, and 1850," in *Massachusetts and the Civil War: The Commonwealth and National Disunion*, ed. Matthew Mason, Katheryn P. Viens, and Conrad E. Wright (Amherst: University of Massachusetts Press, 2015), 47–69.

29. "Declaration of the Colored Citizens of Boston," *Liberator*, Oct. 11, 1850.

30. Theodore Parker, "A Sermon of Conscience," *Speeches, Addresses, and Occasional Sermons* (Boston: Wm. Crosby and H. P. Nichols, 1852), vol. 2: 258.

31. *Liberator*, October 4, 1850.

32. Phillips, *Speeches*, 35, 41, 61, 184, 357.

33. "Speech of Wendell Phillips," *Liberator*, Aug. 17, 1849.

34. "Rocking the Old Cradle of Liberty: Immense Meeting," *Liberator*, Oct. 18, 1850.

35. Phillips, "Sims Anniversary," *Speeches*, 77–78, 81, 88–89; emphasis in original.

36. Albert J. Von Frank, *The Trials of Anthony Burns: Freedom and Slavery in Emerson's Boston* (Cambridge: Harvard University Press, 1998); A. W. Weston to "Folks," May 30, 1854, Ms. A.9.2., Boston Public Library; speech of Charles Slack to the Massachusetts General Court, in *Liberator*, April 20, 1855.

37. See Boston Anti–Man–Hunting League Records, 1846–1887, Massachusetts Historical Society.

38. Phillips, *Constitution a Proslavery Compact*, 6.

39. Phillips, "Sims Anniversary," 86. Probably the most militant black statement on the subject was Henry Highland Garnet's "Address to the Slaves of the United States of America," which was submitted to the Negro National Convention in 1843 and voted down as "insurrectionist." Garnet (in the first published version of the address at least, which he later claimed was much toned down from the original) pronounced armed revolt "inexpedient" and called instead for slaves to go on strike. See Stanley Harrold, *The Rise of Aggressive Abolitionism: Addresses to the Slaves* (Lexington: University Press of Kentucky, 2004), 32–35.

40. Phillips, "Toussaint L'Ouverture," *Speeches*, 468–94. Phillips delivered the lecture for the first time in Boston in December 1857; see Matthew J. Clavin, *Toussaint Louverture and the American Civil War: The Promise and Peril of a Second Haitian Revolution* (Philadelphia: University of Pennsylvania Press, 2010), 42.

41. Phillips, "Toussaint L'Ouverture," 469; newspaper clipping in Phillips, "Toussaint L'Ouverture [Notes and Clippings]," Am 1953 (1590), folder 3, Crawford-Blagden Collection of Wendell Phillips Papers, Houghton Library, Harvard University.

42. Phillips, "Toussaint L'Ouverture," 474. Phillips took this point about the rebel flag from John R. Beard, *The Life of Toussaint L'Ouverture: The Negro Patriot of Hayti* (London: Ingram Cook & Co., 1853), 62, who sees the moment as ironic, as Phillips does not: "Strange reversals! While the colonists hoisted English colours, their slaves exhibited the white flag, with the words on one

side, *Long live the king*; and, on the other, *The ancient system of government.*" Although Phillips apparently had been collecting information on Toussaint since the 1830s, Beard's *Life* seems to have been his principal source for his lecture. Phillips's preparatory notes contain citations to an unnamed work, which turns out to be this British one. See Phillips, "Toussaint L'Ouverture [Notes and Clippings]," Am 1953 (1590), folder 3, citations to pages "153" and "157." Modern historians agree that many (but by no means all) Haitian slaves professed loyalty to the King of France in the early years of their revolution, although not for the reasons Phillips suggests. Instead, they seem to have believed the king sympathized with their cause; also, they hoped to win military support from royalist Spain, which controlled the neighboring colony of Santo Domingo. On the conditional royalism of the slaves, see Laurent DuBois, *Avengers of the New World: The Story of the Haitian Revolution* (Cambridge: Harvard University Press, 2004), 106–8.

43. Lysander Spooner, "A Plan for the Abolition of Slavery" and (verso) "To the Non-Slaveholders of the South," in *The Collected Works of Lysander Spooner*, ed. Charles Shively (Weston, Mass.: M & S Press, 1971), vol. 4: n.p.

44. Stewart, *Wendell Phillips*, 200.

45. Spooner, "Plan for the Abolition of Slavery," "To the Non-Slave Holders."

46. Edward J. Renehan, *The Secret Six: The True Tale of the Men Who Conspired with John Brown* (New York: Crown, 1995), 173–75. For an example of an influential southern secessionist using the Spooner broadside to justify disunion, see John Townsend, *The South Alone Should Govern the South, and African Slavery Should Be Controlled by Those Only, Who Are Friendly to It* (3rd ed.; Charleston, SC: Evans & Cogswell, 1860), 44–47; in another Townsend pamphlet, *The Doom of Slavery in the Union: Its Safety Out of It* (Charleston, SC: Evans & Cogswell, 1860), 34, he alleges (inaccurately) that abolitionists had attempted to put Spooner's "plan" into action in Texas, and had succeeded in producing slave unrest there. The two Townsend pamphlets together sold 165,000 copies in 1860–61; see William W. Freehling, *The Road to Disunion, Volume II: Secessionists Triumphant, 1854–1861* (New York: Oxford University Press, 2007), 394. Townsend apparently learned about the Spooner broadside through a "Manifesto" published by the New York Democratic Vigilant Association, a Democratic Party organization, which publicized the Spooner plan during the 1860 election campaign as part of a broader Democratic effort to link the Republican Party to John Brown and other abolitionists who allegedly wanted "*a war of the races*"; see Townsend, *The South Alone*, 43–44. No doubt, many who dismissed the Spooner plan as preposterous in 1858, when Phillips published it, were far more willing to take it seriously after Brown's attack on Harpers Ferry.

47. Franklin Sanborn, "Theodore Parker and the John Brown Campaign," in Theodore Parker, *Saint Barnard and Other Papers, Works, Centenary Edition* (Boston: American Unitarian Association, 1911), vol. 14: 403. Brown may also have been reluctant to work closely with Phillips because Phillips had been fiercely critical of antislavery interpretations of the U.S. Constitution, a position advocated by both Brown's longtime patron, Gerrit Smith, and Brown's friend Frederick Douglass.

48. Phillips, "Public Opinion," *Speeches*, 50.

49. In this, Phillips may be usefully contrasted with the prominent abolitionist and Unitarian minister Samuel J. May, who in the 1830s believed that all change could be effected by persuasion of individuals alone. May's later decision to back temperance laws represented a falling away

from this position; by contrast, Phillip's decision to back these laws was consistent with his overall views. See Donald Yacovone, *Samuel Joseph May and the Dilemmas of the Liberal Persuasion, 1797–1871* (Philadelphia: Temple University Press, 1991).

50. Phillips, "Public Opinion," 50; Phillips, *Speeches*, "Harper's Ferry," 269.

51. Phillips, "Harper's Ferry," 281.

52. Stewart, *Wendell Phillips*, 200.

53. Phillips, "Harper's Ferry," 263.

54. Ibid., 276.

55. Phillips, "Sims Anniversary," 78.

56. Phillips, "Harper's Ferry," 284–85; emphasis in original.

57. Ibid., 276.

58. Ibid., 272.

59. Phillips, "Under the Flag," *Speeches*, 396–414.

60. Clavin, *Toussaint Louverture and the American Civil War*, 77–79.

61. Higginson, *Contemporaries*, 270.

62. Phillips, "The Scholar in a Republic," *Speeches: Second Series*, 356–57.

63. Leonard Bacon, "Nihilism in America," *Independent*, July 28, 1881.

64. Phillips himself apparently saw no valid comparison between Alexander's assassination and the attack on Garfield. He portrayed the former as a brave political act, while he dismissed the latter as the insane deed of a "pitiable and misbegotten wreck, who is only just within, if indeed he be within, the limits of moral responsibility." See Phillips, "The Death Penalty," *North American Review* 133, no. 301 (1881): 559.

65. Phillips, "The Scholar in a Republic," 359.

5

COMFORTABLE IN HIS OWN SKIN

Wendell Phillips and Racial Egalitarianism

JAMES BREWER STEWART

When Wendell Phillips died in 1884, African Americans all over the nation turned out in massive numbers to mourn his passing. In the decades that followed, as Donald Yacovone shows in this book's essay "Race, Radicalism, and Remembering Wendell Phillips," they honored his memory again and again by naming their schools, fraternal orders, benevolent societies, cultural institutions, and civil rights organizations in his honor. When a young W. E. B. Du Bois addressed his high-school graduation the year of Phillips's death, he chose to speak about the Boston radical, whose example inspired him to take "a long step toward a wider conception of what I was going to do." In addition to Du Bois, an enormous list of prominent African American leaders and common folk alike publicly embraced their memories of Phillips as they continued their quests to secure racial equality well into the twentieth century.[1]

To explain how powerful memories of Wendell Phillips inspired the visions of so many African Americans requires examining how he and his associates with darker complexions dealt with one another in the first place. Such an inquiry seems to present a paradox. Somehow one of Boston's most fully established, most affluent, most highly privileged, most polished, most cosmopolitan, most fully educated, and most publicly recognized "Brahmin aristocrats" also proved to be one of his era's most democratic practitioners of racial equality.

This paradox begins resolving itself, however, once one realizes that Phillips's enormous privilege meshed with his most basic traits of personality. His unusually rich talents, compelling personality, and his deepest abolitionist convictions endowed Phillips with a profoundly stable sense of himself, abiding self-confidence, and enormous emotional security. These qualities of his inner self buffered him against the defensiveness and self-consciousness that so many white Americans (many white abolitionists included) instinctively felt when put in close association with African Americans. At the same time, throughout his career, Phillips espoused a sweepingly egalitarian version of republican ideology in which equality for people of all complexions was the overriding value, a belief in which African American activists fully shared. Empowered by both temperament and conviction, he found himself naturally at ease when collaborating with African American activists, powerfully moved to advocate for their public causes, and unusually effective in addressing their personal concerns. Much in contrast to the vast majority of white Americans, Wendell Phillips truly felt "comfortable in his own skin," whether agitating with black activists against racist bigotry or working quietly on behalf of African Americans who asked for his assistance.

The point of departure in the making of the egalitarian Wendell Phillips is found in the mid-1820s when his opinions of African Americans predictably reflected the deepening white racism of the day. As the nineteenth century opened, wealthy families like the Phillipses began constructing opulent mansions on the crest of Beacon Hill, overlooking the Boston Common. Their compelling motive was to escape the influx of lower-class laborers into their original neighborhoods close by the harbor. On the back side of Beacon Hill, however, near the Charles River, only a fifteen-minute walk from the Phillips family's Charles Bulfinch–designed multistory Georgian residence, there developed a growing black community of politically active, socially engaged artisans, domestic workers, seafarers, and day laborers. Whites commonly called it "Nigger Hill," and proper families such as young Wendell's regarded it as a "place of vague horror."

By the mid-1820s, population growth began rupturing black/white neighborhood boundaries and Beacon Hill "nabobs" now complained of grog shops, prostitution, and other criminal activity. Meanwhile, children of poor families, black children among them, made increasing use of the Common, which for all intents and purposes served as the Phillips mansion's front yard, which was surely how young Wendell regarded it. He clearly resented their presence, and sometimes when black youths appeared he and his high-toned playmates would form into Boston's most privileged neighborhood gang and attempt to drive them off with volleys of rocks. Failing this, they tussled with young blacks who refused to be run off by self-appointed white "superiors."[2]

Phillips clearly had begun acquiring prejudices in favor of wealth and white skin that he would one day be forced to reconsider. And when he finally did so, he was not reflecting enlightened racial views espoused by his family. His mother, Sarah, openly scorned his embrace of radical abolitionism, and his older brother George once gave Wendell a blunt reminder of the family's prevailing views about African Americans when writing in 1836 about the rescue of two presumed fugitives by some courageous black activists: "The idea that the niggers, in open day, carried off from the Supreme Court room two prisoners has something so laughable in it one can hardly appreciate the insult. . . . The nig is uppermost now for sure."[3]

But on levels by far more profound than racist ideology, it was precisely Wendell's upbringing that set him on a path to racial egalitarianism. To understate the matter, Wendell Phillips was fortunate far beyond all expectations because he was the beneficiary of two immensely positive circumstances—an exceptionally supportive, challenging, and empowering childhood and adolescence—and an almost unbelievably rich array of personal gifts and aspirations that marked him in the eyes of practically all who encountered him as someone to be admired, trusted, and emulated. From childhood onward, Phillips became increasingly aware that increasing numbers of people, including himself, expected his to be a significant, even transformational, destiny.

Phillip knew from his ever-attentive parents that he was their "special" child (the youngest of five siblings) and that they expected him to extend a legacy of exceptional leadership that remained unbroken through a line of eminent Phillips patriarchs stretching back through John Winthrop's colony to Oliver Cromwell's England. Most immediately he remembered (and grieved deeply for) his widely admired father, John Phillips, who unexpectedly died just before Wendell's thirteenth birthday. John Phillips was a truly prepossessing figure who had amassed an enormous fortune, conducted himself as an exemplary public servant, and was esteemed throughout the commonwealth as a superb lawmaker and honored for his accomplishments as incorporated Boston's first mayor and as Speaker of the Massachusetts General Court.

Wendell Phillips knew without question, following his whole-souled religious conversion (induced by his supplicating parents and his grandmother), that his sanctified spiritual destiny was assured and that his charge from on high was to fulfill God's obvious designs. He realized as he passed through adolescence to adulthood that he appeared to others to be all but unbelievably handsome, physically gifted, intellectually masterful, and socially accomplished, that he radiated charisma and projected undeniable moral and ethical authority. People found themselves drawn to him, to trust, respect, and defer to him.

Most important of all, he discovered that he was a genius at forensics, not simply a powerful speaker, but someone graced with a rare creative talent that transfixed his listeners and quite often transformed their beliefs and assumptions. Early on, he well understood that his magnetic oratory endowed him with enormous interpersonal effectiveness and public power.

It is little wonder that, when graduating from Harvard's undergraduate program in 1831 and its law school in 1834, none entertained more exalted expectations for Wendell Phillips than Phillips himself. The examples of Cicero, the fabled Roman orator, the hero-patriot Edmund Burke, and the illustrious accomplishments of his own ancestors measured his highest aspirations.[4]

But as Phillips discovered after setting up his law office, pursuing clients, drafting documents, and litigating disputes made for a deeply disorienting comedown for someone who had been lionized by his peers, spoke like the Classical Era's greatest rhetorician, identified with Edmund Burke, felt the urgings of God's intentions, and yearned to match the accomplishments of his ancestors. Wholly adrift, Phillips succumbed to a clinically diagnosable siege of depression that afflicted him for approximately eighteen months, from mid-1834 until November 1836, the only time in his life when the core of his self-understanding slipped away from him. What he desperately lacked was a sense of his life's vocational calling and moral direction as well any confidence in his ability to define and pursue them. So instead of building his law practice he evaded his anxieties by traveling widely and immersing himself in his family's genealogy.[5] After eighteen months of aimlessness, a series of climactic events compelled him to break through his torment to embrace the calling for which all his gifts and aspirations could be mobilized—radically egalitarian abolitionism. How Wendell Phillips became so deeply engaged in pursuing and practicing racial equality can be explained as follows.

In October 1837, he impulsively married fellow "Brahmin aristocrat" Ann Terry Greene, a zealous exponent of immediate abolition. Their union blended their enormous inheritances, their exceptional intellects, and her ideological clarity with his matchless rhetorical gifts. Ann Phillips brought her husband a redemptive opportunity to begin his life anew as a radical abolitionist. Next, in mid-December, in Faneuil Hall, at an enormous meeting convened to protest the murder of abolitionist editor Elijah P. Lovejoy, Phillips rose, unprepared, and sealed his commitment to that cause by delivering one of the antislavery movement's most memorable and frequently cited speeches. As he laid public claim to his calling, he committed his life to the highest purposes he could imagine for his gift of eloquence and for meeting the expectations that his lineage had laid upon him. Every aspect of his recently fragmented life now fused in an empowering synthesis of personal identity with public calling. His personal identity involved a sense of inner self that rendered Phillips all but immune to negative feelings about racial difference and open to fruitful collaborations with people of color. His public calling led him to espousals of a republican ideology in which racial hierarchy had absolutely no legitimacy.[6]

Thanks to his marriage to Ann and the personal consequences of his Lovejoy speech, Phillips reconstituted what had been, prior to his crisis, his unshakeable understanding of who he was and why he had been put on Earth. This act of emotional reconstruction deepened already well-established ways of dealing with others in which insecurity and defensiveness seem to have had no place. Well before Phillips's embrace of abolitionism, his admiring college friends had characterized him as being "perfectly transparent, no subterfuge, no pretense about him," someone who was "known to all to be just what he seemed . . . a sincere, conscientious and devoted friend to all who sought him out." Another remembered Phillips as being "above pretence, without even a word or thought that the purest might not know or listen to."[7]

These were the social instincts and responses that now determined his relationships with his fellow abolitionists, whatever their skin color. In his voluminous private correspondence with Ann Phillips and with any number of confidants spanning the next forty-seven years, never was he even faintly to suggest anything but an instinctive understanding of who he was and an easy acceptance of whomever he engaged, regardless of their race, class, or gender. Even the searing rhetorical vitriol for which Phillips became so (in)famous only reinforced his equanimity. Laced with scathing personal attacks, Phillips's speeches allowed him to redirect whatever anger he might have felt away from close associates and toward socially removed ideological enemies such as Boston's "Cotton Whigs," "doughfaced" congressional politicians, proslavery clergy, and so forth.[8]

So confident was Phillips in his style of interpersonal relations that he even joked about it. "A quiet, moderate, half-way sort of sim-sam fellow" is the way he once laughingly described himself. He also could chuckle at his gentlemanly displays of studied indifference when others tried to provoke him, a Brahmin aristocrat's pose that avoided open conflict through the application of silent scorn. At ease as he was with himself and others, he knew exactly when and how to transmit a full measure of gentlemanly rebuke. "I can truly say," he wrote a close confidant, "I thank God that he made me . . . so that I can shake my head defyingly and [in] uttermost carelessness, even at intended insult since if there is anything about it worth remembering, time will give me means for proving it was passed by only because it was despised. I'm very generous, AHEM!" Among all his wealth of talents, Phillips's skill in social relationships with people from every walk of life was surely one of the most impressive.[9]

When it came to ideology, Phillips, from the first, deviated significantly from most of his fellow abolitionists in ways that led directly to racial egalitarianism. Most immediate emancipationists came from evangelical backgrounds and spoke of slavery in the prophetic language of Jeremiah and Jesus, warning of sin and the holy retribution awaiting an apostate nation. Phillips by contrast condemned slavery, using the language of republicanism, and hated it as a preeminently social and political institution. As he understood it, slavery's destructive impact polluted all of American political culture, religious culture included, with violence, corruption, personal degradation, and political tyranny. Slavery "sends out poisonous branches over the fair land and corrupts the air we breathe. . . . it saps our strength and blinds our foresight," he declared in 1837. The people must rise up "against the tyranny of a many-headed monster uncaged by the South" that snuffed out life and liberty as it pleased. The abolitionists' mission, he insisted in 1839, was to write the Declaration of Independence fully into the nation's statutes, "to enlarge the canvass of law 'till it covers all men both black and white. When, in 1780, our fathers hung up the shield of this declaration in their [Massachusetts] constitution they did not make it broad enough."[10]

To this end, Phillips now began dreaming of powerful codes, as yet unwritten, that would obliterate all distinctions of color everywhere in the nation. Only when the law became irrevocably colorblind would civil liberty, political freedom, economic self-determination, and moral order reign in Massachusetts—as well as in Virginia. These, quite plainly, were visions that African American activists endorsed wholeheartedly. They also made it imperative for Phillips to join such activists in unprecedented acts of defiance against white supremacy as practiced in his own city and commonwealth.

February 1839 brought Phillips his first opportunity to "enlarge the canvas of law" by appearing before the Massachusetts legislature with numerous other abolitionists, black and white, in support of a petition from the women of the city of Lynn to repeal all laws upholding racial discrimination, including those prohibiting racial intermarriage. At the Senate hearing Mary Barker, a black abolitionist, presented the petition, after which Phillips spoke as its and her advocate. In the very chamber where Phillips's father had once presided, Barker and he were dismissed with contempt, which Phillips then condemned with an invective-laced speech that, according to one listener, "tore the legislature to pieces, ground them into atoms, and then strewed them upon the water, and then condemned [Governor Levi] Lincoln as only fit for the representative of scurrilous, licentious profligates." Phillips's verbal assault on the legislature opened a campaign by black and white abolitionists that led several years later to the repeal of Massachusetts's laws against interracial marriage.[11]

Thus did Phillips jettison the last of his Beacon Hill loyalties even as he grew close to other renegade "silk hat" abolitionists such as Maria Weston Chapman, Caroline and Ann Warren Weston, Ellis Gray Loring, and Edmund Quincy, referred to by those outside their circle as "the Boston clique." But at the same time, for the first time, he also began mingling closely with the working poor and the racially oppressed. Venturing into "Nigger Hill" to drum up support for the New England Anti-Slavery Society, he met a highly organized African American community as fully devoted to securing equal citizenship in Massachusetts as to undermining southern slavery. Fully engaged, he next plunged full force into civil disobedience and high-decibel agitation by joining abolitionists black and white in labor-intensive efforts to abolish racial segregation in Massachusetts.

Phillips began venturing into "Negro cars" on passenger trains in defiance of company rules in early 1841 and quickly absorbed close-up some of the day-to-day humiliation experienced by dark-skinned people. What he learned profoundly affronted him. Riding on the Eastern Railroad, dressed in his gentleman's waist coat and top hat, he sat next to William C. Nell, an exceptionally accomplished scholar and a black abolitionist who worked as a printer's assistant for Boston's preeminent journalist/agitator, William Lloyd Garrison, Phillips's close collaborator. Phillips found the car smelly, dirty, and dark with filthy windows that were nailed shut. The conductor behaved churlishly toward them, and as a properly bred "gentleman" Phillips felt these insults deeply. It may well have been that his privileged upbringing with its stress on mannerly behavior actually sharpened his empathy for people with dark skin who endured these degradations and very much worse. In his eyes, blacks who joined him when practicing civil disobedience were just as much gentlemen as he because social and political equality, including all skin colors, was the truest test of a healthy republican state. Those with the courage to join the struggle were, in his view, consummate heroes and therefore gentlemen, every bit as preeminent for their time as the minutemen of 1776.

Conversely, racial hierarchies of any sort constituted as great a danger to the body politic as slavery itself. To draw battle lines against slavery across the nation of necessity meant obliterating boundaries of caste in Massachusetts. Social designs that endured for a lifetime explain why Phillips threw himself into integration struggles during the 1840s, and in this crucial respect Radical Reconstruction began for him then, in Boston, not in the South in 1867. After the Civil War ended and legalized bondage but not black subjugation had ended, Phillips would always insist, "We have abolished the slave, but the master remains." That conclusion, he insisted, applied to Massachusetts, where slavery had been abolished by judicial decree in 1783, as well as to the slave states.[12]

The assault against segregation next led Phillips back to the Massachusetts legislature, where he represented an interracial group of petitioners demanding the repeal of laws enforcing apartheid transportation. Privately owned railroads and coach lines received "special privileges and franchises" from the state, he argued. Therefore the state was bound by law to make these enterprises treat all citizens equally. "These corporations are our public servants," Phillips insisted, and "therefore bound to serve in accordance with the laws of the commonwealth," which had been designed to "secure the rights of the people." The Jim Crow cars constituted a direct violation of African Americans' citizenship as well as a "direct insult' to their persons. "This community, Mr. Chairman, is not one whose theory tolerates privileged classes." Were shabbily dressed whites suddenly forced into segregated seats, Phillips observed, public outrage would stop the practice at once. Since legal equality recognized no limitations of class, it should permit no racial ones either, and to prevent the inequity of segregation the legislature needed only to enforce the principles upon which Massachusetts's Constitution of 1780 had been founded. "We ask not for the creation of new law," he emphasized. "We ask the legislature to say *what is law.*" Since law, according to Phillips, must insure the public good above all else, the legislature must override the private choices of the segregationists. Otherwise, the state was abetting the destruction of the republican liberty of everyone in Massachusetts, black and white, rich and poor.[13]

The legislature failed to respond to Phillips's arguments, and railroads continued to discriminate for several years before succumbing to sustained abolitionist activism. But as Phillips had made clear during this contest, he equated racial equality with the highest public good and insisted that the force of law and the state must suppress an individual's bigoted uses of private property. To a much greater extent than most other Garrisonians, who placed their nonresistant faith in "moral revolution," Phillips had seized the coercive power of the state, not the consciences of the converted public alone, to enforce freedom for all races and classes. This embrace of governmental power over moral suasion surely accorded with the views of many black activists who were growing increasingly skeptical of religious appeals to white people's consciences during the 1840s.

By 1846, abolitionists had again embroiled Boston in racial controversy, this time over segregated public schools, and Phillips began applying his legal axioms to public facilities as well as to those privately owned. For nearly a decade, Boston's black activists had petitioned to end segregation. Finally, they decided on more drastic steps and began removing their children from classes. Suddenly, city authorities showed deep concern and the Boston School Committee agreed to study the issue. Over the protests of its two abolitionist members, Edmund Jackson and Henry Bowditch, the committee concluded that segregation allowed safer, better education for everyone. Boston's city solicitor, Peleg Chandler, endorsed this conclusion, and Horace Mann, secretary of the Massachusetts Board of Education, kept discreet silence while searching for compromise. Phillips lashed out at them all in articles in Garrison's *Liberator.*[14]

"It is a good sign," he remarked sarcastically, that the school committee found it necessary to call in public officials like Mann and Chandler "to share the infamy with them. The post of persecuting colored children becomes too hot for them to maintain it alone." The commissioners were "small men," Phillips charged, and Solicitor Chandler brought shame on his office by supporting an "odious system" as a "tool of a few narrow-minded and prejudiced men." Mann's "timid silence" was also a fair barometer of white Boston's paltry "moral vision," Phillips continued. A year later, Mann's annual report failed to condemn segregation. Phillips renewed his attack, speaking, as usual, in what he considered the harsh personal language of a vigilant republican censor. Referring to the Boston School Committee, he explained to a close friend, "Their report and their conduct deserve scathing—which is the only thing that will reach them."[15]

Phillips's vituperation did not lead to a quick victory over the school committee. Following the 1850 failure of a desegregation lawsuit brought before the State Supreme Court by black abolitionist Benjamin Roberts (*Roberts vs. City of Boston*), a series of legislative maneuvers involving Phillips among others did result in the passage of a statewide school desegregation law. In this long struggle, as in the railway desegregation campaigns, Phillips and other well-heeled white abolitionists cooperated effectively with Boston's most militant blacks, many of whom were working-class members—barbers, cooks, cart men, house servants, artisans, and day laborers. Their interracial coalition had, for some moments at least, obliterated the boundaries of class as well as of caste, just as Phillips's republicanism required. African American activists for their part appreciated the help of high-toned white radicals like Phillips just as much as he admired their tenacious love of freedom.

Thus, when the state antisegregation law finally passed in 1855, John T. Hilton, William C. Nell, and other black leaders arranged a celebration at which Phillips and Garrison were invited to be the only white speakers. The honor certainly confirmed the premises that supported Phillips's devotion to legislated racial equality for, through agitation, a renegade "gentleman" such as himself and working-class blacks like Hilton and Nell had bridged remarkably wide social distances.[16]

As a result, so had Massachusetts's school children, white as well as black, and education had improved for them all now that they studied together. And as Phillips judged it, the republican health of the commonwealth's body politic had also significantly improved—although discrimination clearly remained. He therefore had reasons aplenty to regard his republican brand of abolitionism as a properly combative, socially inclusive formulation that erased distinctions of color or station. Nevertheless, when Phillips joined the inner circle of Boston's white abolitionists in wealthy Maria Weston Chapman's Beacon Hill drawing rooms, the black community's most accomplished spokespersons such as John T. Hilton, Benjamin Roberts, or William C. Nell rarely, if ever, were included. In this private setting, class distinctions seriously undermined Phillips's egalitarianism.

As historian Steven Kantrowitz has amply documented, Phillips often treated Nell as his employee, not his equal. At Phillips's request, Nell carried out numerous menial personal errands such as picking up packages from Phillips's tailor, guarding Phillips's home against burglars when he and Ann were vacationing, or delivering a hand-me-down shawl to one of the Phillips's former house servants. As Kantrowitz explains, the Phillips-Nell relationship was much more economic than personal, an arrangement between patron and client: Nell scratched out a living by performing just such menial tasks for the "clique's" abolitionists and as a result gained access to wealthy sponsors such as Phillips. For his part, Phillips clearly felt comfortable "in his own skin" when treating a talented African American as his paid personal servant despite their public pose of racial solidarity when battling segregation.[17]

But at the same time strong evidence supports the conclusion that Phillips's smug judgments on those "beneath" him such as Nell were, in truth, "color-blind." When, for example, backcountry abolitionists led by white New Hampshire radical Nathaniel Rodgers criticized him and his cliquish friends as "aristocrats," Phillips's impatient response dismissed these critics as "half-educated, impertinent and too misguided to see that if we were aristocratic, we wouldn't employ poor people." In his view, their complaints reflected simple class jealousy: "the Boston clique live in the city—dress in broad cloth and, some of us, been to college." Phillips never stated his Beacon Hill biases more bluntly.[18]

In light of such dynamics, it is hardly a surprise that Phillips and his "cliquish" friends praised just emerging fugitive-slave-turned-abolitionist Frederick Douglass as their own wonderful discovery. Phillips, for example, joined Garrison in writing a preface to Douglass's 1845 *Narrative* that can easily be criticized for its patronizing tone. Moreover, as is well known, when Douglass struck out on his own and began publishing his own independent newspaper, innuendos and racist gossip began circulating in cliquish circles, though there is no evidence of Phillips joining in.[19]

But when Phillips stepped outside the confines of "silk hat" Brahmin abolitionism, his day-to-day relationships with ordinary African Americans actually diminished racial estrangement even as it grew within the movement more generally. This, however, was a complex social process. At first glance, to be sure, the "gentlemanly" Phillips could appear as a formidable "aristocrat" to people of all complexions, and he was certainly given to snobbery. Yet when outside the "Boston clique," he seems to have blended into interracial relationships the same sincerity, openness, and equanimity that his college friends had found so remarkably positive. As a patrician egalitarian whose heroic self-conceptions gave him enormous self-confidence, he earned the respect and admiration of some of the same African Americans he often patronized. Kantrowitz observes that Nell's "deep respect for Phillips was as obvious to outsiders as the inequality between them" and, for Frederick Douglass, Phillips's success in reconciling elitism with egalitarianism was all but overpowering. Writing Phillips in 1846, Douglass revealed that he felt "a great inferiority to yourself" and then hastened to explain that this shocking comment actually bespoke a trust in and respect for the self-possessed Phillips that bordered on awe. "Do not scold me for this," Douglass explained. "I tell you the truth when I say I have for you such grateful regard and admiration that I cannot bring myself to approach you familiarly." Phillips, Douglass revealed, had "been to me like a brother" imparting so much "good counsel that I feel more of a disciple to you than a familiar friend." Phillips, in turn, attributed to Douglass all the qualities of his own gentlemanly style. "Language, taste, fancy eloquence, vigor of thoughts, good common sense are all his," Phillips insisted. "He never thinks of his color and we never do." Though his statement subverts its claim of colorblindness, there is certainly no reason to doubt Phillips's sincerity.[20]

Few black abolitionists addressed Phillips as candidly as did Douglass. William Wells Brown and Lewis Hayden, as well as Nell, generally approached him as a fair-minded colleague in the day-to-day workings of Garrisonian abolitionism, and he managed private business for all of them when they were traveling on behalf of the cause. As general agent of the American Anti-Slavery Society, Phillips set salaries and arranged speaking itineraries for all agents, black and white alike. In discharging these responsibilities, Phillips treated his colleagues equally, and the tenor of their business letters to him was usually friendly and always straightforward regardless of the writer's complexion.[21]

In this regard, however, one unusually revealing incident registers the deeper ambivalences that black abolitionists felt about their working relationships with Phillips. In 1848, plummeting income forced him to terminate the agencies of two abolitionist speakers, black Lewis Hayden and white Erastus Hudson. (Another black lecturer, Charles Lennox Remond, had his position eliminated a few months later.) In candid letters to Phillips, Hayden and Hudson both complained bitterly, even defiantly, about the desperate personal circumstances suddenly facing them. Hayden added testimony that challenged

Phillips in the most personal of terms. When Phillips and the board of the American Anti-Slavery Society had appointed him, Hayden emphasized, they "did not know what I was . . . did not know but what I was a second yourself." But now, without employment, who would ever know what his potential capabilities really were? "[Y]ou all know it is not so you know it is me jest [*sic*] three years from slavery." But he would, he vowed to Phillips, overcome such deficiencies for "If I am not Wendell Phillips now, it ought not to appear what I shall be. . . . I shall do all I can to make myself a man." For all his disillusionment with Phillips, "abolitionism's golden trumpet" still measured his aspirations.[22]

For his part, Phillips had no inhibitions about criticizing his black associates, sometimes in the fullest of Brahmin accents. Charles Lennox Remond, one of his closest associates, struck him as falsely conceited, a trait that Phillips felt "injures him for sober, matter-of-fact, useful home toil." Remond's "foolish ways" sometimes led him to behave like a "wayward child" in Phillips's opinion; he dressed gaudily and tried to emulate Douglass. But however laced with condescension, these were Phillips's judgments on another's taste and comportment, not statements based on Remond's complexion. As Phillips also made clear, he deemed Remond's services to abolitionism as "very valuable and his testimony true and consistent." On another occasion, he had harsh words for James W. C. Pennington, a black anti-Garrisonian who was in Phillips's opinion "self seeking, trimming and utterly unreliable." But again, these were personal and political judgments since Phillips usually assumed the worst about foes of Garrison, whatever their race. Indeed, when Douglass, whom he regarded so highly, defected to the anti-Garrisonian Liberty Party, Phillips criticized the move with great distain but never implied any racial generalizations. During the Civil War and thereafter, Phillips and Douglass easily set their differences aside and resumed the closest of collaborations.[23]

Above all, Phillips never reciprocated the open bigotry and class arrogance that Maria Weston Chapman and Edmund Quincy sometimes conveyed in their letters to him. Quincy especially could wallow in racial crudity. When, for example, a local black commentator criticized his speaking style, Quincy penned the following response "for the Liberator if W.P. approve":

> E.Q returns his grateful acknowledgements to his colored correspondent & assures him that his advice is taken in good part & will be followed as far as possible. He begs to know whether his (his coloured friend's) mother knows

> he's out. He would respectfully inquire of him "*How's yer marm?*" Whether he can truthfully exclaim "O! Crikey don't I love my mother?" He would say that he thinks him (his col'd friend) some pumpkins he does. And that he thinks he is a nigger living in Lynn. That a nigger quite capable of getting this up lives there he (E.Q.) has on good authority of—Pike, Esq. He also thinks that his col'd friend was assisted by a wench living about as far towards the South Shore. You didn't suck in this child, this time. No, *Sirrr*, No *Sirreee*—Horsefly![24]

Phillips did not approve, and the letter never appeared in the *Liberator*.

Whatever Phillips's Brahmin insensitivities toward those "beneath" him, black activists seem to have trusted him enough to complain forthrightly to him about the insensitivity they encountered from white abolitionists, assuming that Phillips would take their complaints to heart. In 1859, for example, Phillips was listed on a roster of exclusively white male speakers who were to pay tribute to the insurrectionist John Brown. Mary Agnes Grant, a black activist from New York City, wrote Phillips bitterly about this exclusionary decision: "*Why is it that White Men* are forever making speeches and glorifying themselves" while eloquent blacks "with their bursting hearts and grand utterances are kept in the background in this so falsely called Free North, as much socially and politically proscribed, almost, as their enslaved Bretheren [*sic*]?" It was a telling indictment, clearly addressed to someone Grant believed would understand and share her complaint. How Edmund Quincy might have replied to Mary Agnes Grant makes interesting speculation. Phillips, she acknowledged, had earned an exemplary reputation among African Americans, as Douglass acknowledged as well in 1852, writing that Phillips had "said more cheering words to me, and in vindication of my race, than any man now living." Grant, then, could find some satisfaction in knowing that Phillips was likely to respect her anger and take it seriously.[25]

Douglass's sentiments were fully justified. No white exceeded Phillips in affirming African Americans' pride in their accomplishments and traditions. In the 1850s, Phillips began delivering two widely repeated speeches, each of which celebrated a black revolutionary and interwove the history of black struggle into a national history of biracial republican freedom. When, for example, he spoke of Crispus Attucks, the black patriot who fell during the Boston Massacre in 1770, Phillips placed him "in the forefront of the men who dared," the figure who was "the emblem of revolutionary violence at its dawn."

As Phillips treated him, Attucks became a revolutionary martyr, every bit the equal of the mob-murdered abolitionist Elijah P. Lovejoy and rightly enrolled in the national pantheon that featured Sam Adams, Patrick Henry, James Otis, and Nathan Hale, heroes "who had liberated *white* colonists from British slavery." Characteristically juxtaposing past with present, Phillips would next identify the leading black abolitionists of his day as Attucks's worthy successors, for they, too, struggled to disenthrall all Americans, but especially whites, from their racism and tolerance of slavery.[26]

Toussaint L'Ouverture, Phillips's second preeminent black revolutionary, had liberated Haiti from French colonial rule in the 1790s by leading the Western Hemisphere's most blood-soaked and longest slave insurrection. As Phillips explained this hero and his accomplishments, Toussaint was an Afro-Caribbean genius who by sheer force of will and the application of transcendent intelligence had created a great black republic out of the tyranny of slavery and the chaos of extended warfare. Toussaint, Phillips declared, had been a more able Oliver Cromwell than Cromwell himself had been when toppling the British monarchy and creating a revolutionary puritan commonwealth. Phillips's Toussaint was a self-taught scholarly genius in the mold of Edmund Burke who had forged once-demoralized slaves into "a thunderbolt" that had "smashed to atoms" the best of British and French armies. "Haiti, from the ruins of her colonial dependency has become a civilized state," he declared, "a very jewel of antislavery testimony and evidence." The story of Toussaint's revolutionary insurrection was, Phillips insisted, "the finest chapter in the history of the race," proving beyond all question the capacity of African-descended people for self-government. No one, ever, should hold up the history of dark skinned people to "pity or contempt," he insisted, for heroes such as Toussaint and Attucks proved beyond all doubt that all black people were "entitled to a place side by side with the Saxon."[27]

Obviously, Phillips had no time for the "scientific" treatises claiming white superiority that began to appear in his day and harbored no sympathy for those who claimed black people to be naturally loyal, good humored, simple minded, imitative, spiritual, deferential, and docile. Harriet Beecher Stowe filled her *Uncle Tom's Cabin* with such generalizations, and Phillips dismissed her book as "mere sentimental excitement." Some of Phillips's close associates during the 1850s, notably Theodore Parker and Thomas Wentworth Higginson, dismissed the enslaved as lacking in initiative and too degraded to be able to strike for freedom on their own. Phillips, by contrast, measured black people, enslaved or free, by his own sternly inclusive republican standards. What counted most was courage, an instinctive love of liberty, and an instinct for striking boldly to overthrow tyranny. By such standards, Phillips was wont to claim, "negro blood, instead of standing at the bottom of the list, is entitled . . . to a place as near our own as any other blood known in history." Sometimes he even claimed that, when it came to courageous action that expressed a love of liberty, black people were superior to whites. "Your Anglo-Saxon blood—it is water," he once told a white audience. In American mythology and history, just as in the schoolrooms and train cars across Massachusetts, Phillips insisted that African Americans take a dignified and equal place. Whatever his biases, this demand set Phillips well apart from the many paternalistic white reformers who trafficked in romantic racialism.[28]

When Phillips involved himself discreetely in the private concerns of African Americans, his gentlemanly instincts often served him surprisingly well. Frequently he was approached by black people struggling with adverse circumstances. For many whites, heavy-handed paternalism would have been the only imaginable response. Phillips, of course, was well known throughout the nation for his wealth and his willingness to champion the oppressed. Ordinary African Americans caught in desperate situations frequently turned to him for financial assistance and direct intervention. Invariably, he responded with great compassion, discretion, and generosity, remaining sensitive to his supplicants' feeling as well as to their needs. He betrayed no symptoms of moral self-congratulation and acted with confidentiality whenever he could. There can be no question that he handed out large sums in small amounts in order to ease his conscience, for he admitted quite openly that his great wealth made him feel terrible guilt. He once remarked that he "hardly dared stand by the side" of the mill workers, artisans, and farmers who constituted abolitionism's rank and file, people who made their living "by drudgery, daily toil, and the sweat of their brow." He wondered, "Who are we that we that we should presume to rank ourselves that are marshaled in that host? What have we done? What sacrifice have we made? Where is the luxury that we have surrendered?" Yet unlike Gerrit Smith or Lewis Tappan, two other abolitionists who could match his fortune, Phillips never attempted to ease his conscience by investing in high-profile projects that testified to his largesse. No one more than Phillips violated the stereotype of the stiflingly moralistic, self-congratulating Victorian philanthropist.[29]

This truth becomes clear in Phillips's response to Anthony Burns, a famous fugitive slave whose case became a cause célèbre across the nation. Phillips unsuccessfully defended him after his arrest in Boston in 1854 and helped to arrange his return from bondage in North Carolina. As this process unfolded, Burns wrote to Phillips in near-illiterate desperation, asking him to "dow [*sic*] all you can for me." Upon his return, Phillips underwrote his matriculation at Oberlin College, and two years thereafter, spelling and handwriting much improved, Burns again wrote Phillips, this time sharing his hopes to become educated. The following year, he sought Phillips's advice about beginning a career in politics. "No one is better able to instruct me in this point than you," Burns assured him.[30]

John Oliver, by contrast, was already enrolled in Oberlin when misadventure struck. He had run up debts, tried and failed to reap easy money in the California gold fields, his talented actress/singer wife Louise De Mortie divorced him, and he faced an Ohio winter without boots and a warm coat. Twice Phillips sent him money and carefully answered his questions about where he might best set up a business in New England. In the post–Civil War years, the same John Oliver repaid his benefactor by sending Phillips news of freed African Americans' struggles for citizenship in Virginia, where he had worked for the American Missionary Association and had become a government official and political activist. By this time, Phillips was editing the *National Anti-Slavery Standard* and had good use for such firsthand reporting.[31]

Phillips's discretion when involved in interracial charity was sometimes as obvious to whites as it was to blacks. In 1860, one William Walker wrote to Phillips in desperation. A white who opposed slavery, Walker nevertheless found himself the executor of the estate of a southern planter and had taken temporary custody of a now-emancipated sixteen-year-old boy who had been part of the inheritance. Could Phillips find an apprenticeship for this young man? No one else seemed able to assist. Walker's second letter to Phillips suggests the quality of Phillips's first response: "I thank you so much for the interest you manifest in this boy. This feeling, this principle which characterize[s] your life I do not find among abolitionists generally. They care much about the slave and nothing about him when he is free." Phillips's meetings with the Boston "clique" were surely lily white, but the wrought-iron fence surrounding Maria Chapman's mansion could not circumscribe his powerfully egalitarian impact within the abolitionist community.[32]

There were other cases such as these, but two in particular illustrate Phillips's markedly constructive approach to interracial philanthropy. The first incident, involving a boy named Bernardo, also offers a rare glimpse of the grassroots abolitionist community during one of its best moments. In 1852, Phillips began to sponsor Bernardo, an illegitimate orphan of mixed parentage, described euphemistically as being of Cuban origins. Bernardo was seriously ill, and Phillips arranged his adoption, paid his expenses, and brought him gifts. Bernardo wrote Phillips only once, for he was ashamed of his poor penmanship, caused by a wracking cough that made his hand shake badly. One of Bernardo's adoptive parents, Mrs. F. H. Drake, resolved to Phillips "to give him a mother's care and kindness and to devote my time to his comfort and enjoyment by reading and conversing" with Bernardo whenever he wished. Soon enough, abolitionists Abby Kelly and Stephen S. Foster, two of Phillips's closest associates, began visiting Bernardo as well, bringing presents of fruit. Bernardo remarked that "no boy could have a kinder friend" than Phillips. After Bernardo's death, another of Phillips's colleagues, Edward N. Davis, delivered the funeral sermon, and many others donated money for the headstone. "Not a word about repentance or condemnation" was uttered during the service, only "a kind and Christian recognition" of Bernardo's "pure life and character" as a "more than ordinary lad." Antislavery friends from all around attended the funeral. Phillips and the other openhearted people who had given their help had also demonstrated that the abolitionist community with which Phillips so closely associated could act with loving inclusiveness.[33]

A case that certainly tested Phillips's discernment to its limit and opened to full view his aristocratic self-confidence involved black, unmarried, pregnant Susan Randall, a stranger who turned to Phillips in desperation in 1858. A traveling entertainer, Carl Formes, had put her "in great trouble," Randall explained, but refused to accept paternal responsibility. Randall was destitute when she wrote Phillips from Hartford, Connecticut, six months advanced in her pregnancy and afraid to turn for assistance to her mother. Formes was now playing Boston, and Randall begged Phillips to find him and make him live up to "what it is his duty to do for me." She also enclosed a medical certificate attesting to her pregnancy. Hers was a desperate and courageous act, and Phillips showed great sensitivity when responding to her plight. As this self-possessed gentleman understood it, duty had nothing to do with sermonizing charity. Responding like a reliable business agent, he first reconfirmed Randall's identity and medical condition by writing to her doctor in Hartford. Then he sought out

Carl Formes and made him agree to support during her pregnancy, delivery, and recovery, obtaining each payment directly from him and sending it on to her. He doubtless complied with Randall's other request, telling Formes never to mention this matter to anyone else. Each month, Phillips sent Randall the money, which she acknowledged with a small note of thanks. In late March 1859 she bore a son, and shortly thereafter Formes's obligations ended. "I shall soon be able to earn my living again," Randall wrote Phillips in her final letter. "I can never forget your kindness to me as a stranger for you can never know the relief your kindness gave my mind at the time. I wish it were in my power, in any way . . . to express my thanks."[34]

Many years after the Civil War, Phillips received a letter from a certain Mary Desmond, who had once visited his and Ann's modest, out-of-the way home on 26 Essex Street. While reminiscing, she remarked of "how little the world or newspapers know of the daily, nay hourly acts of charity that is [*sic*] performed . . . to every preople [*sic*] of every nation" in the Phillips household. She remembered that indigents traveled "constantly . . . upstairs to dear Mrs. Phillips' sick room" and that Wendell had once interrupted his shaving to run next door to give money to someone in need.[35]

Ann Phillips and her husband considered charity a privilege of the privileged, a means for solving the ever-present dilemma of possessing great wealth while championing the poor, black or white. In acts of charity, as in desegregation struggles, in dealings with fellow abolitionists, in speeches extolling great black heroes and, during and after the Civil War, in demanding full citizenship for every black American, Wendell Phillips challenged the boundaries of democracy by obliterating distinctions of race. The exacting standards he demanded of the nation were, in truth, the ones he lived by himself.

NOTES

1. See Donald Yacovone, "Race, Radicalism, and Remembering Wendell Phillips," in this volume.

2. Roger Lane, *Policing the City: Boston, 1822–1875* (Cambridge: Harvard University Press, 1967), 2–25; Andrew R. L. Cayton, "The Fragmentation of a Great Family: The Panic of 1819 and the Rise of the Middling Interest in Boston," *Journal of the Early Republic* 2 (June 1982): 143–67.

3. George Phillips to Wendell Phillips [n.d., 1836], Crawford Blagden Papers, Houghton Library, Harvard University; James Brewer Stewart, *Wendell Phillips: Liberty's Hero* (Baton Rouge: Louisiana State University Press, 1986), 63; Lillie Buffum Chase Wyman, "Reminiscences of Wendell Phillips," *New England Magazine of History* 33 (February 1903): 730.

4. Stewart, *Wendell Phillips*, 1–35.

5. Ibid., 40–42.

6. For fuller explanations of these developments, see James Brewer Stewart, "Wendell Phillips Is the Subtlest, Stubbornest Fact of the Times: Abolition's Golden Trumpet and the Fall of the Slaveholders' Republic," in this volume.

7. Edgar Buckingham, "College Reminiscences," Edgar Buckingham Papers, Harvard University Archives, Pusey Library. Classmate Charles Tappan Pierce quoted in Carlos Martyn, *Wendell Phillips: The Agitator* (New York: Funk & Wagnalls Co., 1890), 43–47.

8. For a fuller explanation of this refocusing from personal stress to public speaking, see Stewart, *Wendell Phillips*, 173–75.

9. Phillips, "1831 Class Questionnaire" [1846], Harvard University Archives, Pusey Library. Phillips to Sidney Howard Gay, July 29, 1846; September [?] 1847, Sidney Howard Gay Papers, Columbia University.

10. *Liberator*, January 29, May 30, 1839.

11. Stewart, *Wendell Phillips*, 72; Ann Warren Weston to Deborah Weston, March 11, 1839, Antislavery Collection, Boston Public Library.

12. *National Anti-Slavery Standard*, July 4, September 12, 1841; February 3, 1866. Oliver Johnson to Phillips, September 12, 1841, Crawford Blagden Papers, Houghton Library, Harvard University.

13. *Liberator*, February 16, 1842.

14. Carleton Mabee, *Black Freedom: The Non-Violent Abolitionists from 1830 through the Civil War* (New York: Macmillan, 1970), 170–81; James O. Horton and Lois E. Horton, *In Hope of Liberty: Culture Community and Protest among Northern Free Blacks, 1700–1861* (New York: Oxford University Press, 1997), 225–46.

15. *Liberator*, August 12, 1846; May 25, 1853. Phillips to Edmund Quincy, August 8, 1846, Sidney Howard Gay Papers, Columbia University. For Phillips's attacks on Mann, see the *Liberator*, December 24, 1847; February 4, 1848.

16. Mabee, *Black Freedom*, 170–81; Steven Kantrowitz, *More Than Freedom: Fighting for Black Citizenship in a White Republic, 1829–1889* (New York: Penguin Books, 2012), 42, 124–33, 167–68.

17. Kantrowitz, *More than Freedom*, 61–62.

18. Phillips to Richard D. Webb, May 25, 1845, Antislavery Collection, Boston Public Library.

19. William H. Pease and Jane H. Pease, "Boston Garrisonians and the Problem of Frederick Douglass," *Canadian Journal of History* 2 (September 1967): 29–48.

20. Frederick Douglass to Phillips, March 25, 1846, Crawford Blagden Papers, Houghton Library, Harvard University. Phillips to Elizabeth Pease, February 25, 1845 (quotation); Phillips to Webb, August 12, 1842; Phillips to Pease, February 24, 1845, Antislavery Collection, Boston Public Library.

21. Consult files for William Wells Brown, Lewis Hayden, William Nell, Charles L. Remond, and William and Ellen Craft and compare with those of Edward N. Davis, Parker Pillsbury, Ste-

phen and Abby Kelly Foster, Erastus Hudson, and Arnold Buffum in Crawford Blagden Papers, Houghton Library, Harvard University.

22. This exchange is discussed in Kantrowitz, *More Than Freedom*, 114–15, 120–21. Erastus Hudson to Phillips, February 3, 1848; Lewis Hayden to Phillips, February 21, 1848, Crawford Blagden Papers, Houghton Library, Harvard University.

23. Phillips to Pease, October [n.d.] 1844; February 24, 1845; February 19, 1850, Antislavery Collection, Boston Public Library, contain Phillips's comments on Remond and Douglass. Phillips to Gay, February 19 [1853], contains Phillips's characterization of Pennington.

24. Maria Weston Chapman to Phillips, June 26 [1846]; Quincy to Phillips, June 19, 1847, Crawford Blagden Papers, Houghton Library, Harvard University.

25. Agnes Mary Grant to Phillips, December 9, 1859, Crawford Blagden Papers, Houghton Library, Harvard University. For a description of the occasion to which Grant referred, see Benjamin Quarles, ed., *Blacks on John Brown* (Champaign-Urbana: University of Illinois Press, 1972), 1–31. Frederick Douglass is quoted in Irving Bartlett, "New Light on Wendell Phillips and the Community of Reform, 1840–1880," *Perspectives in American History* (Cambridge, Mass., Warren Center, 1979), vol. 12: 109 note.

26. "Crispus Attucks" in Wendell Phillips, *Speeches, Lectures, and Letters, Second Series* (Boston: Lee and Shepard, 1894), 69–76.

27. "Toussaint L'Ouverture," in Wendell Phillips, *Speeches, Lectures, and Letters, First Series* (Boston: Lee and Shepard, 1884), 468–94.

28. On Parker and Higginson, see Ethan J. Kytle, *Romantic Reformers and the Antislavery Struggle in the Civil War Era* (New York: Cambridge University Press, 2014); Jeffrey Rossbach, *Ambivalent Conspirators: The Secret Six and a Theory of Slave Violence* (Philadelphia: University of Pennsylvania Press, 1982), and Tilden Edelstein, *Strange Enthusiasm: A Life of Thomas Wentworth Higginson* (New York: Atheneum, 1967). For Phillips on *Uncle Tom's Cabin*, see Phillips to Elizabeth Pease, November 22, 1852, in Antislavery Collection, Boston Public Library. For Phillips's comments on "blood," see Phillips, "Toussaint L'Ouverture," 469; *Liberator*, June 6, 1850.

29. *Liberator*, April 19, 1841.

30. Anthony Burns to Phillips, [n.d.] 1854; August 2, 1856, Crawford Blagden Papers, Houghton Library, Harvard University.

31. John Oliver to Phillips, January 1, August 21, 1857; July 6, 1866, Crawford Blagden Papers, Houghton Library, Harvard University. Donald Yacovone, "Mark R. and Louise De Mortie," *African American National Biography*, www.oxfordaasc.com.ezp-prod1.hul.harvard.edu/article/opr/t0001/e4715?hi=0&highlight=1&from=quick&pos=1. C. Peter Ripley et al., eds., *The Black Abolitionist Papers*, volume 5, *The United States, 1859–1865* (Chapel Hill: University of North Carolina Press, 1992), 136.

32. William Walker to Phillips, April 10, April 21, 1860, Crawford Blagden Papers, Houghton Library, Harvard University.

33. Isaac Mayo to Phillips, November 8, 1852; G. H. Small to Phillips, November 30, 1852; Mary Raymond to Phillips, February 22, 1853; Bernardo to Phillips, August 3, 1856; F. H. Drake to Phillips, September 8, 1856 (quotation), October 2, October 12, November 17, 1856 (quotation), all in Crawford Blagden Papers, Houghton Library, Harvard University.

34. Susan Randall to Phillips, December 15, 1858 (quotation); Phillips to Dr. G. B. Hawley

[draft], December 22, 1858; Hawley to Phillips, December 23, 1858; Randall to Phillips, December 23, 1858, and January 9, February 13, March 14, April 26, 1859 (quotation), Crawford Blagden Papers, Houghton Library, Harvard University.

35. Mary Desmond [Chalmers] to Phillips, July 25, 1876, Crawford Blagden Papers, Houghton Library, Harvard University. Documentation of Phillips's financial support to whites as well as blacks is substantial. See, for example, Thomas Cashman to Phillips, January 16, August 13, 1856; July 22, 1857 (from Westboro, Massachusetts, State Reform School), Crawford Blagden Papers, Houghton Library, Harvard University. Phillips to Samuel J. May, December 4, 1842, Samuel J. May, J. Miller McKim Papers, Cornell University Library, contains a revealing inquiry by Phillips about a possible recipient of his financial support.

6

WENDELL PHILLIPS, THE CONSTITUTION, AND CONSTITUTIONAL POLITICS BEFORE THE CIVIL WAR

MICHAEL LES BENEDICT

They gathered at Tremont Temple to remember Wendell Phillips on April 18, 1884, a couple of months after his death. Surviving Massachusetts abolitionists like Thomas Wentworth Higginson, Elizur Wright, James Freeman Clarke, Julia Ward Howe, and John Greenleaf Whittier greeted each other somberly. The Boston cultural elite—among them Harvard president Charles W. Eliot, William Dean Howells, Thomas Bailey Aldrich, and Edward Everett Hale—joined them. A raft of public officials crowded the pews. Governor George D. Robinson, who had defeated Phillips's old ally, the incumbent Ben Butler, the year before, was there with his whole staff. Along with them were the Governor's Council, the justices of the state's supreme court and judges of the lower courts, federal judges and the U.S. marshal and district attorney—the sorts of people Phillips had lambasted all his life. Clergymen read lofty poems, children sang odes, all inspired by the occasion. A quartet sang "Loyal to the End" and then "Truth," a piece prepared by Minot J. Savage, the progressive pastor of the Church of the Unity.[1]

They had called on George William Curtis, the erudite editor of *Harper's Weekly*, to present a memorial oration. Curtis and Phillips had become friends after the Civil War, even though Curtis had little use for much of Phillips's postwar radicalism and Phillips even less for Curtis's Mugwump reformism.[2] But they had shared a disdain for ordinary politicians, who were always ready to sacrifice principle for political expediency. Throughout his life, Phillips had seen the job of the principled agitator to hold the politicians' feet to the fire. Now, Curtis marveled at the scene. Before the Civil War, Phillips had never voted, never held office, never joined a political party. More than that, until

1861 he had denounced the Constitution of the United States and the Union it fostered. Yet the myriads who have eulogized him "are all loyal to party, all revere the Constitution and maintain the Union, all hold the ballot to be the most sacred trust, and voting to be the highest duty of the citizen." The rite in which they were all participating "is homage to personal character," Curtis said. Phillips had eschewed voting and office, repudiating the Constitution itself, and his agitation had been an "amazing success." His power grew out of his eloquence, but only because that eloquence reflected "a life of transcendent purity of purpose . . . devoted with absolute unselfishness . . . to the welfare of the country and of humanity." That was "a public service so beneficent that, in contemplating them, discordant opinions, different judgments, and the sharp sting of controversial speech, vanish like frost in a flood of sunshine."[3]

Contemporaries had not been so cordial. If Garrisonian denunciation of the Constitution seems quixotic today, it seemed downright perverse at the time. When Phillips first denounced the Constitution in 1842, a correspondent for the Boston *Daily Bee* could not believe his ears. "Our readers will scarcely believe it," he wrote, "yet we assure them that Wendell Phillips had the audacity the shameless self-degradation, TO CURSE THE CONSTITUTION OF THE UNITED STATES in the *Cradle of American Liberty*, before an assemblage of American citizens." "Our blood boiled in our veins," he said. He was not alone. The audience responded with "overwhelming hisses" that almost drowned out the words as they left "his dastardly lips."[4] The *Democratic Review* called abolitionists "reptiles that hiss their venom in the face of the Constitution."[5]

Historians and memorialists have not been very comfortable with Phillips's repudiation of the Constitution and his advocacy of disunion. If cursing the Constitution was "deemed next to cursing Deity" in the 1840s, as Phillips's early biographer Lorenzo Sears observed in 1909, it has been hardly more acceptable since. Sears decided it was "not necessary" to go into detail on the differences over the Constitution between political abolitionists and moral suasionists like Phillips. It was merely "a question of ways and means with some; of conscience with others." He described Phillips's Garrisonian position as essentially idealistic, taking "the high ground of educating the popular mind up to voting for reforming men and measures" while not going into organized politics itself. In Sears's telling, Phillips's goal had been abolition of slavery, and his repudiation of the Constitution and the Union forgivably secondary to that end. "There is no misunderstanding what Phillips's position was at this time. It is easier to understand now [in 1909], however, than in 1849," when it was considered "treason or next to it."[6] When Boston finally erected a statue of Phillips in 1915, no speaker at the dedication even mentioned the embarrassing fact.[7]

Modern historians have done better, but Phillips's condemnation of the Constitution and the Union has rarely been closely analyzed. William Wiecek offered a careful analysis of the Garrisonian position in his study of early antislavery constitutionalism, as have Aileen Kraditor in her study of abolitionist strategy and tactics *Means and Ends in American Abolitionism*, and Louis S. Gerteis in *Morality and Utility in American Antislavery Reform*.[8] Historians have discussed abolitionist abjurations of fidelity to the Constitution in the context of the bitter hostility between political abolitionists and Garrisonians,[9] the closely linked issue of political activism versus "moral suasion" and the distinction between morality and law,[10] or as a principled instance of refusing to obey unjust laws or to participate in unjust institutions.[11] Insofar as repudiation of the Constitution meant repudiation of the Union, historians describe it as an effort to avoid the sin of slavery—"the statement of a moral imperative, a reveille to the conscience." They have seen it as a logical extension of evangelical "perfectionism."[12]

There is plenty of evidence that avoidance of sin played a key role in abolitionist rejection of the Constitution, and that the sinfulness of participating in a proslavery constitutional system was a primary criticism levied at political antislavery. Phillips himself closed his law office rather than practice under the oath to support the Constitution required of attorneys in Massachusetts. He refused to vote. These certainly were personal decisions that reflected his desire to avoid participating in a sinful system. He endorsed the May 1844 resolution of the American Anti-Slavery Society that anyone who voted or held office was "rendering himself an abettor of the slaveholder in his sin."[13] "Immediate ceasing to do evil is our rule," he wrote. That required repudiation of a Constitution that required residents of free states to support the rights of slaveowners. "UNION itself BETWEEN A SLAVE AND FREE STATE IS IMPOSSIBLE, WITHOUT GUILT," he insisted.[14]

However, Phillips denounced the Constitution and the Union not only because they involved northerners in the sin of slavery. He denounced them because he saw no way to abolish slavery as long as ordinary northerners' constitutional commitments were wedded to the document framed in 1787. Americans were dedicated to constitutionalism—a commitment as strong, or even stronger, than their commitment to morality and justice. For Phillips, commitment to constitutionalism was all to the good; it was essential to liberty in a democratic system. Because Americans were committed constitutionalists, one could make arguments for public policy on constitutional grounds, on principles that trumped mere expediency. This was the kind of argument Phillips wanted to make against slavery. He wanted to harness Americans' devotion to the Constitution to augment moral and economic arguments against the peculiar institution. Instead, it was his opponents who appealed to the Constitution, who insisted that it protected southerners' right to slave property. The problem was that Americans were committed to the wrong constitution.

So Phillips's call for disunion was more than what Aileen Kraditor has labeled "strictly an agitational weapon."[15] Phillips was deadly serious. He was elated when the South began seceding in the wake of Lincoln's election in 1860. Disunion had not come in the way he sought, with an abolitionist Massachusetts leading the North out of the slave republic, but the result would be the same if he could persuade northerners to let events run their course. "All my grown-up years have been devoted to creating just such a crisis as that which is now upon us," he exulted.[16] He did not expect that northerners would fight to save the Union. On the contrary, he feared that they might compromise to save it, and he fought with all his might to prevent that from happening. Rather than preserve the Union through another compromise with southerners, he exclaimed that the North should "build a bridge of gold and pay their toll over it."[17]

Whether he was fighting to escape commitments the Constitution imposed on Americans, as he did before 1861, or trying to shape Americans' constitutional commitments as he did thereafter, Phillips was profoundly engaged in a certain kind of politics that present-day observers tend not to see although it is all around us—what analysts in other countries readily see as *constitutional politics*.

For much of the twentieth century and until quite recently, American scholars have tended to see the Constitution as the particular preserve of lawyers and judges. The understanding taught in law schools is that politics and law are separate entities, with the latter setting the constitutional boundaries within which the former can operate. Such a perception has exalted the role of courts, especially the U.S. Supreme Court, in making constitutional policy. This understanding became solidified by the crucial part the Supreme Court played in precipitating the civil rights movement with the *Brown v. Board of Education* decision and by expanding civil liberties afterwards.[18] Since the civil rights era, the Supreme Court has more and more aggressively claimed not only the final authority to interpret the Constitution but the primary and even prescriptive authority to do so. This environment has not been conducive to an appreciation of the degree to which the public engages in the making of constitutional policy through politics.[19]

But nineteenth-century Americans wore no such blinders. They knew that almost every political issue agitating Americans since the founding had been argued in constitutional terms—setting the parameters of the disputes between Federalists and Jeffersonian Republicans, Jacksonian Democrats and Whigs, and Democrats and Republicans over slavery. The Jacksonian Democratic Party claimed a special dedication to constitutional issues. It had been organized explicitly to save the Constitution from the latitudinarian constructions of federal power posited by Federalists and their allies on the Supreme Court, a broad construction of federal power inherited by their Whig successors. As Phillips was becoming active as an abolitionist, the Democrats held their first national party convention. The party's first plank declared "That the Federal Government is one of limited powers, derived solely from the Constitution, and the grants of power shown therein ought to be strictly construed by all the departments and agents of the government, and that it is inexpedient and dangerous to exercise doubtful constitutional powers."[20] That would remain the first plank of every Democratic platform until 1860.

The Supreme Court had weighed in on some of these issues in cases like *McCulloch v. Maryland* and *Gibbons v. Ogden*, which spoke to federal power over economic development; the *Dartmouth College* and *Charles River Bridge* cases, which addressed state legislation and property rights; and in *Prigg v. Pennsylvania*, which barred states from passing laws limiting the ability of slaveowners to recover fugitive slaves under the Fugitive Slave clause of the U.S. Constitution.[21] All these cases have become staples of American constitutional law casebooks, but none of them had settled the broad issues they addressed. They were part of the larger constitutional controversies that roiled American politics—authoritative when they coincided with popular views of the Constitution, less so when they didn't, and sometimes immediately repudiated outright—as when the Supreme Court sought to limit state control over Native Americans.[22]

However, while most antebellum Americans recognized that the people rather than the courts had the final say on what the Constitution meant, Phillips's view was more akin to the modern one, and that fact complicated his approach to constitutional politics before the Civil War. A radical—indeed, a self-described revolutionary—he nonetheless believed that the courts had final authority over constitutional interpretation. Therefore his commitment to popular control of the constitutional system was not manifested in a rejection of judicial authority but rather in his long campaign to persuade northerners to repudiate the Constitution itself, to dissolve the Union and establish a system of government consistent with the commitment to liberty and equality that the revolutionary generation had professed but compromised away in 1787. Only after the South's secession did Phillips concede the possibility of waging constitutional politics under the Constitution of 1787.

Phillips was well aware of the way that ordinary Americans could manifest their constitutional commitments in the public sphere, outside the courtroom. Like a number of others, he was first drawn into the abolition movement in reaction to the mobs that suppressed abolitionist agitation. Ultimately, Americans have come to see such mobs as lawless, but that was not so clear in the 1830s, when mob actions spread like wildfire across the country. For many, what opponents called mobs were the people acting in their most organic and sovereign capacity, led by "gentlemen of property and standing," to protect their communities in an age when many Americans still thought that the people could exert sovereign power outside legal forms. From this perspective, those mobs were authoritative popular statements of the limits of free speech and press, commitment to a Union threatened by disruptive debates about slavery, and conviction that African Americans were outsiders, not entitled to citizenship, its rights, or anything that smacked of "amalgamation."[23]

At first Phillips believed that commitment to the Constitution could be turned against those who sought to silence abolitionists. He first came to public attention at the famed Faneuil Hall meeting called to respond to the murder of Elijah P. Lovejoy by a mob at Alton, Illinois, outside St. Louis. There no less a personage than state attorney general James T. Austin blamed Lovejoy for his own murder. Speaking to an audience leavened with a raucous element come to damn the abolitionists, Austin sympathized with Missourians who had no legal recourse to protect their community against the threat Lovejoy's paper posed to their security. He compared Lovejoy's assailants to the "orderly mob" that dumped tea into Boston harbor in 1773. Outraged, Phillips responded with a ringing appeal to the Constitution's guarantee of free speech and freedom of the press. It was not the mob that murdered Lovejoy, but those who denounced it who could claim the heritage of Massachusetts's revolutionary leaders. Their portraits hung on Faneuil Hall's walls. Could the people of Massachusetts endorse the murder of a freedom-loving editor in the presence of those portraits? His speech clearly energized those who had come to protest Lovejoy's death and may have disconcerted at least some who had applauded Austin. Waves of applause, jeers, hisses, and cheers boomed across Faneuil Hall. "Lovejoy had stationed himself within constitution bulwarks," Phillips said. "He had planted himself on his constitutional rights—appealed to the laws,—claimed the protection of the civil authority,—taken refuge under the broad shield of the Constitution. . . . He took refuge under the banner of liberty . . . and when he fell, its glorious stars and stripes, the emblem of free institutions . . . were blotted out in the martyr's blood."[24]

But if it were possible to appeal to a hostile crowd based on its constitutional commitments, Phillips soon learned how powerfully the same commitments cut the other way. The Latimer case, which played the most crucial role in molding Phillips's constitutional thought, persuaded Phillips that constitutionalism provided a bulwark for slavery rather than freedom. Every legal effort to secure the release of George Latimer, claimed in Boston as a runaway slave, failed. Massachusetts's constitution and laws guaranteed Latimer due process of law. But Lemuel Shaw, the respected chief justice of the Massachusetts Supreme Court, held that all those provisions were superseded by the federal Fugitive Slave Act. No matter how much he detested slavery, Shaw explained, the U.S. Constitution obliged him to enforce the federal law over that of Massachusetts.[25] One of Phillips's early biographers wrote that it was Shaw's decision that led Phillips to realize "that in advocating the rights of the blacks his real antagonist was the Union."[26] Over and again state and federal judges who professed abhorrence of slavery would don what scholars have called "the masks of the law" to sustain federal laws protecting property rights in slaves against state laws trying to preserve African Americans' rights as human beings and state citizens.[27]

Phillips, who had studied law at Harvard, where the great U.S. Supreme Court justice Joseph Story both administered the law school and lectured on constitutional law, understood and accepted the principle that lower courts must follow the precedents and reasoning of higher courts, as well as respect the authority of precedents set by other courts. He knew that under the precedents being set all over the country judges would rule in favor of slavery. The Framers had incorporated provisions protecting slavery into the Constitution. The nation's charter represented a bargain with slaveholders in return for "certain commercial concessions to the North," Phillips observed, and the documents proved "that the nation at large were fully aware of this bargain at the time, and entered into it willingly and with open eyes." "[T]he unanimous decision of all the courts in the land, both State and Federal;—the action of Congress and the State Legislature[s];—the constant practice of the Executive in all its branches;—and the deliberate acquiescence of the whole people for half a century" had reconfirmed the bargain and entrenched slavery in the Constitution even more firmly.[28] Politicians like Daniel Webster say that the Constitution orders the return of fugitive slaves, Phillips observed. "So say we; and that is the reason why we hate the Constitution."[29]

Other abolitionists insisted that the proslavery interpretations judges gave these provisions were wrong, that other provisions counteracted them, and even that the Constitution banned slavery, if only one interpreted it in accord with principles of a higher, natural law of justice and morality.[30] To Phillips this was all bosh. For the purposes of government, law was "a rule of civil conduct prescribed by the Supreme power of a State." A "higher law of justice" might obligate an individual to refuse to abide by unjust laws, but it could not nullify the law itself nor the penalties for violating it. He challenged Lysander Spooner, who insisted that the Constitution must be interpreted to conform with a higher law. Spooner "is at liberty to say that much of what the world calls law is not obligatory, because it is not just in the eye of God," Phillips said. But he was dead wrong if he meant "that in settling what shall be *the rule* of civil conduct, the voice of the majority is not final and conclusive, on its own officers, in *all the departments of government*." Obeying the law of God and justice might require a good man to withdraw his allegiance to the state and suffer the consequences, but it could not justify government officers picking and choosing which law to obey, and certainly not judges. "[I]f the majority enact a wicked law, and the Judge refuse to enforce it, which is to yield, the Judge or the majority?" Phillips asked. "Of course, the first," he answered. "On any other supposition Government is impossible." "The only test . . . to which our courts have any right to submit the action of the Legislature is, to ask, is it constitutional?' Phillips insisted. "If so, it is legally binding on them—no matter how unjust or how unreasonable it is."[31]

The only course for one who believed morality and justice trumped positive law was to refuse to participate in the government that the Constitution had created. This was especially so because the Constitution required officeholders, both state and federal, to take oaths to support it. And since voting was a right intimately bound up with officeholding, one who voted in effect made the same promise. No abolitionist could in good conscience do either, Phillips insisted, and he reserved some of his harshest criticism for the so-called political abolitionists, who had formed antislavery political parties or who claimed to be antislavery Whigs or Democrats. Some of them took oaths to support the Constitution with the reservation that they would not carry out its unjust provisions. Phillips blasted that alternative. The oath was a contract between the officeholder and the people, and it was all or nothing. "[I]t is an oath to support the Constitution—that is, *the whole of it*, there are no exceptions." An oath, whether for public or private purposes, established a solemn obligation. Taking oaths with "reservations" would "destroy utterly that confidence between man and man which binds society together." It was "contrary alike to honor, to fair dealing, and to truthfulness."[32]

Other antislavery politicians took oaths to support the Constitution only as they interpreted it—as an antislavery document. That was just as bad. "The absurdity of . . . laws which have no fixed meaning—but which each man construes to mean what he pleases and obeys accordingly—must be evident to every one," Phillips wrote. Taking such a position, the antislavery politicians made the Constitution "waste paper by construction."[33] The officeholder who swore to uphold the Constitution and the voter who implicitly did the same were promising to support it as it was understood and interpreted by the whole country and articulated by the Supreme Court, which had the power "to affix the proper construction to the instrument, and that construction both parties are bound to abide by, or repudiate the whole contract."[34]

No good man could take that oath. Nor could he obey the laws that the U.S. and state governments enacted under the constitutional obligation to protect slavery. "If the majority set up an immoral Government, I obey those laws which seem to me good, because they are good—and I submit to all the penalties which my disobedience of the rest brings on me."[35] He lauded "the fearless efforts of those who, trampling the laws and Constitution of the country under their feet . . . 'hide the outcast,'" and make their hearths "[in] spite of the law, an asylum for the oppressed."[36]

In criticizing those who posited an antislavery Constitution, Phillips conceded more authority to the U.S. Supreme Court than most contemporaries did. If the Supreme Court gave the Constitution a proslavery interpretation, "[t]his, then is the law of the land," he insisted. "Those who now swear to support that instrument are bound to support it in the sense which the Courts give it." This, he insisted was "the universal Northern doctrine."[37]

It was not as universal as Phillips claimed. Antislavery politicians rejected his views. In a bitter exchange, Horace Mann criticized Phillips for claiming an "extreme prerogative for the Supreme Court" that would destroy the "free agency" of the political branches. It was a "well known legal principle, that even the opinions of the Supreme Court are not the law, but only *evidence of the law.*"[38] Salmon P. Chase, whose antislavery constitutional arguments were constantly repudiated by the courts, blasted "the facility with which the federal judges reach conclusions adverse to freedom over obstacles apparently insurmountable"—that is, the obstacles he fashioned in his compelling constitutional arguments. The future chief justice called upon antislavery activists to be "bold, indignant, and emphatic" in denouncing decisions so inconsistent with the true construction of the Constitution.[39] Republicans adopted the antislavery constitutional arguments that Phillips scorned. "I do not believe slavery can legally exist in this country, a single hour, under an honest interpretation of our national Constitution," orated James M. Ashley, who would manage the Thirteenth Amendment through the House of Representatives a decade later. Slaveholders had "deliberately perverted and judicially misinterpreted our national constitution," he charged.[40]

When he insisted on the final authority of Supreme Court decisions, Phillips was echoing the position that Federalists and Whigs had taken. Both stressed the Supreme Court's special role in interpreting the Constitution. But Democrats—the majority party in most of the country—had generally taken a different view. Their party had organized to resist the broad construction of federal power that had characterized Supreme Court decisions in the 1810s and 1820s, as well as the restrictions it claimed the Constitution imposed on the states.[41] So when Whigs insisted that the Supreme Court's ruling in *McCulloch v. Maryland* authoritatively established the constitutionality of a national bank, Pennsylvania Senator James Buchanan called the claim "preposterous." "[H]e was not . . . willing to rest the liberties of this country on the decision of any earthly tribunal." He was "astonished" at claims of "the infallibility of the decisions of the Supreme Court," claims that the Supreme Court's opinions "were to be incorporated with the text," as if the court's exposition of constitutional law was as authoritative "as our Saviour's exposition of the moral law."[42] Jackson had submitted the question of the constitutionality of the Bank of the United States to the people in the presidential election of 1832. He "had willingly . . . and frankly declared his unalterable opposition to the bank as being both unconstitutional and inexpedient," Jackson told his opponents. "On that ground the case was argued to the people; and now that the people have sustained the President, . . . it is too late . . . to say the question has not been decided."[43]

Reviewing the political principles governing the United States, Jackson's successor referred to "the fallacy" of the idea that the Supreme Court had "a controlling power over the other departments in respect to constitutional questions." One would search the Constitution "in vain" for any provisions "which indicate a design on the part of its framers to give to one of the departments power to control the action of another" in that way. The only way to resolve disagreements among Congress, the president, and the Supreme Court about constitutional interpretation was to appeal to the people.[44]

On the other hand, when faced with South Carolina's claim that it could nullify an unconstitutional congressional law in 1832, Andrew Jackson responded that the judiciary was the institution responsible for determining the constitutionality of congressional laws.[45] And in 1857, Buchanan forgot his earlier words and told Americans that, in the pending Dred Scott case, the Supreme Court would authoritatively resolve whether Congress had constitutional authority to bar slavery in the territories. "[I]t is a judicial question, which legitimately belongs to the Supreme Court." There it will be "speedily and finally settled," he observed, in a decision in which "all good citizens . . . shall cheerfully submit."[46]

But Buchanan's notion that all Americans acknowledged the finality of a Supreme Court interpretation of the Constitution proved optimistic, to say the least. When the Supreme Court came down with yet another trenchantly proslavery opinion in *Scott*, Republicans repudiated the decision.[47] "It is not law, and it has no binding force upon either the people or the government. It is not an authoritative interpretation of the Constitution, nor is it, legally, a decision entitled to any weight whatever," thundered the Republican *Pittsburgh Gazette*.[48] The party's national platform promised to ignore it. The Constitution not only authorized a law barring slavery in the territories, the platform declared, it compelled one.[49]

Phillips welcomed the spirit of the response, but he disagreed with the constitutional reasoning. In his view, the Supreme Court's opinion was the logical exposition of a proslavery Constitution, issued by the institution authorized to define its provisions. "It is infamous," he wrote his friend and co-agitator Theodore Parker. "But it is the law of the United States."[50]

Nonetheless, it was not the judges that were the problem. Phillips's belief in the Supreme Court as final authority over constitutional interpretation was as broad as any adherent of judicial supremacy today, but he scouted the idea that the role of the Supreme Court was to counter abuses of power by democratic majorities. "You may sigh for a strong government, anchored in the convictions of past centuries, and able to protect the minority against the majority,—able to defy the ignorance, the mistake, or the passion as well as the high purpose, of the present hour," he said, "but still the fact remains, that we are launched on the ocean of an unchained democracy, with no safety but . . . the instinctive love of right in the popular heart."[51] After the war, Phillips never suggested relying on the courts to protect the rights of the newly freed people. The only way the freed people could secure their rights was through the ballot. "[N]o citizen is safe without the right of suffrage."[52]

Courts reflected in constitutional law what the people demonstrated they believed about the Constitution through politics. "The penny papers of this State . . . did more to dictate the decision of Chief Justice Shaw" in another fugitive slave case "than the Legislature that sat in the State-House, or the statute-book of Massachusetts," Phillips said. "We live under a government of men." Massachusetts law made no racial qualification for sitting on juries, but no African American had yet been a juror. Why? Because the mayor and aldermen "have been such slaves of [popular] colorphobia" that they won't enforce the law.[53]

The problem was not only that the judges were enforcing a proslavery Constitution. It was that the people were in thrall to the Constitution as well. That was what so impressed and appalled Phillips about the Latimer case. When abolitionists called a meeting at Faneuil Hall to denounce the decision, dozens of rowdy anti-abolitionists filled the seats.[54] They shouted down the African American leader Charles L. Remond—"Down with the darkey! Sell the nigger!" they hooted—and they booed and hissed down abolitionist lawyer Edmund Quincy and Liberty Party leader Joshua Leavitt.

Phillips had the knack for quieting a crowd—he never tried to shout over them; he spoke in an ordinary voice, forcing them to cut down the din to hear whatever outrageous words they wanted to shout down. What he saw was that the crowd, no less than Justice Shaw, was committed to a Constitution that required them to do what they otherwise abhorred. "Many of you, I doubt not, regret to have this man given up, but you cannot help it," he said, because "there stands the bloody clause in the Constitution." He knew that thousands of other northerners felt the same way. As Henry Ward Beecher described the situation, "[F]idelity to the agreements that had been made in the formation of our Constitution . . . was regarded everywhere as a moral obligation by men that hated slavery."[55] This was the context in which Phillips uttered the shocking words that caused such an uproar. "When I look on those crowded thousands and see them trample on their consciences and on the rights of their fellow-men at the bidding of a piece of parchment, I say, my curse be on the Constitution of these United States!"[56] Americans had "no idea" of a higher law, he observed more than fifteen years later. For them, "absolute right means the truth diluted by a strong decoction of the Constitution of '89. They breathe that atmosphere; they do not want to sail outside of it; they do not attempt to reason outside of it."[57] For years, abolitionists would face mobs led by "gentlemen of property and standing" who claimed to be defending the Constitution against those who traduced it and put the Union at risk.[58]

Abolitionist colleagues like Samuel J. May said that the Constitution would be proslavery or antislavery no matter what the Framers intended, "whichever the people pleased to make it."[59] Young Thomas Wentworth Higginson echoed the thought. The Constitution's language provides opportunities for antislavery constructions. "I do not care where the loophole is found. . . . I do not care how small it is; give us a Supreme Court that is favorable to liberty and the Constitution is an anti-slavery document to-morrow. . . . Give us the power, and we can make a new Constitution, or we can re-interpret the old one."[60]

But Phillips and Garrison denied that the Constitution was so malleable. "I think the nation knows what it says, and understands what it says," Garrison replied to Higginson.[61] Phillips was what legal scholars nowadays call an "originalist." If a text admits only one meaning, one must follow it, he insisted. If it admits two meanings, one must discover which of the two the legislators intended, looking at both their words and the context of the time. He argued that the Constitution was in a sense a contract among the people of the

United States, and like all contracts must be enforced with the meaning that the parties intended. And finally, uninterrupted practice carried great weight in confirming an original understanding. In sum, "[T]he understanding of the nation at the time, uniform practice since, and uninterrupted acquiescence by all parties, form one of the most obvious methods of determining with irresistible clearness the meaning of the Constitution."[62]

The Supreme Court had the final, authoritative say on what the Constitution meant, Phillips had insisted, but that did not mean it could interpret it any way it wished. Others have the power to make the laws, he explained. The judiciary has power "only to *construe* and *apply* them."[63] He had proven that Americans had understood that key provisions of the Constitution were proslavery in his *The Constitution a Pro-Slavery Compact*. People, politicians, judges together had maintained that understanding for fifty years and more. Judges could not simply ignore those precedents. The Supreme Court's decision in the Dred Scott case only reconfirmed them. "It is . . . dreadful," he agreed. "It must make you willing to go behind a parchment and say what is justice."[64] The only way to abolish slavery was to abolish the Constitution itself. And the only way to do that was for northerners, beginning with Massachusetts, to break free of the Union.

Other, deeply committed opponents of slavery would not go that far. Every constitution sanctions injustice and wrong, his friend Massachusetts Senator Charles Sumner wrote him. Does that mean I must repudiate my citizenship? he asked. "Shall I not rather . . . by speech, by the pen, by *my vote*, endeavor to procure an alteration of the Constitution, to expurgate the offensive passages?"[65] Phillips insisted that patiently working to amend the Constitution was unacceptable. "[I]mmediate ceasing to do evil is our rule. Dissolution of the Union is a course, by which a man or State may immediately disconnect themselves from the sin of sustaining slavery." Amending the Constitution to abolish slavery was impossible for the foreseeable future. It would take a supermajority in Congress and the states. One might as well hope to cross a stream by waiting for it to run dry. The fool who did so was "wise, not to say . . . impatient . . . , compared with the abolitionist who should remain in the Union."[66] Dissolution of the Union, on the other hand, could be the work of a minority, as long as it was the majority in a single state like Massachusetts.

The clearest example of how the Constitution imposed the sin of slavery on northerners was the enforcement of the Fugitive Slave Act. Abolitionists consistently dramatized the inhumanity of sending African American residents of northern states into bondage without even a legal process to assure they were indeed runaways. They knew that the drama of the attempted rescue, the symbolism of the Boston courthouse surrounded by chains to prevent it, the sight of a squadron of United States soldiers marching the hapless victim through the city's streets, the mob's attempt to suppress criticism at Faneuil Hall, were more powerfully persuasive than dozens of lectures. Garrison burned both a copy of the Fugitive Slave Law and the Constitution that sustained it after local judges and U.S. soldiers sent Anthony Burns south into bondage. His action was clearer, more shocking, and more powerful than Phillips's most eloquent lectures.[67] South Carolina Representative Preston Brooks's assault on Sumner on the floor of the Senate illustrated the impossibility of maintaining the Union between the free North and the slave South more tellingly than anything Phillips could say. Phillips knew it full well. "The cause goes well," he wrote the broken senator. "[W]e thank God that he has given us such texts."[68]

Phillips urged disunion not only to free northerners of sin. "Apart from the desire to keep ourselves pure, . . . our only object is, the abolition of slavery," and dissolution of the Union would bring the abolition of slavery sooner than any agitation within it. By entering into the Union, each state "guarantees peace in the dominions of the other," he pointed out. The Constitution explicitly required the federal government to protect every state against domestic violence.[69] But peace in a slave state "means holding the oppressor's heel firmly on the neck of the slave. . . . This is what a free State actually does, when she links herself to a slaves sister [state]." That guarantee reassured slaveowners that they need not fear slave insurrection. Only the "strong arm" of the North had kept "the prison-door [of slavery] bolted for fifty years," Phillips claimed. "*Cut all loose!*" he exhorted northerners. "Let us not any longer hold back the storm, the very fear of which will, we know, make the trembling master grant his victim A PEACEFUL AND BLOODLESS EMANCIPATION."[70]

Despite Phillips's reassurances that emancipation would come peacefully, Phillips implied that slave violence might be required to shock southerners into abolition. Abolitionists "see nothing but disaster in slave risings," he insisted. But then he added, "How much of active interference the North . . . owes to the three millions, whose prison-door her strong arm alone has kept bolted for fifty years; how much it owes them . . . by way of atonement, we need not say."[71] "Disunion leaves God's natural laws to work their good results," he would say in 1861, as he urged northerners to let the South go. "Under God's law, insurrection is the tyrant's check. Let us stand out of the path, and allow the Divine law to have free course."[72] In another address, he affirmed "that I prefer an insurrection which frees the slave in ten years to slavery for a century. A slave I pity. A rebellious slave I respect."[73] It is no wonder that in the 1850s, Phillips, in the words of biographer James Brewer Stewart, "was trafficking with insurrectionary violence as heavily as he could." He did nothing to discourage friends who conspired with John Brown to precipitate the sort of slave insurrection he believed would frighten slaveowners into emancipation once disunion relieved northerners of the obligation to protect the South against it. For Phillips, the fact that Washington authorities ordered Col. Robert E. Lee and a force of U.S. Marines to capture Brown provided another text—illustrating his point about the Guarantee Clause as powerfully as any words he could muster. He spared no effort in rousing the North to see it as clearly as he did.[74]

In all this, Phillips and other antislavery agitators and politicians were engaging in constitutional politics. Antislavery politicians in the Liberty Party and the Republican Party strove for popular support to reinterpret the Constitution. Phillips and the Garrisonians were unusual in American history for seeking popular support to repudiate the Constitution and to dissolve the Union it created. But they all saw that public opinion lay at the root of constitutional arrangements. Phillips referred scornfully to the "parchment Constitution."[75] Sooner or later, abolitionists would awaken northerners to the travesty it made of liberty. "Institutions . . . are but pasteboard . . . against the thought of the street. Statutes are mere milestones, telling how far yesterday's thought had travelled; and the talk of the sidewalk to-day is the law of the land." You may frame laws as "strong as language can make, but once change public feeling, and through them or over them rides the real wish of the people."[76]

The Garrisonians never persuaded northerners to repudiate the Constitution and dissolve their ties with the Union. Instead it was the South that moved to secede after the election of Abraham Lincoln to the presidency. But it was all the same to Phillips. Preventing the North from saving the Union through another compromise with slavery would achieve the result for which he had been striving for almost twenty years. He urged New Englanders to take the lead and stand for "freedom for every man between the oceans, . . . Union or no Union, Constitution or no Constitution."[77]

Even as he tried to use the crisis to dissolve the North's connection to slavery, however, Phillips began to move toward the understanding that political abolitionists had espoused. He still thought that the Constitution was an artificial construction that had forced Americans "into an unripe union." Real constitutions grow naturally, like the British one, Phillips argued. But now he realized that Americans *had* reinterpreted the Constitution of 1787—that the Constitution was not necessarily the originalist straightjacket he had posited. Americans had already broken the shackles of the Constitution by interpreting its provisions to enable them to annex a continent, to build railroads and dredge out lakes, and protect manufactures. "Some lawyers got together and wrote out a constitution," he observed. "The people and great interests of the land, wealth, thought, fashion, and creed, immediately laid it upon the shelf, and proceeded to *grow* one for themselves." This process had been blocked only with regard to slavery. "[O]ur politicians and a knot of privileged slaveholders are trying to keep the people inside of this parchment band. . . . [T]hey would mould the people to fit the Constitution, instead of cutting the Constitution to fit the people."[78] Now the dam was about to burst.

Everything changed as it became clear that northerners would fight slaveholders rather than see the Union destroyed. "We abolitionists have doubted whether the Union really meant justice and liberty," he acknowledged. "We have doubted whether they could be achieved under the Constitution. Now the people are answering the doubts. They say, 'We believe that the Fathers meant to establish justice. We believe that there are hidden in the armory of the Constitution weapons strong enough to secure it.'"[79] Phillips did not retract his former disunionism. It *had* taken disunion to break northerners' commitment to the proslavery Constitution. Southerners foolishly had done what the Garrisonians could not. In effect, they had destroyed the old Constitution—that is, the old interpretation of the Constitution—and made it possible for Phillips and his sometime antislavery allies to argue for a new one. Within a few months he would be urging Congress to exercise its constitutional war powers to emancipate the slaves.[80]

Phillips had not thought it possible to fight for universal freedom and equality within the framework of the Constitution and the Union. Now he saw the contours of the new constitutional struggle that would absorb his energies during and after the war—to create the popular foundation for a Constitution that would do both. "We are willing yet to try the experiment," he said. "Give us time."[81]

NOTES

1. New York *Sun*, April 19, 1884, 2.

2. My use of "Mugwump" is slightly anachronistic here. The liberal reformers of Curtis's ilk would not gain the epithet "Mugwump" until they bolted the Republican Party to back Democratic presidential candidate Grover Cleveland a few months later.

3. George William Curtis, "Wendell Phillips: A Eulogy Delivered before the Municipal Authorities of Boston, Mass., April 18, 1884," in *Orations and Addresses of George William Curtis*, ed. Charles Eliot Norton, 3 vols. (New York: Harper & Brothers, 1894), vol. 3: 272–73.

4. Boston *Daily Bee*, [October 31, 1842], republished in *Liberator*, November 4, 1842, 174.

5. "The Conspiracy of Fanaticism," *United States Democratic Review* 26 (May 1850): 386.

6. Lorenzo Sears, *Wendell Phillips, Orator and Agitator* (New York: Doubleday, Page & Co., 1909), 102, 108, 128–29.

7. *Exercises at the Dedication of the Statue of Wendell Phillips, July 5, 1915* (Boston: City of Boston Printing Department, 1915).

8. William M. Wiecek, *The Sources of Antislavery Constitutionalism in America, 1760–1848* (Ithaca, N.Y.: Cornell University Press, 1977), 128–48; Aileen S. Kraditor, *Means and Ends in American Abolitionism: Garrison and His Critics on Strategy and Tactics, 1834–1850* (New York: Pantheon Books, 1969), 196–217; Louis S. Gerteis, *Morality and Utility in American Antislavery Reform* (Chapel Hill: University of North Carolina Press, 1987), 43–61.

9. Louis Filler, *Crusade against Slavery: Friends, Foes, and Reforms, 1820–1860* (Alogonac, Mich.: Reference Publications, 1986), 135–71 and passim; James Brewer Stewart, *Wendell Phillips: Liberty's Hero* (Baton Rouge: Louisiana State University Press, 1986), 117–20.

10. Sears, *Wendell Phillips*, 118, 191–93; Merton Dillon, *The Abolitionists: The Growth of a Dissenting Minority* (DeKalb: Northern Illinois University Press, 1974), 124; Gerteis, *Morality and Utility in American Antislavery Reform*, 43–61.

11. William M. Wiecek, "Latimer: Lawyers, Abolitionists, and the Problem of Unjust Laws," in *Antislavery Reconsidered: New Perspectives on the Abolitionists*, ed. Lewis Perry and Michael Fellman (Baton Rouge: Louisiana State University Press, 1979), 219–37.

12. Kraditor, *Means and Ends in American Abolitionism*, 207. See also Wiecek, *Sources of Antislavery Constitutionalism*, 228–32.

13. Phillips, *Can Abolitionists Vote or Take Office under the United States Constitution?* (New York: American Anti-Slavery Society, 1845), 3.

14. Phillips, "Dissolution of the Union," in *Liberator*, January 14, 1848, 7.

15. Kraditor, *Means and Ends in American Abolitionism*, 206.

16. Phillips, quoted in *Liberator*, Mar. 22. 1861, 47 (report of an address at New Haven, Conn., March 14, 1861).

17. Phillips, "Disunion," lecture delivered in Boston Music Hall, January 20, 1861, in *Speeches, Lectures, and Letters, First Series* (Boston: Lee and Shepard, 1894), 354.

18. *Brown v. Board of Education of Topeka*, 347 U.S. 483 (1954). For the Supreme Court's central role in the expansion of civil rights and liberties in the decades following *Brown*, see John E. Semonche, *Keeping the Faith: A Cultural History of the U.S. Supreme Court* (Lanham, Md.: Rowland

& Littlefield, 1998), 262–398; Melvyn I. Urofsky, *The Continuity of Change: The Supreme Court and Individual Liberties, 1953–1986* (Belmont, Calif.: Wadsworth Publishing Co., 1989).

19. Only recently, as constitutional scholars have begun to challenge judicial supremacy, have they begun to recover the crucial role the people of the United States play in setting constitutional policy. See, for example, Bruce Ackerman, *We the People*, 2 vols. (Cambridge: Harvard University Press, 1991–98); Michael Les Benedict, "'The People Themselves': The Constitutional Responsibilities of the American People," *Doshisha American Studies* 43 (March 2007): 1–19; Larry D. Kramer, *The People Themselves: Popular Constitutionalism and Judicial Review* (New York: Oxford University Press, 2004); Wayne D. Moore, "Toward Constitutional Citizenship: Unofficial Commitments," in Moore, *Constitutional Rights and Powers of the People* (Princeton: Princeton University Press, 1996), 37–65; Mark Tushnet, *Why the Constitution Matters* (New Haven: Yale University Press, 2010); Keith E. Whittington, *Constitutional Construction: Divided Powers and Constitutional Meaning* (Cambridge: Harvard University Press, 1999).

20. *National Party Platforms, 1840–1872*, 5th ed., ed. Donald Bruce Johnson and Kirk H. Porter (Urbana: University of Illinois Press, 1975), 3. For constitutional issues and the organization of the Jacksonian Democratic party, see Gerald Leonard, "Party as a 'Political Safeguard of Federalism': Martin Van Buren and the Constitutional Theory of Party Politics," *Rutgers Law Review* 54 (Fall 2001): 221–81.

21. *McCulloch v. Maryland*, 17 U.S. (4 Wheaton) 316 (1819); *Gibbons v. Ogden*, 22 U.S. (9 Wheaton) 1 (1824); *Dartmouth College v. Woodward*, 17 U.S. (4 Wheaton) 518 (1819); *Charles River Bridge Co. v. Warren Bridge Co.*, 36 U.S. (11 Peters) 420 (1837); *Prigg v. Pennsylvania*, 41 U.S. (16 Peters) 539 (1842).

22. For the relationship between Supreme Court decisions and contemporaneous constitutional politics, see Michael Les Benedict, *Political Parties and the Constitution* (Washington, D.C.: American Historical Association, 2015); Mark A. Graber, "Federalist or Friends of Adams: The Marshall Court and Party Politics," *Studies in American Development* 12 (Fall 1998): 229–66; Leonard, '"Party as a 'Political Safeguard of Federalism'"; Gerard N. Magliocca, *Andrew Jackson and the Constitution: The Rise and Fall of Generational Regimes* (Lawrence: University Press of Kansas, 2007). On the Supreme Court's failed effort to prevent Georgia from gaining control of the lands that federal treaties reserved to the Cherokee Nation, see Tim Alan Garrison, *The Legal Ideology of Removal: The Southern Judiciary and the Sovereignty of Native American Nations* (Athens: University of Georgia Press, 2002); Jill Norgren, *The Cherokee Cases: Two Landmark Federal Decisions in the Fight for Sovereignty* (Norman: University of Oklahoma Press, 1996).

23. For the continued salience of the idea that the people could exercise sovereignty outside of legal forms, see Christian Fritz, *American Sovereigns: The People and America's Constitutional Tradition before the Civil War* (New York: Cambridge University Press, 2008). On mobs, see David Grimsted, *American Mobbing, 1828–1861: Toward Civil War* (New York: Oxford University Press, 1998); Leonard L. Richards, *Gentlemen of Property and Standing: Anti-Abolition Mobs in Jacksonian America* (New York: Oxford University Press, 1970); Beverly Tomek, "To Preserve the Integrity of the Union: The 1838 Anti-Abolition Mobbing of Pennsylvania Hall," presented to the Canadian Association for American Studies, Toronto, Fall 2012.

24. Wendell Phillips, "The Murder of Lovejoy," in *Speeches, Lectures, and Letters, First Series,*

2, 6. Austin's speech, an account of the meeting, and another account of Phillips's speech are in *Liberator*, December 15, 1837, 202–3.

25. See Wiecek, "Latimer."

26. Carlos Martyn, *Wendell Phillips: The Agitator* (New York: Funk & Wagnalls, 1890), 165.

27. The classic study is Robert M. Cover, *Justice Accused: Antislavery and the Judicial Process* (New Haven: Yale University Press, 1975). The notion that judges don "the masks of the law," was stated most powerfully and influentially in John T. Noonan, *Persons and Masks of the Law: Cardozo, Holmes, Jefferson, and Wythe as Makers of the Masks* (New York: Farrar, Straus and Giroux, 1976).

28. Phillips, *The Constitution a Pro-Slavery Compact; or, Extracts from the Madison Papers, Etc.*, 3d. ed. (New York: American Anti-Slavery Society, 1856), 5, 7. The first edition was published in 1844.

29. Sears, *Wendell Phillips*, 142.

30. For the standard and best account, see Wiecek, *Sources of Antislavery Constitutionalism in America.*

31. Phillips, *Review of Lysander Spooner's Essay on the Unconstitutionality of Slavery, Reprinted from the "Anti-Slavery Standard," with Additions* (Boston: Andrews & Prentiss, 1847), 9–10, 23.

32. Phillips, *Can Abolitionists Vote?* 10, 15.

33. Ibid., 19.

34. Ibid., 17.

35. Phillips, *Review of Lysander Spooner's Essay*, 26.

36. Phillips to Frederick Douglass, April 22, 1845, in Douglass, *Narrative of the Life of Frederick Douglass, an American Slave* (Dublin: Webb and Chapman, 1845), xvi.

37. Phillips, *Review of Lysander Spooner's Essay*, 5–6, 5.

38. Horace Mann, "Reply of Hon. Horace Mann to Wendell Phillips, Esq. [April 4, 1853]," in *Liberator*, April 8, 1853, 54.

39. Chase to ?, January 5, 1851; Chase to John P. Hale, May 12, 1847, Salmon P. Chase Papers, Manuscripts Division, Library of Congress.

40. James M. Ashley, "Closing Portion of a Stump Speech Delivered in the Grove near Montpelier, Williams County, Ohio, September, 1856," in *Duplicate Copy of the Souvenir from the Afro-American League of Tennessee to Hon. James M. Ashley of Ohio* (Philadelphia: Publishing House of the A.M.E. Church, 1894), 615.

41. Leonard, "'Party as a 'Political Safeguard of Federalism'"; Magliocca, *Andrew Jackson and the Constitution.*

42. *Congressional Globe*, 27 Cong., 1 Sess., Appendix, 157 (July 7, 1841).

43. Andrew Jackson, "Removal of the Public Deposits," September 18, 1833, in *A Compilation of the Messages and Papers of the Presidents, 1789–1897*, ed. James D. Richardson (New York: Bureau of National Literature, 1897), vol. 3: 1226.

44. Martin Van Buren, *Inquiry into the Origin and Course of Political Parties in the United States, Edited by His Sons* (New York: Hurd and Houghton, 1867), 328–52 (quotations at 333 and 335).

45. Andrew Jackson, "Proclamation to the People of South Carolina," December 10, 1832, in *Compilation of the Messages and Papers of the Presidents* 3: 1203–19, at 1205. He added that another alternative was to appeal to "the people and the States," meaning the amending process.

46. James Buchanan, "Inaugural Address," March 4, 1857, in *Compilation of the Messages and Papers of the Presidents* 7: 2962.

47. Don E. Fehrenbacher, *The Dred Scott Case: Its Significance in American Law and Politics* (New York: Oxford University Press, 1978), 417–48.

48. Pittsburgh *Gazette*, March 7, 1857, 2.

49. "Republican Party Platform of 1860," plank 8, in *National Party Platforms*, ed. Johnson and Porter, 32. ("That, as our Republican fathers . . . ordained that 'no person should be deprived of life, liberty or property without due process of law,' it becomes our duty, by legislation, . . . to maintain this provision of the Constitution against all attempt to violate it; and we deny the authority of Congress, of a territorial legislature, or of any individuals, to give legal existence to slavery in any territory of the United States.")

50. Quoted in Martyn, *Wendell Phillips*, 287.

51. Phillips, "Harper's Ferry," in *Speeches, Lectures, and Letters, First Series*, 265.

52. Phillips in the *National Antislavery Standard*, June 6, 1868, 1.

53. Phillips, "Public Opinion," in *Speeches, Lectures, and Letters, First Series*, 41, 47.

54. For the tumultuous Latimer case protest meeting at Faneuil Hall, see Stewart, *Wendell Phillips*, 120–21.

55. Henry Ward Beecher, *Wendell Phillips, A Commemorative Discourse* (New York: Howard and Hulbert, 1884), 418–19.

56. Phillips, "Speech at Faneuil Hall," Oct. 30, 1842, reported in *Liberator*, November 11, 1842, 178.

57. Phillips, "Harper's Ferry," 265.

58. Lorman Ratner, *Powder Keg: Northern Opposition to the Antislavery Movement, 1831–1840* (New York: Basic Books, 1968), 51–64.

59. Samuel. J. May, quoted in Dillon, *The Abolitionists*, 133.

60. Higginson, in *Liberator*, May 22, 1857, 81.

61. Garrison, in *Liberator*, May 22, 1857, 82.

62. Phillips, *Review of Lysander Spooner's Essay*, 28–31 (quoted at 31).

63. Ibid., 10.

64. Phillips speaking at the American Anti-Slavery Society Convention, May 12, 1857, in *Liberator*, May 22, 1857, 82.

65. Charles Sumner to Phillips, February 4, 1845, in *The Selected Letters of Charles Sumner*, ed. Beverly Wilson Palmer, 2 vols. (Boston: Northeastern University Press, 1990), vol. 1: 144.

66. Phillips, "Dissolution of the Union," 7.

67. Donald Yacovone, "A Covenant with Death and an Agreement with Hell," Object of the Month, Massachusetts Historical Society, July 2005, www.masshist.org/objects/2005july.cfm (consulted Nov. 1, 2012).

68. Phillips to Sumner, Aug. 18, 1856, quoted in Irving H. Bartlett, *Wendell Phillips: Brahmin Radical* (Boston: Beacon, 1961), 201–2.

69. U.S. Constitution, Article 4, Section 4.

70. Phillips, "Dissolution of the Union," 7. Emphasis in original.

71. Ibid., 7.

72. Phillips, "Disunion," 362.

73. Phillips, "Progress," in *Speeches, Lectures, and Letters, First Series*, 383.

74. Stewart, *Wendell Phillips*, 200–207 (quotation at 200).

75. Phillips, "Public Opinion," 41.

76. Phillips, "Harper's Ferry," 264–65.

77. Phillips, "Disunion," 354.

78. Phillips, "Progress," 375–76.

79. Phillips, "Under the Flag," in *Speeches, Lectures, and Letters, First Series*, 407–8.

80. Phillips, "The War for the Union," in *Speeches, Lectures, and Letters, First Series*, 435–39.

81. Phillips, "Under the Flag," 408.

7

WENDELL PHILLIPS AND TRANSATLANTIC RADICALISM

Democracy, Capitalism, and the American Labor Movement

PETER WIRZBICKI

Wendell Phillips's political life had been dedicated to the end of slavery. And in 1863, he told a New York audience that emancipation in the South seemed finally in sight. However reluctant, the nation was on the path to freedom and inching closer to real democracy and equal rights. However, he warned that the governments of France or England might jeopardize progress by recognizing the South, turning the conflict from a civil war into a global conflict. And, if the aristocrats of Europe intervened in American affairs on behalf of the southern planters, he warned, the North would be forced to intervene in European affairs on behalf of the European working class, the North's natural ally. "Let us say to Europe," Phillips thundered, "'We are trying the experiment of a popular Government; put but a finger into our machinery, and we extend a right hand to Garibaldi with ten millions, and he uproots Rome; we give fifty to the Chartists, fifty to the Poles, fifty to the Red Republicans of France, and joy to you of your thrones.'"[1]

This gesture of solidarity between a New England Brahmin and the European revolutionary left, along with the broader way in which Phillips saw his abolitionism as naturally affinitive with European working-class and democratic movements, helps shape our understanding of the ideological imaginations of American abolitionists. For years historians have debated the relationship between the antislavery movement and the larger development of industrial capitalism. Especially fraught has been the question of the attitude of the early labor movement toward abolitionism. On one spectrum are historians who emphasize the overlap between the antislavery impulse and the labor and land reformers.[2] Probably more prominent today are historical narratives that emphasize the ways that the abolitionists had an uncomfortable and often hostile relationship with the American labor movement, and operated within the ideological space of free labor. By celebrating the liberty of the northern wage laborer, this historical narrative says, abolitionists, wittingly or unwittingly, defined freedom as self-possession and the ability to sell your own labor in the marketplace.[3] Phillips's affinity with the European Left suggests that the ideological gaps between American abolitionism and labor activism have been exaggerated.

One gap in this debate has revolved around the tendency of scholars to treat this ideological debate as one revolving purely around economic doctrines, missing the significant degree to which both labor and abolitionist reformers could come to agreement on questions of political rights, especially in regard to their shared vision of democracy. Recently historians have begun to consider abolitionists as crucial democratic theorists, participants in broad and transnational conversations about the meaning of democracy.[4] Few abolitionists thought as hard about questions of democracy as Wendell Phillips. For Phillips, the fight to protect democracy linked his antebellum crusade to end slavery with his postwar interest in labor reform. Inspired by transatlantic reformers and radicals, he saw both slavery and unfettered capitalism as threats to democratic self-rule, and he saw the empowerment of politically marginalized groups—slaves, workers, freedpeople, and women—as the solution to a corrupt democracy. Phillips was not a "provincial patriot," as Richard Hofstadter called him, but rather was deeply engaged in an Atlantic conversation about democracy and civil liberties.[5] Understanding Phillips in the context of transatlantic discourses of radical democracy, working-class empowerment, and hostility to entrenched privilege will further our understanding of abolitionist attitudes toward the marketplace. More than anything else, it was the preservation of a fragile democracy—a democracy that implied a radical challenge to entrenched economic and political interests—that linked Phillips's many political interests, especially abolitionism and labor reform.

THE EVOLUTION OF WENDELL PHILLIPS

Wendell Phillips first began to think seriously about issues of class inequality during a trip to Europe in 1841. He wasn't yet thirty, and had only recently been converted to abolitionism, when he toured the continent with his wife, Ann. Phillips, unlike many American tourists at the time, did not view Europe as simply a place to reaffirm American superiority. In Italy, the descendent of Puritan leaders began to appreciate the Catholic Church, where he saw black priests treated as equals, and admired the egalitarianism of a "democratic method of Catholic worship," so unlike the pews separated by race and class back in Boston.[6] But if he admired the racial egalitarianism of Europe, Phillips was horrified by the economic inequality he saw all around him. In a letter to William Lloyd Garrison he marveled at the "wealth beyond that of fairy tales, and poverty all bare and starved at its side" that he saw in Italy. Phillips became more radical in Europe, as his face-to-face encounter with economic inequality convinced him of the threat that accumulated wealth posed to a republican society.[7]

Out of his experience in Europe, Phillips developed two major tropes that would inform his future activism. The first was the image of Europe as a dystopian threat, what America could become if democratic rights were eroded and the power of unaccountable elites was allowed to grow. Throughout his career, he returned to the image of a Europe marked by "accumulated wealth, hungry churches, and old nobles" as an antithesis of the American ideal he valued.[8] The second trope compared the European left, especially as manifested in popular movements like the Chartists and later the revolutionaries of 1848 with the American abolitionist movement, both of which he saw as fighting undemocratic elites. In Europe, then, were two possible futures for America—one unequal, corrupt, aristocratic; another democratic, egalitarian, and progressive.

Many of Phillips's colleagues had similar reactions when they toured Europe. Theodore Parker, the radical antislavery activist and transcendentalist theologian, became increasingly politicized after seeing the poverty, political repression, and inequality of Germany and Italy.[9] Henry I. Bowditch, the future abolitionist and medical pioneer, wrote to his mother from France that his times in the republican crowds of Paris had made him "far more liberal now than . . . before visiting Europe."[10] The Boston reformer most associated with European revolutions was Samuel G. Howe, who spent five years fighting for Greek independence in the 1820s alongside Lord Byron. On a second trip to Europe, he participated in the July 1830 Revolution in Paris. In the early 1850s, Howe even lobbied for American entry into Europe in order to defend the 1848 revolutions, suggesting that America might have to threaten war against European reactionaries because "the intense desire of the bourgeois class all over Europe for *peaceful* pursuit of *business*, let who may govern," was leading to despotism on the Continent.[11] Although black abolitionists rarely had the luxury of European vacations, those that did travel to Europe often found themselves in the company of radicals. William Wells Brown dined with Louis Blanc, the controversial French architect of the socialized national workshops, and many black abolitionists, including Frederick Douglass and Henry Highland Garnet, worked closely with British working-class radicals.[12]

Since abolitionists most often visited Great Britain, they were especially likely to come into contact with the British Chartists. The primary demand of their famous Charter was universal manhood suffrage, but they were widely perceived as seeking to empower the working class economically, as well as politically. The poverty William Lloyd Garrison saw in England outraged him and drew him to the "moral force" wing of the Chartists. He declared that he supported the workers' "labour to effect redemption for themselves."[13] And in the late 1830s key segments of the British working class and the antislavery middle class had converged on a number of shared demands, including expanded suffrage and support for American abolitionism.[14] As William Wells Brown noted when he toured England, there was a direct link between democratic politics and antislavery; abolitionism in Great Britain, he told an American audience, "proceeds, for the most part, from that portion of the British people who admire republicanism, and wish for its propagation."[15] As the example of Wells suggests, black abolitionists seemed to have been particularly interested in the working-class movement, with Frederick Douglass proudly calling himself a Chartist, and Henry Highland Garnet pledging to unify the causes of slaves and white workers.[16] Douglass was instrumental in the formation of the Anti-Slavery League, a British abolitionist organization that explicitly hoped to combine the forces of the working-class Chartists with abolitionists.[17] The Chartists, it should be pointed out, divided between a radical "physical force" wing, which counted Karl Marx among its advocates, and a more moderate "moral force" wing, which American abolitionists tended to support.[18]

Like Garrison and Douglass, when Phillips visited England, he made lifelong connections to the world of British radicalism. Most notably, he befriended Daniel O'Connell, the Irish patriot who had helped to draw up the Charter and who inspired in Phillips a lifelong dedication to the cause of Irish freedom. For the next twenty years, Phillips would make admirable, if quixotic, attempts to convert the Boston Irish community to abolitionism. Other British abolitionists whom Phillips spent time with, like George Thompson and Elizabeth Pease, also would soon advocate the Charter. John Cluer, a British emigrant, who would later become active as an American abolitionist, remembered that "Mr. Phillips [w]as a genuine Democrat. . . . [W]hen Mr. P[hillips] was in England, instead of seeking introductions to the aristocracy, he periled his popularity by finding his way into a loft among the Chartists, and spoke with them and sympathized with them."[19]

Back home in New England, Phillips drew on European themes as fodder for two of his most popular lectures. "Street Life in Europe" dealt mostly in humorous anecdotes and stock images of national traits. "Chartism," on the other hand, was much more serious and explicitly political, clearly in support of the British working-class rebellion. Although strangely forgotten by most historians and biographers, "Chartism" became one of Phillips's most popular lectures, an audience pleaser like his famous lecture on ancient technology, "The Lost Arts." Observers noted that his lecture on Chartism proved far more appealing to abolitionists and other radicals than to the rich. A correspondent to the *Liberator* reported that, when Phillips gave the lecture in Providence, Rhode Island, the "aristocracy" remained unmoved, but he received a warm welcome from "a few of us despised abolitionists, peace men, etc."[20] Phillips's lecture "Chartism" marks an important development in his thought, as he began seriously to consider European democratic movements and implicitly comparing these European radicals to American abolitionists.

Phillips's lecture broadly supported the cause of the Chartists, although he registered some reservations about their socialism and religious heterodoxy. He understood that most Americans—at least among his audience in Whiggish New England—would be skeptical of the Chartists. "At the mention of [the Chartists'] name almost every American lip curls in scorn," Phillips acknowledged. And so Phillips protested his distaste at the "infidelity and licentious doctrines of the socialists," with whom he saw the Chartists were allied "by necessity for they have no other allies." But if the Chartists struck Americans as unorthodox, Phillips reminded his audiences that "the martyrs and heretics of one age are sure to be the Saints of the succeeding." Savvy listeners, of course, would hear in Phillips's language an apology for himself and his abolitionist brethren, likewise tarred as irreligious and politically radical.

Unlike both radical and reactionary critics of the British industrial system, Phillips did not make a voyeuristic spectacle of the British poor. In fact, Phillips only briefly mentioned the material conditions of the British poor: the British working class was "in poverty to the very life," he acknowledged. Instead, he focused on their political oppression, describing them as equally scorned by a nervous middle class and a blindly opulent upper class. A British worker was "almost a pauper battling against the injustice of an aristocracy upon whose employment or mercy he depends for the very means of subsistence."[21] Characteristically, he focused on what he saw as the moral and political consequences of the Chartist rebellion.

Phillips, in other words, sympathized most with those demands of the Chartists rooted in democratic rights and civil liberties. Although a working-class movement, the Chartists primarily were concerned with basic democratic rights, like universal manhood suffrage. In this, the British Left wasn't alone; throughout Europe workers were struggling for basic political rights. Manhood suffrage was, after all, the second demand of Marx's German Communist Party, and Marx, of course, advocated that the working class unite with the bourgeoisie to win political democracy where it had not yet been achieved.[22] Phillips was drawn more to "the perseverance with which they insist on the ballot" and their demand for civil rights.[23] Phillips would later argue that while agitation in England had begun over localized economic issues—which manifested itself in the fight to repeal the Corn Laws and thus reduce the price of bread—reformers had realized that "the cause of the evil is in selfish legislation," and thus had switched tactics to push for universal suffrage.[24] Phillips's relative disinterest in the material dimensions of poverty, and his obsession with political rights, was the exact opposite of the position of southern reactionaries, whose pious fixation on the poverty and degradation of the British industrial poor went hand in hand with a contempt for "free society," democratic equality, and the "mudsill" class.

The years immediately following Phillips's return from Europe were some of the most important to the development of a class-conscious abolitionist movement. The New England labor movement, slowly regaining membership and political initiative after the long economic slump started in 1837, took the lead in reaching out to abolitionists. In June 1845, for instance, the New England Workingmen's Association named Phillips and William Lloyd Garrison to represent labor reformers at a national convention in New York.[25] The *Voice of Industry*, a labor paper published by a cooperative of workers, reported favorably on abolitionist activity. In 1845, for instance, they proudly noted that the line of mill girls in Lowell who signed an antislavery petition was "more than a mile" long.[26] Meanwhile, throughout the 1840s, abolitionists made a concerted effort to appeal to workers. Even William Lloyd Garrison, generally the abolitionist who was least likely to appeal to class tensions, began bemoaning the "merciless employers and sordid monopolists, who are endeavoring to coin money out of the very life-blood of the people."[27] In 1848, Garrison even advocated a law limiting the workweek, "for the protection of labor, that capital may not work up human bodies into profits and dividends."[28]

In the broader New England reform movement, of which Phillips by now was a leader, socialism was taking its place alongside abolition, peace, and women's rights in what abolitionists sometimes called the "sisterhood" of reforms.[29] The same mix of transcendentalist-inspired utopianism, democratic upheaval, and religious questioning that was feeding abolitionism contributed to the creation of a series of utopian communes throughout New England. A number of these, such as A. Bronson Alcott's Fruitlands and the Northampton Association had close ties to abolitionism. The Northampton Association had black members, including, for a time, Sojourner Truth and David Ruggles. Late in his life, Frederick Douglass would remember these utopian socialists fondly. "The men and women who were interested in the work of revolutionizing the whole system of civilization," Douglass wrote about the Northampton commune, "were also deeply interested in the emancipation of the slaves."[30] There was a certain naïveté to many of these utopian communes; Marx's description of schemes like these as "cookshops of the future" and "castles in the air" was not inaccurate.[31]

But even the traits that demonstrated their theoretical weakness—their attempt through sheer moral force of will to transcend the racism and class exploitation of New England society—bespoke the creativity and egalitarian enthusiasm of the moral imagination of New England reformers. Moreover many abolitionists wedded this romantic impulse to more practical solutions for helping the working class. Samuel J. May, a close associate of Garrison, was both a supporter of a number of these romantic socialist organizations, and an advocate of labor rights whose more pragmatic proposals in the 1850s for a confiscatory progressive income tax predicted later social democratic reforms.[32]

As much as Phillips came to appreciate socialism, he also feared that the impulse toward "universal reform"—which inspired activists to move into causes as diverse as vegetarianism, peace movements, and water cures—ran the risk of losing sight of the especially evil nature of slavery. In 1846, Phillips helped to start a debate in the pages of the *Liberator* over the meaning of wage labor, one that helps to clarify how he saw the relationship between class and democracy in the 1840s. Phillips defended Garrison from the charge of George Evans, the prominent land reformer, that abolitionists ignored wage oppression at the expense of chattel slavery. Along with the famous editorial from Garrison's first issue of the *Liberator*, these articles are some of the most often cited pieces of evidence of abolitionist hostility to the labor movement, cited by Eric Foner and Aileen Kraditor, among others.[33]

But a more sympathetic reading of this debate, especially Phillips's role in it, reveals far more closeness between the abolitionists and labor reformers than historical narratives sometimes portray. Phillips's original letter, which set the debate off, was an attack on Evans not because Evans disapproved of wage labor, but for his narrowness in focusing *only* on wage labor as an evil and "sacrificing the rights of one race in the vain hope of more easily securing those of another." In fact Phillips admitted his own sympathy with Evans's land reform goals and declared himself in favor of an ecumenical reform community. "No one ever did much for one reform," Phillips wrote, "who had not a generous sympathy for all."[34] Edmund Quincy, who at this point was closely identified with Phillips's ideological position, agreed, writing in the same issue that abolitionists fought for the slave "not because they are ignorant or careless of the suffering of their own poor at home; but because they see in him the representative of insulted and down-trodden labor everywhere. . . . [I]t is a far reaching philanthropy, not a narrow minded sentimentality."[35] In general the tone was frustrated but friendly, a far cry from the vicious polemics that the *Liberator* was known to hurl at its true ideological enemies.

The most antilabor statement that Phillips ever made came a year later, in 1847, when he clarified his position on wage labor. His argument centered on two ideas. Northern workmen, Phillips began, were not economically oppressed like European workers, and thus deserved less attention from reformers. Here, Phillips betrayed a bit of willed blindness to the conditions of American workers, a myopia that he would soon lose. Second, if American workers ever became so degraded, Phillips claimed, they could "use their own *acknowledged* rights," to defend themselves politically. Phillips, then, justified his distance from the workers' movement on the grounds that they already had democratic privileges, which in 1847 he assumed would guarantee them justice. In a well-functioning democracy, Phillips believed, economic injustice could not last long.

Historians have often made much of moments such as this, when abolitionists like Phillips resisted comparing the plight of white workers to that of black slaves (as did some spokesmen for the white working class). But maintaining conceptual clarity (the oppression of black slaves was different both in form and extent from that of white workers) is not the same as apologizing for an injustice. Before the Civil War, Phillips consistently held that black slavery was the preeminent evil in American society, a form of injustice that required the greatest attention. But dedication to the cause of abolitionism need not imply hostility to the cause of the northern working class. Even Karl Marx had believed that American laborers would never emancipate themselves as long as slavery endured. And if Phillips sometimes minimized the suffering of white workers vis-à-vis the enslaved, he never expressed hostility to the cause of northern labor. He simply wanted to remind his audience of the moral precedence that the abolitionist struggle commanded. Thus, before 1865, many of the conflicts between abolitionists and labor spokesmen emerged over emphasis and priority; abolitionists thought slavery more important and demanded greater attention, while labor and land reformers thought similarly about class issues. But the very fact that each expected the other to be a natural ally illustrates that the two groups actually shared the same ideological terrain.[36]

To a large degree, it would be European examples that provided Phillips and others with a model of behavior and an ideology that could combine working-class issues with antislavery rhetoric. In 1848, revolutionary upheaval threatened nearly every European monarchy, spreading from France all over continental Europe. Amos Bronson Alcott, the quirky transcendentalist, told a British correspondent that the "French affair now absorbs every thing American . . . and invigorates and emboldens" all reformers.[37] The French Revolution, in particular, brought about two revolutionary measures that proved controversial in America—the move to declare the revolution a "social" one, with the "right to work" enshrined in the national workshops of Paris, and the decree which immediately ended slavery in the French colonies.[38] From the start, many Americans cast a skeptical eye upon these aspects of the European revolutions. The conservative Boston *Daily Advertiser* fretted that free slaves in Martinique were burning plantations under the slogan "Liberté, Égalité, Fraternité" while the official organ of the national Whig Party, the *National*

Intelligencer, wrote that the emancipation of the slaves in the West Indies would lead to "the bloodiest scenes" in the French colonies and, worse, inspire the "gravest disorders" in the American South.[39] It was not lost on abolitionists that the most prominent American to be wary of the French Revolution was none other than John C. Calhoun, who declared that both abolitionism and the unrest in Europe sprang from the same "fatal error": that "all men are born free and equal."[40]

The Boston abolitionist community, on the other hand, celebrated the revolutions wholeheartedly.[41] The reform community held numerous triumphant meetings, many of which directly celebrated the social aspects of the revolution. At a Liberty Party meeting, for instance, speakers gloried in the French republicans' attempt to reconcile "the right of *property* with the still more sacred right to *live*." They even went so far as to resolve that "we cannot deny the right of those who will work, to the means of living."[42] Phillips himself, while not a member of the Liberty Party, continued to evoke the 1848 French Revolution as a positive development long after many Americans became nervous at its radicalism. In 1851, he referenced French boldness in giving the lower classes the right to vote as an example that Americans should heed in extending suffrage to women. The next year he described the European revolutions as evidence of how popular opinion could change even undemocratic regimes, and, during the Civil War, used the 1848 French Revolution to remind audiences that popular upheavals and the emancipation of slaves almost always go hand in hand.[43] He even compared his own activities to those of European revolutionaries. In 1851, as he joined other radicals plotting to free fugitive slaves in Boston, he wrote to Elizabeth Pease about the secret conspiracies, complete with guards at the doors, and elaborate maneuvering to protect those who were breaking the law, comparing their activity to "foreign scenes, which have been known to us, transatlantic republicans, only in books."[44]

By the early 1850s, Phillips had developed a remarkably cosmopolitan view of antislavery reform. When welcoming George Thompson, the British reformer, he gave a rousing defense of his international outlook—clearly linking it to a left-wing and anti-imperialist agenda. "The cause of tyrants is one the world over," Phillips thundered, and so "whoever, any where . . . holds out his hand to the oppressed, that man helps the slave." Thanking Thompson for his opposition to British imperialism in India and Ireland, as well as his support "for bread and the ballot" at home, Phillips linked all of these values to support for American abolitionism. For Phillips, "German patriots," Irish nationalists, American slaves, the "starving Hindoo," and British workers all constituted the core of an obvious transatlantic solidarity of the oppressed.[45]

THE BOSTON ABOLITIONIST COMMUNITY

The Boston abolitionist community that Phillips helped lead had become a fascinating and diverse mix of antislavery radicals and labor activists. Phillips would have had repeated interactions with a number of these class-conscious abolitionists. For example, John Cluer was a British worker and Chartist activist who emigrated to New England in the late 1840s. Cluer immediately jumped into reform struggles, agitating on behalf of the ten-hour workday at the same time that he was a member of various abolitionist organizations.[46] Elizur Wright was a former Liberty Party leader who worked to connect working-class struggles to the antislavery fight. In his newspapers, the *Chronotype* and later the *Commonwealth*, he reported on strikes, advocated socialism, celebrated European revolutions, and supported the Liberty and later Free Soil parties.[47] When Phillips and the other abolitionists sought to free fugitive Thomas Sims, they employed the lawyer Robert Rantoul, Jr., who had made his name by arguing the famous *Commonwealth v. Hunt* case, which allowed Massachusetts unions the right to organize without violating conspiracy laws.[48] Phillips also likely knew Ira Steward, perhaps the most important theoretician of the eight-hour-workday movement after the Civil War. Steward had been an abolitionist and had participated in the antislavery actions attempting to free fugitive Anthony Burns in 1854.[49] Perhaps the most important link between the two worlds was William Henry Channing, a leader in the Boston Union of Associationists (the Fourierist organization that developed out of Brook Farm) while simultaneously an active abolitionist.

Boston abolitionism was also a less parochial world than is sometimes imagined. In addition, of course, to the many black abolitionists who played crucial roles, Phillips and other abolitionists had regular contact with a wide range of activists from the nineteenth-century Atlantic world. There were British Chartists, like Cluer, who had moved to Boston and injected their class-conscious rhetoric into the antislavery movement. One of the more interesting antislavery emigrants was Henry Kemp, a Catholic Irish "chair-painter," who brought a pistol to the Anthony Burns rescue attempt in 1854.[50] Kemp, a trusted associate of black radicals like Lewis Hayden, as well as an outspoken defender of the Catholic Church, confounded most narratives that describe Catholics, and the Irish in particular, as rabidly anti-abolitionist.[51] American abolitionism received a particularly important influx of German refugees after the 1848 Revolution. The German historian Mischa Honeck has drawn attention to the radical Karl Heinzen and his influence on Phillips in 1863 and 1864, especially in his support of John C. Frémont's challenge to President Lincoln. German members of the Boston Turners—socialist gymnastic clubs—had served as Phillips's bodyguards during the turbulent winter of 1860, when anti-abolitionist mobs threatened his lectures.[52]

Many Boston abolitionist leaders proved sympathetic to socialism, in one form or another. Thomas Wentworth Higginson, for instance, considered himself "at least a halfway socialist for life."[53] Theodore Parker, renowned for sheltering German intellectuals who were exiled after the failure of the 1848 Revolution, constantly skewered the rich in Boston and rejoiced at the arrival of the ideas of the French socialist Charles Fourier, "because I think our present form of society is irrational and unchristian."[54] In the *Liberty Bell*, an annual periodical of abolitionist essays, poems, and short stories, William I. Bowditch decried the "competition, heartless soul destroying competition" that converted men into "wage slaves in the factories and mines."[55] As early as 1847, Phillips had imbibed this ethos when he declared that "the rights of the peasants of Ireland, the operatives of New England, and the laborers of South America, will not be lost sight of in sympathy for the Southern slave."[56] By 1859, Phillips had moved toward a more sympathetic position on the question of socialism, describing it as "an honest effort, however mistaken, to make all men wholly and really brothers in life, property, and thought!"[57] By the time of Reconstruction, Phillips had become even more radical, submitting a resolution to the Labor-Reform Convention which, after affirming the labor theory of value, resolved that "we declare war with the wages system . . . war with the present system of finance . . . war with these lavish grants of the public lands to speculating companies."[58]

In many ways the abolitionist embrace of a class-conscious language developed out of the demands of their constituents. Rank-and-file Massachusetts abolitionists tended to be of the "middling classes," defined by one historian as "wage-earning workingmen and workingwomen . . . mechanics, small retailers, and petty professionals."[59] As Thomas Wentworth Higginson summed it up, "radicalism went with the smell of leather," referring to the aprons worn by workers.[60] In fact, abolitionists often found that they had far greater support in bustling industrial centers like Worcester, Lynn, and Northampton than in mercantile Boston. Phillips himself described the abolitionist constituency as "the farmers, the mechanics, and the workingmen,—the thinking men of Massachusetts."[61] Studies of those who signed abolitionist petitions or joined antislavery organizations confirm that, while abolitionism drew from a cross-section of New England society, workers were heavily represented. A Lynn, Massachusetts, abolitionist organization, for instance, reported that almost two-thirds of its members were skilled workers, while a study of seven different abolitionist groups showed that between 60 and 70 percent of members owned no real estate.[62]

While some of the abolitionist leadership like Phillips came from privileged classes, they did not reflect the Boston elite, who overwhelmingly repudiated abolitionism. In fact, abolitionists saw the leaders of Boston industry, those who owned the great textile factories and mercantile houses, as their sworn enemies. The "Boston Associates" had supported the Cotton Whig branch of the Whig Party and consistently asked for a more conciliatory policy toward the South, and often led the mobs of "gentlemen of property and standing" who terrorized abolitionists on the streets. Phillips, by the 1850s, was convinced that, in the abolitionist struggle, the "merchants" would always be on the side of slavery.[63] Theodore Parker correctly asserted that a Harvard education and financial success made a Bostonian less likely to support the abolitionist struggle and less likely to support racial egalitarianism.[64] Certainly, by the late 1840s, as Charles Sumner famously charged, the "Lords of the Loom" had formed a bond with the "Lords of the Lash."[65]

PHILLIPS AND DEMOCRACY

The roots of Phillips's commitment to the cause of labor can be seen in the rhetoric he had used as an abolitionist. While Phillips's censure of the city's elite for its complicity with slavery provided much motivation for his support of labor rights, in fact, the deeper roots lay in his finely honed theory of democracy.

Phillips's concern for the fragility of American democracy emerged out of his abolitionism. In ways both formal (such as the Three-Fifths Clause) and informal, slavery had distorted and perverted American democracy. Southerners or their northern lackeys had enjoyed nearly unbroken control of the federal government since the nation's founding. In recent years the Slave Power had forced a new Fugitive Slave Law upon the nation, driving the federal bureaucracy to enforce it; attempted to seize Kansas and the federal lands in the West as slave territory; issued the Dred Scott Decision to not only deny African Americans any rights whatsoever, but to deny the right of government to restrict the growth of slavery anywhere in the Union; and savagely beaten Senator Charles Sumner while he sat in the U.S. Senate chambers. The Slave Power's allies in the North, especially in the Democratic Party, supported legislation favorable to the South and strengthened black racial subordination by excluding blacks from voting and using mobs to silence dissent. Phillips and his coadjutors saw slavery as aided and abetted by concentrated wealth throughout the North. "Except in our Northern State governments," Phillips declared, "we have never had a Democracy in this country."[66] The fight for abolitionism, then, was a fight not just to protect, but in many ways, to *create* a true American democracy.

Phillips came to understand the ways that wealth, power, and inequality corrupted civil society—the nongovernmental institutions which created public opinion and made democracy a reality. The churches prostrated themselves to the slaveholders, and newspapers like the Boston *Daily Advertiser*, "behind whose editorials," Phillips wrote, "a keen ear can always catch the clink of the dollar"—were loyal to the demands of the Cotton Whigs.[67] Combating the corrupting influence of wealth and slavery fortified Phillips's conception of his role as an agitator and simultaneously drew him closer to a theory of class conflict that resembled the ideas of labor radicals and transatlantic revolutionaries. "Capitalists," he charged as early as 1853, "are our feudal barons," a claim which both demonstrated his growing awareness of how class inequality threatened democracy and revealed language drawn from European radicals.[68]

Unlike earlier generations who had hoped that disinterested republican statesmen and citizens could rise above petty local interests to speak for the whole nation, Phillips openly embraced the idea that Americans would frequently vote in their own perceived "selfish" interests, "by which the greatest political questions have been carried."[69] He possessed a keen grasp of the power of interest groups and how to use them for public good. An effective reformer, Phillips argued, "must embody his principle in something which the community loves."[70] If all Americans acted out of "the average selfishness . . . of all classes," they would end up "neutralizing each other, and tending towards that fair play which Saxons love."[71] He assumed the presence of multiple and overlapping publics—working-class, rich, black, white, abolitionist, northern, and southern—that would compete and negotiate. In the 1850s, he had worried that abolitionism would fail because it was unable to "get the selfishness of men of its side."[72] Like many abolitionists, he quickly discovered that his arguments became most effective when he could link the threats that slavery posed to the interests of white northerners. And the most powerful threat that slavery posed to white northerners was to their own democratic rights.

Phillips, then, agitated in hopes of rallying northern public opinion and crafting it into a political force that would demand the end of slavery and the restoration of democratic equality. Temporizing politicians would, Phillips hoped, eventually quake before the "many little men who, at various points, are silently maturing a regeneration of public opinion."[73] In one of his clearest statements of political philosophy, Phillips declared that, since the abolitionists' "aim is to alter public opinion," they could not wait until all men were saints, but instead, accepting a world made up of "self-conceit, and self-interest, of weak men and wicked," they would use all appropriate rhetorical tools to move the public.[74] By doing so, Phillips believed, they were creating a force far more powerful than any politician or political party. Once reformers had secured public opinion, Phillips argued, "there will always be lawyers enough, and aye Courts enough, and ministers enough, to express and enforce this sentiment."[75] During the Civil War, Phillips repeatedly described Lincoln's progress on slavery and civil rights as the consequence of this abolitionist agitation. "You know very well that he is a growing man," Phillips told an audience about the president, "Why did he grow? Because we watered him."[76]

Phillips never wrote a systematic theory of politics, but from his published essays and speeches, it is clear that he held a view of democracy that emphasized the privileged place of ideas in public and political discourse. In a major address in 1862, Phillips distinguished between the "political" form of power—he used Lincoln as a representative—which simply follows what the people want, and the "intellectual" form of power, which attempts to expand one's influence through "his principles of investigation, his fearlessness of examination, his boldness of attitude."[77] The decisions of Lincoln, then, were little more than the surface permutations of a much deeper reality—the opinions of millions of everyday Americans. True power, then, lay in the ability to convince, mobilize, and give voice to these everyday Americans. In his appreciation for the tangible power of abstract ideas, Phillips came the closest as he would to the transcendentalism that surrounded him in the Boston reform community. "We live not under a government of laws," he told the students at Union College in 1857, "but a Government of Ideas. . . . [T]he business of abolitionists is to mould the ideas of the Nation."[78]

Because of this interest in public opinion, Phillips interpreted the Civil War as about more than just the military dominance of the South, but as a conflict for the meaning of democracy. As Thomas Bender and other have argued, the American Civil War must be put in the context of the democratic revolutions that were rocking the entire North Atlantic world in the middle of the nineteenth century.[79] Many European radicals supported the abolitionists and the northern side during the Civil War. These European revolutionaries formed part of a broad trend of liberal nationalism that pushed for formal equality, expanded citizenship, and, in many cases, socialized markets. Across the Atlantic world, liberals and radicals attacked forms of private and local power—sometime explicitly comparing European aristocrats to southern slaveowners. In both America and Europe, they asserted that strengthening the national state would prove the only effective means of guaranteeing equal rights to all citizens.

Like other transatlantic radicals, Phillips interpreted the Civil War as a grand contest between "two powers; Aristocracy and Democracy, which *shall hold the belt of the continent*," a struggle he explicitly compared to the French Revolution.[80] As early as September 1861 he declared, "It seems to me we are passing through the trial-day of democracy."[81] A victory of northern democracy would demonstrate, once and for all, the superiority of democratic governance over the aristocratic polices of the South. "To-day, in this storm and convulsion," Phillips told a Boston audience, "Democracy vindicates its title to be a government."[82]

A Union defeat, Phillips argued, would empower European reactionaries. He increasingly gestured toward transatlantic solidarity, arguing that the Civil War was one outpost of a battle "between free institutions and caste institutions," and because of this, "where class power lives, whether it be on the banks of the Thames or the Seine, whether by the side of the Ganges or the Danube, there the South has an ally."[83] In 1862, he worried about "the impression made upon Europe" by the North lacking the "moral strength" to emancipate the slaves. "France, with one foot planted in Mexico, plots for a weak neighbor that cannot hem in her aggressive designs."[84] Phillips's concern with French imperialism in Mexico was widely shared, but his solution proved unique. If monarchial Europe intervened in the Americas, the United States would be forced to intervene in European affairs. "The right hand of our resistance," he told a New York audience in 1863, "is clasped in brotherhood with the radicals of Europe to upset every throne on the continent."[85]

If Phillips was expressing solidarity with European radicals, some European revolutionaries were themselves coming to appreciate his antislavery work. Defending Phillips from the attacks of the conservative *London Times,* Karl Marx lauded Phillips as a "leader of the Abolitionists in New England . . . combining an iron character with powerful energy and purest conviction." According to Marx, "in the present state of affairs, Wendell Phillips' speech is of greater importance than a battle bulletin."[86]

Phillips's arguments for black suffrage developed out of his theory of democracy. He clearly believed in African American suffrage both as an expression of an abstract right and as a reward for their loyalty during the Civil War. Just as frequently, however, his support for black suffrage represented a brute tool of realpolitik. Painting a picture of a postwar South in which the white "half million leading minds" remained as dedicated to racial subordination as before the war, Phillips worried that northern indifference would jeopardize the legacy of the war. Empowering black voters, Phillips argued, represented the only way to counteract the continued power of southern whites, and in that way "fortify justice . . . [and] render posterity possible."[87] Extending suffrage to freedmen, in other words, was both the right thing to do and essential to the future of American democracy.

With emancipation and the defeat of the Confederacy, Phillips could rightfully claim to have played a major role in the epochal change. But the war's end did not usher in a millennium of democratic freedom and equality. While experiments in multiracial democracy in the South seemed to promise a better future, the war had dramatically empowered a new industrial and financial elite in the North. The very upheavals that had ended one threat to democracy (slavery), had empowered a new threat: a generation of war financiers (like Jay Gould), railroad barons, and industrial tycoons who found in the Republican Party a fertile base from which to amass tremendous fortunes and political power. Few abolitionists saw as clearly and as early as Phillips that this contradiction threatened their democratic victory. The nation had degenerated, Phillips declared, and increasingly took on the class characteristics of Europe. In the industrial factories and urban slums of the Northeast, he said, America "betrays its weakness, and copies Europe," with New York becoming like London and Lowell like Manchester.[88] The adverse changes fueled Phillips's radicalism and, increasingly, he celebrated the European Left, shocking his audiences with praise for the Paris Commune and Russian Nihilists. He would even dabble in electoral politics during the postwar period, including an unsuccessful run at the Massachusetts governorship.

As he struggled to attain the vote for southern freedmen, it was exactly on the terrain of democracy that he framed many of his postwar criticisms of capitalism. The labor movement, Phillips declared, deserved his support because "it is my only hope for democracy."[89] The combined power of capitalists, especially the railroad barons, had become the new enemies of democracy in the 1870s, comparable, he thought, to the power of antebellum slaveholders. "Everybody knows that the laws of the State of New York are not made at Albany," he told an audience while campaigning for Benjamin F. Butler, "they are made in Vanderbilt's count-room."[90] Face-to-face with what he called "the power of wealth, the inordinate power of capital," Phillips simply redirected his ideas and rhetoric from the antislavery movement to the labor movement, reasserting his belief that the protection of democracy required that public opinion must be organized and rallied to defend society against another elite hegemony.

Phillips consistently described the labor movement as following in the footsteps of the abolitionist struggle. Having determined that an employer could not own a laborer, Phillips told an audience, "we fitly commence a struggle to define and to arrange the true relations of capital and labor."[91] Phillips wasn't alone in this. Labor advocate Ira Steward, for instance, used the same logic that had given "the slave his freedom" to try to win workers an eight-hour workday.[92] Another prominent postwar labor activist who got his start in the abolitionist movement was Ezra Heywood, one of the most important anarchist intellectuals of postwar Massachusetts. As a young activist, Heywood had been an agent for the American Anti-Slavery Society, and almost had been expelled from Brown University after convincing a literary society to elect Wendell Phillips as its anniversary orator.[93] William Henry Channing joined fellow veteran abolitionists like Stephen Foster and Josiah Warren as a leader in the postwar New England Labor Reform League, men who linked prewar abolitionism to postwar labor politics.[94]

The New England labor movement, influenced by homegrown theorists like Steward, as well as by international discourse, made a fight for a shorter workday the central plank of its demands in the postwar years. Phillips threw his support to the eight-hour-day cause, but, characteristically, he did so because he saw in the issue a way to defend the ability of the democratic masses to participate in self-rule. Endorsing the slogan, "eight hours for labor, eight hours for sleep, and eight hours for what we will," Phillips reminded the audience that "where the government rests on the people," those people needed time to participate in public affairs. If Karl Marx looked forward to a future where the worker could use his or her time to hunt in the morning, rear cattle in the evening, and write literary criticism after dinner, Phillips hoped that, with a decrease in the workday, the average laborer could now find the time to read a long Charles Sumner speech.[95]

The labor movement was important both because its goals like the eight-hour workday strengthened democracy, but also because an organized working class would serve as a countervailing power, what Phillips called "the rallying of men against money," in order to balance the power of the corrupt elite.[96] Phillips even embraced the reduction of the workday because of its instrumental value toward protecting democracy.[97] He compared the fight for the eight-hour day to recent debates about slavery, pointing out that, like the newly freed slaves, the worker should have the right to a certain amount of leisure time, because "his freedom belongs to him, and he is responsible for its use."[98] For Phillips, democracy was naturally egalitarian, something that, if functioning, would necessarily lead to a more equitable society. "I want to see a Democracy educated to the level of the Roman boast, that it pulls down the oppressor, and lifts up the oppressed," he told an audience during the Civil War.[99]

Embracing the labor movement was one thing, but Phillips's Brahmin friends were aghast when he began advocating the end of a strict gold standard, the stable rock upon which the Gilded Age bourgeoisie built their empire. Throughout the 1870s, he tirelessly advocated that the government print paper currency and lend it to any individual or business at 2 or 3 percent interest, well below what they could get from private banks. "For this greenback question," he told the elite Radical Club, "only means whether we shall trust the

Declaration of Independence—that all men are created equal in money matters, as in everything else," adding that "it *will* be the first work needed by a *true Democratic* party."[100] Essentially, Phillips was suggesting the nationalization of the financial industry, a program that would have as much political force as it would economic.

The more Phillips incorporated practical politics and an appreciation for the democratic masses into his rhetoric, the more he understood the ways wealth and power perverted politics and subverted democracy. Since the power of the elite had grown so great, there was all the more need for an empowered public that would counter this elite, which now had "their knives on the throat of the Government."[101] Some former abolitionists interpreted the corruption of the Gilded Age as evidence of the need for more elite control—and perhaps even less working-class participation in government. Phillips, on the other hand, saw the need for greater working-class empowerment. By 1872, he would defend Marx's Internationalists, declaring, "when they tell me it is a system by which the working-men from London to Gibraltar, from Moscow to Paris, can clasp hands. Then I say God speed."[102] He even refused to condemn the Paris Commune.[103]

Wendell Phillips became one of the most consistent and outspoken advocates for a vigorous and active democracy. He found inspiration in the words of European radicals who moved him toward more a vigorous defense of the working class and a more strident criticism of the wealthy and their corporations that so dominated American society in the years after the Civil War. What makes Phillips's vision so effective, and relevant today, was his understanding of how public opinion is formed and how he could wield it for radical democratic ends. He accepted modern means—including labor unions, immigrants' rights, mass labor parties, and even inflationary monetary policy—to insert old democratic values into the new industrial world.[104] In this he presaged later progressives, who would attempt to use the means of the federal government to recreate the ends of Jeffersonian equality.

NOTES

1."Wendell Phillips on the Political Situation; His Views of the President's Message and Proclamation," *New York Times*, December 20, 1863.

2. Early interpretations of this relationship stressed the variety of possible reactions. Williston H. Lofton, writing in the 1940s, stressed that, while abolitionists often reached out to the labor movement, workers reciprocated with a range of opinions, from outright hostility to open embrace. Herbert Aptheker was optimistic—perhaps naively so—when he described abolitionists as eager critics of capitalism. With more rigor, local studies, such as Bruce Laurie's analysis of the Massachusetts Liberty Party, have demonstrated that local activists for antislavery political parties sought the votes of workers by advocating measures such as limitations on the working day. Whether this embrace of labor's goals was opportunistic or sincere, it demonstrated the overlapping constituencies for antislavery and labor reform. Finally, scholars often find that individual abolitionists' own experiences in the vagaries of antebellum capitalism led them to question the marketplace. John Stauffer, for instance, finds that Gerrit Smith, John Brown, and James McCune Smith grew skeptical of the free market after the trauma of the Crash of 1837. Williston H. Lofton, "Abolition and Labor: Appeal of the Abolitionists to the Northern Working Classes: Part 1," *Journal of Negro History* 33 (June 1948): 249–61; Herbert Aptheker, *Abolitionism: A Revolutionary Movement* (Boston: Twayne, 1989), 42; Bruce Laurie, *Beyond Garrison: Antislavery and Social Reform* (New York: Cambridge University Press, 2005); John Stauffer, *The Black Hearts of Men: Radical Abolitionists and the Transformation of Race* (Cambridge: Harvard University Press, 2004); Jonathan A. Glickstein, *American Exceptionalism, American Anxiety: Wages, Competition, and Degraded Labor in Antebellum United States* (Charlottesville: University of Virginia Press, 2002).

3. See, for instance, Thomas Bender, ed., *The Antislavery Debate: Capitalism and Abolitionism as a Problem in Historical Interpretation* (Berkeley: University of California Press, 1992); John Ashworth, *Slavery, Capitalism, and Politics in the Antebellum Republic*, vol. 1: *Commerce and Compromise, 1820–1850* (New York: Cambridge University Press, 1996); Eric Williams, *Slavery and Capitalism* (1944; Chapel Hill: University of North Carolina Press, 1994); Eric Foner, *Politics and Ideology in the Age of the Civil War* (New York: Oxford University Press, 1980), 57–76; Amy Dru Stanley, *From Bondage to Contract: Wage Labor, Marriage, and the Market in the Age of Slave Emancipation* (New York: Cambridge University Press, 1998). The degree to which this narrative may be dominant can be seen in Jonathan Levy's interpretation of Elizur Wright. For Levy, Wright is a figure who represents two mutually constitutive ideologies—the "liberal self-ownership" of the capitalist man and the "freedom" of the abolitionist. See Jonathan Levy, *Freaks of Fortune: The Emerging World of Capitalism and Risk in America* (Cambridge: Harvard University Press, 2012).

4. See, for instance, Caleb McDaniel, *The Problem of Democracy in the Age of Slavery: Garrisonian Abolitionists and Transatlantic Reform* (Baton Rouge: Louisiana State University Press, 2013).

5. Richard Hofstadter, *The American Political Tradition: And the Men Who Made It* (1948; New York: Vintage, 1989), 139.

6. "Letter from Wendell Phillips," *Liberator*, May 28, 1841.

7. James Brewer Stewart, *Wendell Phillips: Liberty's Hero* (Baton Rouge: Louisiana State University Press, 1986), 79.

8. Wendell Phillips, *Speeches, Lectures, and Letters* (Boston: James Redpath, 1863), 47.

9. Dean Grodzins, *American Heretic: Theodore Parker and Transcendentalism* (Chapel Hill: University of North Carolina Press, 2002), 397.

10. Quoted in John Cumbler, *From Abolition to Rights: The Making of a Reform Community in the Nineteenth Century* (Philadelphia: University of Pennsylvania Press, 2007), 25.

11. Howe lobbied Charles Sumner and Horace Mann especially. See Samuel G. Howe, *Letters and Journals of Samuel Gridley Howe: The Servant of Humanity*, ed. Laura E. Richards (Boston: Dana Estes and Co., 1909), vol. 2: 354, emphasis in original.

12. R. J. M. Blackett, *Building an Antislavery Wall: Black Americans in the Atlantic Abolitionist Movement, 1830–1860* (Baton Rouge: Louisiana State University Press, 2002); William Wells Brown, *Three Years in Europe; or, Places I Have Seen and People I Have Met* (London: Charles Gilpin, 1852), 113.

13. Quoted in Betty Fladeland, *Abolitionists and Working Class Problems in the Age of Industrialization* (Baton Rouge: Louisiana State University Press, 1984), 142. Fladeland argues, writing about Chartist and abolitionist Joseph Barker, that "An area in which British Abolitionists, among them Barker, took the lead in influencing American abolitionists was in recognizing that the denial of rights to the labouring classes in Great Britain had an intrinsic connection with chattel slavery in America."

14. See Betty Fladeland, '"Our Cause Being One and the Same': Abolitionists and Chartism," in *Slavery and British Society, 1776–1846*, ed. James Walvin (Baton Rouge: Louisiana State University Press, 1982), 69–99.

15. "Sketch of W. W. Brown's Lecture," *National Anti-Slavery Standard*, December 30, 1854.

16. See Richard Bradbury, "Frederick Douglass and the Chartists," in *Liberating Sojourn: Frederick Douglass and Transatlantic Reform*, ed. Alan Rice and Martin Crawford (Athens: University of Georgia Press, 1999), 169–186; Fladeland, '"Our Cause Being One and the Same,'" 97.

17. William S. McFeely, *Frederick Douglass* (New York: W. W. Norton, 1991), 138–40.

18. For Marx's view of Chartism, see Karl Marx, *Surveys from Exile* (New York: Verso Press, 2010), 22–24, 262–71.

19. "Twenty-ninth Annual Meeting of the Massachusetts Anti-Slavery Society," *National Anti-Slavery Standard*, February 1, 1862.

20. "Wendell Phillips," *Liberator*, February 9, 1844.

21. "Chartism," Wendell Phillips Papers, MS Am 1953 (1585), Houghton Library, Harvard University.

22. See "The Demands of the Communist Party in Germany," in Karl Marx, *The Revolutions of 1848* (New York: Verso Press, 2010), 109–11.

23. "Chartism," Wendell Phillips Papers.

24. Wendell Phillips, "Reformers," *North Star*, December 3, 1847.

25. "First Annual Meeting of the New England Workingmen's Association," *Voice of Industry*, June 12, 1845.

26. "A Mile of Girls," *Voice of Industry*, December 26, 1845.

27. William Lloyd Garrison et al., *Proceedings of the Anti-Sabbath Convention, Held in the Melodeon, March 23d and 24th* (Boston: Published by the Order of the Convention, 1848), 38.

28. Ibid., 34.

29. William Henry Channing, *The Gospel Today: A Discourse Delivered at the Ordination of T. W. Higginson* (Boston: Crosby and Nichols, 1847), 11.

30. Frederick Douglass, "What I Found at the Northampton Association," in *The History of Florence, Massachusetts. Including a Complete Account of the Northampton Association of Education and Industry,* ed. Charles Arthur Sheffield (Florence, Mass.: Charles Sheffield, 1895), 129–30.

31. Karl Marx, *Capital* (New York: Penguin, 1976), vol. 1: 99; Marx, *Revolutions of 1848,* 96.

32. Donald Yacovone, *Samuel Joseph May and the Dilemmas of the Liberal Persuasion, 1797–1871* (Philadelphia: Temple University Press, 1991), 126.

33. Foner, *Politics and Ideology in the Age of the Civil War,* 71; Aileen Kraditor, *Means and Ends in American Abolitionism: Garrison and His Critics on Strategy and Tactics, 1834–1850* (Chicago: Elephant Paperbacks, 1989), 248–51.

34. "Wages and Chattel Slavery," *Liberator,* Sept 4, 1846.

35. "Wendell Phillips and 'Young America,'" *Liberator,* Sept 4, 1846.

36. James Russell Lowell, for instance, responded directly to the land reformers by arguing that abolitionists and land reformers simply chose different, but not contradictory, reform goals: "Let us endeavor, brother land-reformers, not only to be satisfied, but even to be thankful for each other, and go about our respective works with a better heart." James Russell Lowell, *The Anti-Slavery Papers of James Russell Lowell* (Boston: Houghton, Mifflin, 1902), vol. 2: 135, emphasis in original.

37. A. Bronson Alcott to Charles Lane, April 16, 1848, *The Letters of A. Bronson Alcott,* ed. Richard Herrnstadt (Ames: Iowa State University Press, 1969), 137.

38. See Edward Berenson, "American Perspectives on the French Republic," in *The French Republic: History, Values, Debates,* ed. Edward Berenson, Vincent Duclert, and Christophe Prochasson (Ithaca: Cornell University Press, 2011), 358.

39. "Martinique—Murder!—Incendiarism!—Abolition of Slavery!" Boston *Daily Advertiser,* June 24, 1848; Berenson, "American Perspectives on the French Republic," 359.

40. Quoted in "John Calhoun vs. The Declaration of Independence," *Liberator,* July 14, 1848. Calhoun's position was probably in the minority in the South, where most whites and almost all the blacks supported the revolution (for very different reasons). But Calhoun, who Richard Hofstadter once called the Marx of the Masterclass, represented a growing and influential worldview in the South. See also Charles Wiltse, "A Critical Southerner: John C. Calhoun on the Revolutions of 1848," *Journal of Southern History* 15 (August 1949): 299–310.

41. For instance, William Henry Channing's address, "Sketch of the Speech of Mr. Channing," *Liberator,* April 14, 1848.

42. "Sympathy for the French," *Liberator,* April 21, 1848, emphasis in original.

43. Phillips, *Speeches, Lectures, and Letters,* 15, 47, 411.

44. Wendell Phillips Garrison and Francis Jackson Garrison, *William Lloyd Garrison, 1805–1879; The Story of His Life Told by His Children* (Boston: Houghton Mifflin: 1894), vol. 3: 324.

45. "Grand Reception Meeting in Lynn," *Liberator,* December 6, 1850.

46. Albert von Frank, *The Trials of Anthony Burns: Freedom and Slavery in Emerson's Boston* (Cambridge: Harvard University Press, 1998), 137.

47. On Wright, see Laurie, *Beyond Garrison,* 17–19, 67–70; Lawrence Goodheart, *Abolitionist, Actuary, Atheist: Elizur Wright and the Reform Impulse* (Kent, Ohio: Kent State University Press, 1990).

48. Rantoul's arguments can be read in Robert Rantoul, Jr.; Charles Loring; and George T. Curtis, *The Trial of Thomas Sims, on an Issue of Personal Liberty, on the Claim of James Potter, of Georgia, against Him, as an Alleged Fugitive from Service* (Boston: William S. Damrell, 1851), 3–23.

49. Von Frank, *The Trials of Anthony Burns*, 158; David Roediger, "Ira Steward and the Anti-Slavery Origins of Eight-Hour Theory," *Labor History* 27 (Summer 1986): 410–26.

50. Von Frank, *The Trials of Anthony Burns*, 64; George Adams, *The Boston Directory for the Year 1852, Embracing the City Record, A General Directory of the Citizens, and Business Directory, with an Almanac* (Boston: George Adams, 1852), 145.

51. Thomas Wentworth Higginson called Kemp an "energetic Irishman." See Thomas Wentworth Higginson, *Cheerful Yesterdays* (Boston: Houghton, Mifflin, 1898), 148; "Annual Meeting of the Massachusetts A.S. Society," *Liberator*, February 2, 1855.

52. See Mischa Honeck, *We Are the Revolutionists: German-Speaking Immigrants and American Abolitionists after 1848* (Athens: University of Georgia Press, 2011), 137–71; Stewart, *Wendell Phillips*, 214. For his collaboration with Heinzen and others, see J. Müller to Wendell Phillips, May 2, 1864; Heinzen to Wendell Phillips, February 4, 1864, Wendell Phillips Papers, Houghton Library.

53. Thomas Wentworth Higginson, *The Magnificent Activist: The Writings of Thomas Wentworth Higginson, 1823–1911*, ed. Henry Meyer (New York: Da Capo Press, 2000), 7.

54. Theodore Parker to Dr. Francis, March 13, 1844 in *Life and Correspondence of Theodore Parker*, ed. John Weiss (New York: Appleton, 1864), vol. 1: 229.

55. William I. Bowditch, "Faith in Human Brotherhood," *Liberty Bell*, 1852, 104.

56. "The Question of Labor," *Liberator*, July 9, 1847.

57. Phillips, *Speeches, Lectures, and Letters*, 250.

58. Wendell Phillips, *Speeches, Lectures, and Letters, Second Series* (Boston: Lee and Shepard, 1900), 152–53.

59. Laurie, *Beyond Garrison*, 7.

60. Higginson, *Cheerful Yesterdays*, 115.

61. Phillips, *Speeches, Lectures, and Letters*, 90.

62. Edward Magdol, *The Antislavery Rank and File: A Social Profile of the Abolitionists' Constituency* (New York: Greenwood Press, 1986), 68, 61.

63. As an example, see "Wendell Phillip's Lecture," *National Anti-Slavery Standard*, January 20, 1855.

64. Theodore Parker, *Saint Bernard and Other Papers* (Boston: American Unitarian Association, 1911), 297.

65. Charles Sumner, *Orations and Speeches in Two Volumes* (Boston: Ticknor, Reed, and Field, 1850), vol. 2: 257.

66. "The Times: A Lecture by Wendell Phillips, ESQ., Delivered in the Fraternity Course, at Tremont Temple, Boston, Tuesday Evening, January 7th, 1862," *National Anti-Slavery Standard*, January 25, 1862.

67. Phillips, *Speeches, Lectures, and Letters*, 215.

68. Ibid., 143.

69. Ibid., 83.

70. "Speech of Wendell Phillips," *Pennsylvania Freeman*, June 8, 1848.

71. Phillips, *Speeches, Lectures, and Letters*, 265.

72. Ibid., 82.

73. Ibid., 37.

74. Ibid., 110.

75. "Nineteenth Anniversary of the American Anti-Slavery Society," *Pennsylvania Freeman*, May 20, 1852.

76. "Speech of Wendell Phillips at the Cooper Institute, New York, on Tuesday Evening, December 22, 1863, on President Lincoln's Message and Proclamation," *Commonwealth*, January 1, 1864.

77. "Address of Wendell Phillips, Delivered before the Twenty-Eighth Congregational Society, at Music Hall, Boston, July 6, 1862," *National Anti-Slavery Standard*, July 12, 1862.

78. Wendell Phillips, "Ideas and Laws," *National Anti-Slavery Standard*, August 19, 1854.

79. Thomas Bender, *A Nation among Nation: America's Place in World History* (New York: Hill and Wang, 2006), 116–81.

80. Phillips, *Speeches, Lectures, and Letters*, 427, 421, emphasis in original.

81. "Speech of Wendell Phillips, Esq., Delivered at Allston Hall, Boston on the Anniversary of the Birthday of Theodore Parker, August 23," *National Anti-Slavery Standard*, September 7, 1861.

82. "The Times: A Lecture by Wendell Phillips, ESQ."

83. Phillips, *Speeches, Lectures, and Letters*, 525.

84. "Address of Wendell Phillips, Delivered before the Twenty-Eighth Congregational Society, at Music Hall, Boston, July 6, 1862."

85. "Speech of Wendell Phillips at the Cooper Institute, New York, on Tuesday Evening, December 22, 1863."

86. Karl Marx, *On America and the Civil War*, ed. Saul Padover (New York: McGraw Hill, 1972), 215–16.

87. "The Anniversaries," *New York Herald-Tribune*, May 9, 1866.

88. Phillips, *Speeches, Lectures, and Letters, Second Series*, 164.

89. Ibid., 175.

90. Wendell Phillips, *The People Coming to Power! Speech of Wendell Phillips, Esq., at the Salisbury Beach Gathering, September 13, 1871* (Boston: Lee and Shepard, 1871), 13.

91. Phillips, *Speeches, Lectures, and Letters, Second Series*, 139.

92. Roediger, "Ira Steward and the Anti-Slavery Origins of Eight-Hour Theory," 422.

93. Martin Henry Blatt, *Free Love and Anarchism: The Biography of Ezra Heywood* (Urbana: University of Illinois Press, 1989), 17.

94. David Montgomery, *Beyond Equality: Labor and the Radical Republicans, 1862–1872* (New York: Alfred Knopf, 1967), 410.

95. Phillips, *Speeches, Lectures, and Letters, Second Series*, 173.

96. Ibid., 175.

97. See Brian Greenberg, "Wendell Phillips and the Idea of Industrial Democracy in Early Postbellum America," in *The Struggle for Equality: Essays on Sectional Conflict, the Civil War, and the Long Reconstruction*, ed. Orville Vernon Burton, Jerald Podair, and Jennifer L. Weber (Charlottesville: University of Virginia Press, 2011), 137–52.

98. Phillips, *Speeches, Lectures, and Letters, Second Series*, 140.

99. "The Times: A Lecture by Wendell Phillips, ESQ."

100. Mrs. John T. Sargent, ed., *Sketches and Reminiscences of the Radical Club of Chestnut Street, Boston* (Boston: John R. Osgood, 1880), 164, emphasis in original.

101. Sargent, ed., *Sketches and Reminiscences of the Radical Club*, 165.

102. Phillips, *Speeches, Lectures, and Letters, Second Series*, 169,

103. Ibid., 154.

104. Phillips supported inflationary proposals, including printing paper money. This was a radical measure at the time, one mostly held by the far left. See "Charles Bradlaugh's Views on Finance—Wendell Phillips Answered—A Few Words about Butler," Hartford *Daily Courant*, October 12, 1875.

8

THE PEOPLE COMING TO POWER!

Wendell Phillips, Benjamin F. Butler, and the Politics of Labor Reform

MILLINGTON W. BERGESON-LOCKWOOD

Wendell Phillips had been dead six years, buried alongside his wife, Ann, in Milton, Massachusetts, before aging former Civil War general and Massachusetts governor Benjamin F. Butler took the stage in December 1890. At Boston's Tremont Temple he shared recollections of his work with the famous orator, antislavery leader, and social reformer. Butler recalled his long relationship with the renowned activist and paid special attention to their association during the final decade of Phillips's life. Clear in Butler's words was the central thread connecting Phillips's lifetime of advocacy. "He became a champion of labor," Butler told the packed audience. "He classed black and white labor together. In that he and I stood together."[1] From Phillips's fight against slavery through his battle for just labor policy and against moneyed interests in politics, causes that occupied him until the end of his life, he stood with common people against forces that would rob them of their economic autonomy and political voice. In the last decade of his life, Butler became one of his most constant allies and a recipient of Phillips's support.

Butler's presence on the dais in 1890, however, did more than merely provide a thoughtful recollection of the life of a great man. Rather, Butler and his political career served as the living embodiment of Phillips's postwar political philosophy, which condemned major parties and moneyed control in politics. Phillips imbued Butler's campaigns for public office with rich meaning and viewed the general as the best hope for challenging the political status quo.

Exploring Phillips's support of Butler in his campaigns for Massachusetts governor exhibits how much Phillips's ideology of social democracy drove his politics, and departed from his rejection of electoral political action during his antebellum years. Further, it shows how his calls for labor and finance reform in the last decade of his life went beyond bettering the condition of working people and became part of a broader political strategy. In Phillips's view, Butler was the politician most likely to lead a movement toward a new political order where common people, black and white, and not the wealthy elite drove the political system.

Phillips's vision of electoral politics reflected how he viewed the relationship between labor and capital in the American economic system. Just as workers should have full control and benefit of their labor, voters should be able to shape society without interference from party machines or moneyed corruption. In labor, selfish business owners who privileged profit above all else oppressed the worker. In politics, party bosses and the influence of money compromised the power of the popular vote. Phillips advocated a labor system wherein capital and labor worked as partners. The voice of labor should have a decisive role in determining business decisions, and profits from workers' efforts should be spent on comfortable wages first before going into the owner or shareholders' coffers. Likewise, in politics, the rights and voice of the everyday voter should drive the political system, not the interests of the party organizations or their wealthy backers. Phillips advocated labor and financial reform, not only for specific issues per se, but to weaken the power of the economic and political elite while elevating the power and influence of everyday working people.

Focusing on the intersections between Phillips's labor reform and electoral activism expands understandings of his actions in the final decade of his life. Previous scholars of Phillips's labor activism focus primarily on his involvement in the eight-hour-workday movement and the Labor Reform Party, culminating with the failed election of Benjamin F. Butler as Massachusetts governor in 1871.[2] These studies of his early activities are crucial in understanding Phillips, but overlook the persistence of labor reform and electoral activism in his later advocacy. Scholars have neglected the persistence of Phillips's dedication to electoral activism and the crucial role support for Butler played as the embodiment of his political philosophy in the last decade of his life.

Phillips continued to play a central role as candidate and spokesperson in campaigns on behalf of workers until his death in 1884. During these later years he allied himself with the Greenback Party and again supported Butler during his campaigns for governor. With Phillips's support, Butler, returning to the Democratic Party, finally succeeded in 1882. Even months before his death, Phillips publicly supported Butler in his reelection campaign and continued to speak out against the Republican Party.

In the final decades of his life, Phillips embraced electoral politics as a primary means of social change. This was a stark departure from his antebellum rejection of party politics as a corrupt compromise with a political system tainted by the stain of black enslavement.[3] After emancipation and with the passage of the Reconstruction amendments, however, Phillips looked to voting as a pure expression of an individual's will and a way to transform society without the unrest and disorder of violent revolution.

Phillips's political philosophy was rooted deeply in his faith in the power of democracy and sanctity of the ballot to achieve meaningful change. Americans, Phillips praised, were fortunate in their electoral system and right to vote. Working people should turn to voting first and use physical confrontation and strikes only as a last resort. If properly organized and motivated, oppressed people could make the ballot and elections more powerful than any strike. The failure of political leaders to respond to electoral pressure, however, would come with dire consequences as the only option.

Although only occasionally a candidate, Phillips campaigned actively for people and parties that best expressed his ideologies of economic and political equality. In doing so, he rebuked the Republican Party in favor of independent and third parties. Phillips was a hesitant supporter of Republicans from the party's creation in the 1850s and supported their candidates begrudgingly. Ideology continued to drive Phillips's partisan choices following the war, during a time when the Republican establishment had turned away from support of African Americans and workers' rights. Phillips remained committed to the use of government power and policy at a time when liberal reformers within the Republican Party opposed state intervention to protect workers and to guarantee African Americans' economic rights.[4] In Phillips's mind, the Republican Party faced a choice: either reform and dedicate itself to radical action, or face the consequence of spokespeople like himself leading voters to emerging third parties, or even the Democrats.

It was this conflict that brought Phillips to embrace Butler as a candidate and conduit for his ideas. During the 1870s, Republican opponents maligned Butler for his support of economic reforms. Although elected as a Republican to the U.S. Congress during Reconstruction, Butler campaigned openly against the Republican establishment and provided a way for Phillips to take a stand against the party without having to stand as a candidate himself. Butler's opponents decried the perceived corruption of his policies, labeling them

"Butlerism." According to historian Eric Foner, this term "became a shorthand for a new kind of mass politics that had infused American public life with 'the spirit of the European mob.'"[5] This embrace of mass politics was exactly what attracted Phillips to Butler.

Even as his strategies shifted to embrace electoral activism, Phillips remained faithful to his principles of full equality and justice for all people, an agenda radical for his era. Hardly naive to the challenges ahead, Phillips had been inspired by the victory against the Slave Power. The abolition of slavery and the subsequent efforts to protect black civil and political rights in the Constitution empowered Phillips to attack labor and economic equality as well. If slavery, America's greatest sin, could be destroyed, then perhaps even more sweeping change was possible.

As in his antislavery work, Phillips sought to awaken the public to the moral indignities of political and economic corruption. Using his powerful skills as an orator, he moved audiences with utopian visions of political justice and economic equality where everyday people, not political leaders or bosses, shaped the destiny of the nation. Phillips vowed to remake American society in the postwar years, and he dedicated the final decades of his life to a purification of the political and labor system based on the rights and autonomy of American people as voters and workers.

Phillips's political ideology intertwined his dedication to labor reform, hatred of financial corruption in politics, and faith in the electoral process. All three came together during the campaigns of Butler for governor of Massachusetts. With Butler on the ballot and Phillips at the campaign podium, the two friends and political allies attempted to remain ideologically true to their cause of economic equality and labor reform, while challenging an electoral order they perceived as immoral and corrupt.

THE ORATOR AND "THE BEAST"

Prior to their postbellum alliance, Phillips recognized Butler as a radical ally during the Civil War. Although Butler was a Democrat and opposed abolition before the war, the realities of wartime and witnessing slavery firsthand had transformed him. As a result, he became a powerful antislavery force during the conflict. Notably, he pioneered the labeling of fugitive slaves as "contraband" so as to secure their protection by Union forces. Additionally, as the general in charge of Union-occupied New Orleans, he treated Confederates harshly, most famously Confederate women, bringing him high regard from African Americans and radical northerners, but utter disdain from white southerners who named him "Beast Butler."

These actions helped draw Phillips to Butler and began to cement the relationship that featured so prominently in his political life over the next two decades. Phillips praised Butler's decisive actions on behalf of enslaved people and against the South. This was in stark contrast to what he perceived were weak policies of compromise and inaction from the Lincoln administration.[6] "Lincoln drifts, Butler steers," Butler's brother-in-law recounted Phillips saying. "Five years ago I thought Lincoln a better man," Phillips continued, "but when this war broke out, Butler's New England mind burst the trammels of party, and comprehended this whole great question."[7] In an 1863 speech, he commended Butler as the only man who "had organized victory."[8] A year later, Phillips praised Butler in a letter the general would continue to show off even after Phillips's death. In 1890, Butler read Phillips's words to a captivated Boston audience. A wide circle, Phillips wrote in 1864, "regards you as the genius whom the war has thrown to the surface. . . . [W]e look upon you as a very large part of our capital for the future."[9]

Butler would not disappoint in the immediate aftermath of the war. He emerged as one of the most powerful radical voices in Congress and continued, like Phillips, to champion a broad radical civil rights agenda.[10] As Phillips was hesitant to enter elected office himself, Butler became a formal political vehicle into which Phillips could channel his activism. Butler openly challenged the Republican establishment, and party leaders despised what they viewed as his corrupt populist politics. In the postwar era, Butler embodied the radicalism quickly dwindling among other Republicans. His courage to confront the establishment demonstrated to Phillips the power of Butler as an ally. With their radical bona fides in place, both men turned increasingly toward issues of labor, finance reform, and independent politics—issues that would consume the rest of their lives.

"THE QUESTION FOR THE NEXT TEN YEARS"

On September 4, 1871, Phillips took the stage at the Labor Reform Convention in Worcester, Massachusetts. "We affirm, as a fundamental principle," Phillips declared, "that labor, the creator of wealth is entitled to all it creates."[11] On behalf of the convention, he advocated "the overthrow of the whole profit-making system, the extinction of all monopolies, the abolition of privileged classes, universal education and fraternity, perfect freedom of exchange, and, the best and grandest of all, the final obliteration of that foul stigma upon our so-called Christian civilization,—the poverty of the masses."[12] Among the conventioneers' demands were a ten-hour day for factory work (with the ultimate goal of an eight-hour day), equal pay for women, and the restriction on contract importation of Chinese labor.[13] Phillips continued with his thoughts on the labor reform movement, "the grandest and most comprehensive movement of the age."[14] Less than one week later, he told an audience at Salisbury Beach during a campaign stop for Benjamin Butler, "the question for the next ten years is the relation of labor to capital."[15]

Phillips, who had garnered immense attention, and much notoriety, from his antislavery work, brought the weight of a national leader to the labor reform movement, increasing its national profile. He believed strongly in the empowerment of working people and angrily opposed their exploitation by employers. He believed that workers should be the focus and main recipients of the benefits of industry and that profits should go to wages first before paying dividends to owners or shareholders. "The meaning of the labor question," Phillips told the Salisbury Beach gathering in 1871, "is this: Whether you on these acres, on yonder waves, or in the mills shall work honestly, industriously, soberly, for seventy long years, and then die worth a thousand or two thousand dollars, a small house, forty acres of land, or nothing, while some financial sponge sucks up millions."[16]

Phillips connected the struggle against slavery and for African Americans' rights to the future of the labor movement. "The anti-slavery cause was only a portion of the great struggle between capital and labor," Phillips wrote to a group of prominent black Bostonians in 1872. Speaking to African Americans as working people, he continued, "capital undertook to own the laborer. We have broken that up. . . . [T]hat dispute and all questions connected with it sink out of sight . . . and a clear field is left for the discussion of the labor movement. . . . I see . . . the retiring of old issues and the securing of a place for new ones." "Workingmen," Phillips announced, "rally now, to save your great question from being crowded out and postponed."[17]

While Phillips advocated increased power for black and white working people, he recognized that both labor and capital were necessary for a thriving economy. He did not oppose capital outright; he argued that workers' conditions, not owners' profits, should be the priority. "There is no antagonism between Man and Money—between Capital and Labor," Phillips explained, "they are friends, not foes; partners, not competitors; they are two parts of one scissors—each useless without the other."[18] Phillips did not seek a total upending of the free market, but wanted the power dynamic shifted toward workers' benefit.

While labor and capital were in partnership, it was the workers who took precedence. Phillips demanded "an equalization of property," which he called "the meaning of the Labor Movement."[19] The present system, Phillips argued, threatened the stability of the nation. "The safety of our institutions, justice and Christianity dictate that out of common profits, capital should have less and labor should have more than it now does."[20] "Labor," Phillips explained, "as it is human life, has to be the first claim."[21] A corporation should first pay its workers a comfortable wage before allocating money to settle its debts or pay stockholders. But just what wage "men can comfortably live on" and how this should be determined were the central questions facing the labor movement. "This is ground of the present quarrel," Phillips argued, "and peace will never come till this is settled."[22]

The best way to resolve this dispute was for corporations and laborers to meet as equals in mutual conference. Phillips rejected "the babble and chaff of 'supply and demand,'" which he argued, "forgets God, abolishes hearts, stomachs, and hot blood, and builds its world as children do, out of tin soldiers and blocks of wood."[23] A system that placed wage-making authority purely in the hands of capital and offered unemployment, poverty, and starvation as the only alternative was tantamount to slavery. Such policies were unsustainable and planted the seeds of violent discord. The best solution for Phillips was a mutual bargaining between labor and capital. A joint committee of business representatives and workers would examine the details of the business and then decide on a reasonable amount of wages. This Phillips explained was "the only just, safe, and lasting basis of peace."[24]

In addition to building more amicable relations between labor and capital, Phillips was concerned with securing time for workers to rest, enrich, and educate themselves. He was dedicated to the growth and empowerment of workers as individuals apart from their labor. Increased leisure time, he believed, would ultimately make them more enlightened and thoughtful citizens. Phillips's advocacy of reduced hours connected directly to his faith in the power of workers as voters. With time for self-improvement, workers would ultimately become better and more informed voters, inclined to shape their own electoral destiny. With no time outside of work, however, they were destined toward poverty and incivility.

One of Phillips's first causes following the Civil War, therefore, was the advocacy of an eight-hour day for workers. In 1865, Phillips joined with labor activist Ira Steward in publically supporting the creation of a Massachusetts commission to study labor issues and called for legislation enforcing an eight-hour workday. Although he and Steward would have a public falling out years later over priorities in the movement, Phillips remained committed to limited hours as a key part of labor reform.[25] Reduced work hours, he argued, would provide workers with time to improve themselves through education, leisure, and self-reflection. Phillips explained, "Give me a million of men in Massachusetts working eight hours a day and studying three, adult schools, open libraries, free lecturers, larger interest in politics, a little glimpse of art, [and] a little love of adornment."[26] With a shorter day, workers would have more time to enjoy arts and culture, increase their education, and help build a better society.

By 1870, labor reform rose in national significance, and Phillips emerged as one of the nation's most prominent activists. In May that year, the Eight Hour League held its first convention, in Boston's Horticultural Hall. Among the speakers was Phillips, who, the press argued, "embodies and eloquently presents the philosophy of the new movement, which . . . is taking root here, and certain before long to make itself felt both in our State and National politics."[27] Phillips named wealth inequality the greatest danger and condemned the rising influence of the "monied aristocracy" on American politics and government. In the long term, the protection of working people would benefit the wealth of all. "Whenever the capital of New England," he continued, "is borne up by the educated energies of eight-hour men, it will make better dividends than it does today."[28] He argued that no person had the right to amass unlimited wealth while there were those nearby in poverty.

During these early campaigns, Phillips endorsed a strategy of political independence. In 1869, he endorsed the creation of the Massachusetts Labor Reform Party. To this new party and the Eight Hour League, Phillips brought his reputation as an abolitionist and a powerful speaker, increasing the attention to labor issues and elevating his profile as an advocate of working people. During his time with these groups, Phillips promoted an increasingly broad version of labor reform that included not only a reform of working hours but significant transformation of taxation, currency, and financial policy.[29]

Phillips's involvement with labor reform and electoral politics merged in more than rhetoric when he accepted the nomination for governor from the Massachusetts Labor Reform Party in September 1870.[30] Phillips humbly accepted the nomination in a letter, writing, "I have no wish to become Governor of Massachusetts. . . . I thoroughly dislike to have my name drawn into party politics, for I belong to no political party. But I see nothing in your platform from which I dissent, and the struggle which underlies your movement has my fullest and heartfelt sympathy. . . . If my name will strengthen your movement, you are welcome to it."[31] Phillips continued to reiterate his opposition to the influence of capital on politics and advocated that the law "should do all it could to give the masses more leisure, a more complete education, better opportunities, and a fair share of profits."[32]

The formation of the Labor Reform Party fulfilled Phillips's vision of using the ballot to strike against corporate interests. "I feel sure," he wrote, "that the readiest way to turn public thought and effort into this channel is for the working men to organize a political party. No social question ever gets fearlessly treated here till we make politics turn on it. . . . [O]n questions like these a political party is the surest and readiest, if not the only way, to stir discussion and secure improvement."[33] For Phillips, organizing a political party and making a considerable showing on Election Day was as important as actually winning. He hoped to show the major political parties, especially Republicans, that voters would bolt in the name of labor reform. "Though working for a large vote," he concluded, "if we fail, we should not be discouraged by a small one. . . . [T]he antislavery movement proves how quickly a correct principle wins assent if earnest men work at it."[34]

Phillips's acceptance of the nomination from the Labor Reform Party generated fear among the Republican establishment. "There is no telling how large a vote Mr. Phillips may poll," wrote a correspondent to the *New York Times*. "There is good reason for our Republican friends in the Bay State to rouse themselves, and organize a vigorous campaign without further loss of time."[35] Phillips, they argued, would likely draw Republican voters to his campaign and, although it was unlikely he would win, his candidacy might dilute the

Republican electorate, securing a Democratic victory. "There is a danger," they concluded, "that the Republican majority may be seriously impaired."[36] If Phillips worried about Republican concerns, he did not let it show as he continued his campaign in October.

Throughout his speeches leading up to the election, he openly condemned the Republican Party. In an October 18 speech at Boston's Music Hall he condemned both major parties for "having no living idea to purpose."[37] Phillips criticized the Republican Party for refusing to take up the planks of the Prohibition and Labor Reform parties. The causes of temperance and labor were the future of the party, and Republicans refused to embrace them at their own peril. Phillips argued that Republicans campaigned only on their record of antislavery activism and had little to contribute to the pressing issues of the day. "All the party aimed at now," he declared, "was to watch its own growth."[38] "It had since nothing to do but die; was dead; and must be buried," Phillips continued at a speech in November, "It must rot before it would produce anything."[39] By embracing the ballot and voting for the Labor Reform candidates, voters could leverage their electoral power and press the Republican Party to embrace a pro-labor agenda.

Political observers expected a big turnout on Election Day, and when the votes were tallied Phillips had won nearly 22,000 votes out of over 150,000 cast.[40] Although defeated, Phillips was confident that voters had sent a message of support for labor reform. "We are still elated—more than satisfied with our success," he remarked.[41] He praised the political independence of his supporters and hoped that his campaign would inaugurate a new era of politics. By leaving the Republican Party, voters "showed advanced thought and the highest morals protesting against the lower plane of party purpose. . . . It has breathed more earnestness into our State politics, and the seed planted will give good account of itself."[42] Phillips braced supporters for continued challenges, but remained confident in the ultimate success of labor reform voters. "Associated wealth—the selfish union of wealthy corporations," he concluded, "is to do its utmost to undermine or strangle popular liberty. In that contest popular institutions need the fullest use of all the forces within their control . . . the power which comes from the organized and disciplined ranks of Labor, are the great bulwarks against this peril."[43] Phillips remained active in the Labor Reform Party following his defeat. The following year, however, he declared he would refuse the nomination if it were offered to him again.

Phillips argued that success depended less on the governor and more on the strength of labor reform in the legislature. He hoped that increasing the cohort of sympathetic legislators could bend the Republican Party toward their cause. Indeed, Phillips rejected the idea that labor reformers were "selling out" to the Republicans; quite the opposite. "It wasn't the Republican Party that was to swallow the Labor Reformers; but the Labor Party was to absorb the Republican."[44] He argued that only by embracing labor reform would the Republican Party survive. "The labor question," he predicted, "is to be the inspiration, groundwork, and front upon which American politics is to turn for the next generation."[45] Phillips would never again stand as candidate for major political office, but rather channeled his efforts into the election of candidates who embodied his ideology. In this, Benjamin Butler was his man.

"NEVER FORGIVE AT THE BALLOT BOX!"

The solution to both the oppression of American workers and the oversized power of the wealthy, for Phillips, was the political organization of voters. In his 1871 pamphlet *The People Coming to Power!* Phillips declared that "I am determined, as far as I am concerned that the brains of this generation shall try to tear that system open and let the light into it, and the readiest way I know is by political action." Through electoral activism, rather than strikes or violence, voters could negate the corrupting influence of wealth and partisan interest. Here again, Butler became the conduit for Phillips's advocacy. Butler, Phillips declared, has "revealed the dry-rot" of the Republicans.[46] The general's campaign, he argued, "is the first blow to knock the Republican Party to pieces."[47] Butler's election would show the Republican Party establishment that voters were paying attention and willing to push in a more radical direction. "The reason why we want Butler put into the [governor's] chair," Phillips explained, "is, because it will teach the Republican party what instruction lingers in the hearts of the people. . . . [The party] needs disturbing; it needs a storm."[48] Phillips was confident that if given the opportunity a majority of Massachusetts voters would support Butler.[49]

In Butler, Phillips found the one candidate who could take his radical message to the voters as an elected official. Although Phillips supported Butler's work in the Congress since the end of the war, he became especially politically involved with Butler during his 1871 campaign. Butler contested the Republican nomination for Massachusetts governor that year and ran on a platform supporting labor reform. Butler's campaign embodied the issues most supported by Phillips, including a coalition of various reform movements like temperance and women's suffrage. Butler, Phillips told an audience in 1871, "represents *an idea*."[50] For Phillips, Butler's campaign could be the catalyst for the universal political transformations he sought.

Despite Phillips's support, at the October 1871 Republican convention in Worcester the delegates rejected Butler's candidacy. As the convention concluded, Butler refused to bolt the party and agreed to support the eventual Republican candidate and current governor William Claflin. Although he disagreed, Phillips understood Butler remaining with the party and was confident that Butler "wouldn't have taken the step he did if he didn't think it was best thing for the causes he advocated as well as himself."[51] Phillips continued to support Butler, and their alliance grew in the late 1870s as both men joined the Greenback Party. In these campaigns, Phillips channeled his continued advocacy of workers' rights into a more pronounced denunciation of moneyed influence in politics.

Phillips remained confident that change could come through electoral organizing, but it was up to workers to mobilize. In April 1872, he spoke before a meeting of the International Grand Lodge of the Knights of Saint Crispin. During his speech he called the audience to action. Phillips declared: "If you want power in this country; if you want to make yourselves felt; if you do not want your children to wait long years before they have the bread on the table they ought to have, the leisure in their lives they ought to have, the opportunities in life they ought to have; if you don't want to wait yourselves,—write on your banner, so that every political trimmer can read it, so that every politician, no matter how short sighted he may be, he can read it, 'We never forget! . . .' So that a man, in taking up the Labor Question, will know he is dealing with a hair-trigger pistol, and will say, 'I am to be true to justice and to man; otherwise I am a dead duck.'"[52]

Uniting behind a candidate and for a specific policy would help deemphasize the differences among workers. By pressing a specific issue, like the eight-hour workday, the demands of the movement could be clearly understood. Phillips concluded that workers should be unequivocal in their support of candidates and hold them accountable for supporting labor reform. "Inscribe it in letters of gold over every ballot-box, 'Here labor never forgives.' . . . I wish I had every primary school, to teach the children their first lesson; I wish I could write a ballad. . . . [T]he refrain of the music should be, 'Never forgive at the ballot-box!'"[53]

Phillips argued that wielding political power via the ballot box was the peaceful and thus preferred method. Workers, he urged, should reject violent overthrow in favor of "agitation, discussion, and . . . associations for mutual help and protection."[54] In particular, he advocated workers uniting as voters and using their electoral strength to sway the platforms of the major parties. "Voters under a representative government," he announced, "let them unite in political action, and appeal to the moral forces of the age. The necessities which underlie free institutions and the soundest maxims of political economy are their strong allies, and the conscience of mankind is on their side."[55] He had great faith in American democracy and was confident that, if organized, American workers and their allies could use it to reform society. "In the name of Heaven, and with the ballot in our right hands," Phillips declared, "we shall not need to write our record in fire and blood; we write it in the orderly majorities at the ballot box."[56]

Political action could lessen the need for potentially violent confrontation. To achieve their goals, workingmen and women should use the ballot to exert political influence and turn to strikes and violence only as a last resort. "Strikes," Phillips declared, "are an admissible and a defensible remedy. . . . Never let a man say a word against strikes, therefore. Always insist that in the last resort of self-defense that is your power."[57] Holding the right to vote, however, American workers should use the ballot primarily to achieve their goals.

Without political action through the ballot, American workers might resort to more extreme violent means. "Politics is the safety-valve," Phillips advised.[58] "If capitalists do not act wisely," he warned, "a revolution will take place which will be nothing to the revolution of 1791."[59] The only solution Phillips concluded is "for capital and labor to meet at once on equal terms, and, acknowledging each other's rights, to arrange their relations on the basis of justice and a fair division of the common profit."[60]

Much of Phillips's ire was targeted at the Republican Party, who he felt had departed from their earlier work on behalf of oppressed people. Phillips argued that the present Republican Party was weak and lacked the principled focus of its earlier years. "The Republican Party is dead," he wrote, "the only mistake is that it fancies itself alive."[61] When the party fought slavery, Phillips argued, its vocal members were united by principle. At present, he lamented, party leaders cast about for prominence and diminished the power of the party. "The men whom the Republican Party has created are not men of convictions," Phillips complained, "they seek only to use for party or personal ends the power they have inherited. . . . [T]he party is falling apart."[62] Meanwhile, a southern Democratic Party united by white supremacy and the cause of black disenfranchisement was gaining power rapidly.

Of additional concern was the increasing embrace of soft-money policy and causes of labor by Democrats, policies attractive to northern working-class voters. If the Republican Party did not move quickly to advocate these reforms, Phillips warned, the Democrats would advance their southern agenda as they rode to power on the strength of northern and western voters. The Republican Party, he declared, "should place itself at the head of the new movement."[63] By becoming the party of labor and financial reform, Phillips urged, Republicans could restore their principled convictions and stem the rising tide of southern Democratic power.

By the early 1870s, Phillips's agitation was beginning to pay off. In 1872, he told a meeting of the International Grand Lodge of the Knights of Saint Crispin that, by organizing voters in labor unions and workers' organizations, calls for labor reform had grown into a national movement. In just three short years, Phillips celebrated, issues of labor reform had gone from marginal discussions of strikes to robust debates in the pages of the national press.

He continued to declare the labor reform movement one of the only hopes for American democracy. The power of labor reformers was the last defense of American government from moneyed interests. "Unless there is power in your movement, industrially and politically," Phillips warned, "the last knell of democratic liberty in this Union is struck. . . . Now, there is nothing but the rallying of men against money that can contest with that power."[64]

Capital had the resources to wait out labor reformers. As continued activism depleted reform coffers, business opposition had the money for a protracted fight. For Phillips, the only way to overcome this challenge and to continue to draw the attention of the nation was to organize on a large scale. "By gathering together by hundreds of thousands, no matter whether it be on an industrial basis or a political basis, and saying to the nation," Phillips commanded, "'We are the numbers, and we will be heard,' and you may be sure that you will."[65] Through this unity, he argued, American workers could make the difference in every state and national election and swing the power away from wealthy political power brokers.[66] Phillips girded his followers for a protracted fight. "You do not kill a hundred millions of corporate capital, you do not destroy the virus of incorporate wealth by any one election," Phillips declared.[67]

"MAN FIRST—MONEY, THE WEEK AFTER"

As Phillips's activism continued, he championed workers' rights while focusing increasingly on the problem of the undue influence of the wealthy on politics. Wealth exploited not only the labor of workers, but it compromised electoral politics as the primary tool for change. In an 1878 pamphlet, Phillips asked, *Who Shall Rule US? Money or the People?* For him the answer was obvious. The only way to achieve meaningful change and improvement of the conditions of American workers was to defeat the outsized influence of money on United States politics. Unless voters acted, the levers of government power would remain in the hands of those sympathetic, not to workers, but to the wealthy bosses and shareholders who exploited them. For Phillips, the best remedy was the mobilization of everyday people. "I believe in the people," Phillips wrote. "If corruption seems rolling over us like a flood, mark, it is not the corruption of the humbler classes. It is the millionaires who steal banks, mills, and railways; it is defaulters who live in palaces, and make way with millions; it is money-kings who buy up Congress. . . . These are the spots where corruption nestles, and gangrenes the state. . . . It is not the common people in the streets, but the Money Changers who have intruded into the temple, that we most sorely need some one to scourge. If the hills will cease to send down rottenness, the streams will clean and clear on the plains."[68]

Phillips's hatred of moneyed influence in American life was related closely to his labor reform work. At the annual convention of the Massachusetts Eight Hour League in 1871, Phillips presented resolutions denouncing corruption. "The labor movement," he began, "is one which deals with principles lying at the very root of democratic institutions. . . . [I]ts solution will tend to overturn and remold society, supplanting old systems of monopoly and fraud with the sway of justice and love."[69] He argued that the recent defeat of a bill in the Massachusetts Legislature mandating a ten-hour workday was "fresh evidence that in this struggle between privileged capital and unfairly burdened labor, there are no Republican and no Democratic lines; but that for us are all the just and fair-minded men, and against us are all the greedy and unscrupulous, who sacrifice justice to party and interest, and make haste to be rich by any means."[70]

Phillips was especially concerned with the outsized influence of corporate money on American politics, which he warned was oppressing the political power of everyday people and undermining American democracy. "The great danger that threatens us in the future," he cautioned, "is the money power."[71] During a March 1871 speech in New York City, Phillips condemned "the power of capital and large corporations, and the influence which they exercised over the Legislature."[72] "The Republican Party itself," he continued, "is rotten to the core with its servility to rank and wealth in Washington."[73]

Phillips cautioned that the wealthy were consolidating power as a new aristocracy and wielding undue influence on government. He publically celebrated the rise in support of labor reform among legislators in the House of Representatives and called upon the audience to resist rising opposition and influence from corporate capital. He warned, during a meeting at Boston's Music Hall in March 1871, that a "great money power looms over the horizon at the very moment when . . . the power of the masses concentrating in the House of Representatives is to become the sole omnipotence of the State."[74] Phillips feared that little could be done to stem the rising tide of incorporated wealth. "No statesman, no public man yet," he explained, "has dared to defy it. Everyman that has met it has been crushed to powder."[75]

Phillips declared the object of labor reformers once elected was to "save the Congress of the Nation from the moneyed corporations of the State."[76] In order to weaken the power of the wealthy, he advocated a system of progressive taxation. The wealthy should be taxed until they "shall not have anything more than a moderate lodging and an honest table."[77] "We'll crumble up wealth by making it unprofitable to be rich," Phillips declared, "The poor man shall have a larger income in the proportion he is poor. The rich man shall have a lesser income in the proportion he is rich. . . . Land, private property, all sorts of property, shall be so dearly taxed that it shall be impossible to be rich; for it is in wealth, in incorporated, combining, perpetuated wealth, that the danger of labor lies."[78] By transferring money from the rich to public coffers, Phillips and other labor reformers would strengthen public programs, like education, and weaken the ability of corporations to influence lawmakers.

The only hope, Phillips argued, was the unification and mobilization of like-minded voters. "It is the working masses that are really about to put their hands to the work of governing. . . . [The labor movement] is the last noble protest of the American people against the power of incorporated wealth."[79] Such a movement could inaugurate a new era, Phillips predicted, "in which we will cut the hamstrings of capital, undermine the tyranny of corporations, and restore the legislatures their independence."[80]

Extending his opposition to the influence of wealth in politics, by the mid-1870s Phillips became a vocal advocate for finance reform and supported specie currency. Hard-money policies, he argued, concentrated wealth in the hands of a few corporate interests and did little to help working people. Again, Phillips was concerned that these policies concentrated too much power in the hands of a wealthy elite few and took financial control away from the populace. He explained his advocacy of finance reform as an outgrowth of his labor reform advocacy. "My interest in finance grew out of the effort to rally a workingman's party," he wrote in a letter to the *Boston Globe.*

> Every wage laborer desired a fair division of the joint product of labor and capital. . . . In our effort to secure a fairer division we soon saw that the dollar in which the labor was paid was one of the most important, if not the most important element, in the solution of this problem. . . . [W]e saw it was currency which, rightly arranged, opened a nation's well springs, found work for willing hands and filled them with a just return, while honest capital, daily larger and more secure, ministered to a great prosperity; or it was currency, wickedly and selfishly juggled, that made merchants bankrupt, and starved labor into discontent and slavery, while capital added house to house and field to field, and gathered into its miserly hands all the wealth left in a ruined land.[81]

As he entered the second half of the decade, Phillips rejected the two major political parties and backed third-party efforts, especially the Greenback Party, as vehicles for labor and financial reform. The Greenback Party, which grew into prominence nationally during the 1870s, advocated the elimination of bank notes in favor of a national paper currency convertible into government bonds bearing a low interest rate.[82] Support for the Greenback Party, with its transfer of currency control to the federal government, was highly controversial, especially in Massachusetts, which was increasingly dominated politically by wealthy Republicans loyal to the banking system and opposed to expanded federal economic authority.[83]

Phillips was attracted by the controversy and viewed the Greenback Party as a vehicle to strike against forces that limited popular control of politics. The greenback movement, as Phillips explained, "is a revolt against a system of finance which rests the power of inflation in the hands of a few hundred bank directors, and lets them play with values at their pleasure . . . a revolt against the notion that, in ordinary matters, the people can govern themselves, but on questions of finance they must be kept under perpetual guardianship, and be the wards of rich men."[84] As with his advocacy of labor reform, Phillips fought any attempt to consolidate power in the hands of the wealthy. The most effective weapon in this battle, he argued, was the ballot, and throughout his advocacy he called on voters to use it to crush the political status quo and place power in the hands of working people.

Phillips channeled his confidence in electoral power into the support of political parties dedicated to the interests of workers and opposition to moneyed corruption. In a speech at the New England convention of the Greenback Party, Phillips argued for the need to consolidate workers' interests into the new party. "To my mind," he explained, "the great object of the Greenback party today should be to show its strength. You want to make the public respect and fear you."[85] Phillips argued that it was unsustainable to maintain a labor party "because no sharp line can be drawn between capital and labor"[86] "We are not against the manufacturers or the merchants," he continued, "We are against the men that live by making corners; that live by making a tail of the nature of currency."[87] Therefore, he called on the Greenback Party to absorb and represent labor interests. Phillips and the party moved forward as the National Greenback and Labor Party.

In supporting the Greenback Party, Phillips repeated his criticisms of Republicans and affirmed his independent stance. "The Republican Party today," Phillips accused, "is inspired and ruled by the money power. . . . Today the greatest danger is the Republican Party, wolves in sheep's clothing. . . . I hail their coming defeat."[88] He concluded, "The best possible thing that could happen in the political field is the disappearance of both the old parties and the rallying of men on new lines . . . that will produce on the stage at once the struggle between (not capital but) capitalists, the money power and the people."[89] He declined the nomination of lieutenant governor, much to the disappointment of party supporters, on the grounds that he could "serve [the greenback movement] more efficiently by remaining outside of party lines, where

Figure 8.1. Phillips embraced Benjamin Butler as "the Beast" come to terrorize the Massachusetts Republican establishment. *Harper's Weekly,* April 11, 1874, Library of Congress.

my whole life has been passed."[90] Phillips's strengths were better used as a leader and an orator. As in earlier efforts, he lent these talents to the service of Benjamin Butler, this time as a Greenback candidate.

"HIS SUCCESS WILL BE THE PEOPLE'S TRIUMPH"

Once again Benjamin F. Butler became the electoral vehicle for Phillips's ideology. In the 1878 gubernatorial campaign, Butler led the Greenback Party ticket, and Phillips traveled the campaign trail on his behalf.[91] "His success," Phillips wrote, "will be the people's triumph."[92] The election of Butler, Phillips often told packed audiences, would begin a national movement to overthrow the current political order and place workers' interests first. "There need be no doubt of the success of the Greenback Party," he said in a *Boston Globe* article. "Its presence is everywhere, in local and national elections."[93]

For Phillips, Butler was essential to the movement's success: "I shall vote for General Butler because he represents the determination of the people to take the currency out of the control of the money kings . . . and keep it for themselves."[94] Phillips reminded voters of the general's longtime support of labor and his early endorsement of financial reform. During a rousing speech at Boston's Mechanic's Hall, Phillips named Butler "a leader of the working men—the manhood of the Northern States."[95] As such, he argued, Butler was best equipped to respond to the most pressing issues of the day, labor and financial reform. "On this great question will turn the welfare of this Commonwealth," he emphasized. "Under what system of finance shall the poor man be endowed and protected? This is the question that is to be decided."[96] Although Butler failed to win, Phillips rededicated himself to the greenback cause and endorsed Butler again the next year.[97]

In 1879, Butler stood again as Greenback candidate for governor. Phillips joined the general briefly on the initial ticket as the nominee for lieutenant governor, but would ultimately decline the nomination. During their annual convention, the party endorsed pro-labor policies, such as a reduction in work hours, restrictions on child labor, and a prohibition on convict labor. During the campaign, Phillips and Butler received support from workingmen against biting criticisms that their personal wealth made them ill-suited as candidates. Their supporters lauded their political independence. "The Greenbackers selected the names for the ticket solely on the ground that they represented not a class," a "greenback workingman" explained in a letter to the *Boston Globe*, "but the interests of the whole people. . . . [Butler] and Wendell Phillips are the two prominent men of all others in Massachusetts who owe no allegiance to party, but go before the people as the candidates of that people, regardless of partisan politics."[98]

Phillips was hopeful that, with Butler at the helm, the Greenback Party could upset the prevailing political order. Both Democrats and Republicans, he argued, were bolting their respective parties to support Butler, who, more than any man, "has been so watchful for the people's interests." "No workingman or poor girl ever was turned away from him. . . . [H]e is loved by all."[99] Despite Phillips's predictions, love for Butler did not win him the governor's seat in 1879—capping off a decade of losses during the 1870s. Butler regrouped, however, and won the office as a Democrat in 1882. In this election his challenge to the status quo finally prevailed. Building on a growing feeling of discontent with the Republicans, Butler's working-class and immigrant supporters helped secure his victory.[100]

Butler's victory after so many years did not lessen Phillips's activism or cause him to temper his rhetoric. Phillips, now infirm and in the final year of his life, continued to support his old friend and ally. Additionally, Phillips persisted to fight for Massachusetts's working people. For example, he testified at a hearing of the state committee on labor in support of legislation increasing the liability for employers whose workers were injured on the job. He criticized current laws as biased in favor of capital.[101] He infused his advocacy of Butler's reelection with these continued critiques of the undue influence of money in politics.

During Butler's reelection campaign in 1883, Phillips prominently campaigned through letters read at public rallies. He explained why, after nearly a decade supporting third parties, he had returned to backing major-party candidates, this time a Democratic Butler. He reflected on his long career and his attempts to establish a successful third party in favor of labor, temperance, or finance, but concluded that "the time has not come to rally a party on either of those lines, and the idea loses more than it gains by such premature attempt. . . . [A]t present there can be only two political parties."[102] Having learned firsthand the dominance of the well-funded machines of the major parties, he saw the best way forward as transforming the parties from within.

The election of Butler to the governor's seat seemed to be a clear step in that direction, and Phillips used the moment to again attack Republicans. During a crowded pro-Butler meeting at Boston's Music Hall on October 10, 1883, Boston Mayor Albert Palmer read a letter from Phillips, who, due to illness, was not able to take part in public meetings.[103] As Phillips declared his support for Butler, he again condemned the influence of corporate money on the Republican Party. He criticized the party's pro-business agenda and the present exploitation of American workers. "I remember that the Republican Party . . . when it had a conscience," Phillips's letter read, "But I see that now, the willing tool of capital and the banks, and with a thimble-rig system of national bonds, it is doing far more to undermine our institutions and enslave the white man."[104]

Echoing years of activism, Phillips argued that moneyed interests continued to control the Republican Party and "hoodwinked" young voters. Butler was the only candidate willing to challenge their power. "The battle today is between men and money. . . . Privileged and incorporated wealth is one of the two great dangers that here threaten popular institutions, and the Republican Party is its servant and organ. Every lover of liberty should therefore toil and pray for its destruction."[105] Therefore, Phillips concluded, "I shall vote for the man who, years and years ago, advocated a system of finance which would have saved us from this bondage to the Shylocks, and would now go far to avert our danger."[106] "I shall hail his re-election this year," he wrote in a letter to the *Boston Globe*, "as a vast stride toward relieving the State from the Republican incubus which weighs so heavily upon it."[107] He lauded the movement behind the Democratic Butler as "the protest of earnest men against all this."[108]

Despite Phillips's best efforts, Butler lost reelection. Less than three months following Butler's defeat, Phillips, suffering from heart disease and after a series of severe seizures, died of a heart attack on February 2, 1884.[109] Significant remembrances highlighted his political independence and dedication to labor reform. At a large public memorial service at Faneuil Hall held under the auspices of the Labor Reform Party, labor reform leader and Minister Jesse H. Jones spoke on Phillips's service on behalf of workers. Phillips, Jones declared, "was genuinely and earnestly a labor reformer as he had been before an antislavery reformer." He praised Phillips's work for "land, time, and finance reform" as "each a true measure to set right the wrongs in the structure or conduct of society to make the life of the laboring man easier on earth."[110]

Other workingmen and labor leaders also joined in remembering Phillips for his work on behalf of the oppressed and as an advocate of independent politics. A speaker at a trade-union meeting declared, "Just as long as the word emancipation exists in the English language, just so long will the name of Wendell Phillips shine on our pages of history. . . . To him there was dignity in labor, in him the oppressed had a bulwark against unjust and discriminating laws.

No plea so powerful to move him as the plea founded on truth, on honesty, on right."[111] Members of a local chapter of the Knights of Labor resolved "that at this critical point in our history the clarion voice of our tried leader is silent. . . . [A]s the representatives of organized labor in this town, while we sorrow for our loss, we will ever cherish . . . the sympathetic heart, the eloquence and the lofty inspiration which made this unequalled man the personal friend of each one of us."[112] At the state convention of the Greenback-Labor Party, organizers memorialized Phillips as rising "high above the petty quibbles of superficial minds, of party lines . . . freeing and elevating the people of his country by infusing them with a higher consciousness of duties and responsibilities toward one another."[113]

The final decade of Wendell Phillips's life brought his passion for economic justice together with his deep belief in electoral democracy as a method of change, although without allegiance to either of the major political parties. In a marked change from his antebellum days, he had come to place his faith in the rise of new parties, led by advocates like Benjamin Butler, who would stand as a bulwark against the moneyed interests that controlled American politics. In both his advocacy for labor reform and his opposition to the corruption of money in politics, he sought the empowerment and autonomy of ordinary people to shape their own economic and political destinies. American voters, like workers, were to shape their own world on their own terms, free of oppression or influence from business interests or political party bosses. Captains of industry and high-level elected officials achieved power only through the workers' production or through the voters' will. Therefore, real power in American society lay not in the halls of government or corporation's boardrooms, but in the hands of the average worker and the voter. The greatest threat facing the United States, Phillips concluded, was greed, and he died dedicated to the struggle toward a nation where workers were treated justly and capital and labor united toward a common good.

NOTES

1. "General Butler," *Boston Daily Globe*, December 14, 1890.

2. James Brewer Stewart, *Wendell Phillips: Liberty's Hero* (Baton Rouge: Louisiana State University Press, 1986); David Zonderman, *Uneasy Allies: Working for Labor Reform in Nineteenth Century Boston* (Amherst: University of Massachusetts Press, 2011); Timothy Messer-Kruse, "Eight

Hours, Greenbacks and 'Chinamen': Wendell Phillips, Ira Seward, and the Fate of Labor Reform in Massachusetts," *Labor History* 42 (2001): 133–58; Brian Greenberg, "Wendell Phillips and the Idea of Industrial Democracy in Early Postbellum America," in *The Struggle for Equality: Essays on Sectional Conflict, the Civil War, and the Long Reconstruction*, ed. Orville Vernon Burton, Jerald Podair, and Jennifer L. Weber (Charlottesville: University of Virginia Press, 2011), 137–52.

3. Stewart, *Wendell Phillips*, 119–20.

4. Eric Foner, *Reconstruction: America's Unfinished Revolution, 1863–1877* (New York: Harper and Row, 1988), 469–99; Heather Cox Richardson, *The Death of Reconstruction: Race, Labor, and Politics in the Post–Civil War North, 1865–1901* (Cambridge: Harvard University Press, 2001).

5. Foner, *Reconstruction*, 491.

6. Stewart, *Wendell Phillips*, 244.

7. Quoted in Fisher A. Hildreth to General Butler, March 24, 1864, in Benjamin F. Butler, *Private and Official Correspondence of Gen. Benjamin Butler During the Period of the Civil War*, 5 vols. (Norwood, Mass., Plimpton Press, 1917), vol. 3: 574.

8. J. O. A. Griffin to Benjamin Butler, January 18, 1863, in *Private and Official Correspondence of Gen. Benjamin Butler* 2: 580.

9. Wendell Phillips to Benjamin Butler, December 11, 1864, quoted in "Gen. Butler," *Boston Daily Globe*, December 14, 1890.

10. Stewart, *Wendell Phillips*, 297–98.

11. Wendell Phillips, *Speeches, Lectures, and, Letters, Second Series* (Boston: Lee and Shepard Publishers, 1891), 152.

12. Phillips, *Speeches, Lectures, and Letters, Second Series*, 152.

13. Ibid., 153.

14. Ibid.

15. Wendell Phillips, *The People Coming to Power!: Speech of Wendell Phillips, Esq., at the Salisbury Beach Gathering, September 13, 1871* (Boston: Lee and Shepard, 1871), 9.

16. Ibid., 9.

17. "Wendell Phillips' Letter," *New York Times*, August 21, 1872.

18. Phillips, *The People Coming to Power!* 17.

19. Phillips, "The Foundation of the Labor Movement," *Speeches, Lectures, and Letters, Second Series*, 163.

20. Phillips, *The People Coming to Power!* 10.

21. Wendell Phillips, "The Outlook," *North American Review* 127 (July–August 1878): 112.

22. Ibid., 112.

23. Ibid., 113.

24. Ibid., 114.

25. Messer-Kruse, "Eight Hours, Greenbacks and 'Chinamen.'"

26. "The Eight Hour Movement," *New York Times*, May 24, 1870.

27. Ibid.

28. Ibid.

29. Zonderman, *Uneasy Allies*, 141.

30. "Massachusetts Labor Reform Convention," *New York Times*, September 8, 1870; Zonder-

man, *Uneasy Allies*, 158–59. In 1870, Phillips was also nominated by the Prohibition Party; see "Massachusetts: Formation of Prohibition Party," *New York Times*, August 18, 1870.

31. "Wendell Phillips," *New York Times*, September 13, 1870.

32. Ibid.

33. Ibid.

34. Ibid.

35. "Massachusetts Politics," *New York Times*, August 29, 1870.

36. Ibid.

37. "Wendell Phillips," *New York Times*, October 19, 1870.

38. Ibid.

39. Ibid., November 4, 1870.

40. "The Campaign at Boston," *New York Times*, November 8, 1870; "The Official Vote of Massachusetts," *New York Times*, November 28, 1870.

41. "Wendell Phillips," *New York Times*, December 1, 1870.

42. Ibid.

43. Ibid.

44. "Massachusetts," *New York Times*, August 10, 1871.

45. Ibid.

46. Phillips, *The People Coming to Power!* 10–11.

47. "Massachusetts," *New York Times*, August 10, 1871.

48. Phillips, *The People Coming to Power!* 19–20.

49. "What the Champion of a Demagogue Thinks of Him Now," *New York Times*, October 4, 1871.

50. Phillips, *The People Coming to Power!* 6.

51. "What the Champion of a Demagogue Thinks of Him Now."

52. Phillips, *Speeches, Lectures, and Letters, Second Series*, 177.

53. "The Eight Hour Movement," *New York Times*, May 24, 1870.

54. Phillips, "The Outlook," 114.

55. Ibid.

56. Phillips, *Speeches, Lectures, and Letters, Second Series*, 154.

57. "The Eight Hour Movement," *New York Times*, May 24, 1870.

58. Phillips, *Speeches, Lectures, and Letters, Second Series*, 158.

59. "The Questions of Today," *New York Times*, March 8, 1871.

60. "The Reform League," *New York Times*, May 10, 1871.

61. Phillips, *The People Coming to Power!* 8.

62. Phillips, "The Outlook," 97.

63. Ibid., 114.

64. Phillips, *Speeches, Lectures, and Letters, Second Series*, 175.

65. Ibid., 170.

66. Ibid., 176.

67. Ibid., 154.

68. Wendell Phillips, *Who Shall Rule US? Money or the People?* (Boston: Franklin Press: Rand, Avery, and Co., 1878), 8.

69. "The Eight Hour League," *New York Times*, June 1, 1871.

70. Ibid.

71. Phillips, *The People Coming to Power!* 12.

72. "The Questions of Today."

73. Ibid.

74. Phillips, *Speeches, Lectures, and Letters, Second Series*, 157.

75. Ibid., 157.

76. Ibid., 167.

77. Ibid.

78. Ibid.

79. Ibid., 157.

80. Phillips, *The People Coming to Power!* 18.

81. "Wendell Phillips," *Boston Daily Globe*, October 27, 1878; Phillips, *Who Shall Rule US?* 5.

82. Foner, *Reconstruction*, 478.

83. Gretchen Ritter, *Goldbugs and Greenbacks: The Antimonopoly Tradition and the Politics of Finance in America, 1865–1896* (New York: Cambridge University Press, 1997), 147.

84. Phillips, "The Outlook," 110.

85. "Greenbacks and Labor," *Boston Daily Globe*, January 3, 1879.

86. "Greenbacks in Conference," *New York Times*, January 3, 1879.

87. Ibid.

88. "Phillips Declines," *Boston Daily Globe*, September 29, 1879.

89. Ibid.

90. Ibid. On reaction to Phillips declining the nomination, see "The Greenbackers," *Boston Daily Globe*, October 12, 1879.

91. The Greenback Party nominated Phillips for Congress from Massachusetts's Fourth District, but he did not accept. See "The Bay State Greenbackers," *New York Times*, October 25, 1878; "Phillips and Greenbackers," *Boston Daily Globe*, November 2, 1878.

92. Phillips, *Who Shall Rule US?* 8.

93. "That New Party," *Boston Daily Globe*, May 11, 1878.

94. "Wendell Phillips," *Boston Daily Globe*, October 27, 1878; Phillips, *Who Shall Rule US?* 4.

95. "At Mechanics Hall," *Boston Daily Globe*, November 1, 1878.

96. Ibid.

97. "Just Before," *Boston Daily Globe*, November 5, 1878.

98. "General Butler and Wendell Phillips," *Boston Daily Globe*, September 26, 1879.

99. "Wendell Phillips," *Boston Daily Globe*, October 24, 1879.

100. Richard Harmond, "The 'Beast' in Boston: Benjamin F. Butler as Governor of Massachusetts," *Journal of American History* 55 (September 1968): 268–69.

101. "Wendell Phillips," *Boston Daily Globe*, March 14, 1883. He also sent letters in support of a telegraph workers' strike; see "From Absent Sympathizers," *Boston Daily Globe*, August 15, 1883.

102. "Wendell Phillips on Butler," *Boston Daily Globe*, September 15, 1883.

103. "Wendell Phillips," *Boston Daily Globe*, October 11, 1883.

104. Ibid.

105. Ibid.
106. Ibid.
107. "Wendell Phillips on Butler."
108. Ibid.
109. "Wendell Phillips Ill," *New York Times*, February 2, 1884; Stewart, *Wendell Phillips*, 333–34.
110. "Wendell Phillips," *Boston Daily Globe*, February 9, 1884.
111. "Among the Laborers," *Boston Daily Globe*, February 5, 1884.
112. "Action of the Knights of Labor Assemblies," *Boston Daily Globe*, February 7, 1884.
113. "Equality in All Things," *Boston Daily Globe*, April 26, 1884.

9

THE RIGHTS OF OTHERS

Wendell Phillips and Women's Rights

HÉLÈNE QUANQUIN

In 1869, supporters of woman suffrage split over support for the Fifteenth Amendment.[1] Wendell Phillips's advocacy of the amendment sparked accusations from his former allies that he had abandoned the cause of woman suffrage. In 1866, he had opposed the Fourteenth Amendment, which defined United States citizenship and granted equal protection under the law, on two grounds. First, he did not believe that it offered enough protection for the rights of African Americans against "the dominant race of the Southern Territories." Second, he opposed the introduction of the word "male" for the first time in the Constitution, which, he feared, "confin[ed] us in the onward march of the suffrage question to one sex."[2] Three years later, in an article published in the *Woman's Advocate* and the *National Anti-Slavery Standard*, he argued that the Fifteenth Amendment, which prohibited disfranchisement on the basis of "race, color, or previous condition of servitude," did not explicitly enfranchise women, but differed from the Fourteenth Amendment. The word "male"—"odious to all, in laws and constitutions"—was not mentioned in it: "Wherever and whenever women vote," he claimed, the Fifteenth Amendment "will protect their rights as fully as those of men, and be as valuable to them as to men." He then called for a Sixteenth Amendment to ban disenfranchisement on the basis of sex.[3]

In the same article, Phillips targeted such activists as Elizabeth Cady Stanton and Susan B. Anthony, who had been actively campaigning against the passage of the Fifteenth Amendment and had attacked him as president of the American Anti-Slavery Society for the organization's refusal to include woman suffrage in its platform.[4] Phillips maintained that "ignorance" and "selfishness" blinded those who failed to recognize the important difference between the Fourteenth and Fifteenth amendments and condescendingly deplored women's rights activists' insufficient "education in reform." They did not see, he claimed, what was really at stake in the debates—namely, the instability of the South and the threat to the safety and lives of African Americans, making their enfranchisement an urgent priority.[5] He contended that at this crucial point in American history women's rights represented "essentially a selfish" movement as "women [were] contending for their own rights." By contrast, he viewed abolitionism as "disinterested," with free people who battled on behalf of those without liberty and would gain nothing personally by success. He regretfully added that, "[w]hen women emphasize this selfishness by turning aside to oppose the rights of others, it is, in truth, no generous spectacle."[6]

Phillips's postwar critique of the women's rights movement revolved around the idea that a movement's legitimacy came as much from the disinterestedness of its supporters—the ability to see beyond their own group and fight for the "rights of others"—as from the cause itself. Phillips lectured the feminist adversaries of the Fifteenth Amendment, asserting that the "true reformer" would never view progress for one group as detrimental to that of another.[7] He maintained that people could fight for their own rights, but should never impede the advancement of the "rights of others." But was Phillips's assessment unproblematic?

Until 1860, Phillips had epitomized the figure of the "true reformer," and his commitment to women's rights had been virtually unquestioned by his contemporaries, even those women's rights activists who opposed him after the Civil War. Although not present at the Seneca Falls Convention in July 1848, he did sign calls for national woman's rights conventions in the 1850s and attended some of them. He had become such a constant fixture at those conventions that in 1861, Anthony, who attempted to organize a meeting that year against the opposition of most reformers (including Stanton), pleaded with him that "[w]e surely cannot get through a W[oman's].R[ights]. Con[vention]. without you or Mr. Garrison & others of the A[nti].S[lavery]. friends as speakers & audience."[8] His presence at a women's rights convention still embodied the close link between abolitionism and the women's rights movement.

Since the end of the nineteenth century, Phillips's biographers have considered his commitment to women's rights mostly as an integral and uncomplicated part of his reform activism—the logical continuation of his abolitionism. Carlos Martyn, who had known Phillips and published his biography in 1890, asserted that the reformer was proud that women's rights "should have been the issue of the Abolition movement—as Eve was taken from the side of Adam."[9] Yet, as the division of the antislavery movement in the late 1830s and the post–Civil War debates over the Fifteenth Amendment show, the relationship between abolitionism and the women's rights movement was never so straightforward. The two movements interacted with each other, but the phrase "woman's rights"—used during Phillips's lifetime—encompassed complex and intertwined issues ranging from woman suffrage to women's education to a host of divisive issues surrounding marriage and definitions of gender. It meant different things to different people, including abolitionists and women's rights activists.[10]

Phillips wrestled with the political and personal implications of his feminist ideas. His stand on women's rights, informed by his abolitionist convictions and understanding of American democracy, also depended upon more personal elements. In *The Second Sex*, Simone de Beauvoir noted that women's condition differed from other oppressed groups as they live in close proximity to their oppressors and are isolated from one another.[11] For Phillips, this meant that "the rights of others" also included his relationship with his wife, and correlated to a certain extent with dominant cultural and self-definitions of masculinity and femininity. His women's rights commitment did not provoke a drastic "modification in [his] own gender identity," but certainly involved personal queries and challenges that his other engagements did not necessarily imply.[12]

WOMEN'S RIGHTS, ABOLITION, AND DEMOCRACY

In an undated letter, Anna Greene Alvord, the wealthy financial backer of Brook Farm, asked Phillips about the origins of his women's rights convictions: "I saw your name in the papers, and you were considered very radical on the woman question—when did you adopt such views?"[13] We do not have Phillips's answer to this question, but in keeping with other male abolitionists he gradually moved toward women's rights activism. As the abolitionist movement's "leading public intellectual" when the women's rights movement emerged in the 1840s and 1850s, he helped formalize a discourse on women's rights.[14] Grounded in his antislavery convictions and views on democracy, Phillips's advocacy of women's rights increasingly chafed against the feminist interpretation and goals of such activists as Elizabeth Cady Stanton, who advocated a "stand-alone feminism" and devoted "her considerable intellect solely to developing the philosophy and promoting the cause of woman's rights."[15]

Phillips advocated the cause of women's rights very early on in his career as a reformer. His many powerful speeches became influential landmarks of the movement. In particular, his remarks on the first day of the World's Anti-Slavery Convention in London in June 1840 in defense of the right of American female delegates to speak at the proceedings earned him, according to the authors of *The History of Woman Suffrage*, "the sincere gratitude of all womankind."[16] He quickly became an authoritative voice for the movement, and in the mid-1850s Lucy Stone even claimed that he had converted Theodore Parker to women's rights: "On his return from one of these conventions, Wendell Phillips met Theodore Parker, who said to Mr. Phillips, hearing that he had been to a Woman's Rights Convention: 'Wendell, don't make a fool of yourself.' Mr. Phillips replied: 'Theodore, this is the gravest question of the age. You ought to understand it.' Thus admonished, Theodore Parker studied the subject, and before the close of the year he saw, as Wendell Phillips did, that it was 'the gravest question of the age.' He preached four sermons on it."[17]

His "conversion" of Parker—a considerable intellectual force in reform circles at the time—and the fact that people at the time might have believed Stone's story testified to Phillips's authority and persuasive powers. Women's rights activists also looked to him for guidance and reliable information, for instance regarding the law. In 1855, reformer Caroline Healey Dall asked him for "a list of all the laws in Mass. which bear unjustly or unequally on women" for an article she was to write for the women's rights periodical *Una*, adding that she "presume[d] that [he] may have such a list."[18]

Phillips first became drawn into women's rights during the acrimony of the late 1830s over the role of women within antislavery organizations, a well-documented controversy that ultimately divided the American Anti-Slavery Society in 1840.[19] Garrison's support for equal roles for women in the abolitionist movement had been inspired by his 1833 trip to England and the agitation of British female abolitionists.[20] Thereafter, he personally encouraged the participation of American women and, after hearing about the formation of the Boston Female Anti-Slavery Society in October 1833, he informed its members that "[his] heart was cheered" by the news.[21] Before his engagement to Helen Eliza Benson, he urged her to organize a women's abolitionist society, as he "rel[ied] upon female influence to break the shackles of the bleeding slave."[22]

As noted by W. Caleb McDaniel, British abolitionist George Thompson's tour of the United States in the summer of 1835 "helped catalyze the growth of American women's antislavery societies" and "converted" many women to abolitionism, including Angelina E. Grimké and Sarah Pugh.[23] Thereafter, women played central roles in the abolitionist movement, especially through the organization of antislavery fairs, which "provided crucial financial support for abolitionist activities."[24] In 1837, probably impressed by the action of the many abolitionist women he knew, Garrison "began arguing that women could hold official positions in mixed antislavery societies."[25]

Resistance began almost immediately. In July 1838, for instance, the Boston reformer Anne Warren Weston described a committee meeting of the Massachusetts Anti-Slavery Society in which she and her sister Caroline Weston noted instant disagreement over the "woman question." "[T]hey asked us if we wished to take seats with the Committee," Anne wrote. "Caroline said that she threw the whole burden of introducing women into the Committee upon Mr. Phelps. This made a laugh but was a constrained one on the part of Mr. P." Concerning Amos A. Phelps, she wrote, "I'd say the truth, he is so sensitive about this subject that he cannot laugh about it."[26] Animosity became so heated that many of Garrison's former colleagues, as Maria Weston Chapman observed, simply dismissed him as "a Fanny Wright man—an infidel—a Sabbath-breaker—a bad and dangerous man—promulgating the doctrines of the French Jacobins, &c. &c."[27]

The battle over women's role in the movement culminated at the annual meeting of the American Anti-Slavery Society in New York City in May 1840. The election of Abby Kelley to the society's executive committee—with 557 votes for and 451 against—accelerated the split. John Greenleaf Whittier described Kelley's election as "the affair—the bomb-shell that exploded the society."[28] Refusing to serve with a woman, Lewis Tappan, Amos A. Phelps, and Charles W. Denison resigned.[29] Whittier claimed that Phelps did "not hesitate to [compare Kelley's] conduct to that of old Mrs. Adam in [Eden], Delilah shearing Sampson, etc—," showing the extent of both the rift and the prejudice surrounding women abolitionists.[30]

Garrison's nonresistance, which implied both pacifism and nonparticipation in government, as well as his opposition to capital punishment, became primary bones of contention between the warring sides, leading to what W. Caleb McDaniel has called "a tactical gap that proved impossible to bridge."[31] But the unbridgeable divide also focused on the question of women's equal role in the society, raised by the election of Abby Kelley, which sent the society's more conservative members packing. Lewis Tappan and his fellow conservatives then organized the male-dominated American and Foreign Anti-Slavery Society. His brother Arthur became the society's president and justified the move by explaining that the American Anti-Slavery Society had been founded by men only, and not by "a mixed society of men and women," adding that the role of women should be confined to that of auxiliaries.[32] To link abolition and women's rights, Tappan asserted, would be to create an unwanted and uncalled-for "innovation," which would only "divert the minds of abolitionists from the cause of the slave." He appealed to custom, arguing that women's equal participation "was contrary to the usages of the civilized world."[33] While reflecting increasingly combative relations among the various abolitionist factions, the split did give the American Anti-Slavery Society greater ideological coherence and, equally important, critical roles for women.[34]

From the very beginning of the conflict, Phillips supported Garrison and the presence of women in leadership roles. Although he never accepted non-resistance philosophy, he did support the peace movement and attended the Boston Peace Convention of September 18, 1838, which founded the New England Non-Resistance Society, and was appointed to the business committee after male members walked out to protest against the admission of women as delegates.[35] In June 1839, he received a letter from Sarah Baker, a Danvers, Massachusetts, abolitionist, who thanked him for "open[ing] [his] mouth for the dumb of [her] sex."[36]

At the time of the contentious New York meeting of the American Anti-Slavery Society, Phillips and his wife, Ann Greene Phillips, had been traveling in Europe for almost a year. Suffering from what would become a lifelong affliction which began in 1836, she endured crippling pains that no medical treatment could alleviate. She improved somewhat before their wedding in 1837 and for a time appeared to enjoy good health, but it did not last. By the early summer of 1839, shooting pains returned. Her physicians suggested a European tour—a common recommendation to promote recuperation. Through numerous letters and copies of the *Liberator*, the Phillipses kept abreast of the growing divisions among the American abolitionists. While staying in London they discussed with George Thompson the organization of the World's Anti-Slavery Convention, scheduled for June 1840. In a letter to Garrison published in the *Liberator* in August, Phillips referred to the upcoming London meeting, writing that Thompson had "insist[ed] on you coming, accompanied by many of the men and women of our ranks."[37]

Several American organizations, both mixed-gender and women's associations, sent female delegates to London.[38] Warned by American opponents of women's participation that their colleagues intended to send female delegates, the organizing committee of the London convention issued a statement prior to the convention's start that only male delegates would be admitted. According to Phillips and his Garrisonian colleagues, the ban contradicted the "inclusive rhetoric" of the convention's initial call, which had been addressed to "the friends of the slave of every nation and of every clime."[39] According to Lucretia Mott, when asked about this contradiction, the convention organizers replied that "the name 'The World's Convention' was merely 'poetical license.'"[40] When they arrived in England, the American delegates learned that the exclusion of women would stand.[41] The day before the opening of the convention, the female delegates from Pennsylvania issued a protest, denouncing their exclusion as an injustice.[42] Unwilling to disrupt the convention, however, they decided not to present their credentials since, as James Mott noted, "[t]he privation seemed to them trifling, in comparison with the oppression of those whose rights they were willing and desirous to aid in restoring."[43] Yet, the credentials of the female delegates of the Massachusetts Anti-Slavery Society, such as Ann Phillips, were "harder to ignore, as men carried authorizations from the same body." Phillips and his wife were delegates of the same organization.[44]

The London convention opened at Freemason's Hall, at 11 a.m. on Friday, June 12. The women present, including Ann Phillips, sat apart from the men, in "[t]he upper end and one side of the room," the only place where they had been allowed to sit.[45] The topic of women's participation had already dominated the conversations among delegates before the opening, and expectations had been building as to how the convention would handle the controversy. The first day's session started with Reverend Thomas Scales's "exposition of the objects of the Convention," which warned against the introduction of "topics of a foreign and irrelevant character," a clear allusion to the different issues which had split the American abolitionist movement, including nonresistance and women's participation in the debates.[46]

Wendell Phillips then introduced the question of the participation of female delegates in the proceedings by calling for the preparation of an official membership roll. He moved that "a committee of five be appointed to prepare a correct list of the members of this Convention, with instructions to include in such [a] list all persons bearing credentials from any Anti-Slavery body."[47] The preparation of an official membership roll had been a tactic used for almost two years by American proponents of women's admission as a way to introduce the issue at the conventions they attended, including non-abolitionist ones. At the 1838 Peace Convention, Garrison wrote his wife, explaining that "When the roll of members was about being made out, I rose and suggested, that, as mistakes often occur in procuring signatures, each individual should write his or *her* name on a slip of paper, &c.; thus mooting the vexed 'woman question' at the very outset."[48] Calling for the "roll" had been a well-worn tactic for both advocates and opponents of women's participation. Garrison noted that, after introducing his resolution, "There was a smile on the countenances of many abolition friends, while others in the Convention looked very grave." But "[o]f course," he proudly noted, "women became members, and were thus entitled to speak and vote."[49] Similarly, at the acrimonious May 1839 annual meeting of the American Anti-Slavery Society, participants had divided over a resolution that called for "the names of all persons, male and female, who are delegates from any auxiliary society, or members of this society," to be placed on the roll of the meeting.[50]

Phillips had been present at both meetings, and in London he adopted the same tactic. He asserted that it was not "just or equitable" to exclude women from the membership rolls. Moreover, "We stand here in consequence of your invitation, and knowing our custom, as it must be presumed you did," he argued, "we had a right to interpret 'friends of the slave' to include women as well as men." He refused to allow the English to impose their "custom" on Americans: "We have not changed by crossing the water. We stand here the advocates of the same principle that we contend for in America. We think it right for women to sit by our side there, and we think it right for them to do the same here."[51]

Undoubtedly, the American delegates had planned the protest and deliberately chose Phillips to present the case for seating the women. His renowned talent for oratory, his high social standing—appreciated by both American and British delegates, who had chosen him as one of two American secretaries of the convention—and the fact that his wife had been officially chosen as a delegate probably governed his selection. Moreover, he may have sought out the opportunity to reengage with the movement after so long an absence because of his wife's illness.[52]

On the first day of the convention, Phillips tried to strengthen his case for the seating of the female delegates by exposing it as part of a larger effort by his American opponents to discredit Garrison for his unorthodox social and political views. As early as January 1839, Garrison had been denouncing "a conspiracy going in our midst . . . in the hope of subverting the Liberator, and thus driving *me* from the field."[53] Phillips, hoping to deemphasize American dissension over the role of women in the movement, maintained that "[i]t was political action which divided us [Americans], and not the introduction of the woman's question."[54] He hinted at some of the issues that American abolitionists had fought over in the previous months, specifically involvement in party politics and opposition to nonresistance principles. He sought to answer what he saw as the misleading comments made earlier by James G. Birney, the Kentucky abolitionist and Liberty Party candidate for president, and an opponent of women's participation, who had claimed that "there were other grounds of separation deemed more obnoxious than the one now under discussion [women's participation]; but it was *one* of the grounds, and considered by no means an unimportant one."[55] In his reply to Birney, Phillips suggested that the "woman question" had not been the decisive factor in the split within the abolitionist movement.

In the published proceedings of the convention, however, we find a footnote to Phillips's comments: "Mr. Phillips has since expressed a desire that an acknowledgment should be made on his behalf that he was in error here. The alleged causes of the division in America have been the introduction of women into the meetings, and differences about resolutions on political action."[56] Phillips confirmed a disagreement over "political action" but then qualified his previous statement, which diminished the importance of the "woman question" in dividing American abolitionists. He conceded that "the introduction of women into the [abolitionist] meetings" had proved contentious, a reference to the already noted debates over the presence of women in the same associations as men.

Although there is evidence of some communication between Phillips and the Committee of the British and Foreign Anti-Slavery Society after the convention, it is not clear when, why, or in what manner he asked for the correction.[57] The very fact that he did, however, is evidence of the importance he placed on the issue and how it appeared in the convention proceedings—

and especially the way his comments would be interpreted. He might have prompted the correction after discussing the issue with his colleagues or after reading the "Both Wrong" article in the August 14 issue of the *Liberator*, which appeared to place equal weight on "the woman question" and "politics" for the divisions among abolitionists. To account for Phillips's "mistake," the author of the article added that the quotation from his speech might have been "an error of the reporter," which Phillips's correction contradicts.[58]

In London, Phillips stood firm for the female delegates and drew attention to the invaluable and equal contribution of women to the American antislavery movement. He claimed, "We could not go back to America to ask for any aid from the women of Massachusetts if we had deserted them, when they chose to send out their own sisters as their representatives here."[59] Additionally, he drew an obvious parallel between the situation of women at the convention and that of blacks in the United States. "When we have submitted to brick-bats, and the tar tub and feathers in America, rather than yield to the custom prevalent there of not admitting colored brethren into our friendship," he asked, "shall we yield to parallel custom or prejudice against women in Old England?"[60]

The day before, Lucretia Mott had used the very same argument with Samuel Jackman Prescod, a black delegate from Barbados, who had been sent to the American women delegates' boarding house in order "to persuade [them] not to offer [themselves] to the Convention." Prescod had argued that "it would lower the dignity of the Convention and bring ridicule on the whole thing if ladies were admitted," to which American delegates had answered "that similar reasons were urged in Philadelphia for the exclusion of colored people from our meetings—but had we yielded on such flimsy arguments, we might as well have abandoned our enterprise."[61]

Phillips intended to create a sense among the audience that the fight for justice required close attention to all prejudices, an argument similar to the one he developed thirty-nine years later when criticizing women's rights activists' opposition to the enfranchisement of freedmen. Phillips's remarks, however, did not take into account the fact that some abolitionists were not necessarily intent on promoting equality between the races, let alone between the sexes. English painter Benjamin Robert Haydon, commissioned to render a painting of the convention, recalled in his diary the difficulties he had in convincing the English abolitionist John Scoble, also an opponent of women's participation, to be represented next to a black delegate, William Knibb.[62]

While Phillips's and other American delegates' comments in London do not show clear indications that his defense of women's participation was part of a larger discourse on women's rights, his opponents certainly thought so. In London, Birney mentioned in the proceedings that the question was necessarily linked to that of "the perfect equalization of the sexes as to rights, duties, &c., &c."[63] In a letter published in the *Pennsylvania Freeman* in November 1840, the Quaker abolitionist and poet John Greenleaf Whittier described the British abolitionists as sincere reformers who had come to London expecting to discuss emancipation, not "Yankee doctrines of Equality, or sexless democracy."[64]

The convention voted overwhelmingly against admitting women as delegates. When George Thompson asked him publicly if he would comply with the decision, Phillips replied with grace: "There is no unpleasant feeling in our minds," he assured him. "I have no doubt the women will sit with as much interest behind the bar as though the original proposition had been carried in the affirmative. All we asked was an expression of opinion, and, having obtained it, we shall now act with the utmost cordiality."[65] Fifty years later, and despite their praise for Phillips's advocacy of women's equal participation in the proceedings, Stanton and Anthony nevertheless interpreted the remarks as evidence of Phillips's—and men's—failure "to understand what liberty means for woman."[66]

This view, published in 1881, probably reflected Stanton's and Anthony's resentment over Phillips's position on women's rights after the Civil War. In fact, no evidence exists from American supporters of women's participation criticizing Phillips's conciliatory remarks at the time. On the contrary, he was admired for his courage. Abby Kelley, who did not attend the London convention, had criticized Lucretia Mott's decision not to present her credentials, which for her meant that "Mott ha[d] sacrificed *principle* on the altar of Peace." Mott's rather crisp answer in a letter to her sister Martha C. Wright praised the Phillipses' conduct. She was "glad however that Wendell Phillips & Ann were not so easily put by & that he came forward & manfully plead for the right—I shall ever love Ann Phillips for her earnest appeals to her husband to stand firm in that hour of trial—and him for doing so—Tell Abby Kelly [*sic*] if I am not much bold myself I respect those who are so."[67]

Garrison's conduct at the convention stands in sharp contrast with that of Phillips. Garrison had taken part in the New York annual meeting of the American Anti-Slavery Society in May and because of poor weather arrived almost a week after the opening of the meeting. When he learned of the convention's decision, he and his three fellow-travelers, including Charles L. Remond, the only African American delegate, forfeited their credentials to protest women's exclusion from the debates.[68] Garrison's silence proved deafening. His fellow American delegates tried to convince him to participate, but they failed, as Lucretia Mott confided to her diary: "met William L[loyd] G[arrison] & Co. 'with joy & sorrow too'—they had resolved not to enter the Convention where we were excluded—reasoned with them on the subject—found them fixed."[69] Despite the injustice he perceived, Phillips (with the support of Mott and other women) did not follow Garrison's stand and disrupt the first world's antislavery convention further.[70]

Although he was clearly disappointed by the London meeting, the experience became a stepping stone upon which Phillips—and other male abolitionists—developed support for the emerging women's rights movement in the 1840s. The broadening conversation on women's position in society became integral to Phillips's larger discourse on democracy and republicanism in the United States. In July 1846, he observed, "In regard to the civil position of women, it is especially true that the western States have drunk deeper of the fresh spirit of the age." He advocated that women should have "the full and unfettered control of all her property and earnings, whether she were married or unmarried, claiming that it "developes [*sic*] character and intellect."[71] He also expressed his support for woman suffrage and found receptive ears in Garrison, who predicted ultimate success for the cause of women's rights: "There's 'a good time coming' for the whole human race, yet. In this faith, I mean to live, and hope to die."[72] Several of Phillips's coadjutors agreed. In 1845, Samuel J. May had become the first American minister to advocate women's enfranchisement.[73]

At the Second National Woman's Rights Convention, in 1851, Phillips gave a speech that women's rights activists considered the perfect synthesis of reformers' views on the antebellum movement. Phillips's first biographer, George Lowell Austin, called it a "remarkable address," while his memorialist George William Curtis claimed that "more than any other single impulse, [it] launched that question upon the sea of popular controversy. In the general statement of principle nothing has been added to that discourse; in vivid and effective eloquence of advocacy it has never been surpassed."[74] In the mid-1850s, Lucy Stone included the address in a compilation of what she considered to be the era's most important "woman's rights tracts."[75]

Phillips used his force of conviction and unmatched oratorical skills to develop a feminist discourse based on universal rights and republicanism—a popular approach among women's rights activists.[76] The Declaration of Sentiments adopted at Seneca Falls in July 1848, for instance, borrowed heavily from the Declaration of Independence, and an 1846 petition presented at the New York State Constitutional Convention, asking for "the extension of the elective franchise to women," also manifested a "stunning grasp of democratic republican rhetoric."[77] In 1851, Phillips, as he would do in most of his speeches, asserted that justice dictated that "the civil rights and privileges which man enjoys," including suffrage, and the right "to choose for herself her profession, her education, and her sphere" should be similarly open to women.[78]

Women's alleged inferiority did not constitute legitimate grounds for excluding them from full-fledged citizenship, he asserted, as women's true potential nature could not be assessed until they had access to the same rights and privileges as men, an argument which abolitionists also used to support equal rights between whites and blacks. For him, "All that woman asks through this movement is, to be allowed to prove what she can do; to prove it by liberty of choice, by liberty of action, the only means by which it ever can be settled how much and what she can do." He underscored the value of "responsibility" as "one instrument—a great instrument—of education, both moral and intellectual," a comment reminiscent of his 1846 remarks on property rights as a means to educate women. If "female profligacy" existed, he asserted, the fact that "all the other powers [of women] are dormant for want of exercise" explains why. Woman suffrage and women's equal rights thus fit in with Phillips's vision of the three pillars of democratization: "individual thought, constant agitation, and education."[79]

For Phillips, women's condition became "the test of civilization," a central component of the development of American democracy and part of the history of human and political progress.[80] In his 1851 oration, he described his vision of the general movement toward equality: "The law has been always wrong. Government began in tyranny and force, began in the feudalism of the soldier and bigotry of the priest; and the ideas of justice and humanity have been fighting their way, like a thunder-storm, against the organized selfishness of human nature. And this is the last great protest against the wrongs of the ages. It is no argument to my mind, therefore, that the old social fabric of the past is against us."[81]

Phillips's discourse, however, exhibited certain limitations in light of the growing movement for women's rights before the Civil War. When Stanton attempted to introduce reform of laws regarding marriage and divorce into the debate, Phillips recoiled. At the Tenth National Woman's Rights Convention in May 1860—the last one to take place before the Civil War—delegates divided over Stanton's resolutions calling for legislation on marriage reform and divorce rights. In his speech at the convention, Phillips, who asked for the resolutions not to be included in the "journal" of the meeting, argued that the convention "ha[d] nothing to do with them, any more than with the question of intemperance, or Kansas." For him, the object of women's rights meetings was first and foremost the discussion of "the laws that rest[ed] unequally upon women," while "whether a man and a woman [we]re married for a year or a life [wa]s a question which affect[ed] the man just as much as the woman." Although he still conceded that "the results of marriage, in the present condition of society, [were] often more disastrous to woman than to men," for him, it was "not the fault of the statute-book." In his comments, he went as far as saying that "this Woman's Rights Convention [was] not Man's Convention," which made the resolutions on divorce irrelevant for him as they affected men and women equally.[82]

Anthony's response to Phillips was unequivocal and exposed the contradictions of his line of reasoning. "Marriage," she replied, "has ever been a one-sided matter, resting most unequally upon the sexes. By it, man gains all—woman loses all."[83] On June 1, 1860, the *Liberator* published a letter by Stanton, who argued extensively against Phillips's position at the convention. She claimed, "The contract of marriage is by no means equal. . . . In entering this compact, the man gives up nothing—he is a man still; while the legal existence of the woman is suspended during marriage."[84]

Phillips was well aware of the unequal nature of divorce laws in the United States. As a temperance activist, he was familiar with tales of the abuse women suffered at the hands of their husbands. In the mid-nineteenth century, states began passing legislation to allow divorce on the basis of incompatibility between the two spouses. In a letter to James Freeman Clarke, a radical Unitarian minister, Phillips asked if he would perform the wedding ceremony of Eleanor F. Davis, a "young friend" of his. At the end of the letter, he added that Davis was divorced and that the trial judge had described the case as "the most atrocious case of abuse that ever came before him."[85] Clearly, Phillips understood the issues at stake and was sympathetic to the fate of women in the hands of abusive husbands.

Yet Phillips and other activists, including some women, resisted including Stanton's call for revision of current divorce laws into the women's rights movement. They understood and largely accepted society's conviction that marriage was "something unique and sacred" and, equally important, feared any association of the movement with the stigma of "free love." In his speech at the Seventh National Woman's Rights Convention in 1856, Phillips alluded to the popular views among women's rights activists at the time, seeing marriage as a "perfect union" and "symmetrical development" between men and women. "God meant that a perfect human being should be made up of man and woman allied," he claimed.[86] At the 1851 National Woman's Rights Convention, Phillips had underscored his conviction that the women's rights movement struck at the very foundation of American society. "It is a great social protest against the very fabric of society," he claimed.[87] For personal and tactical reasons, Phillips was not ready to include the reform of laws regarding marriage and divorce into the women's rights movement.

Phillips developed a discourse on women's rights consistent with his vision of republican ideals, but he also relied on more traditional ideas that complicated his and other activists' feminist convictions. He accepted the popular concept of "woman's influence" based on presumed specific qualities unique to the gender, a common nineteenth-century notion that defined—and restricted—women's role in American society. "Influence" had been a major argument in favor of women's commitment to abolitionism, and it remained as important in the women's rights movement. Historians have shown that, in the 1830s, female antislavery societies exhibited both conservative views on the role of women and a desire to create "a new female political culture."[88] Nancy Isenberg describes the presence within the antebellum women's rights movement of a discourse that advocated both difference and equality, which she calls "coequality."[89]

The idea of women's "unique influence" informed a major part of Phillips's discourse on women's rights. On March 19, 1847, for instance, he discussed the elevation of the black race and women's influence to the Adelphic Union, a Boston African American literary society founded in 1838 and open to both women and men.[90] He credited "the influence of woman" for social progress and insisted that women must play a major role in social development not only for the sake of society, but for their own education. When "she stretches forth an arm to relieve the necessities of society, and enlighten its ignorance," Phillips asserted, woman "is sure to find her own heart holier, her own mind brighter, and her capacity for moral and intellectual effort increasing every day." The ambiguity of his speech lay in the reliance upon orthodox social values.[91] In May 1869, he reiterated his stand, arguing that "a woman enjoyed now an influence . . . as large, or nearly as large, as the ballot would give her."[92]

Phillips's support for women's rights before the Civil War remained consistent with, and allied to, his abolitionist principles. He held that expansion of suffrage represented a positive good and could play an instrumental role in the general uplift of the masses, including women.[93] With a tradition-bound, rights-centered vision of reform, however, Phillips could not keep pace with activists such as Stanton who advanced a much wider agenda for the women's rights movement after the Civil War.

THE POLITICAL IS PERSONAL

Other potent forces also shaped Phillips's feminism, particularly his understanding of gender and his relationship with his wife. While John Tosh posits that "[m]en do not decide to work for a major change in the position of women without experiencing a modification in their own gender identity," Phillips's example reveals a complex interaction between women's rights activism and gender performance, and helps us understand some of the possible limits of his support. Phillips set great store upon the idea of disinterestedness in assessing activists' strategy and their ability to fight for "the rights of others." But the centrality of abnegation and selflessness in his discourse on activism should not conceal the personal elements that also shaped his women's rights activism.[94]

Ann Terry Greene Phillips had inherited the fortune of her father, the merchant Benjamin Greene, after both her parents died during her childhood. At the time she met her future husband, she lived quite comfortably near the Phillips family estate with her wealthy cousin, the prominent abolitionist Maria Weston Chapman. Reminiscing about his few encounters with Ann when he was a boy, Wendell Phillips Garrison recalled, "Her good looks always impressed me, and I liked the slight cast in her eyes, which I thought no blemish. You do not exaggerate her cheerfulness and vivacity in congenial company."[95]

When Phillips met Ann Terry Greene, she was an abolitionist, and Phillips's modern biographer James Brewer Stewart argues that she bore much responsibility for his participation in the antislavery movement. In a January 1836 letter, written before Phillips's engagement, Maria Weston's sister Deborah described the twenty-four-year-old Phillips in laudatory terms: "Wendell I like. There seems to be a great deal of straightforwardness & simplicity about him." But she also added, "Intercourse with the Abolitionists will I think do him good."[96] The remark clearly reveals that Weston thought Phillips too "conservative" on the slavery issue. It also likely indicated that Phillips needed "education" and maturing and that Ann Greene would certainly guide him in that direction.

As Stewart abundantly showed in his biography, Ann's influence on her husband was manifest in many ways. As their correspondence reveals, despite her chronic invalidism, she played a major role in her husband's life and they discussed all matters related to his reform activities. Their collaboration began at the start of their marriage and took an interesting turn at the London convention. Phillips's comments on the first day of the meeting reflected the interaction of private conversations among delegates behind the scenes and those carried in public. During the convention debates, Prescod opposed women's admission as official delegates, claiming that he knew with a certainty "that the ladies themselves did not come here with a certain expectation of being received amongst us. I had this fact from the ladies themselves." The remark sparked two important reactions. The first reflected Reverend W. Bevan's "protest against mere private conversations being repeated before a public assembly." Prescod replied that the conversation had taken place at "a preliminary meeting at which persons, not delegates, were present." The chairman rebutted Prescod's answer, asserting that he was "decidedly out of order in giving the details of private conversations; he has clearly no right to do so."[97]

The second reaction came directly from the American women delegates, who had been deprived of the right to speak for themselves. Their position emerged from the dialogue between husband and wife on the first day of the convention. Ann Phillips encouraged her spouse and gave him at least one note that we know of, penciled on a convention program:

> Wendell
>
> Please to maintain the floor—no matter what they do dont give up y[ou]r right to—Please deny for *me* who never saw Mr Prescott [*sic*] his assertion with re-

gard to the women saying they *doubted* whether they sh[ou]ld be accepted & Massachusetts was appointed *conditionally*—

Ann[98]

When Phillips corrected Prescod's misleading assertion, he not only responded to a perceived lie but also to his wife's injunction. Just as she directed, Phillips protested the idea that the women never expected to sit at the convention: "I deny it. They may have said that they did not expect to be in a majority if it went to a division."[99] Phillips played the role of his wife's voice and defended what he saw as women's invaluable contribution to the antislavery movement. She warned him against any prevarication: "'Don't shilly-shally, Wendell!" or so Francis Jackson Garrison cast the incident, painting Phillips as following his wife's demand.[100] As Stewart observed, these words have been accepted as tradition without real documentation.[101] Yet, they certainly testify to the way the Phillipses' contemporaries saw their close and equal partnership.

Our understanding of the Phillips marriage has evolved in critical ways over the past decades. Irving H. Bartlett's early judgment, based on Ann Phillips's undiagnosed maladies, that the two endured "a marriage practically without social life, with no children, and perhaps with no sex," is no longer accepted. Over the last forty years, the depth of the new women's history as well as the recovery of critical new family papers in 1977 have helped historians reconsider her disability and the Phillips marriage more subtly. Because of the revealing primary sources, Bartlett developed a far more nuanced understanding of Phillips's relationship with his wife, which has influenced all subsequent historians. The new documentation clearly revealed that "despite her illness they were able to sustain a long, affectionate, and mutually supportive marriage in which she remained fully engaged in his career."[102]

The Phillips correspondence, as James Brewer Stewart fully detailed, revealed how well the two managed to overcome Ann's invalid state. The letters document their affectionate relationship by the exchange of nicknames—"dearest," "darling," "Bessie Gra," "char," "Good little baby." His constant inquiries as to her well-being and concern over the food they both ate dominate his letters. Allusions to physical intimacy also appear, as when in the 1860s Phillips confessed that "I wish I were to be near to tuck my baby up & warm her clothes in the morning. How long you will be washing your face when I am not by to hurry you."[103] When on yet another lecture tour, he sent her a dinner menu from Dubuque, noting, "I have drawn a pencil mark round all those things I ate for *my* health's sake & put admiration marks to those I longed for but abstained from for your blessed baby's sake."[104] Evidence of care and physical intimacy can be seen in another letter, in which Phillips enclosed "a precious relic—a veritable bit of Gra's *toenail*." Phillips added, "It will remind you of his cutting yours—& is quite as good a vehicle of sentiment as a lock of hair—You need not tell of it for nobody will understand it but Char & Gra." The remarkable letter casts light on the physicality and idiosyncrasy of the Phillipses' relationship, which they thought "nobody w[ould] understand."[105]

Phillips's contemporaries easily might have read his wife's condition as hysteria, "a condition whose clinical criteria could be modified in order to diagnose all the behaviours which did not fit the prescribed model of Victorian womanhood."[106] Her letters to her husband, however, show otherwise, revealing her intense pain and discomfort. They also detail how frequently Phillips played his wife's nurse, waking up several times during the night to tend to her, and protecting her from outside disturbances. Phillips might have epitomized ideals of manhood to his contemporaries, but he also exhibited qualities commonly assigned to women.[107]

Phillips's family life resonated with his women's rights commitment in other ways. In his speech at the National Woman's Rights Convention of 1851, he confronted the physiological consequences of women's unequal position in society. "Our dainty notions," he claimed, "have made woman such a hot-house plant, that one half the sex are invalids."[108] The reference to women's invalidism might have sounded familiar to the audience, many of whom knew of Ann Greene Phillips's condition. At the same time, in Phillips's mind, the term "invalid" might have implied mental and intellectual dependence, a description that Phillips never would have applied to his wife. The use of this word, however, shows that Phillips's marriage and relationship with his wife informed his vision of women's rights. This is not to imply that without his wife Phillips never would have become a "woman's rights man." Rather, as in the case of all other women's rights activists, feminism resonated with certain aspects of his personal life more than with others. The "rights of others" were also personal in that respect.[109]

In his 1851 speech in Worcester, Phillips referred to the roles of men and women in the movement, which required women to stand for their own rights.

"Why ask aid from the other sex at all?" he asked: "I say, TAKE your rights!" he exclaimed, adding, "It is for you but to speak, and the doors of all medical hospitals are open for the women by whom you make it known that you intend to be served." As with other male women's rights activists, Phillips often expressed his admiration for strong women, such as Elizabeth Blackwell, the first woman to graduate from a medical school in the United States.[110] Phillips clearly enjoyed the society of strong-minded women; perhaps they reminded him of his mother, Sarah Phillips, whom Anne Warren Weston once described as "a perfect Dragon."[111] He was also close to the strong-willed women of the "Boston Clique," which included female abolitionists such as Maria Weston Chapman and his own wife, Ann, all of whom came from the same social class.[111] He also formed strong bonds with other female abolitionists, such as Abby Kelley Foster, whose letters evidenced mutual admiration and affection.

Phillips's friendships with women involved mostly white women, and what little evidence exists does not reveal that he treated black women any differently.[113] His concern for the abuse, dependence, and victimization black women endured in slavery was genuine, as a resolution he introduced at the First National Woman's Rights Convention shows: "That the cause we are met to advocate,—the claim for woman of all her natural and civil rights,—bids us remember the million and a half of slave women at the South, the most grossly wronged and fully outraged of all women; and in every effort for an improvement in our civilization, we will bear in our heart of hearts the memory of the trampled womanhood of the plantation, and omit no effort to raise it to a share in the rights we claim for ourselves."[114]

Clearly, Phillips's commitment to women's rights also included the enslaved—at a time when many feminists considered only *white* women's rights. This accounts for the controversy around Phillips's resolution, as Jane Swisshelm, the white editor of the Pittsburgh *Saturday Visiter,* claimed that race could not be discussed at a women's rights convention.[115] His remarks also indicated how Phillips's feminism remained deeply rooted in his abolitionism.

Phillips agreed with the popular notion among women's rights activists that gender equality benefited men as well as women. Moreover, he accepted the idea that true men would welcome women's entry into the public sphere on an equal footing. While he admitted that women were supposed to be the primary actors of their own emancipation, he believed that not all of his sex were "man enough" to accept gender equality: "It is generally the second-rate men who doubt,—doubt, perhaps, because they fear a fair field," he claimed.[116]

Phillips's comment reversed the popularly held belief that those who advanced women's rights "unsexed" themselves, denying assumed definitions of true manhood and womanhood. Phillips's "eloquence of abuse" on behalf of women's rights sometimes made him the target of derogatory remarks grounded in certain gendered assumptions.[117] An 1867 article in the *New York Times* reflected an orthodox construction of masculinity and directly challenged Phillips's manhood. "Shall MR. PHILLIPS," the author asked, "say what he pleases, abuse personal character when he chooses, and always be passed by like an old scolding woman? I confess I had some difficulty to determine this question, especially since most gentlemen thus afflicted by him, seem in favour of considering him on the feminine hypothesis."[118]

The comment reflected competing versions of masculinity in the nineteenth century. Phillips could be lampooned for acting like a stereotypical old woman. However, among abolitionists in particular, as Donald Yacovone has written, very often "the most esteemed style of manhood combined elements commonly assigned separately to each gender." The over-emphasized notion of "separate spheres" ignores the differing constructions of nineteenth-century gender, which combined and blurred what some historians have assumed to be clear distinctions between the feminine and the masculine.[119] This explains why male activists like Phillips did not view women's rights as threatening to their masculinity. Indeed, they presumed that their disinterested support for women's rights displayed their true manhood and in fact showed them to be "better men" for siding with the women.[120]

Phillips's definition of masculinity came into play at the September 1853 World's Temperance Convention in New York City, a meeting that excluded women from the proceedings. One delegate exclaimed that "the women and niggers had already met in Convention, and that he desired that white people might be let alone." Phillips answered "that such language does not befit the lips of a gentleman." Later on, replying to criticisms against his own language, he claimed, "Whatsoever I have felt it my duty to say, either one thing or the other, I have never yet spoken, and I never mean to speak, so that any man can say that I have not conducted myself in a manner becoming a gentleman."[121]

The term "gentleman" used here twice can be read as an allusion to Phillips's social background as a true representative of the Boston Brahmin class. It may also refer to certain acquired assumptions on his part concerning the conduct of a true man. Stewart emphasized the centrality of control in Phillips's education, both at home and at school. One of his teachers at Harvard, Edward Channing, professor of rhetoric and oratory, "place[d] rhetorical authority within the mind and heart—the character—of the speaker or writer," and for whom "morality was linked to education defined as mastery of knowledge and mastery of emotions." Oratory in particular fell within what society would have defined as a man's realm.[122]

This might explain why Phillips found it possible to sustain a marriage in which, as Stewart suggests, "sexual fulfilment was almost certainly rare, maybe impossible."[123] Phillips and his wife's sexuality might not have corresponded to the norm of both marital sex and male potency, but scholars have warned us against trying to impose our "modern form of sexual subjectivity" onto past events and characters.[124] For example, Peter Coviello has investigated the possibility, expressed by Walt Whitman and Henry David Thoreau, of considering sex apart "from the market-based logics of liberal individualism and individual productivity."[125]

The qualities that Phillips exhibited in public earned him the respect of unlikely admirers, especially "the small cluster of southerners at Harvard." To this group, Phillips's "masculinity, his mastery of fencing and horsemanship, and his oratorical power reminded them of the 'natural aristocracy' they expected to enter upon their return home."[126] An even more surprising example came from France, in a correspondence by Elizabeth Bates Langel, a niece of Ann Warren Weston. After the First National Woman's Rights Convention in 1850, Langel informed Phillips that, when an amusingly named "Mlle Wild" read his remarks at the convention in Victor Hugo's newspaper, *L'Evénement*, she "exclaimed with effusion 'Voilà un homme que j'aime. Je voudrais lui serrer la main que je l'aime cet homme là.'"[127] The enthusiastic Miss Wild might have been surprised to read about a man advocating women's rights so eloquently, but she also revealed that in France also defending the women's cause did not necessarily contradict notions of manly qualities.

Phillips's commitment to women's rights revealed the complexity of nineteenth-century gender relations—the interaction of (self-)images of masculinity, combining fluid notions of manhood and womanhood—and displayed the inseparable relationship between the personal and the political. His women's rights discourse, grounded in his abolitionism, also reflected his larger vision of American democracy—and therein lay the problem.

CONCLUSION

Phillips's clash with the more radical elements of the women's rights movement after the Civil War has to be considered within a twofold context. His remarks about the "selfishness" of female women's rights activists and their opposition to "the rights of others" indicate his awareness of an elementary change taking place within the movement. Ellen Carol DuBois has identified "[t]he shift from universal suffrage to woman suffrage," which to "independent feminism" meant that a movement *for* and *by* women had grown apart from the abolitionist movement.[128] To Phillips, the refusal of women's rights activists like Stanton to endorse the Fifteenth Amendment contradicted the "disinterestedness" that he considered an essential bulwark against tyranny.[129] He might also have considered that Stanton's choice of "racialist logic" and "hierarchical rhetoric" to promote her goal of woman suffrage after the Civil War was a betrayal of abolitionist ideals.[130]

Yet Phillips's own position after the Civil War did not conform so closely to his own ideals of "selflessness." His concerns for the potential consequences of the disfranchisement of African Americans and the threat it posed to their safety moved him to violate his own first principles. In addition to his castigations of Stanton and her allies, he not only gave priority to one cause over another, but in 1867 he actively sought to damage the women's rights movement when he withdrew funds that should have gone to women's rights campaigns and instead employed them to finance the *National Anti-Slavery Standard* and the American Anti-Slavery Society.[131] These actions might have been in response to the personal attacks he endured during the debate over the Fifteenth Amendment, ones which he undoubtedly considered unfair given his long commitment to women's rights. His bitterness and anger are evident in his snub of Stanton at a meeting in 1870, when he allegedly told his niece in Stanton's presence: "Mrs Stanton & I are not friends."[132] Additionally, his flagging interest in women's rights also may have resulted from his traditional belief in the "influence" of women. If, as Phillips and others including his own wife claimed, women exerted great "influence," then their disfranchisement might have been less problematic than that of African Americans.

NOTES

1. I would like to thank A J Aiséirithe and Donald Yacovone for their comments, insightful revisions, and great patience. I am also grateful for the anonymous reviewer's extremely helpful remarks. On the split among reformers, see Ellen Carol DuBois, *Feminism and Suffrage: The Emergence of an Independent Women's Movement in America, 1848–1869* (Ithaca: Cornell University Press, 1978).

2. "'Reject the Amendment—Depose the President.' Address by Wendell Phillips, at the Cooper Institute, New York, Oct. 25, 1866," *National Anti-Slavery Standard,* November 3, 1866, 1. When dealing with apportionment, Section 2 of the Fourteenth Amendment referred to "male inhabitants," suggesting that only men could be enfranchised.

3. Wendell Phillips, "The Fifteenth Amendment," *National Anti-Slavery Standard,* July 3, 1869, 1.

4. James Brewer Stewart, *Wendell Phillips: Liberty's Hero* (Baton Rouge: Louisiana State University Press, 1986), 283. See for instance the report of the thirty-fourth annual meeting of the American Anti-Slavery Society in *National Anti-Slavery Standard,* May 25, 1867, 1–2.

5. In a speech to the American Anti-Slavery Society in May 1869, Phillips claimed that women, labor, and capital "never can either one of them have it until this element of discord, hatred of race, is banished from the statute-books of the Republic. Why I am interested in that question is because I want the epoch finished; I want the seal put on the idea" ("Meeting of the American Anti-Slavery Society," *National Anti-Slavery Standard,* May 29, 1869, 2).

6. Phillips, "The Fifteenth Amendment," 1.

7. Ibid.

8. Susan B. Anthony to Wendell Phillips, Rochester, April 28, 1861. In a follow-up letter sent the next day, Anthony wrote Phillips that Elizabeth Cady Stanton "is *decided,* that it is best to postpone our W.R. Convention—says it is impossible for her to think or speak on anything but the War," emphasis in original. Susan B. Anthony to Wendell Phillips, Seneca Falls, April 29, 1861. Wendell Phillips Papers, 1555–1882 [MS Am 1953], Houghton Library, Harvard University.

9. Carlos Martyn, *Wendell Phillips: The Agitator* (New York: Funk and Wagnalls Co., 1890), 235. Phillips's biographies include George Lowell Austin, *The Life and Times of Wendell Phillips* (Boston: Lee and Shepard Publishers, 1888); Martyn, *Wendell Phillips*; Oscar Sherwin, *Prophet of Liberty: The Life and Times of Wendell Phillips* (New York: Bookman Associates, 1958); Irving H. Bartlett, *Wendell Phillips: Brahmin Radical* (Boston: Beacon Press, 1961); and Stewart, *Wendell Phillips.* This limited view of the relationship between abolition and women's rights might be related to Donald Yacovone's remark that "[p]erhaps the profession's emphasis upon traditional biography diverts individuals from more innovative approaches" in his "Review: *Captain Charles Stuart: Anglo-American Abolitionist* by Anthony J. Barker; *Wendell Phillips: Liberty's Hero* by James Brewer Stewart," *The Pennsylvania Magazine of History and Biography* 112 (July 1988): 468.

10. This is what Arianne Chernock's work on British male feminists suggests. See Chernock, *Men and the Making of Modern British Feminism* (Stanford: Stanford University Press, 2010).

11. "Elles vivent dispersées parmi les hommes, rattachées par l'habitat, le travail, les intérêts économiques, la condition sociale à certains hommes—père ou mari—plus étroitement qu'aux autres femmes." Simone de Beauvoir, *Le deuxième Sexe* (Paris: Gallimard, 1949), vol. 1: 20.

12. John Tosh, "The Making of Masculinities: The Middle Class in Late Nineteenth-Century Britain," in *The Men's Share? Masculinities, Male Support and Women's Suffrage in Britain, 1890–1920*, ed. Angela V. John and Claire Eustance (London: Routledge, 1997), 39.

13. Anna Greene Alvord to Wendell Phillips, May 26, [n.d.], Phillips Papers.

14. W. Caleb McDaniel, *The Problem of Democracy in the Age of Slavery: Garrisonian Abolitionists & Transatlantic Reform* (Baton Rouge: Louisiana State University Press, 2013), 92.

15. Lori Ginzberg, *Elizabeth Cady Stanton: An American Life* (New York: Hill and Wang, 2009).

16. Elizabeth Cady Stanton, Susan B. Anthony, and Matilda Joslyn Gage, eds., *The History of Woman Suffrage*, 6 vols., 2nd ed. (Rochester, N.Y.: Anthony and Mann, 1889), vol. 1: 60–61.

17. Lucy Stone, Preface, in *Woman's Rights Tracts*, comp. Lucy Stone (Rochester, N.Y.?: Steam Press of Curtis, Butts?, 1854?), Massachusetts Historical Society.

18. Caroline Healey Dall to Wendell Phillips, March 18, 1855, Phillips Papers. The information he provided also may have influenced Dall's well-known *Women's Rights Under the Law* (Boston: Walker, Wise, 1861).

19. On the split of the abolitionist movement, see Aileen S. Kraditor, *Means and Ends in American Abolitionism: Garrison and His Critics on Strategy and Tactics, 1834–1850* (New York: Pantheon Books, 1969); James Brewer Stewart, *Holy Warriors: The Abolitionists and American Slavery* (1976; New York: Hill and Wang, 1996); and more recently McDaniel, *The Problem of Democracy in the Age of Slavery.*

20. McDaniel, *The Problem of Democracy in the Age of Slavery*, 50.

21. William Lloyd Garrison to the members of the Boston Female Antislavery Society, April 9, 1834, Boston Female Antislavery Society Letterbook, April 9, 1834, to January 7, 1838, Massachusetts Historical Society.

22. William Lloyd Garrison to Helen Eliza Benson Garrison, January 18, 1834, Garrison Family Papers, Houghton Library. In her answer to Garrison's suggestion, Helen Eliza Benson answered that she did not feel up to the task: "You say that you look to me for the formation of an antislavery society; but you are not aware how extremely limited my influence is, and inefficient my efforts would be in such a cause" (Helen Eliza Benson Garrison to William Lloyd Garrison, February 18, 1834).

23. McDaniel, *The Problem of Democracy in the Age of Slavery*, 58.

24. Ibid., 82.

25. Ibid., 69–70.

26. Anne Warren Weston to Mary Weston, Boston, July 9, 1838, Anne Warren Weston Correspondence, Boston Public Library.

27. Maria Weston Chapman, *Right and Wrong in Massachusetts* (Boston: Dow & Jackson's Anti-Slavery Press, 1839), 51.

28. John Greenleaf Whittier to his sister, May 30, 1840, published in John B. Pickard, "John Greenleaf Whittier and the Abolitionist Schism of 1840," *The New England Quarterly* 37 (June 1964): 253. Although the letter is dated "30th of 6th 1840," John B. Pickard dates it to a month before (252).

29. *Seventh Annual Report of the Executive Committee of the American Anti-Slavery Society* (New York: American Anti-Slavery Society, 1840), 10.

30. Whittier to his sister, May 30, 1840, in Pickard, "John Greenleaf Whittier," 253.

31. McDaniel, *The Problem of Democracy in the Age of Slavery*, 66.

32. *American and Foreign Anti-Slavery Reporter*, June 1840, 4.

33. Ibid., 5.

34. Stewart, *Wendell Phillips*, 64; Donald Yacovone, *Samuel Joseph May and the Dilemmas of the Liberal Persuasion, 1797–1871* (Philadelphia: Temple University Press, 1991), 69–70.

35. "Proceedings of the Peace Convention," *Liberator*, September 28, 1838, 54.

36. Sarah Baker to Wendell Phillips, June 4, 1839, Phillips Papers; Julie Roy Jeffrey, *The Great Silent Army of Abolitionism: Ordinary Women in the Antislavery Movement* (Chapel Hill: University of North Carolina Press, 1998), 184.

37. Stewart, *Wendell Phillips*, 46–53, 76; "Letter from Wendell Phillips," in *Liberator*, August 23, 1839, 135.

38. For a detail of the affiliations of the American women delegates, see Kathryn Kish Sklar, "'Women Who Speak for an Entire Nation': American and British Women at the World Anti-Slavery Convention, London, 1840," in *The Abolitionist Sisterhood: Women's Political Culture in Antebellum America*, ed. Jean Fagan Yellin and John C. Van Horn (Ithaca: Cornell University Press, 1994), 332–33. Some female delegates also had credentials from more than one society. For instance, Lucretia Mott was a delegate from the American Anti-Slavery Society, the Philadelphia Female Anti-Slavery Society, and the American Free Produce Association. See Carol Faulkner, *Lucretia Mott's Heresy: Abolition and Women's Rights in Nineteenth-Century America* (Philadelphia: University of Pennsylvania Press, 2011), 92.

39. Sklar, "'Women Who Speak for an Entire Nation,'" 305.

40. Lucretia Mott to Maria Weston Chapman, July 29, 1840, in *Selected Letters of Lucretia Coffin Mott*, ed. Beverly Wilson Palmer (Urbana: University of Illinois Press, 2002), 78. For a discussion on the meaning of a World's Anti-Slavery Convention for Garrisonians, see McDaniel, *The Problem of Democracy in the Age of Slavery*, 74.

41. Sklar, "'Women Who Speak for an Entire Nation,'" 305.

42. June 11, 1840, Frederick B. Tolles, ed., *Slavery and "the Woman Question," Lucretia Mott's Diary of Her Visit to Great Britain to Attend the World's Anti-Slavery Convention of 1840, Journal of the Friends' Historical Society*, supplement no. 23 (1952): 28.

43. James Mott, *Three Months in Great Britain* (Philadelphia: J. Miller McKim, 1841), 18.

44. Karen I. Halbersleben, *Women's Participation in the British Antislavery Movement, 1824–1865* (Lewiston, Maine: Edwin Mellen Press, 1993), 35. The exact status of Ann Greene Phillips at the London Convention is still a matter of debate. Not all the sources mention her as a delegate. See Sklar, "'Women Who Speak for an Entire Nation,'" 333.

45. *Proceedings of the General Anti-Slavery Convention, Called by the Committee of the British and Foreign Anti-Slavery Society, and Held in London From Friday, June 12TH, to Tuesday, June 23RD, 1840* (London: British and Foreign Anti-Slavery Society, 1841), 1.

46. Ibid., 15, 16.

47. Ibid., 23.

48. William Lloyd Garrison to Helen Benson Garrison, Boston, September 21, 1838, in Wendell Phillips Garrison and Francis Jackson Garrison, *William Lloyd Garrison, 1805–1879: The Story*

of His Life Told by His Children, 4 vols. (New York: Century Co., 1885), vol. 2: 227, emphasis in original.

49. Garrison and Garrison, *William Lloyd Garrison* 2: 227.

50. *Sixth Annual Report of the Executive Committee of the American Anti-Slavery Society* (New York: American Anti-Slavery Society, 1839), 28.

51. Stanton, Anthony, and Gage, eds., *The History of Woman Suffrage*, vol. 1: 55, 58.

52. *Proceedings of the General Anti-Slavery Convention*, 8–9. The other American appointed secretary was Henry B. Stanton, Elizabeth Cady Stanton's husband. As mentioned by Lori D. Ginzberg, his position on women's participation in London is still a matter of debate as, contrary to what Elizabeth Cady Stanton later claimed, her husband did not take a position publicly on the question during the official proceedings. Ginzberg argues, however, that "[g]iven Henry Stanton's opposition to Garrison's leadership . . . his negative vote seems more likely" (Ginzberg, *Elizabeth Cady Stanton*, 37).

53. Letter from William Lloyd Garrison to Samuel J. May, January 4, 1838 [1839], in *The Letters of William Lloyd Garrison: A House Dividing Against Itself*, ed. Louis Ruchames (Cambridge: Harvard University Press, 1971), vol. 2: 415, emphasis added.

54. *Proceedings of the General Anti-Slavery Convention*, 45.

55. Ibid., 41, emphasis in original.

56. Ibid., 45.

57. In a letter dated August 28, 1840, I. H. Tredgold, the secretary of the Committee of the British and Foreign Anti-Slavery Society, forwarded "a copy of a Vote of Thanks unanimously passed during the sittings of the late Anti-Slavery Convention, expressive of the sense entertained by that body of the valuable services rendered by [Phillips] and [his] respected colleagues on that interesting and important occasion" (Tredgold to Wendell Phillips, August 28, 1840, Phillips Papers).

58. "Both Wrong," *Liberator*, August 14, 1840, 131.

59. *Proceedings of the General Anti-Slavery Convention*, 36.

60. Ibid.

61. June 11, 1840, Tolles, ed., *Slavery and "the Woman Question,"* 29.

62. Willard Bissell Pope, ed., *The Diary of Benjamin Robert Haydon*, 5 vols. (Cambridge: Harvard University Press, 1963), vol. 4: 642. Haydon also notes in his diary that a certain "Scobell [*sic*]" refused to be represented next to a black man: "He sophisticated immediately on the propriety of placing the Negro in the distance, as it would have greater effect." Haydon however added, "I'll do it though" (Pope, ed., *The Diary of Benjamin Robert Haydon*, 644). On Haydon's painting, see Hélène Quanquin, "'Question de la femme' et 'question de l'homme': Les Américains à la Convention mondiale contre l'esclavage de 1840," in *L'engagement des hommes pour l'égalité des sexes (XIVe–XXIe siècle)*, ed. Florence Rochefort and Eliane Viennot (Saint-Etienne: Publications de l'Université de Saint-Etienne), 74–76.

63. *Proceedings of the General Anti-Slavery Convention*, 42.

64. Quoted in McDaniel, *The Problem of Democracy in the Age of Slavery*, 74.

65. Stanton, Anthony, and Gage, eds., *The History of Woman Suffrage*, vol. 1: 60.

66. Ibid., 60–61.

67. Mott to Chapman, Dublin, July 29, 1840, in *Selected Letters of Lucretia Coffin Mott*, ed. Palmer, 79, emphasis in original.

68. For the reactions of Remond's "African constituency" on his return from London, see Martha Jones, *All Bound Up Together: The Woman Question in African American Public Culture, 1830–1900* (Chapel Hill: University of North Carolina Press, 2007), 53–54.

69. June 17, 1840, Tolles, ed., *Slavery and "the Woman Question,"* 36. On the significance of Garrison's silence, see Quanquin, "'Question de la femme' et 'question de l'homme,'" 83.

70. In a letter to the *Liberator*, however, Phillips expressed his disappointment with the convention: "the meeting has been in many respects a failure," he wrote ("Letter to the *Liberator*," *Liberator*, July 24, 1840, 119). Later, when he mentioned the convention and the debates on women's participation in letters to his mother, it was to let her know that "the Convention did not go as [he] wished & [his] remarks on many occasions were strenuously opposed by nine tenths" (Wendell Phillips to Sarah Phillips, July 24, 1840, Phillips Papers).

71. Wendell Phillips, "Capital Punishment—Women's Rights," *Liberator*, July 3, 1846, 107.

72. William Lloyd Garrison to Wendell Phillips, Boston, June 30, 1846, Phillips Papers.

73. Yacovone, *Samuel Joseph May and the Dilemmas of the Liberal Persuasion*, 120.

74. Austin, *The Life and Times of Wendell Phillips*, 156. George William Curtis, *Wendell Phillips: A Eulogy Delivered before the Municipal Authorities of Boston, Mass., April 18th, 1884* (New York: Harper & Bros., 1884), 32.

75. Stone, comp., *Woman's Rights Tracts*.

76. Consider the resolution introduced at this same convention: "we hold these truths to be self-evident: that all men are created equal; that they are endowed by their Creator with certain inalienable rights; that among these are life, liberty and the pursuit of happiness; that, to secure these rights, governments are instituted among men, deriving their just powers from the consent of the governed; and we charge that man with gross dishonesty or ignorance, who shall contend that 'men,' in the memorable document from which we quote, does not stand for the human race; that 'life, liberty and the pursuit of happiness,' are the 'inalienable rights' of *half* of the human species; and that, by 'the governed,' whose consent is affirmed, to be the only source of just power, is meant that *half* of mankind only who, in relation to the other, have hitherto assumed the character of *governors*" (Resolution 8 in Stone, comp., *Woman's Rights Tracts*, 2–3), emphasis in original.

77. Jacob Katz Cogan and Lori D. Ginzberg, "1846 Petition for Woman's Suffrage," *Signs* 2 (Winter 1997): 437. On the petition, see also Lori D. Ginzberg, *Untidy Origins: A Study of Woman's Rights in Antebellum New York* (Chapel Hill: University of North Carolina Press, 2005).

78. "Speech of Wendell Phillips, Esq., at the Convention Held at Rochester, October 15 and 16, 1851," in Stone, comp., *Woman's Rights Tracts*, 17, 6.

79. Ibid., 6–7, 15–16, 19–20; McDaniel, *The Problem of Democracy in the Age of Slavery*, 104.

80. "Wendell Phillips on the Rights of Woman," *Liberator*, January 16, 1857, 12.

81. "Speech of Wendell Phillips, . . . 1851," 4.

82. Stanton, Anthony, and Gage, eds., *The History of Woman Suffrage*, vol. 1: 732.

83. Ibid., 735. In an article published in the *New York Tribune* on May 14, 1860, Horace Greeley suggested that "hereafter these meetings shall be called not by name of Woman, but in the

name of Wives Discontented" (Stanton, Anthony, and Gage, eds., *The History of Woman Suffrage* 1: 740).

84. Elizabeth Cady Stanton, "Marriage and Divorce," *Liberator,* June 1, 1860, 88.

85. Wendell Phillips to J. F. Clarke, October 1, 1877 (bMS Am 1569.7), Phillips Papers. I thank A J Aiséirithe for the quotation.

86. William Leach, *True Love and Perfect Union: The Feminist Reform of Sex and Society* (New York: Basic Books, 1980), 3, 145; "Wendell Phillips on the Rights of Woman," 12.

87. "Speech of Wendell Phillips, . . . 1851," 21.

88. Ruth Bogin and Jean Fagan Yellin, "Introduction," *The Abolitionist Sisterhood,* ed. Yellin and Van Horne, 10.

89. Nancy Isenberg, *Sex and Citizenship in Antebellum America* (Chapel Hill: University of North Carolina Press, 1998), 71–74. On the different meanings of women's "influence" in the antebellum period, also see Lori D. Ginzberg, *Women and the Work of Benevolence: Morality, Politics, and Class in the Nineteenth-Century United States* (New Haven: Yale University Press, 1990).

90. Jones, *All Bound Up Together,* 227, note 11.

91. Ibid., 63.

92. "35th Annual Meeting of the American Anti-Slavery Society," *The National Anti-Slavery Standard,* June 6, 1869, 1.

93. McDaniel, *The Problem of Democracy in the Age of Slavery,* 104.

94. Tosh, "The Making of Masculinities," 39. On the place of "disinterestedness" in Phillips's thought, see McDaniel, *The Problem of Democracy in the Age of Slavery,* 106–7.

95. Stewart, *Wendell Phillips,* 44; Wendell Phillips Garrison to Francis Jackson Garrison, August 6, 1886, Wendell Phillips Garrison Papers (bMS Am 1169.2–5), Houghton Library, Harvard University.

96. Stewart, *Wendell Phillips,* 44–45; Deborah Weston to Anne Warren Weston, January 22, 1836, Deborah Weston Correspondence.

97. *Proceedings of the General Anti-Slavery Convention,* 43.

98. Ann Terry Greene Phillips to Wendell Phillips, [n.d.] 1840, Phillips Papers.

99. *Proceedings of the General Anti-Slavery Convention,* 45.

100. Francis Jackson Garrison, *Ann Phillips, Wife of Wendell Phillips: A Memorial Sketch* (Boston: printed for private circulation, 1886), 8; Stewart, *Wendell Phillips,* 81.

101. Stewart, *Wendell Phillips,* 81.

102. Irving H. Bartlett, *Wendell and Ann Phillips: The Community of Reform, 1840–1880* (New York: W. W. Norton, 1979), 41.

103. Wendell Phillips to Ann Greene Phillips, 1866–68, Phillips Papers.

104. Ibid., n.d., between Dubuque and Waterloo, Phillips Papers.

105. Ibid., April 10, n.d., Phillips Papers.

106. Jane Wood, *Passion and Pathology in Victorian Fiction* (Oxford, U.K.: Oxford University Press, 2001), 12.

107. Chris Dixon, *Perfecting the Family: Antislavery Marriages in Nineteenth-Century America* (Amherst: University of Massachusetts Press, 1997), 116.

108. "Speech of Wendell Phillips, . . . 1851," 17.

109. Hélène Quanquin, "'Wendell [Phillips], don't make a fool of yourself': Feminist Consciousness as Dialogue and Process in the American Antebellum Society," in *Exchanges and Correspondence: The Construction of Feminism*, ed. Claudette Fillard and Françoise Orazi (Newcastle upon Tyne, U.K.: Cambridge Scholars Publishing, 2010), 184–85.

110. "Speech of Wendell Phillips, . . . 1851," 13.

111. Stewart, *Wendell Phillips*, 8–9. Anne Warren Weston to Deborah Weston, October 17, 1837, Anne Warren Weston Correspondence.

112. For a discussion of the "Boston Clique," see Lawrence J. Friedman, *Gregarious Saints: Self and Community in American Abolitionism, 1830–1870* (Cambridge, U.K.: Cambridge University Press, 1982).

113. Stewart, *Wendell Phillips*, 107; also see Stewart's "Comfortable in His Own Skin: Wendell Phillips and Racial Egalitarianism," in this collection.

114. *Proceedings of the Woman's Rights Convention Held at Worcester, October 23d and 24th, 1850* (1851; rpt. Charleston, S.C.: BiblioBazaar, 2010), 17.

115. For a summary of the controversy, see Jones, *All Bound Up Together*, 92–93; Hélène Quanquin, "'There Are Two Great Oceans': The Slavery Metaphor in the Antebellum Women's Rights Discourse as Redescription of Race and Gender," in *Interconnections: Gender and Race in American History*, ed. Carol Faulkner and Alison M. Parker (Rochester, N.Y.: University of Rochester Press, 2012), 86.

116. "Speech of Wendell Phillips, . . . 1851," 6.

117. E. Anthony Rotundo, *American Manhood: Transformations in Masculinity from the Revolution to the Modern Era* (New York: Basic Books, 1993), 271–72; Irving H. Bartlett, "Wendell Phillips and the Eloquence of Abuse," *American Quarterly* 11 (Winter 1959): 509–20.

118. "Reply of Gen. Rousseau to Wendell Phillips," *New York Times*, May 10, 1867.

119. Donald Yacovone, "'Surpassing the Love of Women': Victorian Manhood and the Language of Fraternal Love," in *A Shared Experience: Men, Women, and the History of Gender*, ed. Laura McCall and Donald Yacovone (New York: New York University Press, 1998), 209; Yacovone, "Abolitionists and the Language of Fraternal Love," in *Meanings for Manhood: Constructions of Masculinity in Victorian America*, ed. Mark C. Carnes and Clyde Griffen (Chicago: University of Chicago Press, 1990), 85–95.

120. I want to thank Donald Yacovone for the revisions of this paragraph.

121. "Disgraceful Scenes at the World's Temperance Convention," *Liberator*, September 16, 1853, 146.

122. Stewart, *Wendell Phillips*, 25; Dorothy C. Broaddus, *Genteel Rhetoric: Writing High Culture in Nineteenth-Century Boston* (Columbia: University of South Carolina Press, 1999), 24; Isenberg, *Sex and Citizenship in Antebellum America*, 58.

123. Stewart, *Wendell Phillips*, 86.

124. Peter Coviello, *Tomorrow's Parties: Sex and the Untimely in Nineteenth-Century America* (New York: New York University Press, 2013), 20.

125. Coviello, *Tomorrow's Parties*, 64.

126. Stewart, *Wendell Phillips*, 22.

127. "Here's a man that I like. I'd like to shake his hands how I love that man." Elizabeth

Bates (Chapman) Langel to Wendell Phillips, (October?) 19 1850, Phillips Papers. I want to thank W. Caleb McDaniel for this quotation.

128. Ellen Carol DuBois has conceded a change in her own interpretation of this shift. "The shift from universal suffrage to woman suffrage, which I had once regarded as the moment that independent feminism had 'emerged,' now appeared more a political defeat, with reactionary consequences for both the suffrage movement and the American constitutional tradition." See DuBois, "The Last Suffragist: An Intellectual and Political Autobiography," *Woman Suffrage and Women's Rights* (New York: New York University Press, 1998), 10–11.

129. McDaniel, *The Problem of Democracy in the Age of Slavery*, 107.

130. Michele Mitchell, "'Lower Orders,' Racial Hierarchies, and Rights Rhetoric: Evolutionary Echoes in Elizabeth Cady Stanton's Thought during the Late 1860s," in *Elizabeth Cady Stanton, Feminist as Thinker: A Reader in Documents and Essays*, ed. Ellen Carol DuBois and Richard Càndida Smith (New York: New York University Press, 2007), 134.

131. On the Hovey Fund, see Ann D. Gordon, ed., *The Selected Papers of Elizabeth Cady Stanton & Susan B. Anthony*, vol. 2: *Against an Aristocracy of Sex, 1866 to 1873* (New Brunswick, N.J.: Rutgers University Press, 2000), note 3, 43–44. I thank the anonymous reviewer for pointing out this fact.

132. Susan B. Anthony to Anna E. Dickinson, February 22, 1870, in Gordon, ed., *The Selected Papers of Elizabeth Cady Stanton & Susan B. Anthony* 2: 204.

10

WENDELL PHILLIPS AND THE AMERICAN INDIAN

ANGELA F. MURPHY

On January 26, 1870, members of the American Anti-Slavery Society met at Horticultural Hall in Boston for the Thirty-Sixth National Anti-Slavery Festival. At this meeting they celebrated the news that the Fifteenth Amendment, to secure black male suffrage, would likely be ratified. Despite this accomplishment, abolitionists recognized that there was still work for them to do. Rev. John T. Sargent, who presided over the meeting, said that "it was not so much the 15th amendment they required as amendment in the hearts of the people." He remained concerned about continued color prejudice against African Americans, but he remarked that they also "had still to secure the rights, the privileges and equality of all the independent races of America." Wendell Phillips, who was a keynote speaker at the event, built upon this last idea. In response to the abolitionists' self-congratulation at the impending ratification of the Fifteenth Amendment, Phillips said that "in one point of view there was scarcely anything to be said, and yet from another point of view there seemed everything to be said." He urged members of the society to keep working. "Alps rise on Alps," he exclaimed, explaining that "they had no sooner risen and done one portion of their work than it lifted them to just that level which revealed to them the work that lay beyond." Now that they had secured "freedom of the race" for African Americans, Phillips asserted that they needed to work not just for justice for the freedmen, but for "every good cause." He argued that "the anti-slavery struggle was merely a school to fit them for future work." Part of this work, he said, was to seek justice for the American Indian population.[1]

American Indian affairs drew the attention of Phillips in the aftermath of the Civil War because the "Indian Question" loomed large in the American consciousness at that time. An explosive situation existed in the western United States during these years, as white settlers moved into lands inhabited by native peoples. Violent conflicts arose as the two cultures collided. For western settlers, the Indian Question was a pressing one. Many westerners called for policies that would remove the impediments to western settlement presented by the presence of American Indians. Some even advocated a policy of extermination. The conflicts also attracted the attention of eastern reformers who wanted to end the violence and promote the eventual integration of Indian nations into the American republic. As various groups of Americans debated what to do about the status of the American Indian population, questions arose about land rights, the reservation system, citizenship, education, race, religion, and violence.

Some former abolitionists, including Phillips, saw parallels between the plight of the American Indian and that of the freedmen, and they sought to address the needs of both populations through organized reform efforts.[2] In many ways, Phillips's experience as an abolitionist was a great boon for the Indian reform movement. He was able to employ many of the lessons learned from the school of antislavery when he turned his attention to the American Indian. Phillips's antislavery background, however, also shaped his idea of what reform for this population should mean. While citizenship rights, individual ownership of land, the establishment of schools, and assimilation into American society were central to the aspirations of many African Americans after the Civil War, this agenda was less attractive to members of the Indian nations who wanted to retain their cultural identity and independence from American governance.[3] Thus, while Phillips had the best of intentions, his plan for American Indian reform ignored the desires of many of those he wished to help. Although ahead of his time in recognizing that America's race problem did not exclusively involve justice for African Americans, Phillips did not recognize fundamental differences between Native and African American populations, which blinded him to the unique cultural and political requirements of American Indians.

Phillips was not alone in his inability to envision a solution to the Indian Question that would preserve the cultural identity and the autonomy of the various Indian nations within the United States. Few white Americans considered this a reasonable goal. Most reformers interested in American Indian affairs argued that traditional Indian cultures could not survive the pressures of American expansion and modernization. They believed that American Indians should be "civilized" and absorbed into the American populace for their own good as well as for the good of the American nation. Although they differed in their visions of when and how this should happen, assimilation was the end goal of the nineteenth century humanitarian reformers—not preservation of Indian ways.

Phillips, like other white humanitarians, advocated reforms that would lead to the eventual absorption of the Indians into the American republic. For Phillips, this approach primarily grew out of his desire to free the American public from racial prejudice; and because his focus was on white racism as the problem, he tended to lump nonwhite groups that were excluded from the benefits of American citizenship together. His blueprint for racial justice was inclusion in the American republic on an equal basis with white Americans.

As his speech at the antislavery festival indicates, Phillips's involvement in American Indian reform was part of a general expansion of his reform interests after the Civil War. Phillips remained committed to promoting black equality and continued to be one of the most prominent spokesmen for black rights after the war, but in the wake of emancipation and the passage of constitutional amendments to protect those rights, causes that had been peripheral to his abolitionist agenda during the antebellum era became more important to Phillips. Among these were labor reform, women's rights, temperance, immigrant rights, Irish home rule, and the abolition of capital punishment, to name a few. One of his first modern biographers, Irving Bartlett, has aptly characterized him as a "universal reformer" during these years.[4]

Because Phillips saw so many parallels between the American Indian population and African Americans, Indian reform was high on his list of concerns in the postbellum years; but because his attention to Indian reform accompanied so many of his other efforts, and because his postwar reform work in general has been treated as a postscript to his career as an abolitionist, there has been little scholarship on Phillips's role in the movement.[5] The emphasis on Phillips as an abolitionist is appropriate, for his agitation for black rights was undoubtedly his most significant contribution to American history. He was nonetheless an important voice in nineteenth-century Indian reform. His involvement in that arena deserves more attention not only because he helped to shape the Indian policy that emerged in the United States in the decades after the Civil War but also because his approach reveals so much about Phillips's views on racial justice in American society.

Phillips's agenda for the American Indian encompassed four major goals, all of which were also central concerns in his efforts on behalf of African Americans: equal protection under the law, citizenship with the right of suffrage, provision and protection of individual land rights, and access to education in order to promote uplift and the "progress of the race." These goals, highlighted in Phillips's speeches and writings on the Indian Question, became the agenda of the majority of white Indian reformers in the postwar years. Phillips's view of Indian reform was shaped during the antebellum era, and in the two decades after the Civil War, Phillips became one of the loudest advocates for the cause, agitating on the subject frequently. He continued to do so up until his death in 1884, just three years before the passage of the Dawes Severalty Act and the establishment of a new Indian policy that put many of his ideas into practice.

Phillips adapted the techniques he had used during his days with the American Anti-Slavery Society to promote the reform of American Indian policy. His approach is best summed up in his own words. In 1876, he wrote a letter of encouragement to a fellow Indian reformer. He closed it with these words: "Agitate, write, talk; hope on. Never give up."[6] That is the course that Phillips himself followed. He gave speeches, contributed to books, sponsored speaking tours, agitated for new government policies, and worked with various voluntary associations to promote justice for the American Indian population. He addressed many specific issues that were associated with Indian reform using these methods. He called attention to the problem of white encroachment on Indian lands, the violent conflicts that took place between the American military and western tribes, and the lack of legal protections for the rights of individual Indians. He was a proponent of President Ulysses S. Grant's Peace Policy and the federal government's use of humanitarian reformers to promote the "civilization" and Americanization of members of the tribes.

Underlying all of these efforts was Phillips's desire to attack what he called the problem of "caste" in American society. It was because he viewed Indian policy through this lens that Phillips tended to equate the needs of American Indians with that of African Americans. They were both groups that had been excluded from the benefits of American citizenship due to white racial prejudice and who had therefore been denied the opportunity to rise up to a position of legal, economic, and social equality with American whites. He believed both groups would benefit from a greater inclusiveness in the American republic and an end to the caste system that had developed as a result of white racism in the United States. One can see this underlying belief in all of Phillips's rhetoric regarding the American Indian, from the antebellum period through the end of Reconstruction.

While his focus remained largely on slavery and black equality during the antebellum era, Phillips did speak out for Indian rights in the years preceding the Civil War. He was not the only abolitionist to do so. Many antebellum reformers who are remembered primarily for their work on behalf of the American slave had been involved in protesting Cherokee Removal from Georgia during the early 1830s.[7] Phillips was just entering adulthood at this time and was not part of this protest, but in 1849 he became involved in the movement to promote state citizenship and suffrage for Massachusetts Indians—an effort that eventually led to the Massachusetts Enfranchisement Act of 1869.

The Massachusetts Enfranchisement Act declared that members of Native American tribes in Massachusetts would no longer be considered wards of the state. Instead, they would be "entitled to all the rights, privileges, and immunities, and subject to all the duties and liabilities of citizenship."[8] The act also allowed for the sale of Indian tribal lands, encouraging private land ownership as an alternative. The Massachusetts Enfranchisement Act was an early effort at "Americanization"—the policy that would come to dominate the efforts of Indian reformers in the late nineteenth century. It foreshadowed, at the state level, the policy the federal government would put in place with the passage of the Dawes Act in 1887. The cost of citizenship in both cases was that members of Indian nations must relinquish special claims associated with their tribal identity, including that of holding land in common, and melt into the larger population. According to a commission appointed by the Massachusetts legislature in 1869, the policies put forth in the Massachusetts Enfranchisement Act would contribute to the effort to end "all distinctions of race and caste" in the state.[9]

Wendell Phillips supported the effort to Americanize the native population of Massachusetts because he too saw it as a way of ending the evils of caste. He was one of the first voices to call for the new approach to Indian affairs in his state. In December 1849, he published a piece on "The Massachusetts Indians" in the *Massachusetts Quarterly Review*, responding to a report on the "condition of the Indians in Massachusetts" that the state legislature had requisitioned the previous winter. In it, Phillips articulated his ideology concerning Indian reform.

In "The Massachusetts Indians," Phillips criticized the state's policies toward "the feeble and scattered remnant of those once powerful tribes" of Massachusetts. He argued that, because Massachusetts held them under guardianship, denied them the vote, and did not encourage individual ownership of tribal lands, the state's Native American population had become "practically children, with all the confirmed bad habits, in many cases, of mature age." He blamed what he saw as the stunted condition of the Massachusetts Indian population on the conduct of Massachusetts citizens who "have neglected and despised them according to the true American model of treating all races not blessed with a color like their own." The same feeling of "caste" that was "the fruitful parent of so many evils to the negro race in our land," he argued, "lies at the root of all the mistakes and wrongs which affect the Indian." Phillips believed that the solution to these wrongs lay in "the two great elements of national progress and individual growth . . . education and the management of property." Because both African and Native Americans had been denied equal access to these resources, they had not had the opportunity to improve their condition as white Americans had. Phillips thus advocated that the state provide these populations with equal access to public schools and encourage private land ownership among American Indians as well as the freedmen. In addition, he argued that individuals within both groups must have equality under the law, including the right to vote, so that they could protect their own interests in the future. Thus, in "The Massachusetts Indians," Phillips articulated his core prescription for American Indian Reform: education, property rights, equal rights under the law, and suffrage. His ultimate goal: the acceptance of an excluded group into the American populace and the end of "caste" distinctions in American law. "Had these feeble remnants been crumbled up into the general mass of society," he said of the Massachusetts Indians, they would have "partaken in the common warmth and growth" it provided. The problem, he said, was that "the white race has held them at arm's length."[10]

"The Massachusetts Indians" also reveals much about Phillips's views on race, racism, and caste in the United States. To modern eyes, Phillips's description of the American Indian population as a "feeble" and childlike race may seem to contradict his criticisms of the American caste system, but they were consistent with the views of race held by many nineteenth-century humanitarians.[11] Phillips's rhetoric reveals his acceptance of Enlightenment-era racial thinking, which rejected the idea that racial characteristics were biologically determined but accepted the general concept of distinctive racial categories, arguing that environmental factors were the reasons for such distinctions. He thus believed in the notion of a continuum among the races from savagery to civilization. He embraced the concept of racial progress and believed, along with many others of his day, that education and inculcation with modern values could allow "barbaric" races that occupied an earlier stage on this continuum to achieve civilization.[12] In sum, Phillips accepted the argument that the American Indian had not yet become fully civilized, but he argued that the Indian race was as capable of civilization as the Anglo-Saxon.

Phillips first addressed the issue of American Indian rights at the national level in 1859 when John Beeson introduced the Indian Question into the abolitionist agenda. That year Beeson, who was an abolitionist as well as an advocate for American Indians, spoke at several American Anti-Slavery Society meetings. In his talks, he condemned the American government's militaristic approach toward American Indians who resisted white encroachment on their lands in the western United States, and he blamed the American government for the violent skirmishes that increasingly erupted in that region. Beeson urged his fellow abolitionists to join him in promoting a reform of American Indian policy. Phillips, along with approximately one hundred other members of the American Antislavery Society, responded to this call by attending an October meeting in Boston's Faneuil Hall. The explicit purpose of the gathering was to lay the groundwork for a national Indian reform movement by initiating a series of mass meetings in various eastern cities. Central to their agenda was greater attention to Christianizing and "civilizing" members of the tribes so that they could be incorporated peacefully into the United States. Those attending the meeting elected a committee, which included both Beeson and Phillips, and charged it with the duties of organizing the new movement and formulating a more specific policy.[13]

At this meeting, Phillips joined Beeson in his criticism of the American people for the current state of affairs in the West. He expressed sadness because, although many Americans agreed that American policies toward Native Americans had been unfair, "none, or few, would lift a single finger in behalf of this feeble . . . race." Expounding on this theme further, he lamented that "the Church sends them nothing but religion; the Government sends them nothing at all." America's Indian policy had been a "national sin," and he hoped that an organized reform movement could help bring about change.[14]

The effort to kick off a movement on behalf of Indian reform in 1859, however, was cut short. Although Beeson attempted to publicize the cause widely, his call coincided with John Brown's raid on Harpers Ferry and the heightening of sectional tensions over slavery in the United States. When Beeson inaugurated a journal that was meant to promote Indian reform, *The Calumet*, on February 1, 1860, he failed to gain traction for the movement as tensions mounted between the North and the South and the nation spiraled toward Civil War. The first issue of the journal was the only one published.[15] Wendell Phillips's attention, like that of the rest of the nation, was absorbed with the issues of secession, emancipation, and war.

Soon after the war's end, however, Phillips addressed the Indian Question again. His first postwar publication on the subject, which appeared in the *National Anti-Slavery Standard* in 1868, illustrates how the context of Reconstruction affected his views on American Indian policy. His editorial emphasized what he believed to be the barbarism of American policy toward the Indian population, saying it was based on greed and bloodthirstiness in the West and apathy in the East. He asserted that Indian wars were not just immoral and costly in terms of lives lost, but also were financially draining. He lamented the government's removal of troops from the unreconstructed South in order to fight Indians in the West. In his view, they were being removed from a place where they might be a force for good to a place where they did evil. Phillips argued that the movement of these troops was part of a conspiracy to loosen up military control in the South and allow the old Slave Power to regain authority in the region—thus the title of his editorial, "The Indian Plot." At the heart of his critique of the situation in the West, however, was Phillips's long-standing concern with American racial prejudice. He compared American views of the Indian to those regarding the African American. "We shall never be able to be just to other races, or reap the full benefit of their neighborhood till we unlearn contempt," he said.[16]

In the postwar years, Phillips also expressed deep concern about the impact of railroad construction on the western tribes. His interest in this problem was ignited by outbreaks of violence along the new transcontinental railroad as Plains Indians destroyed railroad tracks and telegraph lines, and, in some cases, attacked railroad workers and passengers. In 1869, responding to the anger Americans expressed over these attacks, Phillips wrote a controversial editorial in the *National Anti-Slavery Standard*. In it, Phillips asserted that Americans should abandon the building of railroads on the Plains. As was his practice in his antislavery writings and speeches, Phillips was purposefully provocative in his rhetoric. He called on American Indians to resist white encroachment, but his real goal was to confront white Americans with the Indian point of view. There was "great good," he said, in the Indians' tearing up of rails and in their threats to passengers and conductors, for this showed that they refused to be victims. Phillips called on members of the western tribes to continue their actions so long as protests and complaints about their treatment went unheard. Although he wished that they could make headway without the use of violence, he advised them to continue to agitate against the "pet plaything of the American people"—the railroad. He ended his piece with an especially provocative appeal: "Would our words could reach every Indian chief, we would tell him, lay down your gun, but allow no rail to lie between Omaha and the mountains. . . . Haunt that road with such dangers that none will use it."[17]

As with his speech of 1868, this editorial sheds light on the ways in which the issues of Reconstruction helped to shape Phillips's point of view regarding the American Indian. He wrote it at the same time that he agitated for the passage of the Fifteenth Amendment. In a rhetorical twist, Phillips used the Indian Question to comment on the inadequacy of the Fourteenth Amendment, which guaranteed equality before the law for male citizens regardless of race but did not guarantee the right of suffrage. "Heaven forbid we should betray the Indian to such protection as 'Citizenship' gives to the Georgia negro and loyalist," he said, "No. We are thankful that the Indian has one defense that the Negro never had. He is no citizen and has the right to make war." He expressed the hope that the Indian tribes would use that right "and never yield till 'citizenship' means more than it does now."[18] These statements were not inconsistent with Phillips's belief that citizenship was necessary for both African Americans and American Indians. In his remarks, Phillips made the point that citizenship without the vote did not adequately protect the interests of these groups. His rhetoric also furthered his argument that violent conflict with western tribes would remain a threat to the American republic as long as American Indians were considered aliens in the United States.

Phillips's *National Anti-Slavery Standard* piece drew a great deal of attention and criticism. A month after the editorial appeared, *Harper's Weekly* printed an illustration by Thomas Nast, entitled "All Hail and Farewell to the Pacific Railroad," that depicted Wendell Phillips in Indian garb, lying across railroad tracks

Figure 10.1. "All Hail and Farewell to the Pacific Railroad." Thomas Nast, wood engraving, *Harper's Weekly*, July 10, 1869, Library of Congress.

in the path of an approaching train, knife in hand.[19] A writer for the *New York Times* accused Phillips of being full of "sickly sentimentality" for the tribes and of promoting the "butchery" of white Americans.[20] Conversely, an editorial in the *Vermont Chronicle* argued that Phillips put the American Indian population in danger with his counsel. "The [railroad] line will be protected, if need be, with forces that will sweep away the whole race," it argued. "We yield to none, in the measure of our sympathy for the Indian under the grievous wrongs done to him in a long series of years, but we cannot approve that sort of counsel which leads to his inevitable destruction."[21]

Phillips's 1869 editorial also sheds light on another major issue of the Reconstruction Era: the end of slaveholding among the Five Civilized Tribes of Indian Territory. In addition to his comments on the railroad, Phillips contrasted the postwar actions of white and Indian holders of black slaves in his piece. He pointed out to those who criticized the western tribes that slaveholding Indians had capitulated to the terms of Reconstruction with less resistance than white southerners. Slave-owning tribe members in Indian country, he said, upheld their honor when they freed their slaves by immediately absorbing them as equal members of the tribe upon emancipation. Phillips also praised the Indian Territory population for allowing women to have a voice in tribal affairs, and he asserted that Indian women had more influence than American women did in their own governance. "An abolitionist may well glory in these Red Men," he said. He believed there was a better solution to the Indian problem than "sending butchers to waste treasure and blood in the vain effort to exterminate a braver race than ours."[22]

Central to Phillips's vision of Indian reform, then, were the promises of the Fourteenth and Fifteenth amendments to the Constitution. He wanted to extend them more broadly. For Phillips, absorbing African Americans into the republic on an equal basis was only the beginning of the application of these amendments. He called for guarantees for the American Indian population, as well as other excluded groups such as the growing Chinese American population. As abolitionists successfully concluded their agitation for the ratification of the Fifteenth Amendment, Phillips addressed his fellow Americans on the subject of equality under the law: "With infinite toil, at vast expense, sealing the charter with 500,000 graves, we have made it true of the negro. With what toil, at what cost, with what devotion, you will make it true of the Indian and the Chinese, the coming years will tell."[23]

The wording of the Reconstruction amendments, in fact, highlighted the ambiguous relationship between the American Indian and the United States government. White reformers regarded the explicit exclusion from citizenship of "American Indians, not taxed," which applied to all tribal Indians, as an impediment to their goal of integrating members of those tribes into the republic. A year after the ratification of the Fifteenth Amendment, a shift in Indian affairs made Phillips even more convinced that citizenship status was a necessity. On March 3, 1871, the government announced that, although old treaties would remain in effect, it would no longer make new treaties with the tribes. Thus, in future negotiations with Indians, they would not be treated as members of independent political entities, but they also were not American citizens.[24] In Phillips's view, this ambiguous status left them unprotected, and he stepped up his advocacy for the incorporation of Indians into the republic with the same rights that the Fourteenth and Fifteenth amendments guaranteed to African Americans.

Phillips encouraged other former abolitionists to agitate for these goals. In October 1870, after the Fifteenth Amendment was secured, the American Anti-Slavery Society, over which Phillips had presided in its last years, proclaimed its abolitionist mission a success and disbanded. Many of the former abolitionists became involved in a new organization, the Reform League, which was meant to be an umbrella association for the other causes into which they shifted their energy. One of the first gatherings of the Reform League was a special meeting to address the need to work on behalf of "a class of people who are now even greater sufferers than the colored people from the American pride of race, selfishness, and greed of gain." As part of its commitment to "issues pertaining to human welfare and progress," it would promote citizenship rights for the American Indian population. "For them," the organizers of the meeting proclaimed, "there is no alternative other than extermination, or a recognized membership in our body politic upon terms of equal citizenship and protection."[25]

The Reform League overlooked or ignored the wish of many members of American Indian nations to remain outside of the polity of the United States. This was the great limitation in their approach. The centrality of the Reconstruction amendments to the proposed reforms, however, did have a positive effect as well. It encouraged Phillips and many other former abolitionists to address the issue of institutionalized racism in a broad sense. They were no longer focused so tightly on black rights, turning instead to what they called the "race question" and the "question of caste." They promoted political equality in the United States, broadly conceived.

Wendell Phillips's attention to Indian reform did not grow only out of a desire to explore new areas of social justice after the achievement of abolitionist goals for African Americans. It was also a response to the crisis in American Indian affairs that existed in the West in the aftermath of the Civil War. During the 1860s and 1870s, warfare with the tribes escalated as the swelling tide of western settlement put pressure on more groups and threatened their tribal independence. Phillips's postwar efforts on behalf of the American Indian began at the same time in which reformers both within and outside of the American government began to advocate a new "Peace Policy" in Indian affairs in order to put an end to the wars with Indians.

In particular, this peace movement emerged in the aftermath of the infamous Sand Creek Massacre of November 29, 1864. After a Colorado militia attacked a peaceful encampment of Cheyenne and Arapaho Indians, slaughtering men, women, and children, many Americans called for investigations of American Indian policies.[26] In 1865, Congress established a committee under the leadership of Senator James Rood Doolittle to investigate the situation with the tribes in the West. The committee's report, published in 1867, emphasized that tribal societies were experiencing decay, and it called for an expansion of the reservation system and for enhanced efforts to acculturate Native Americans.[27] In 1867, the U.S. government sent out an Indian Peace Commission to negotiate treaties in order to end warfare with the western tribes, which continued to be a problem. Their task was to end conflict over white western expansion by convincing Indian tribes to settle on reservations.

The Indian Peace Commission was made up of three generals and four civilians. The mixed makeup of this commission would reflect the government's future approach to Indian affairs, which relied on a combination of military expertise and the efforts of civilian humanitarian reformers. General William Tecumseh Sherman was one of the military representatives. Balancing the military presence were civilians like Samuel F. Tappan, who was the younger cousin of famous abolitionist brothers Arthur and Lewis Tappan. Tappan came to the committee with experience, for he was an army veteran who had served in New Mexico during the years of the Civil War. He had led the official investigation of the Sand Creek Massacre, which condemned the actions of white

Americans during that affair. He was also a committed abolitionist and Indian reformer, and a friend of Wendell Phillips. Phillips, in fact, used his influence with government officials to encourage Tappan's appointment as an Indian agent in the 1870s.[28]

In time, the Peace Commission was successful in establishing treaties—one with tribes on the southern Plains and another with tribes on the northern Plains. The treaties would confine tribe members to reservations where, the American representatives promised, they would receive government support and protection from white encroachment on their land. In addition to negotiating the treaties, the commission submitted a report to the president calling for the government to send aid and agents to establish assimilative practices on the reservations. Their hope was that individuals on reservations would eventually be absorbed into American society.[29]

The Doolittle and Peace Commission reports inspired a more activist Indian reform movement in the eastern United States. Eastern reformers pressed the government to promote the civilization of American Indians and to employ humanitarian reformers as agents who would encourage this process. These calls helped to encourage the official implementation of the Peace Policy.

During the 1870s, then, Peace Policy advocates called for changes similar to those espoused by the Reform League after the passage of the Fifteenth Amendment. They wished to end the warfare with Indians, encourage the integration of Indians into the republic as individuals, and bestow them with the rights of citizenship. The Peace Policy advocates, however, placed more emphasis on the use of reservations as training grounds for civilization and assimilation than did Phillips and other members of the Reform League. They believed that the rights and responsibilities of citizenship could only come after missionaries and educators had prepared Indians to exercise them wisely. They argued that humanitarian agents must properly Christianize and "Americanize" the Indians in order to integrate them into the republic on an equal basis with other citizens, and they viewed reservations as institutions where they could implement this transition.[30] Wendell Phillips never emphasized the reservation system in his own speeches concerning the American Indians. Although he conceded that reservations could serve a valuable role in the effort to educate and Americanize Indians, he opposed forced removal to reservations, and he argued that citizenship and the vote should be made immediately available to the Indian population. He believed that citizenship itself would be the best way to hasten

Americanization because the bestowal of its protections would encourage a dedication to republicanism—the hallmark of American identity.

Although most Indian reformers promoted the goal of Americanization, there was no unified reform agenda in the years immediately following the Civil War. Early reform efforts were mostly individual ones. Reformers such as John Beeson and William Whipple gained prominence as westerners who spoke out in the East and brought attention to the need for a humane Indian policy.[31] English-born Beeson had been affected by Indian wars after he settled in Oregon in the 1850s, and Whipple was an Episcopal bishop in Minnesota who became an advocate for the tribes of his region. Living in close contact with American Indian populations, both sought to promote the fair treatment of members of the western nations. The activities of these men captured the attention of former abolitionists like Phillips, Samuel Tappan, Lydia Maria Child, and Lucretia Mott, all of whom also spoke out for Indian reform as conflicts with the western tribes drew more and more attention.[32]

Increasingly, however, reformers began to organize themselves into groups. The most influential of these early groups was Peter Cooper's U.S. Indian Commission, which met in New York City during the late 1860s and early 1870s. After the investigations of Sand Creek became public, the commission sent a memorial to Congress on July 14, 1868, declaring that all Indian wars had been the fault of white Americans who promoted fraudulent treaties, occupied Indian lands illegally, and pursued a policy of extinction. This private group with an official-sounding name was the loudest voice for the Peace Policy, and Wendell Phillips contributed to their efforts to promote reform. At a meeting held in New York at Cooper Union on May 19, 1870, a letter from Phillips was presented in which he proclaimed that the extension of the vote was the only way to ensure that Indians would become good and industrious citizens.[33] Phillips was more active, however, in an organization that sprang up in Boston in 1870, the Massachusetts Indian Commission. He spoke at its meetings, using his prominence to promote its goals, and he remained involved in its organizational activities through the 1870s.[34]

When Ulysses S. Grant was elected president in 1868, reformers in these two organizations were anxious about the former general's approach to the Indian Question, supposing that his wartime background might lead him to adopt a militaristic stance. To their surprise, Grant embraced many of the proposals of the reformers, and because of this his approach became widely known as "The Peace Policy." When Grant assumed the presidency, he surprised everyone with the creation of a Board of Indian Commissioners made up of Christian citizens. These commissioners were meant to serve as watchdogs who would work with the secretary of the interior to insure that Indian policy would operate fairly and free of corruption. Although he did not shy away from using military officers as Indian agents or from using military might to respond to outbreaks of violence in the West, Grant also supported the federal government's employment of humanitarian reformers as agents who would help to Christianize and educate the American Indian on reservations. In many ways these agents had the same role as Freedmen's Bureau agents who were charged with helping African Americans in the South make the transition from slavery to freedom in the aftermath of the Civil War. Grant also endorsed the larger goal of the humanitarian effort on behalf of American Indians, which was to prepare them for assimilation into the republic as citizens. Wendell Phillips supported Grant's presidency, largely because of his support for the Fifteenth Amendment and for Indian reform. "Let him cover the Indian with this shield [of citizenship]," he said, "and give him . . . a Department in the Cabinet which shall watch . . . [the Indians'] rights."[35]

There were many skirmishes with the Indian nations of the West that caught the attention of the Peace Policy advocates during the decades after the Civil War, and each one invigorated their demands for reform. Phillips became especially involved in calls for change in the aftermath of a series of conflicts with the Modoc nation on the Pacific coast in the early 1870s, which in 1873 culminated in a Modoc attack on peace commissioners that left several American officials dead. The conflict with the Modoc challenged Grant's efforts to implement his Peace Policy with the tribes, as it sparked a demand for a more warlike approach from many Americans, especially those living in western territories. Some demanded a transfer of Indian affairs to the War Department, and a growing number of westerners pushed for a policy of extermination.[36] Reformers were therefore justifiably concerned that advances made under Grant's Peace Policy, which relied heavily on humanitarian reformers' efforts to provide aid and uplift, would be reversed in favor of more military reprisals.

Wendell Phillips helped to counter this reaction to the Modoc affair by sponsoring talks by Alfred B. Meacham, a peace commissioner who had suffered injuries during the Modoc attack. Meacham, in fact, had been partially scalped, and he commenced his lectures on Indian reform in the eastern cities as he was still recovering from his wounds. He blamed white policies for creating the frustrations among the Modoc that led to the violent conflict, and, largely at Phillips's prompting, he became a vocal advocate of Indian reform throughout the 1870s.

In 1874, Phillips invited Meacham to speak at Park Street Church in Boston. Many Bostonians came, hoping to learn the gruesome details of the attack. Meacham did not disappoint, but his main thrust was an indictment of American Indian policy, which he said was to blame for the conditions that led to the Modoc violence. Phillips spoke after Meacham, marveling that a man who was "covered all over with wounds received at the hands of the Indians" could still speak the truth about white responsibility for the problems of the West. The public response to Meacham's visit led Phillips to plan a larger lecture tour the following year to promote Indian reform, and this was followed by still more elaborate tours in later years. Meacham's testimony, Phillips noted in a letter to a colleague, "will largely help our question."[37]

In addition to his work as a lecturer, Meacham wrote a book, *Wigwam and War-Path; or, the Royal Chief in Chains,* that promoted reform through what one reviewer described as "extra-harrowing descriptions of injustice done to the Indians by government agents and the semi-savage white adventurers into Indian country."[38] Phillips contributed by writing the introduction for Meacham's seven-hundred-page book. He praised the author as one who was particularly "qualified to speak with authority concerning the Indian character and the treatment of the Indians by the United States," and he lauded Meacham for his fight against the "hideous current of national indifference and injustice." He asserted that the book was important not only for its exposure of the injustices in American Indian policy, but also because it provided a "picture of a race fast fading away and melting into the white men's ways." He believed that Meacham's account would vindicate the Americanization efforts of reformers and draw needed attention to the Indian Question. "Except for the negro," Phillips said, "no race will lift up at the judgment near, such accusing hands against this nation as the Indian."[39]

During Meacham's 1875 lecture tour to promote his book, he brought with him several members of different western tribes to draw in an audience. He went out of his way in his talks to emphasize the progress of the Peace Policy in civilizing the Indian population and to depict tribes like the Modoc as properly "pacified." In a talk he gave in San Francisco, for example, he recounted his visit to the Modoc reservation, where he observed the way in which the Modoc people were becoming Americanized. As proof of the changes taking place, he described the new western dress of Modoc tribe members and related how they played "the peaceful and effeminate game of croquet" during his visit. He claimed that the Modoc people seemed "comfortable and contented," and he expressed optimism that their lives would only improve as they became more educated in the ways of civilization. "All of the children attend school and are making satisfactory progress," he said; "the country about the Modocs' home is settled, railroad depots are within twelve miles of them, and their associations are such that they cannot fail to lose identity as a warlike people within a very short time."[40]

With Phillips's sponsorship, Meacham reprised his lecture tour in 1876. He drew in audiences by promising an exposition on American Indian culture and beliefs, entitling his speech "Religion of the Red Men." Again, he used the talk to promote reform. He characterized American Indians as an honest, upright people who only resorted to violence in the face of white dishonesty. Along with his anecdotes and descriptions of Indian culture, he expressed strong opposition to a military solution to Indian affairs.[41]

On this tour he again brought with him an Indian delegation, and this one included a particularly inspirational individual, a Modoc woman named Wi-ne-ma. Wi-ne-ma had intervened during the 1873 attack on the Peace Commission after Meacham was injured but before he could be killed. She drew great attention as the woman who saved Meacham's life, and Phillips and other Massachusetts reformers widely publicized her presence on the tour. She took the stage with Meacham and Phillips as they gave their speeches, and she appeared at a reception given in her honor after the talks. In response to this tour, one newspaper proclaimed that Pocahontas and John Smith were now replaced in the American imagination with a new couple who symbolized interracial cooperation: Wi-ne-ma and Colonel Meacham, "whose hair would have been lifted but for the interposition of the dusky heroine."[42] Meacham brought further attention to Wi-ne-ma's actions by writing her biography, which was published in 1876.[43]

The engagement of Indian associates like Wi-ne-ma on Meacham's tour was particularly helpful in drawing in audiences and adding impact to his accounts by humanizing the problems he addressed. In using this mode of persuasion,

Phillips and Meacham drew upon methods that had successfully been used by abolitionists before the Civil War. Black speakers, many of whom were former slaves, had been among the most effective weapons that abolitionists held in their arsenal during the antebellum era, for they personalized the issue of slavery for northeastern audiences. Likewise, the inclusion of Indians from the West in the eastern reformer's meetings proved to be a powerful tool for promoting sympathy for the Indians' plight.

Meacham's talks were not the only events where Phillips employed this strategy. In 1871, a particularly memorable gathering took place at a meeting of the Massachusetts Indian Commission at Tremont Temple in Boston. There, a number of leaders from the Cheyenne, Arapaho, and Wichita tribes gathered with Indian reformers. Among them were Little Raven, Buffalo Good, and Stone Calf, who joined Phillips and various government officials on stage, where they addressed the audience about their hopes and grievances. Among the topics they covered were the threat that the railroad posed to Indian societies and the right of Indian tribes to resist encroachment on their lands by white settlers. They expressed frustration with their loss of independence, the broken promises of the American government, their depletion in numbers, and their increasing confinement. Having had to accept such losses, however, they said they now wished for the establishment of churches and schools on tribal lands since the buffalo, on which the Plains Indian cultures had depended, had been driven away. They also wished the government to honor promises for supplies in order to help them become self-supporting through agriculture. Finally, they demanded that the borders of reservations be honored and that railroads be kept out of Indian lands in order to prevent conflict between whites and Indians. Peace, they said, was what they wanted.[44]

These tribal leaders appealed for reforms that were on Grant's Peace Policy agenda, and Indian reformers used their appearance in Boston in order to encourage the continuance of that policy. Of special concern to the Massachusetts Indian Commission was the upcoming presidential election. They feared that Grant might be voted out of office in 1872 and that his Peace Policy would subsequently be overthrown. When Phillips spoke at the end of the meeting, he thus appealed to the audience "to uphold the President in his pacific policy, and to do what could be done to educate and elevate the Indian race." He characterized Indian reform as a cause that should rise above party politics, for peace in the West was a bipartisan issue. Any politician who promoted it, he argued, would be sure to gain public favor.[45]

Not all of the Plains Indians, however, would agree to live on the reservations imposed by the U.S. government under Grant's Peace Policy. Factions within various groups, such as the Lakota Sioux led by Sitting Bull, resisted confinement during the 1870s. These rebels hoped to preserve their status as members of independent nations, and they refused to cooperate with the American government's plans for them. Violent conflicts therefore continued to erupt on the Plains even as members of many tribes agreed to live on reservations. Although the government's Indian policy had newly been labeled the "Peace Policy," members of the military stationed in the West sometimes resorted to violence as they dealt with off-reservation Indians. Phillips addressed this issue on several occasions, blaming American policies for provoking the violence with the tribes and using inflammatory language to great effect. In all of his talks, Phillips criticized what he exaggeratedly called the military's policy of "extermination" in the West. He was a great advocate of ending the military's involvement in Indian affairs. He did not believe in the use of force to compel members of Indian nations to move onto reservations, and he worried that the Indian wars that broke out over the reservation system would become an excuse to pursue a policy of exterminating those who resisted confinement.

In a speech to the Reform League in 1870, Phillips responded to western complaints about "Indian savagery" and to settlers' calls for a more militaristic policy against the western tribes. Proclaiming that the leaders of the American military were the only savages on the Plains, he promoted the continued use of humanitarian reformers that was central to Grant's Peace Policy. "Thank God for a President in the White House," he said, "whose first word was for the negro, and the second for the Indian. Who saw protection for the Indian, not in the rude and blood-thirsty policy of Sheridan and Sherman, but in the ballot, in citizenship, the great panacea that has always protected the rights of Saxon individuals."[46]

Despite Grant's reelection and the continuation of the Peace Policy through the 1870s, violence in the West escalated. In 1876, after George Armstrong Custer's death at the Battle of Little Bighorn, the army's policy of treating off-reservation Indians as outlaws gained even more support in the West. In response to this state of affairs, Phillips wrote an open letter to the commanding general of the army, William T. Sherman. In this letter, originally published in the New York *Herald,* Phillips accused the army of warmongering and of promoting the massacre of innocent Indian women and children. Phillips also complained specifically about Sherman's policy of waging war against Sitting Bull and the Lakota Sioux and their allies, and he called on Sherman to reply to the charge that he was waging a war of extermination against the western tribes.[47]

Sherman responded to Phillips's criticism in a letter to Samuel Tappan, with whom he had served on the Indian Peace Commission. In it, Sherman defended his policy on the frontier, saying that his duty was to uphold the reservation system—which he characterized as beneficial to American Indians. The army did not seek out violence with the tribes and only punished "outlaws," like Sitting Bull, who refused to remain confined.[48] The American press widely reprinted and commented upon the letters of the two men, with some editorials supporting Phillips's position and others defending Sherman.[49]

Because the U.S. military continued to treat them as outlaws, Sitting Bull and his followers eventually sought refuge in Canada. When some Americans suggested that the U.S. government pursue the extradition of Sitting Bull, Phillips wrote to the Canadian governor general, urging him to refuse any such request. "It has been England's pride for centuries that her borders were ever a shelter for the victims of political misrule," he said. Phillips drew a parallel between the British refusal to return fugitive slaves to the United States during the years before the Civil War and the provision of sanctuary for the Sioux in Canada. Sitting Bull and his followers, he believed, were in a situation equivalent to the persecuted black Americans who had sought the protections of the British government when they fled from slavery in the United States. "Every reason which made England refuse to give up the fugitive slave exists in the Indian's case," he said. Phillips argued that, because Sitting Bull was not a citizen, he could not be treated "like an ordinary criminal and reckoned within the purview of international treaties on such subjects," for "to surrender him is to surrender one in arms, not against his own acknowledged government, but one in arms against a government which, in large degree, shuts him out from the limits of its civil policy; a government which he disavows and repudiates, and which you know will do him no justice."[50]

Phillips also contrasted Canadian and American Indian policy in this letter, arguing that the big distinction was the Canadian strategy of "making the Indian a full citizen and melting him into the common mass."[51] This statement refers to the Canadian Enfranchisement Act of 1869, which was aimed at promoting the rapid assimilation of Indians into Canadian society. According to historian Roger L. Nichols, the passage of the Enfranchisement Act "signaled the Canadian officials' desire to dismember the tribes and move the native people into the general society as quickly as possible."[52] Nichols points out that most Indians in Canada did not embrace the Enfranchisement Act. They were, according to one Indian representative, "wholly adverse to their people taking the advantages offered" by the law. The act was thus a great failure.[53] From Phillips's perspective in 1877, however, the Canadian policy was a model for the United States. He believed that a policy of rapid assimilation backed up with the legal protections that accompanied citizenship would improve the condition of the American Indian population and bring an end to the violent conflicts between white Americans and western tribes. He pointed out that such conflicts were not as commonplace in Canada as in the United States. The problem with U.S. Indian policy, he said, was that "we have always put force in the place of law, and shutting the Indian out from the shelter of law, have treated him as an alien and an outlaw."[54] This contrast between American and Canadian policies was a continuing theme in Phillips's speeches. Phillips painted a rosy picture of Indian affairs in Canada and clung to the distinctions between Canada and the United States in order to draw attention to injustice toward the tribes in the United States and to suggest a model for U.S. policy.[55]

Phillips's willingness to condemn American policy toward the tribes put him in the vanguard of American Indian reform; however, despite his genuine commitment to fair treatment for the American Indian, his vision of social justice was bounded by nineteenth-century ideas about reform and racial difference. If Phillips's opinions illustrate his commitment to egalitarianism and his faith in the protections of American citizenship, they also reveal the racial essentialism that guided his thinking. As in his earliest writings on Indian affairs in Massachusetts, Phillips tended to lump all the tribes together as one Indian "race" in his postbellum addresses. He continued to characterize American Indians as lower on the continuum of civilization but capable of progress. The shortcomings that he saw in this race—whether it be a childlike or a warlike temperament—he continued to attribute to white racism. On the other hand, while at times he pointed out what he believed to be their shortcomings, Phillips also romanticized American Indians, characterizing them as more honest, loyal, and courageous than Anglo-Saxons.[56]

The speech Phillips gave as he shared the stage with the Plains Indian visitors in 1871 is representative of his romantic racialism. After the Indian speakers finished their talks, Phillips expressed satisfaction that the "extremes of the earth meet on this platform tonight," and he spent much of his time on the platform elaborating upon the genius of the Indian race. As he did in numerous speeches, he spoke of the honesty of the American Indian population, contrasting their behavior with the lies and broken treaties of the white men in their dealings with the tribes. No "aboriginal race, brought into conflict with a great civilized wave," has behaved better, he said.

In addition to the trait of honesty, Phillips argued, the American Indian had a natural eloquence about asserting his rights and an inborn courage in his willingness to defend them. "No race ever outdid him" in this regard, he said. Phillips believed that, no matter what the circumstances, American Indian peoples were in the right when they defended themselves, and he placed the blame for the nation's "Indian Problem" squarely on the shoulders of white Americans. He declared that it was "the Indian who taught us what this American continent can make of manhood" with his record of resistance and argued that Americans owe their revolutionary tradition to these lessons. "I am only proud of my country as a continent," Phillips said, "because the race that preceded us was no race to yield up tamely their rights." He commended the American Indian because he did not appeal to pity. Instead, he demanded justice.[57]

In 1875, Phillips began giving a formal lecture on the Indian question that elaborated upon his conceptions of the Indian race and in many ways echoed his rhetoric concerning the Massachusetts Indians in 1849. The lecture focused on how relations between whites and Indians fit into the larger history of contact between "the Civilized Man and the Barbarian" since classical times. He argued that the tendency to think of the Indian as naturally inferior prevented peace with and justice toward the tribes. Phillips explicitly criticized the emerging scientific racism of his day that assumed the innate inferiority of nonwhite groups. According to Phillips, the American Indian had been hindered from developing a more advanced society by the greed of white policies in the New World since European arrival. The Indian, he felt, could be civilized and brought into the populace if Americans abandoned the policy of "ostracism" that placed him outside of the law and failed to recognize his rights as either foreigner or citizen. Phillips advocated the establishment of schools as a key to Indian civilization and the absorption of Indians into the American republic as citizens. According to Phillips, white men bore the responsibility for any savagery that might exist among the American Indian population, and the only way to rectify their wrongs was to provide education and equal protection under American law. Justice for the tribes depended upon their assimilation into the American republic on an equal basis.[58]

Along with his own oratory upon the Indian question, Phillips continued to encourage others—both Native American and white westerners—to speak out on behalf of Indian reform. Phillips's final, and perhaps most effective, employment of speakers from the West occurred between 1879 and 1881, when he sponsored the tour of a delegation of western reformers and Plains Indians who promoted the rights of the Ponca tribe.

In 1879, the case of the Ponca elevated the issue of Indian rights under American law in the public eye. The American government had removed members of this tribe from a reservation in Nebraska that it had granted them by treaty, sending them to a new reservation in Indian Territory in 1877. The removal took place after the American government transferred the Ponca lands to the Dakota Sioux, traditional enemies of the Ponca, in order to appease the more powerful tribe. The Ponca never consented to the move, but American officials forced them to relocate despite their claim to their reservation. The Ponca obeyed the order to resettle, but a number then quickly became dissatisfied with their new lands, where they suffered disease and hardship. Under the leadership of the Ponca chief, Standing Bear, a faction of the tribe left Indian Territory and began to make their way back north, but they were soon arrested and detained for leaving the reservation. After their release from detention, they settled in with Omaha Indian allies rather than return to their assigned reservation.[59]

Their plight captured the attention of white reformers in Nebraska, and the assistant editor of the Omaha *Herald*, Thomas Tibbles, publicized the government's injustice toward the Ponca. The Omaha reformers urged Standing Bear to take his people's case to the federal courts since the U.S. government had broken a treaty and acted illegally. In order to provide aid and publicity for the Ponca, Tibbles and other white reformers formed the Omaha Ponca Relief

Committee. In a report of this committee issued in 1880, the Omaha reformers promised to assist the Ponca in pursuing the return of their lands "from which they had been unjustly and inhumanely ejected." They criticized government policy under which the Ponca were "imprisoned in the Indian Territory" and "kept there against their will," and they demanded the restoration of the old Ponca reservation and fifty thousand dollars to help repair it from its dilapidated state.[60] With the aid of the Omaha reformers, the Ponca won a writ of *habeas corpus* at a U.S. District Court in Omaha, where Judge Elmer Dundy referenced the Fourteenth Amendment guarantee of equal protection under the law to "any person within its jurisdiction." He ruled that "an Indian is a person within the meaning of the law," and thus had the right to pursue justice in the American courts. Standing Bear acted on this ruling immediately, making preparations to take the case against the Ponca removal to the Supreme Court. Concurrently, the U.S. district attorney set out to appeal the writ of *habeas corpus* granted to the Ponca.

When Wendell Phillips learned of the Omaha committee's efforts, he linked up with Tibbles to encourage eastern support for the Ponca as they pursued their legal battles. First, Phillips made arrangements to provide financial support for Tibbles to visit the eastern states to give a series of lectures on behalf of the Ponca. After Tibbles's first eastern tour, Phillips helped to arrange a second one in which he was accompanied by Chief Standing Bear and two Omaha Indians—Bright Eyes and her brother Wood Carver.[61] Bright Eyes, who would become Tibbles's wife in 1881, served as interpreter on the tour. Following the model that Meacham's tour during the 1870s had provided, special receptions were held after the delegation's appearances, at which prominent members of society were invited to mingle with the Indian visitors.[62]

Again, in these efforts one can see evidence of the reformers' abolitionist legacy. At one point during the tour, Standing Bear expressed an interest in cutting his hair and wearing western clothes, but white reformers talked him into waiting until the conclusion of his scheduled appearances. Despite their commitment to Americanizing the Indians, eastern reformers wanted to promote their cause by drawing audiences in to see an authentic tribesman appealing for justice. The promotion of Standing Bear's "Indian-ness" can be compared to abolitionists' interest in accentuating the slave background of black antislavery speakers such as Frederick Douglass and Sojourner Truth during the antebellum period. Both of these famous black abolitionists were urged, sometimes to their chagrin, to present an image that conformed to white America's conception of the slave, for this sense of authenticity drew in audiences and provoked a sympathetic response.[63]

In conjunction with lecture tours, which Tibbles and his entourage conducted between 1879 and 1883, the reformers also followed precedent in another activity. As Meacham had for the Modoc several years before, Tibbles wrote a book to publicize the plight of the Ponca. *The Ponca Chiefs* was published in 1880 under the pseudonym "Zylyff," and Bright Eyes contributed an introduction to the volume. Wendell Phillips wrote the dedication for the book, in which he described the narrative of the Ponca tribulations "as a fair specimen of the system of injustice, oppression, and robbery, which the Government calls *Indian Policy.*" He dedicated the book "to the people of the United States, those who love liberty and intend that their government shall protect every man on its soil and execute justice between man and man." The proceeds from the book's sale went to finance the legal expenses of the Ponca.[64]

As a result of eastern reformers' involvement with the Ponca, Boston became the center of activity on behalf of their cause. Reformers raised almost seven thousand dollars in the city for court expenses—more than enough to cover what was necessary. In addition, the Massachusetts governor appointed a committee made up of prominent citizens to investigate the removal of the Ponca and to comment on Indian affairs in general. Members of this committee included Phillips, Unitarian minister Edward Everett Hale, publisher Henry O. Houghton, mayor of Boston Frederick O. Prince, and poet Henry Wadsworth Longfellow.[65] The committee concluded that the Ponca were unlawfully removed from their reservation and that the result of the forced removal had been "most disastrous to them as a people." It determined that the tribe held just claim to their old reservation, that the American government was bound to restore their claim and pay restitution to the Ponca, and that Congress should form a committee to investigate the case.[66]

In response to the attention from Boston, President Rutherford B. Hayes engaged a committee to conduct such an investigation, and it recommended redress for the Ponca. On March 31, 1881, Congress appropriated $165,000 to compensate the tribe for losses during removal and allowed tribal members to choose either their old reservation in Nebraska or the new land in Indian Territory as their home. Because of Congress's action, the Ponca case never went to the Supreme Court. This recognition of Ponca grievances and attempt to make restitution marked a major turning point in the movement for reform of American Indian policy. Not only had the Ponca won their right to return to their reservation, but they had succeeded in forcing the justice system to recognize Indian rights under federal law.

The Ponca case was Phillips's crowning effort in his work on behalf of the American Indian. It became his last great push for Indian rights. He would retire from public life after the resolution of the Ponca conflict, and he died soon after, in 1884. The Ponca case proved an appropriate end to Phillips's work on behalf of Native Americans as the national government conceded that the Ponca had rights under American law, representing a first step toward his goal of citizenship for the American Indian.

The case set the stage for a new era of Indian reform, bringing into the movement fresh voices that would redefine Indian policy in the 1880s. Among the new reformers was Helen Hunt Jackson, who became interested in Indian affairs after hearing Ponca Chief Standing Bear speak in Boston. His talk inspired her to conduct research on the American government's past dealings with the Indian tribes, which in turn led to the publication of her influential indictment of these dealings, *A Century of Dishonor*, in 1881. In it Jackson criticized the American reservation system as a force that worked against civilization and assimilation. New Indian reform organizations also sprang up to promote the goal of Indian citizenship in the 1880s. Among them were the Indian Rights Association, which was formed in Philadelphia in 1882, and the Boston Indian Citizenship Committee, which emerged out of the agitation for Ponca rights. In 1883, a number of influential "Friends of the Indian" established annual meetings at Lake Mohonk Lodge in upstate New York to discuss Indian affairs. Their meetings became known as the Lake Mohonk Conference. At these annual meetings, reformers discussed ways to end the reservation system, provide education that would promote assimilation, and integrate the Indians into the American republic as citizens.[67]

Thus, in his last major effort, Phillips helped to launch the involvement of the next generation of Indian reformers—a generation that would promote a vision similar to Phillips's own. Their efforts helped to spur congressional action and culminated in the Dawes Severalty Act of 1887, named for its sponsor, Henry Dawes. The act provided allotments to tribe members to promote individual ownership of land and bestowed citizenship upon those who abandoned tribal claims. Coinciding with the passage of the Dawes Act was the development of a more extensive Indian educational program, in which the federal government entered into partnership with church groups in order to provide schools that would Americanize Indian children.[68]

Nineteenth-century Indian reformers saw these changes in policy as a great triumph, but in practice they were destructive to tribal identity. While reformers emphasized the protections that the Indian population would gain by becoming citizens of the United States, many American Indians instead saw the new policy as a loss, for they were forced to give up their tribal rights and cultural ways in order to lay claim to the benefits of citizenship. Although white humanitarian efforts had arisen out of a genuine interest in providing justice for the Indian population and promoting an egalitarian republic, the vision of Phillips and other reformers was limited by their faith in the universal applicability of equal inclusion in the republic as the foundation for racial justice.

Phillips's goals for the American Indian population reflected both his abolitionist background and the context of Reconstruction Era racial politics, but most of all they reflected his belief that the problem of a racial caste system was the central one that all nonwhite groups, including Native Americans, faced in the United States. Phillips believed that education, citizenship, the vote, and land rights were the keys to ending this system of caste, and thus reforms in these areas were the backbone of his agenda for all excluded groups.

This vision predisposed him to much the same rhetoric in his speeches concerning the American Indian and the African American. Because of the different historical relationship of the two groups to the American republic, however, these themes played out in very different ways. While many African Americans supported reformers' efforts to encourage land ownership among freedmen, American Indians often did not share this interest in private property, wishing instead to assert tribal rights. Similarly, while education and citizenship rights were central to African American integration into the American polity, many American Indians wished to remain outside of that polity. Thus, although the Dawes Act represented a success in achieving some of the immediate goals of the reform movement in which Phillips participated, its provisions have been among the more widely criticized Indian policies in American history.[69]

Phillips's work on behalf of African Americans thus provided a double legacy for his Indian reform efforts. While he was able to bring in much knowledge and experience from his antislavery past, those very experiences limited his vision. Even so, Phillips helped to bring attention to the need for the reform of American Indian policy, which arguably was at its nadir in the years following the Civil War. His efforts on behalf of the American Indian also made him one of the first reformers of the postwar era to emphasize that Americans had a "race problem" that went beyond black and white.

NOTES

1. Boston *Daily Advertiser*, January 27, 1870.

2. On Indian reform during the second half of the nineteenth century, see Robert Winston Mardock, *The Reformers and the American Indian* (Columbia: University of Missouri Press, 1971); Francis Paul Prucha, *American Indian Policy in Crisis: Christian Reformers and the Indian, 1865–1900* (Norman: University of Oklahoma Press, 1976); Christine Bolt, *American Indian Policy and American Reform: Case Studies of the Campaign to Assimilate the American Indians* (Boston: Allen & Unwin, 1987); C. Joseph Genetin-Pilawa, *Crooked Paths to Allotment: The Fight over Federal Indian Policy after the Civil War* (Chapel Hill: University of North Carolina Press, 2012); Linda K. Kerber, "The Abolitionist Perception of the Indian," *Journal of American History* 62 (1975): 285–95. Bolt, Mardock, and Kerber emphasize the links between the abolition and Indian reform movements, while Prucha deemphasizes them. Kerber provides a particularly compelling discussion of the way in which abolitionists approached Indian reform. Genetin-Pilawa focuses on those who proposed alternatives to the mainstream assimilationist approach to Indian reform that most former abolitionists, including Wendell Phillips, promoted. For general accounts of the nineteenth-century American conflicts with the tribes in the West, see Robert Marshall Utley, *The Indian Frontier, 1846–1890*, rev. ed. (Albuquerque: University of New Mexico Press, 1984); Philip Weeks, *Farewell, My Nation: The American Indian and the United States in the Nineteenth Century*, 2nd ed. (Wheeling, Ill.: Harlan Davidson, 2001).

3. Although the general current of reform among African Americans emphasized equality within American society, some African Americans also had separatist inclinations. For a discussion of American Indian visions of reform in the late nineteenth century, see Lucy Maddox, *Citizen Indians: Native American Intellectuals, Race, and Reform* (Ithaca: Cornell University Press, 2005). See also Genetin-Pilawa, *Crooked Paths to Allotment*, for a discussion of some of the reformers who had a more nuanced understanding of Indian reform.

4. Irving H. Bartlett, *Wendell Phillips: Brahmin Radical* (Boston: Beacon Press, 1961), 367–85.

5. Although his work on behalf of the American Indian is acknowledged by Phillips's biographers, it is not explored. See Bartlett, *Wendell Phillips*, 380; Lorenzo Sears, *Wendell Phillips: Orator and Agitator* (1909; Whitefish, Mont.: Kessinger Publishing, 2010), 303; James Brewer Stewart, *Wendell Phillips: Liberty's Hero* (Baton Rouge: Louisiana State University Press, 1986), 292–93. In addition to the tendency to focus on Phillips as an abolitionist, another likely reason why Indian reform does not figure prominently in the Phillips biographies is that there is scant mention in the Wendell Phillips Papers at Harvard University's Houghton Library of his work on behalf of

Indian rights. Instead, much of his involvement is documented in the newspapers of the era, and only recently has the digitization of many nineteenth-century papers made it possible to easily excavate information on his Indian reform work. The best scholarly discussions to date are references to his work that are embedded in more general treatments of the connections between the abolition movement and Indian reform. See Kerber, "The Abolitionist Perception of the Indian," 285–87; Mardock, *The Reformers and the American Indian.*

6. Phillips to Rev. R. West in St. Louis *Globe-Democrat*, August 20, 1876.

7. On abolitionist involvement in protests against Indian Removal, see Mary Hershberger, "Mobilizing Women, Anticipating Abolition: The Struggle against Indian Reform in the 1830s," *Journal of American History* 86, no. 1 (June 1999): 15–40; Alisse Portnoy, *Their Right to Speak: Women's Activism in the Indian and Slave Debates* (Cambridge: Harvard University Press, 2005); Kerber, "The Abolitionist Perception of the Indian," 272–75.

8. Quoted in Ann Marie Plane and Gregory Button, "Massachusetts Indian Enfranchisement Act: Ethnic Contest in Historical Context, 1849–1869," *Ethnohistory* 40 (Autumn 1993): 587. This article provides a good overview of the issues surrounding Massachusetts Indian enfranchisement.

9. Plane and Button, "The Massachusetts Indian Enfranchisement Act," 588.

10. Wendell Phillips, "The Massachusetts Indians," *Massachusetts Quarterly Review* 3 (December 1849): 105–17. See commentary on the article in *Liberator*, December 7, 1849.

11. For a good discussion of the idea of the infantalization of the American Indian among humanitarians of the nineteenth century, see Gregory Eiselein, *Literature and Humanitarian Reform in the Civil War Era* (Bloomington: Indiana University Press, 1996), 139–43.

12. On nineteenth-century thinking about race, see Reginald Horsman, *Race and Manifest Destiny: The Origins of American Racial Anglo-Saxonism* (Cambridge: Harvard University Press, 1981).

13. *Liberator*, May 27, July 8, October 14, 1859; Prucha, *American Indian Policy in Crisis*, 5.

14. *Liberator*, May 27, July 8, October 14, 1859; Prucha, *American Indian Policy in Crisis*, 5.

15. Mardock, *The Reformers and the American Indian*, 11. The women's rights movement experienced a similar hiatus during the Civil War.

16. *National Anti-Slavery Standard*, September 19, 1868.

17. Ibid., June 12, 1869.

18. Ibid.

19. *Harper's Weekly*, July 10, 1869.

20. *New York Times*, June 11, 25, 1869.

21. *Vermont Chronicle*, June 19, 1869.

22. *National Anti-Slavery Standard*, June 12, 1869. Slave emancipation among Indians and the granting of tribal rights was actually a more complicated and conflict-ridden process than Phillips's comments would suggest. See Thomas F. Andrews, "Freedmen in Indian Territory: A Post Civil War Dilemma," *Journal of the West* 4 (July 1965): 367–76; Walt Wilson, "Freedmen in Indian Territory during Reconstruction," *The Chronicles of Oklahoma* 49 (Summer 1971): 230–44; Claudio Saunt, "The Paradox of Freedom: Tribal Sovereignty and Emancipation During the Reconstruction of Indian Territory," *The Journal of Southern History* 70 (2004): 63–94. On gender

roles, see Theda Perdue, *Cherokee Women: Gender and Culture Change, 1700–1835* (Lincoln: University of Nebraska Press, 1998).

23. Milwaukee *Daily Sentinel,* May 17, 1870.

24. For a discussion of the end of the treaty system, see Francis Paul Prucha, *American Indian Treaties: The History of a Political Anomaly* (Berkeley: University of California Press, 1994), 289–358.

25. *National Standard,* October 15, 1870. In May 1870, the editors of the *National Anti-Slavery Standard* changed the name of the paper to *The Standard* to reflect the shift in its content to the broad reform agenda of the Reform League following the dissolution of the American Anti-Slavery Society. At the end of July 1870, the paper's name again changed to the *National Standard.*

26. Utley, *The Indian Frontier,* 85–98; Prucha, *American Indian Policy in Crisis,* 11–13; Eliott West, *The Contested Plains: Indians, Goldseekers and the Rush to Colorado* (Lawrence: University Press of Kansas, 1998), 287–308.

27. *Condition of the Indian Tribes* (Washington, D.C.: Government Printing Office, 1867).

28. Mardock, *The Reformers and the American Indian,* 26, 137; Samuel Forster Tappan, letter to Wendell Phillips, November 5, 1871, Crawford Blagden Papers, Houghton Library, Harvard University.

29. Vine Deloria, Jr., and Raymond De Mallie, eds., *Proceedings of the Great Peace Commission of 1867–1868* (Washington, D.C.: Institute for the Development of Indian Law, 1975); Kerry R. Oman, "The Beginning of the End: The Indian Peace Commission of 1867–1868," *Great Plains Quarterly* 22 (2002): 35–51.

30. The reservation policy has some admitted parallels to the policies of white colonizationists who promoted removing black freedpeople from the United States and encouraging their settlement in Africa. Phillips was critical of the colonization movement, and although he supported the Peace Policy in general, reservations were not his solution to Indian affairs. He consistently supported legal equality within the republic as the appropriate goal. For more on colonization and Indian policy during the early nineteenth century, see Portnoy, *Their Right to Speak.*

31. Robert H. Keller, *American Protestantism and United States Indian Policy, 1869–82* (Lincoln: University of Nebraska Press, 1983), 9–10.

32. Mardock, *The Reformers and the American Indian,* 30–35.

33. Bangor *Daily Whig & Courier,* May 19, 1870.

34. *The Standard,* July 1870; Mardock, *The Reformers and the American Indian,* 78.

35. *New York Times,* March 11, 1869. On Grant's Peace Policy, see Keller, *American Protestantism and United States Indian Policy,* 17–30.

36. For more information on the Modoc conflict, see Keith A. Murray, *The Modocs and Their War* (Norman: University of Oklahoma Press, 1959); Utley, *The Indian Frontier,* 168–71.

37. Wendell Phillips to E. S. Tobey, June 30, 1874, quoted in Mardock, *The Reformers and the American Indian,* 135–36. On Meacham's activity, see also Prucha, *American Indian Policy in Crisis,* 85–90.

38. Boston *Daily Advertiser,* July 29, 1875.

39. Alfred Benjamin Meacham, *Wigwam and War-Path; or, the Royal Chief in Chains* (Boston: J. P. Dale and Co., 1875), iii–iv.

40. San Francisco *Daily Evening Bulletin*, January 20, 1875.

41. Lowell *Daily Citizen*, September 4, 1876.

42. Galveston *Daily News*, February 16, 1876; *Frank Leslie's Illustrated Newspaper*, February 26, 1876.

43. Alfred Benjamin Meacham, *Wi-ne-ma (the Woman Chief) and Her People* (Hartford: American Publishing Co., 1876).

44. Lowell *Daily Citizen and News*, June 7, 8, 1871.

45. *Daily Citizen and News*, June 8, 1871; *National Standard*, June 17, 1871. On party politics and American Indian policy, see Heather Cox Richardson, *Wounded Knee: Party Politics and the Road to an American Massacre* (New York: Basic Books, 2010).

46. *National Anti-Slavery Standard*, April 16, 1870.

47. New York *Herald*, July 19, 1876.

48. Lowell *Daily Citizen*, July 24, 1876.

49. Boston *Daily Advertiser*, July 20, 1876; St. Louis *Globe-Democrat*, July 21, 1876; Milwaukee *Daily Sentinel*, July 21, 25, 1876; Bangor *Daily Whig and Courier*, July 24, 1876; Denver *Daily Rocky Mountain News*, July 28, 1876; Galveston *Daily News*, August 15, 1876.

50. Boston *Daily Advertiser*, August 27, 1877. Sitting Bull and his followers eventually returned to the United States of their own accord in 1881. Buffalo depletion in Canada meant that the Sioux refugees could not support themselves in traditional independence, and the Canadian government was unwilling to provide land or material aid for them.

51. *Daily Advertiser*, August 27, 1877.

52. Roger L. Nichols, *Indians in the United States and Canada: A Comparative History* (Lincoln: University of Nebraska Press, 1998), 211.

53. Ibid., 212.

54. Ibid.

55. For references to the Canadian comparison, see *National Anti-Slavery Standard*, September 19, 1868; Boston *Daily Advertiser*, August 6, 1879. On Canadian policy toward the tribes, see Nichols, *Indians in the United States and Canada*; L. F. S. Upton, "The Origins of Canadian Indian Policy," *Journal of Canadian Studies* 8, no. 4 (1973): 51–61; John L. Tobias, *Protection, Civilization, Assimilation: An Outline of Canada's Indian Policy* (Toronto: University of Toronto Press, 1991).

56. For a discussion of the importance of the American Indian as a symbol to abolitionists, see John Stauffer, *The Black Hearts of Men: Radical Abolitionists and the Transformation of Race* (Cambridge: Harvard University Press, 2002), 182–307.

57. Lowell *Daily Citizen and News*, June 8, 1871; *National Standard*, June 17, 1871.

58. Boston *Daily Advertiser*, October 21, 1875.

59. For an overview of the Ponca story, see Mardock, *The Reformers and the American Indian*, 169–89.

60. Thomas Henry Tibbles, *Report of the Omaha Ponca Relief Committee* (n.p., 1880).

61. Mardock, *The Reformers and the American Indian*, 175–79.

62. [B. W. Williams], *Invitation to Meet Standing Bear and Miss LaFlesche, October 27, 1879* (Boston: City of, 1879). Bright Eyes was educated in American schools, and she also was known by the western name "Susette LaFlesche."

63. Frederick Douglass, *The Life and Times of Frederick Douglass: From 1817–1882* (London: Christian Age Office, 1882), 185–86; Augusta Rohrbach, "Profits of Protest: The Market Strategies of Sojourner Truth and Louisa May Alcott," in *Prophets of Protest: Reconsidering the History of American Abolitionism*, ed. Timothy Patrick McCarthy and John Stauffer (New York: The New Press, 2006), 242–55.

64. Thomas Henry Tibbles and Kay Graber, *Standing Bear and the Ponca Chiefs* (Lincoln: University of Nebraska Press, 1995), 2, 138, emphasis in original.

65. Ibid., 130.

66. William H. Lincoln, *The Indian Question: Report of the Committee Appointed by Hon. John D. Long* (Boston: F. Wood, 1880).

67. Prucha, *American Indian Policy in Crisis*, 132–55; Helen Hunt Jackson, *A Century of Dishonor: The Early Crusade for Indian Reform* (1881; New York: Harper & Row, 1965).

68. For a discussion of these policies, see Prucha, *American Indian Policy in Crisis*, 227–352.

69. See, for example, Angie Debo, *And Still the Waters Run: The Betrayal of the Five Civilized Tribes* (Norman: University of Oklahoma Press, 1984); Emily Greenwald, *Reconfiguring the Reservation: The Nez Perces, Jicarilla Apaches, and the Dawes Act* (Albuquerque: University of New Mexico Press, 2002); Wilcomb E. Washburn, *The Assault on Indian Tribalism: The General Allotment Law (Dawes Act) of 1887* (Malabar, Fla.: R. E. Krieger Pub. Co., 1986).

11

RACE, RADICALISM, AND REMEMBERING WENDELL PHILLIPS

DONALD YACOVONE

FROM COLLECTIVE MEMORY TO HISTORICAL MEMORY

The horse-drawn hearse rolled to a stop as the February sun set over Boston's Park Street Church. Escorted by black and white soldiers, the pallbearers carried Wendell Phillips's mahogany casket into the old Granary Burial Ground, where the great orator's remains would rest along with those of Crispus Attucks, Samuel Adams, John Hancock, Paul Revere, and so many other Boston legends.[1] The solemn ceremony capped a daylong series of events to honor one of the city's most famous residents and unquestionably the nation's best-known reformer. Even for those who had disdained Phillips in life, his passing marked an unsettling generational change. As the *Congregationalist* newspaper remarked, Phillips's death removed yet "another of the few remaining links which bind the great man and great speakers of a former generation to the present." Phillips, far more than William Lloyd Garrison or any other former antislavery leader, had been the region's high priest of the temple of reform. He seemed to Rev. Henry Ward Beecher no complex organ, but rather a trumpet, "sharp, wide-sounding, narrow and intense," a man like Moses, "called of God."[2]

Beecher, who stood on the steps of the city's famed Parker House hotel to observe the funeral procession on its way to Faneuil Hall—where Phillips's body would lie in state—seemed stunned by the enormity of the crowds and the outpouring of grief. Everyone he saw had tears in his or her eyes. African American soldiers with down-turned muskets led the march, followed by a silent band and army officers bearing reversed-held swords. As he stood watching amid the deluge of emotion, the New York minister—the nation's leading clergyman—could not help but think that those who "persecuted and would have slain him . . . [are] now exceedingly busy in building his tomb and rearing his statue." Those who would not permit the name of that man to

Figure 11.1. Old Granary burial of Wendell Phillips, *Harpers Weekly*, February 16, 1884. Courtesy of the Hutchins Center for African and African American Research, Harvard University.

"defile their lips . . . are thanking God today that he lived. He has taught some lessons," Beecher concluded. Phillips's career evoked the life of Jesus, "bathed in the providence of God" and dedicated to the oppressed. Phillips, Beecher explained, is a "rising son—a sun that will never set."[3]

For nearly half a century, the sun did not set on the memory of Wendell Phillips. His name resounded throughout the popular press; lecturers traveled the country, even in the Deep South, to recount his career to eager audiences. Populists, socialists, communists, labor leaders, reformers, progressives, feminists, literary figures, biographers, and social commentators—even orators at high-school graduations—all invoked his name and celebrated his example. Hardly a day passed without his popular quotations or mentions of him appearing in the country's newspapers. Phillips's legacy counted, playing a central role in the conflict over the changing meaning of the Civil War, the fight against resurgent racism, and in the radical critique of American capitalism. Yet, by the mid-1920s, references to him, his accomplishments, and his opinions had disappeared from the daily press, relegating his memory—and influence—to a shrinking number of African American, labor, socialist, and scholarly communities. Although historical memory of Phillips persisted in his native Boston and, critically, among post–World War II civil rights advocates, well before the close of the last century even the birthplace of radical abolitionism had largely forgotten one of its most influential sons.

Phillips's life, or more precisely his long and consequential afterlife, is a remarkable example of the workings of popular memory. Analyzing the changing ways we remember the past has become a central feature of modern historical scholarship—and the literature related to it is vast. At times, the terms "history," "memory," "public memory," "collective memory," "historical memory," "memorialization"—even "prosthetic memory"—are confusingly invoked as scholars attempt to define these terms' various and overlapping meanings. No one, however, has written more or with better clarity on the relationship between memory and history than David Blight. History and memory are not the same, he avers, but are two separate and interrelated streams of historical consciousness. Formal history, the written record of the past grounded in evidence, is largely the necessary but inevitably problematic domain of scholars. Collective (or public) memory, however, represents the efforts of groups (or nations) to construct usable versions of the past "and employ them for self-understanding and to win power in an ever-changing present." Memory of the past is, as Blight reminds us, less about thinking about the past as it is thinking with it, revealing how "social memory, becomes political." It is a process—shared by professional historians—of remembering *and* forgetting, a public struggle "in which versions of the past are used as instruments of power." What gets remembered (and forgotten) matters, revealing society's contending values and priorities.[4]

"The remembered past is a much larger category than the recorded past," as John Lukacs once wrote, and it is a far more personal one. Indeed, as one survey discovered, Americans maintain a special connection to the past, and appear to require a first-person account to fully appreciate a historical event—perhaps because, as Louis Menand observed, we greatly rely on history "to inspire the present."[5] In large measure, this helps explain why a city that so loathed Wendell Phillips—to the point that by 1860 he required bodyguards and carried a pistol for his protection—forgot its own actions and at his death honored him as intensely as his surviving antislavery colleagues. The Civil War and the demise of slavery had changed everything, including memory, making it cohere into a new collective memory that better served, as Maurice Halbwachs once wrote, "our ideas of the moment." In some way, the public response to Phillips's passing acknowledged that in a larger sense Phillips and the abolitionists had been right and the city—and much of the North—wanted to lay claim to that legacy which gave their own sacrifices a more transcendent meaning.[6]

What began in Boston exemplifies the national process of collective memory formation, and one that illuminates the legacy of Wendell Phillips, who remembered him, what they remembered him for, and why. It is a process that begins with the creation of popular or "collective memory," which requires personal or first-person experience with a person or event. In time, it moves toward "historical memory," in which received opinion (not personal experience) becomes the primary force in public memory formation. Current theory on public memory in the electronic age theorizes that "consumers of electronic mass media" can experience "a common heritage with people they have never seen" and can "acquire memories of a past to which they have no geographic or biological connection," a circumstance that one scholar has labeled "prosthetic memory." If true, its durability—if not authenticity—raises troubling questions. In the case of Wendell Phillips, however, the many people who knew him shaped his public memory, forming a lasting and influential legend that they eagerly passed on to the succeeding generation. In this way, Phillips remained a powerful cultural force, shaping opinions and events throughout the country and assuming a central role in the nation's culture wars from the end of the nineteenth century through the Progressive Era. The subsequent decline of historical memory of Phillips, if nothing else, casts light on its previous centrality to American culture and upon the fading place of social and economic justice in modern political debates.[7]

CREATING MEMORY

At 6:15 p.m. on February 2, 1884, Wendell Phillips died after a massive heart attack. On the morning of February 6, Phillips's coffin was placed in a hearse and arrived in a train of twelve carriages for services at the Hollis Street Chapel. Along the route from Phillips's home, the streets filled with thousands of mourners of every "race, creed and prominent measure" of those that Phillips had championed throughout his life. The services, led by the Rev. Samuel Longfellow of North Cambridge (Henry Wadsworth Longfellow's brother), included the state's governor and political elite and nearly every surviving reformer of any note, including Henry B. Blackwell, Lucy Stone, Julia Ward Howe, Thomas Wentworth Higginson, Elizur Wright, Theodore Dwight Weld, John Greenleaf Whittier, Ednah Dow Cheney, Abby W. May, Louisa May Alcott, Susan B. Anthony, Sarah Orne Jewett, Harriet H. Robinson, Frederick Douglass, and George T. Downing. Even the sculptor Anne Whitney, author Edward Everett Hale, and jurist Oliver Wendell Holmes, Jr., attended. After the Unitarian minister and abolitionist Samuel May, Jr., offered a final prayer, the casket was escorted back to its carriage by pallbearers Dr. Oliver Wendell Holmes, John Murray Forbes, William I. Bowditch, Samuel E. Sewall, Lewis Hayden, Charles K. Whipple, Richard Hallowell, and Wendell Phillips Garrison. Boston never had seen anything like it before, nor would it ever again.[8]

As the Reverend Beecher observed, tearful mourners packed the route from the chapel to Faneuil Hall; thousands considering it their duty to stand in the cold and wait for an opportunity to pass by Phillips's casket in the location that had launched his abolitionist career forty-seven years earlier. Four African American soldiers from the Robert Gould Shaw Guards stood at attention around the casket, covered in black broadcloth topped with a sheaf of wheat wrapped in ivy. The battle flag of the famed Fifty-fourth Massachusetts Regiment hung alongside floral arrangements provided by Phillips's colleague in the radical labor movement, Gen. Benjamin F. Butler, and two Irish organizations.

According to one estimate, by 4 p.m. at least 15,000 mourners had passed through Faneuil Hall, including hundreds of schoolchildren and Boston's en-

Figure 11.2. Wendell Phillips lying in state in Faneuil Hall. *Frank Leslie's Illustrated Newspaper,* February 16, 1884. Original image owned by author.

tire African American population. On the evening of February 8, the phalanx of aging reformers reconvened at Faneuil Hall for another ceremony to honor Phillips. Before a life-size bust of Phillips accented with bright green vines of smilax, the throng heard several of his former colleagues, Howe, Cheney,

Downing, along with William Wells Brown and Edward G. Walker—son of the famed David Walker—orate on each phase of Phillips's career. John Hutchinson, the last survivor of the singing antislavery family, performed familiar abolitionist songs. All participants inculcated the same message: Phillips never quit, and when others did, he "marched on alone."[9]

Two days after his death, the Boston board of aldermen rushed to make plans for a public memorial to honor one of the most "illustrious men of our times," an unmatched example of "unflinching devotion to the cause of human liberty, and uncompromising advocacy of the poor and oppressed of every race, creed, and color." The city recruited one of the nation's most influential editors, authors, and social commentators, George William Curtis, to deliver the keynote address on April 18 at Tremont Temple. The former Brook Farmer, political abolitionist, Republican activist, and related by marriage to the martyred Robert Gould Shaw, Curtis would certainly appeal to the commonwealth's social and political elite that would pack one of the city's prime venues. He understood his role well and intended to make Phillips's "death like his life, most serviceable to young Americans." Additionally, the city printed five thousand copies of the handsomely bound version of the memorial services, a kind of *memento mori* that Boston periodically produced for such events between 1853 and 1911 and meant to be examples of the purposeful life that would inspire the young.[10]

In words that would be reprinted around the country, Curtis relished the irony that he and many of those seated before him, unlike Phillips, voted religiously and revered the Constitution and the Union. Moreover, many had been the objects of his attacks, feeling the "sharp sting of controversial speech." But today, he observed, it all vanished "like frost in a flood of sunshine." Curtis admonished the younger sons and daughters of the city that they could not understand Wendell Phillips without grasping that, twenty-four years earlier, "Slavery sat supreme in the White House and made laws in the Capitol. Courts of justice were its ministers and legislatures its lackeys. It silenced the preacher in the pulpit, it muzzled the editor at his desk, and the professor in his lecture-room . . . and denounced the vital principles of the Declaration of Independence as treason." The new generation would be astonished to know that men like Wendell Phillips had been "reviled as lunatics and anarchists. . . . But history, looking before and after, readjusts contemporary judgments of men and events." Phillips and his ilk, although hated in their day, Curtis reminded his audience, turned out to be necessary alarm bells who possessed a "transcendent purity of purpose" and advanced the "welfare of the country," and whose names are now written "with a sunbeam."[11]

Phillips's passing proved most consequential for African Americans, especially those in Boston who knew him so well and benefited so much from his equalitarianism and philanthropy. Shortly before his funeral, city blacks led by George Lewis Ruffin—the state's first African American judge—met and proclaimed that "our people all over the land, deeply feel the irreparable loss which our race and all others for whom he labored."[12] From the beginning of his antislavery career, Phillips had allied himself with Boston's black community, not only by supporting their struggle for freedom but by eagerly engaging with it. He not only knew and socialized with all the city's black leaders but spoke before their cultural societies, such as the Boston Adelphic Union, on a wide range of topics and addressing audiences that included all age groups, from children to the elderly. They all in some way could know and form lasting memories of the great orator.[13]

When William Lloyd Garrison's colleague William C. Nell left for Rochester, New York, in 1847 to assist Frederick Douglass in publishing the *North Star*—fracturing relations between Douglass and Garrison—Phillips betrayed no arrogance and only offered praise. Nell, Phillips wrote, possessed "an enviable character for urbanity, high moral character, and integrity above suspicion." He retained his close friendship with Nell and in the 1850s wrote the foreword to his pioneering history of black military service. Correspondingly, the respect Phillips showed African Americans rebounded in countless ways.[14]

Recognizing Phillips's service to the race, the black sculptor Edmonia Lewis executed a marble portrait medallion of him after the Civil War, which the future African American educator and diplomat Richard T. Greener proudly owned while a student at Harvard. The year before Phillips died, the twenty-six-year-old journalist T. Thomas Fortune visited Boston to report on the city's black community for his New York readers. But he went to Boston primarily to see Wendell Phillips. Fortune, born a slave in Florida, cherished Phillips as having done more to end bondage than anyone else. His admiration for Phillips grew even more when the aging abolitionist told him that once he had been denied lodging in New York because of who he was, "treated as a colored man," and, thus, understood the African American struggle for full freedom in ways other white leaders did not. Few influences, however, proved more consequential for American history than what was revealed in western Massachusetts a few months after Phillips's death. At his high-school graduation in Great Barrington, the young W. E. B. Du Bois delivered his first formal address and chose to speak about Phillips. While his original text does not survive, Du Bois later explained that Phillips's "life and work" had exerted formative influence upon him and that the great Bostonian's quest for racial and economic justice helped him take "a long step toward a wider conception of what I was going to do."[15]

African Americans found a wide variety of ways to commemorate Phillips's life. Many communities, as Boston had done earlier, formed Phillips clubs, literary societies, or lyceums. A James H. Davis in Troy, New York, published at least one issue of a newspaper, the *Wendell Phillips Enterprise*. A family of former Virginia slaves named their son after him, and Wendell Phillips Dabney went on to become a successful businessman and, as if foreordained, the first president of Cincinnati's branch of the NAACP. Black fraternal orders met specifically to honor Phillips as a model of "unswerving devotion to the right." Boston's Wendell Phillips Club, first formed in 1876 and the only society that Phillips permitted to use his name during his lifetime, carried on Phillips's work for social justice. It provided a venue for speakers like Frederick Douglass and waged a citywide campaign to expose white businessmen who refused to hire even well-educated African American males.[16]

Black workers in New York City organized the Wendell Phillips Labor Club, and in the fall of 1884 joined with twenty thousand white workers to demonstrate for higher wages and shorter hours—a story that even appeared in papers of the Deep South. Given the radicalism of Phillips's postwar career, it is no surprise that labor deeply mourned his death. Labor leaders regarded him as their best champion, just as had African Americans. New York's Central Labor Union proclaimed that, if Phillips had been "a Russian he would have been a nihilist; had he been a German he would have been a socialist; had he been a Frenchman he would have been a communist; and had he been a Irishman he would have been an invincible."[17]

Black communities around the country, from Massachusetts to New York, from Alabama to Oregon, held ceremonies to mark Phillips's death, most notably in Washington, D.C., and in Boston. In the nation's capital, Rev. Francis J. Grimké at the Fifteenth Street Presbyterian Church and Frederick Douglass at the city's Congregational Church both addressed interracial services which included most of the city's black elite, such as Blanche K. Bruce; Richard T.

Greener; John F. Cook; and John Wesley Cromwell, Sr.; as well as Massachusetts's former governor John D. Long. Both Douglass and Grimké lamented that African Americans had lost their most able and effective advocate, an event that struck Grimké as the "unexpected coming of a great catastrophe."[18]

In Boston, Grimké's better-known brother, the Harvard-trained lawyer and activist Archibald, on April 9, 1884, addressed a large interracial gathering at Tremont Temple. For Grimké, the loss was as much personal as political, and one can only guess as to how much of the current state of black rights weighed on his mind as he addressed so many former abolitionists and reformers. He had met Phillips while attending Harvard Law School in the 1870s, and the two grew close as Grimké labored in the law office of William Bowditch. The men often were seen walking hand in hand on city streets, forging strong bonds of friendship. As Judge George Lewis Ruffin observed, older African Americans had gravitated toward Garrison, but young blacks went directly to Phillips for advice and assistance, especially during the contentious 1850s. Grimké remarked that Garrison and Phillips represented the mother and father of their movement against slavery. But during the 1850s, Garrison's feminine nonresistance had lost its appeal: "the time for argument had passed; the time for arms had arrived," Grimké asserted. Phillips had come to symbolize action—"Godlike action." Doing nothing amounted to surrender. "Peace was slavery, and sleep was death. . . . His speeches were the first billows breaking in prophetic fury against the South." Grimké saw Phillips as the man of the hour who bravely called for the guns when others hesitated. Only "Wendell Phillips comprehended the gravity of the situation." He understood, Grimké asserted, that "the only hope for freedom lay now in the finger that could pull a trigger."[19]

Word of Phillips's passing spread at lightning speeds not significantly slower than in the so-called modern information age. Death announcements appeared the very next day in Galveston, Texas, and St. Louis, Missouri; within five days, from New England to Colorado to California, notices of the great man's passing had reached every region of the country, soon followed with detailed accounts of his funeral and related commemorations.[20] Pulpits across the country, both liberal and orthodox, considered the meaning of Phillips's life. In Chicago, the Georgia-born Presbyterian minister John Henry Barrows packed the city's Central Music Hall and used his oration to educate the city's younger generation about the "great agitator's life," a vital lesson for the new age of "mammon-worship." In New York, the Rev. Edward Beecher spoke at Shiloh Presbyterian Church, a pulpit once filled by Henry Highland Garnet. In an event covered by newspapers across the country, Felix Adler, founder of the Ethical Cultural Movement, spoke to a thousand people at Union Square's Chickering Hall, proclaiming that Phillips "knew how to sweep the chords of moral indignation with a power like that of the ancient Hebrew prophets."[21] Ministers, orators, social leaders, and poets—black and white—tried to capture the meaning of Phillips's life of service to a new generation dominated by what the Reverend Barrows called "this vortex of mechanic arts and luxury" in a "metropolis of materialism."[22]

While positive assessments of Phillips's life mushroomed, in fact, the controversies sparked by Wendell Phillips in life followed him in death, and his meaning in popular memory remained a battleground. The Boston elite never forgave him for any of his reform work, especially abolitionism and his incendiary critiques of capitalism. The Adams brothers, Henry and Charles Francis, detested Phillips and measured a person's worth by the level of abuse Phillips flung at them. Brother Charles reviled Phillips for the ridicule he poured on him for advocating literacy and educational tests to prevent the political dominance of the Irish, Chinese, and southern blacks. Henry Adams loathed Phillips to the end of his life and in his famed *Autobiography* warned that "Wendell Phillips on a platform was a model dangerous for youth." The classic Mugwump reformer George Frisbie Hoar found it impossible to forgive Phillips for his attacks on his brother E. Rockwood Hoar, who had rejected all Radical Reconstruction plans. When he published his memoirs in 1903, Hoar charged that Phillips lacked all "common honesty." Phillips, Hoar asserted, "never gave the people wise counsel, and rarely told them the truth." When his brother learned of Phillips's death in 1884 and was asked if he had plans to attend the funeral, he told Henry Cabot Lodge that he could not attend, "but I entirely approve of the proceedings."[23]

Many of his former close associates, at the mildest, confessed that Phillips "had his faults." The popular Boston poet, journalist, and author Nora Perry could make no excuses for "his sharp assaults, flung seemingly heedless from his quivering bow and heedless striking either friend or foe, . . . launched with eyes that saw not foe or friend, but only, shining far, some goal or end." Thomas Wentworth Higginson, as a backer of John Brown and the former colonel of the First South Carolina Volunteers, took second place to no abolitionist; nevertheless, he rejected Phillips's disunionism and found his postwar radicalism intolerable. He accused Phillips of treating all reforms with the same single-minded moralism of the antislavery movement. "You cannot settle the relations of capital and labor off-hand, by saying, as in the case of slavery, 'Let my people go.'" At his immensely popular Monday lecture series at Tremont Temple, ongoing for twenty years, the Rev. Joseph Cook confessed that most Bostonians believed with Higginson that Phillips had lost his way since the close of the Civil War and simply didn't understand economics. The charge enraged Cook: "You say he didn't understand the relations between labor and capital? Wait fifty years and then ask if Wendell Phillips understood the case."[24]

Phillips's flair for the invective, always aimed at specifically named targets like Hoar, Rufus Choate, or Daniel Webster, became memorable because they hurt, and Bostonians could not forget, or much forgive. One critic, a Dr. Bartol, likely Dr. Cyrus Augustus Bartol, a Unitarian minister and transcendentalist, could not forgive the "master of invective" who used words as "swords. . . . His tongue was a scourge. His intonations were detonations." Phillips's former antislavery colleague James Freeman Clark, in a piece entitled "His Virtues and Defects" published right after Phillips's death, recounted what would soon become established as the core mythos of Phillips's life—that, born to privilege, he abandoned "fame and distinction" to dedicate his life to a cause "which was very repugnant to the society in which he moved." Like Jesus, Clark noted, he had dedicated himself to the oppressed. But Clark focused on that which had disturbed so many who had heard Phillips speak. According to Clark, Phillips too often turned his invective on those who were innocent of his accusations, and was often as wrong on policy matters as he was right, as when he predicted a peace compromise after the Battle of Gettysburg. While much talk of building a monument to Phillips circulated in Boston, Clark would have none of it. We don't need "tombs to the reformers," he advised, but action to accomplish needed change.[25]

Another former colleague proved even more unforgiving. Kentucky abolitionist Cassius M. Clay refused to join in the chorus of praise heaped on Phillips. According to Clay, as a critic of Lincoln and a disunionist, Phillips did not deserve praise. He considered Phillips's refusal to support the Union to be inexcusable and only proved the defect in his judgment when after secession he reversed course and backed the national government. When Chicago Congressman John F. Finerty, an Irish veteran of the Civil War and the Indian Wars in the West, introduced legislation to mark Phillips's death, opposition came not from the South, but from Connecticut. Representative William W. Eaton, a former U.S. senator and Hartford journalist, objected, telling a reporter that "I do not see what this government has got to be sorry about in the death of Wendell Phillips. He has been a life-long enemy of the government . . . [and] advocated the secession of the free states on the ground that it was impious to live under a constitution that tolerated slavery." When Finerty offered his resolution on the floor of the House, Eaton shouted out, "I object," and the measure was referred to the Committee on the Library, where it died.[26]

The further south and west one went, the greater the chorus of criticism. The Baltimore *Sun* considered him the "boldest and most eloquent and most aggressive" of the abolitionists and the force behind John Brown—which it considered as an indictment. The paper labeled him the "stormy petrel" of the era, a man who wished to keep the South in complete subjugation. It also believed that the new constitutional amendments to protect black rights had sent the "born agitator" looking for new ways to foment trouble, and soon found women's rights, greenbacks, labor, and temperance to fill his time. If one needed additional proof of his "utter wont of judgment," the paper declared, one need only look at his faith in Benjamin F. Butler. In St. Louis, Phillips seemed completely unbalanced and attending his lectures made one feel "in the neighborhood of a dynamite bomb, or in front of a runaway locomotive about to carry everything to smash."[27] The Macon, Georgia, *Weekly Telegraph* admitted that Phillips was earnest, even courageous, and certainly eloquent, but ironically criticized him for seeking to "overthrow the republic." In assisting African Americans, the paper predictably asserted, he had "sown the seeds of dissolution in our body politic." In New Orleans, critics recognized "his broad philanthropy" which covered the world, but considered it "so thin any near-sighted person could see through it." Those in Dallas, Texas, marveled at the number of heretics and "delettanti" [*sic*] that showed up for his memorial services. "How his satanic majesty's fingers must have ached to cast his net at the animated miscellany."[28]

The Memphis *Appeal* expressed its willingness to forget Phillips the abolitionist and, instead, remember him favorably "as a citizen of the world." While never dominant in the South, such a view proved more widespread than one might at first imagine. The Wheeling, West Virginia, *Register* went so far as to warn that it would be a mistake to think that all southern white men disdained

Phillips. The paper did not avoid the fact that Phillips had been an implacable enemy of a southern institution "now extinct," but at least he "was an honest one." More important, the paper contended that Phillips "held in equal abhorrence negro slavery and white vassalage." Given the growing strength of populists, grangers, and workingmen's groups in the 1880s, a man that opposed the "monopolists of Fall River and the iron founders of Pennsylvania" who compelled men to work for sixty-five cents a day "and support their families on that pittance or starve" merited serious attention. Moreover, the paper maintained that Phillips's attacks on the Republican Party as the "instrument and auxiliary of corporations and capital, . . . used by the rich to oppress the poor," should get the attention of all the South. That his labor radicalism could gain Phillips fans below the Mason-Dixon Line might have struck the Boston rebel as one of his greatest triumphs.[29]

THE CONTEXT OF MEMORY

By the time of Phillips's death, Reconstruction had long since ended, and while some African Americans had made advances—even in the South—the overwhelming number faced rapid disenfranchisement, thwarted social and economic progress—if not virtual re-enslavement—and rampant political violence. As farmers demanded just pricing and freedom from the monopoly of the railroad magnates, industrial workers organized for higher wages, shorter hours, and safer working conditions, women sought the vote, and Irish nationalists insisted on independence for their homeland, radicals of all stripes turned to the legacy of Wendell Phillips to advance their cause. Given the ubiquity of Phillips's reputation and accomplishments, there simply was no one else to whom activists could turn to marshal authority and precedent.

Never was such influence more needed. From Supreme Court to village square, most white Americans had concluded that the nation's "experiment" with "negro rule" in the South had utterly failed. Moreover, insistence on southern black rights appeared to stand in the way of national reconciliation and reunification. E. L. Godkin, the flinty editor of the *Nation*, one of the North's most liberal journals, had concluded as early as 1872 that Reconstruction had become "morally a more disastrous process than rebellion." Along with the majority of the North, Godkin rejoiced in the 1877 Compromise that put the Republican Rutherford B. Hayes in the White House and "peace" in the South. No more, he sighed, would the nation be troubled with "the negro"; the "nation as a nation, will have nothing more to do with him." As proof of Godkin's assertion, when Gen. Robert E. Lee died in 1870, Frederick Douglass found an abundance of "*nauseating* flatteries" of him in the nation's newspapers. In the year of Phillips's death, the civil rights advocate, judge, and social novelist Albion Tourgée would justifiably lament that, while "the South surrendered at Appomattox, the North has been surrendering ever since." In his notorious 1895 Memorial Day address, "The Faith of a Soldier," Oliver Wendell Holmes, Jr. (a distant Phillips relative), appeared to drive a final stake into the heart of the North's transcendent antislavery interpretation of the war with his disturbing paean to the soldier's combat experience.[30]

At every level and in every quarter of social thought, most Americans at the turn of the century concluded that the very term "Reconstruction" stood for failure and foolhardy idealism. southern polemicists and racial supremacists in the North recast the nation's understanding of the meaning of the war, even why the sections came to blows in the first place. For those in the New South, "Lost Cause" dogma came to symbolize the Old South's moral superiority and ultimately its views on race. In a North already suffused with distorted views of the former slaves and of Reconstruction, "Lost Cause" ideology transformed and narrowed its understanding of the Civil War, allowing a path forward for national reconciliation and, seemingly, final answers to the vexing national race question. As one scholar characterized the "Lost Cause" *mentalité*, it saw "victory as a curse and defeat as moral purification and salvation," combining "the ancient idea of hubris with the Christian virtue of humility, catharsis with apocalypse." This irresistible appeal helped to transform popular memory of the bloodiest conflict in the nation's history, one that had concluded only twenty years earlier.[31]

"Today the South is in the saddle, and with the single exception of slavery, everything it fought for during the days of the Civil War, it has gained by repression of the Negro within its borders. And the North has quietly allowed it to have its own way." The Baltimore *Afro-American*'s assessment of the state of national affairs in 1913 erred only in maintaining that the North quietly acquiesced in the South's victory in the culture wars. In fact, northern journals and magazines competed to present the most extreme Lost Cause views of the Old South and the war. Even the *Atlantic Monthly* and *Harpers*, which had led the visual war against the South and slavery, threw off their old antislavery patina and printed some of the most hideous characterizations of southern blacks and depicted emancipation as a catastrophe. Some national journals even published first-person accounts by "former abolitionists" who claimed that they had gone south after the war and then revisited the region in the 1880s. They concluded that southerners had been right all along: blacks could not successfully live in freedom. Even Mark Twain's colleague Charles Dudley Warner asserted that blacks remained too ignorant to vote and, thus, southern whites knew best and should be permitted to "manage their blacks."[32]

As Albion Tourgée keenly observed in his compelling account of his own time in the Reconstruction South, *A Fool's Errand, By One of the Fools*, the North's acceptance of the term "Carpetbagger"—northerners who went south during Reconstruction—into its common vocabulary proved especially damaging. The term, with a "quaint and ludicrous sound" associated with abolitionists, stood for the very "incarnation of Northern hate, envy, spleen, greed, hypocrisy, and all uncleanness." Astonished at the North's apostasy, Tourgée confessed his disgust that "there is no other instance in history in which the conquering power has discredited its own agents, denounced those of its own blood and faith, espoused the prejudices of its conquered foes, and poured the vitals of its wrath and contempt upon the only class in the conquered territory who defended its acts, supported its policy, promoted its own, or desired its preservation and continuance." A ferocious battle over the past had begun, instigated by the needs of what Halbwachs had referred to as "our ideas of the moment."[33]

Memory, thus, had become a prime battleground, one that placed Wendell Phillips at the heart of the conflict. While decidedly southern views of the war and its aftermath dominated the landscape, especially in school textbooks and in scholarly studies, they did not go unchallenged. Many former abolitionists, some who had been in their twenties during the war, and their children continued to defend an emancipationist interpretation of the conflict. African American and some white members of the Grand Army of the Republic contested southern revisionism and crafted their own memoirs to challenge prevailing views. Black writers, poets, editors, and their white allies sternly resisted American reconciliation and reunification "forged out of the betrayal of the Civil War constitutional amendments and the deepening racial inequality." Their persistence, especially in focusing on the memory of one whose reform interests spanned so wide a horizon, made Phillips a durable and powerful figure, which ultimately helped gain the modern civil rights movement acceptance.[34]

BOSTON'S COLLECTIVE MEMORY

In Boston, Phillips's funeral and commemorative services only began a memorialization process that grew continuously to 1915. The year after his death, many of the old abolitionists reconvened in November at the South Boston home of William Sumner Crosby, a wealthy Boston hay and grain merchant, to hear the eighty-two-year-old Theodore Dwight Weld remember Phillips. Two years later on Memorial Day, under the auspices of the Wendell Phillips Club, the Parnell Branch of the Irish National League, and the Central Labor Trades Union, African Americans, Irish, and union activists—accompanied by the Hyde Park Drum, Fife, and Bugle Corps—marched the short route from near the city line to Phillips's final resting place in neighboring Milton. Led by John Boyle O'Reilly and William H. Dupree, a black Civil War veteran of the Fifty-fifth Massachusetts Regiment, the procession memorialized Phillips and held a decoration ceremony at his grave. That evening, the multitudes reassembled at Faneuil Hall to celebrate Phillips's career. For the first time, Phillips's labor activism took center stage, with speakers highlighting his attacks on "greedy monopolists who, controlling legislation in their pecuniary interests, oppressed the hard working people of all races—the factory Lords, the bank lords, and the railroad lords." The crowd exclaimed that Phillips had championed the Indian, "the Irishman, the Russian and the Hindoo." When Archibald H. Grimké began his praise, Gen. Benjamin F. Butler startled the audience by appearing unannounced, strutting from the rear of the hall directly to the stage, sparking an uproar of applause. Butler, sidelining Grimké, praised Phillips for standing up for all the oppressed "of whatever race or nation."[35]

During the late 1880s, two Boston groups competed to erect a memorial hall in Phillips's name. The Wendell Phillips Hall Association, established by reformers and progressives in cooperation with the city's black leadership, developed elaborate plans to establish the city's equivalent of New York's Cooper Union. Boston's socialist "Labor and Reform Societies," on the other hand, proposed to build a "Wendell Phillips Hall" to house its various groups that promoted Christian socialism and labor rights. Benjamin F. Butler—who soon joined the competing group—quickly endorsed their project which, he asserted, could be built through the contributions of working people—not the rich—and erect a hall "as has never yet been raised to the Goddess of Liberty." The project languished but then revived in the spring of 1891 under the direction of a W. D. P. Bliss. The "Wendell Phillips Union" opened on the city's busy Washington Street for meetings, lectures, and education, with rooms holding one hundred people or more for "all classes of society." For a time, the WPU hosted a wide array of lecturers, including the abolitionist, temperance advocate, and suffragist Mary Livermore as well as Henry C. Spaulding, an unacknowledged founder of the city's subway system. Spaulding, a peripatetic businessman and inventor, used the Phillips Union to make one of the earliest calls for the construction of an underground "rapid transit" system. Other lecturers, in Phillipsian breadth, covered women and reform, the prison system, labor, and a form of Christian socialism that denounced capitalism and competition as the new slavery.[36]

Bliss and many other workers also lived in the building, creating a settlement house, one of the first in the city. Aiming to have the facility become the focus of reform in Boston, Bliss sought to attract "the workingman, the lettered student, [and] the woman of culture, in one true brotherhood . . . for social regeneration." The group briefly published a newspaper, *The Dawn*, and opened its library of reform literature to the public. For a time, the facility attracted the Central Labor Union, the Socialist Labor Party, the Brotherhood of Carpenters, Knights of Labor, the American Health Associates, and others while also featuring a "Ladies Night" to promote suffrage and women's rights.

The Washington Street Phillips Union soon became home to the Wendell Phillips Women's Club, an organization that lobbied the state legislature to examine labor conditions in the commonwealth. In the spirit of Phillips, the organization marshaled a number of groups to establish a cooperative sewing shop to manufacture children's clothing, hoping to offer better conditions and fairer wages than those found in local factories. It employed twenty-five women, sharing all profits, which for a time actually forced the local manufacturers to raise wages. Unfortunately, within two years the Wendell Phillips Union began to collapse under the weight of a recession and a contagion that killed Bliss's daughter and sent workers fleeing in a panic.[37]

In the fall of 1887, the Wendell Phillips Hall Committee, which would eventually transform into the Wendell Phillips Hall Association, met to develop plans for a permanent memorial to the great reformer. White leaders like Butler, John Boyle O'Reilly, Rev. Jesse H. Jones, and Mary Livermore met with African Americans Archibald Grimké, Mark R. DeMortie, J. C. Chappelle, and others to develop plans for the hall and formally incorporate. Other groups with similar plans also met during this same period, including one at Tremont Temple with Hamlin Garland's Boston Anti-Poverty Society, Benjamin F. Butler, Lt. Gov. John Quincy Adams Brackett, and about a hundred labor activists. The Wendell Phillips Hall Association, however, developed the most elaborate and ambitious plans of any of the many efforts proposed in the city.[38]

Between 1889 and 1891, an unusual alliance of African Americans, white reformers, and the newly elected governor, John Quincy Adams Brackett, joined to create what they envisioned as Boston's "Cooper Union": "a model institute and school of social, political, and industrial science,—a vital centre of the moral and progressive forces of New England, standing to the American Republic as did the Acropolis to Greece, by even what the Temple at Jerusalem was to Judea." The proposed hall, its promotional literature declared, should be "the Mecca of hope and promise." The association leadership believed the proposed institution would stand not just as a monument to Phillips but a symbol of an era, as powerful as Pilgrim Hall, Bunker Hill, Old South Meeting House, and Faneuil Hall. As those institutions symbolized the region's founding and the American Revolution, Wendell Phillips Hall would evoke the new era of freedom won in the Civil War. They imagined numerous stained-glass windows and bas-reliefs which would, like Stations of the Cross, commemorate "the most thrilling episodes in Phillips's life." The association proposed to raise an astonishing $500,000 to honor the abolitionist and, it hoped, restore New England's declining intellectual influence with classes in social, economic, and industrial training, a library, and an archive of items from the antislavery movement. After incorporating, it set up offices at 74 Tremont Street and immediately began contacting abolitionist survivors as potential donors. It held promotional dinners and in 1890 organized an event to commemorate Phillips's 1837 maiden speech at Faneuil Hall and John Brown's execution in 1859. To raise funds and promote the hall, the association reprinted Phillips's Lovejoy speech with an engraving of the orator.[39]

The association's leadership, however, included Benjamin F. Butler, Governor Brackett, Mary Livermore, Edwin M. Chamberlain, William H. Dupree, among several others, none known for their vast wealth or social connections. Instead, they hoped to reach their goal through small contributions from

100,000 individuals. The association's promotional pamphlets, meetings, dinners, and commemorative celebrations at Tremont Temple all focused on Phillips's key role in the antislavery movement and advancement of civil rights for all. As the city's mayor proclaimed at one of its interracial events, Phillips "stood for free speech, free labor, and free voting, for equal rights and equal duties. It is for this that we honor him. It is for this that he has been chosen to represent to coming generations the cause of emancipation and equal rights." Organizers even held elaborate events at Faneuil Hall with local black leaders on Phillips's eightieth birthday, enlisting the support of the city's black churches to help fulfill the association's grand plans. They drew out surviving abolitionists, black leaders like Edward G. Walker, and the popular Boston reporter and lawyer George Fred Williams to whip up support for the project. Williams urged those at the December 1890 gathering at Faneuil Hall to emulate Phillips. "Think you have no duty to humanity? What have you done for your country? If nothing, then you do not understand the meaning of this occasion. . . . [Phillips] fixed his upon [the ideal] and pressed forward. . . . He died with his arm pointing to the loadstar of human destiny."[40]

The plans for Boston's new "Cooper Union" to honor Phillips attracted much support, even beyond the commonwealth. The editor of the influential *New England Magazine* and head of the World Peace Foundation, Edwin D. Mead, urged the city to commemorate its antislavery past with this "living monument, a monument ever in service." The Boston *Advertiser* urged citizens to send funds to Governor Brackett, and the Springfield *Republican* supported the project, even if the vexing Benjamin Butler was leading the organizing committee. T. Thomas Fortune's New York *Age* publicized the effort, reporting that the former African American drummer boy of the Fifty-fourth Massachusetts Regiment, Rev. Henry A. Monroe, asserted that "Freedom has never had a more eloquent or unselfish champion than Wendell Phillips." Even the Detroit *Plain Dealer* reported on the effort to establish the memorial hall for Phillips.[41]

By the close of 1890, however, the fundraising campaign had raised only $2,145.[42] The organizing committee attempted a variety of strategies to gain contributions and increasingly muddled the appeal, deemphasizing Phillips's abolitionism and focusing on his support for free speech, labor reform, temperance, women's rights, and "currency reform." Unclear on how to proceed, discussions gravitated toward simply naming a building after Phillips (a school named for him already existed), or erecting a hotel—one similar plan shockingly proposed to erect a segregated hotel named for Phillips near the present-day Christian Science complex. The association's ambitious plans certainly reflected the importance of Phillips to the region's collective memory of the Civil War era. Prominent involvement of the controversial Butler, however, the poverty of those most likely to support the project, and the unlikelihood of attracting funds from the city's elite—the very people Phillips spent his life criticizing—doomed the ambitious project from the start.[43]

MONUMENTAL SUCCESS

While Boston failed to establish a center of progressive social learning in Phillips's honor, local efforts kept the emancipationist vision of the Civil War era very much alive. In addition to plans for what would become St. Gaudens's masterpiece bas-relief of Robert Gould Shaw and the Fifty-fourth Massachusetts Regiment, the city found a variety of ways to memorialize Phillips. Before a large interracial crowd in November 1894, the city and the reorganized Wendell Phillips Memorial Association unveiled a large marble tablet at the Essex Street site of Phillips's former home.[44] The black Wendell Phillips Club joined with the "Wendell Phillips Association" to honor his legacy, and members of both groups met with the Central Labor Lyceum in hopes of reviving the move to erect a memorial to Phillips. Tremont Temple instituted a Wendell Phillips lecture series, which featured the famed Civil War correspondent Charles C. Coffin, the New York African American lawyer T. McCouts Stewart, who praised Phillips's condemnation of worker exploitation and "the iron heel of soulless corporations," and sponsored readings of Phillips's best known orations. In 1895, fifty Russian refugees collected at Phillips's Milton gravesite to decorate it with a large star, and two years earlier even Harvard University established the Wendell Phillips Debating Club in his honor. Since few alumni thought well of the radical, the club's name was soon changed to the Harvard Forum, and to this day the university has declined to memorialize one of its most famous graduates.[45]

The centennial of Phillips's birth in 1911 became a pivotal moment in the era's collective memory, riveting his life to contemporary efforts to reverse the growing tide of racial oppression. Centennial celebrations took place across the country, as the Philadelphia press noted, especially where "New England blood dominates" and in major African American communities. While some criticism of Phillips's career persisted, the small amount carried little weight amid the chorus of memorialization. Phillips had become not just an important figure from the past, but a vital element in the first decades of the twentieth century. The issues central to him—racial discrimination, women's rights, labor rights, and unrestrained capitalism—had become central to a new generation of Americans.[46]

Assessments of Phillips's career by individuals like the Harvard-trained scholar and literary critic George E. Woodberry embodied the Bostonian's continued relevance. For Woodberry, Phillips was the indispensable American. His warnings against the power of corporations represented the most gripping issue of the times: "unless our children have more patience and courage than [that which] saved this country from slavery, republican institutions will go down before moneyed corporations. The corporations of America mean to govern; and unless some power more radical than ordinary politics is found, will govern inevitably." Because of Phillips, Woodberry asserted, labor rights, women's suffrage, and temperance have advanced. Ireland would achieve home rule, democracy would sprout in Russia, improvements in the criminal justice system had occurred, and popular initiative and recall were progressing, strengthening democracy. These elements, Woodberry contended, "are but the precipitation of his thought." He also drew special attention to Phillips's repudiation of the "color line," linking the country's rampaging racism and lynching to its colonialism and exploitation of Africans and Asians, and tied industrial education to the desire to demean and dominate the poor and people of color. In a remarkable advance since Phillips's death, the Boston radical was, in Woodberry's estimation, the model American.[47]

African Americans used the Phillips centennial to rally the nation against the growing threat of racism. The African American press reported on the many commemorative events around the country, especially in Boston, and urged the staging of more. AMEZ Bishop Alexander Walter pressed William Monroe Trotter's National Independent Political League to increase the number of Phillips commemorations around the nation, each event becoming a rally against the color line. In Washington, D.C., the American Negro Academy, and in New York and Boston, the newly formed NAACP organized several commemorations in conjunction with Trotter's group and the New England Suffrage League. At New York's St. James Presbyterian Church, former Louisiana governor P. B. S. Pinchback appeared with Roscoe Conklin Simmons and others to praise Phillips. At Henry Ward Beecher's old Plymouth Church in Brooklyn, the NAACP organized a celebration featuring Oswald Garrison Villard, Charles Edward Russell, and the Rev. Reverdy C. Ransom.[48]

Ransom, who would become one of the AME Church's most important bishops, filled many pulpits across the United States, edited the church's journal, the *Review*, was a member of the Niagara movement, and later became an ally of Boston's William Monroe Trotter. At Plymouth Church, he drew a direct line between Phillips's era and his own. Just as in the years before the Civil War when appeasement prevailed and only a sanctified few spoke out against slavery, in the twentieth century the North again adopted its previous attitude of "concession and compromise, while the South, through these means and an obliging United States Supreme Court, has regained all it lost upon the field of battle. . . . The question of the South's method of dealing with the Negro has come to be as sacred as was the question of slavery in the days of Mr. Phillips. To demand the enforcement of the Fifteenth Amendment today is to be branded as 'an enemy of both races,' 'a fanatic,' 'a mischievous agitator.' To all outside interference the South says, Leave the Negro to us, we understand him, and we know best how to deal with him, both for his own good and the peace and the welfare of the South." Ransom's eloquence filled Beecher's old church, not to recount what Wendell Phillips had done, but to tell "what we, who would honor his memory, should do now." He insisted that the audience take up Phillips's call to arms, "the cause of justice and equality [not just] to the Negro, but to humanity, without regard to race or sex, to color or to creed."[49]

One of the NAACP's founders, Charles Edward Russell, in the December issue of *The Crisis*, characterized Phillips's life as a challenge to the new generation. He had given up wealth and privilege and for twenty-five years endured "incessant abuse and vilification" to end slavery. "Would there were a Wendell Phillips today!" he cried.[50] The NAACP's Boston branch and Trotter's National Independent Political League took the lead in organizing the nation's largest and most extensive series of events commemorating Phillips's life. On the morning of November 29, a large interracial crowd, "descendants of puritans and descendants of slaves," convened at the Milton cemetery for services and to place a wreath. They then traveled to the Essex Street location of Phillips's former home to see the marble memorial and afterward headed to the Boston Public Library for a dedication of a new bust of Phillips. At noon, a large crowd convened at the Joy Street Synagogue, a structure that for most of its existence housed the city's most important black congregation. Members of the city's "Anti-Lynching Society" spoke, and one woman addressed the crowd on "Phillips and Temperance." William D. Brigham, NAACP member and new secretary of the Wendell Phillips Memorial Association, spoke, and then all adjourned to Faneuil Hall where Trotter's League gathered about three hundred individuals to hear Archibald Grimké, Francis Jackson Garrison, Alice Stone Blackwell, and Franklin B. Sanborn. At the Faneuil Hall ceremony, Mayor John Francis "Honey Fitz" Fitzgerald formally proposed that the city erect a statue to Phillips.[51]

But the day before, a smaller body of Garrison and Hallowell family members, sculptor Anne Whitney, William D. Brigham, and former abolitionists, convened under the auspices of the NAACP at the Park Street Church. Moorfield Storey set the stage, explaining that "few men have sacrificed more for their country than Wendell Phillips [and] few men who have lived to see the triumph of their cause have received less public gratitude."[52] He then introduced the event's keynote speaker: Wendell Phillips Stafford. As if embodying the answer to Russell's plea for a modern Wendell Phillips, Stafford had amassed an impressive record of civil rights activism. Massachusetts's former attorney general Robert E. Pillsbury in fact saw him as a modern Phillips, just the man to fight the "'cotton whigs of today.'"[53] Unrelated to his namesake, the Vermont-born Stafford was the grandson of ardent Massachusetts abolitionists, a writer, poet, and orator who sat on the state's Supreme Court before becoming a district judge in Washington, D.C. Unjustly forgotten, Stafford proved a zealous enemy of Jim Crow and at New York's Cooper Union denounced "Northern indifference and Southern injustice [which] strike hands to keep the black race in a new bondage as helpless and hopeless as the old." He regularly participated in a large number of civil rights conventions, knew W. E. B. Du Bois and the leadership of the NAACP, and became one of the few white members of the association's Washington, D.C., branch. A progressive Unitarian who supported prison reform and a minimum wage, he earned the reputation of being the "most liberal white man in Washington on the race question."[54]

With stern eyes, a large mustache, a high-neck Edwardian collar, and a reputation as a great exponent of human freedom and "Defender of the Constitution," Stafford spoke before a full-length portrait of his namesake. He began with the irony that the very church that hosted the centennial celebration had been closed to Phillips and his antislavery coadjutors. Perhaps it might still be closed to him, as Stafford reminded the audience that no matter when he lived Phillips would have been a reformer and "at war with the evils that surround us now, and if he should return to earth a thousand years hence, it would be the same."[55]

Stafford savored the contradictions in Phillips: the aristocrat who cherished democracy; the Anglo-Saxon who devoted himself to African Americans; a devout Christian who spurned Boston's churches; a great intellect bound for power and privilege, which he refused; a Harvard-trained lawyer who spurned his profession and the Constitution; intensely political, he never wanted to run for office; a despised abolitionist who lived to see slavery end, then refused to celebrate and instead went on the attack against injustice and "new battlefields for human suffering." In one of the era's most eloquent and impassioned defenses of the antislavery movement, Stafford pointed to the city of Boston, which had repudiated Phillips and his message, even threatened to kill him. While the city blankets Phillips with love today, he asserted, when it mattered, Boston sons like Daniel Webster were "deaf to the voices of humanity." And now, a new generation faces the same difficult choices, he warned, and is making the same calculation as in 1850: "Today not a state of the old Confederacy records the Negro vote," Stafford charged. "The Fifteenth Amendment is sneered at by millions at the North as the greatest blunder of the age."[56]

Mindful of the censures Phillips earned for his sharp tongue, Stafford proclaimed that history had proven Phillips correct, even at his most acerbic. The "black race, in less than fifty years of freedom, has justified every claim of the Abolitionists. It has shown itself brave in battle, faithful in peace, eager to learn, capable of acquiring and controlling wealth, and able to produce noble and far-sighted leaders of its own blood. . . . Its progress during the last half-century will be one of the marvels of history." Despite such enviable progress, Stafford reminded his audience that the treatment of African Americans by whites had grown worse, as exemplified by the brutal lynching of Zachariah Walker, not in Georgia, but in "the Quaker commonwealth." The cold-blooded murder of Walker, burned alive in Coatesville, Pennsylvania—action sustained by the courts—cried out for a Wendell Phillips; "one blast upon that silver bugle would be worth a hundred men." At the centennial of his birth, Phillips could not have been more relevant to the nation.[57]

The centennial also rekindled efforts to erect a permanent memorial to Phillips, coming at a time of intense local and national monument building.

In 1877, the city had erected a monument to the commonwealth's Civil War soldiers and sailors on Boston Common. Two years later a copy of Thomas Ball's controversial "Emancipation Group" was placed in Park Square, and between 1880 and 1917, the country's most active era of monument building, the city erected statues to Crispus Attucks and the Boston Massacre, Garrison, Sumner, Theodore Parker, and most prominently to Robert Gould Shaw and the Fifty-fourth Massachusetts Regiment. Around the country, however, questions arose as to why Phillips was "left to the last." Perhaps, as Fortune's *Age* speculated, at first whites had left the task to the city's African Americans. As early as 1889, black leaders Edward Walker, John J. Smith, Charles L. Mitchell (a Fifty-fifth Massachusetts Regiment veteran who also briefly served in the State House), and several others organized a petition campaign to convince the legislature to erect a Phillips statue.[58] In fact, calls for such a monument had begun shortly after Phillips's death and arose periodically thereafter, even during the campaign to establish the ill-fated Wendell Phillips Hall. After that project's demise, demands for a Phillips monument increased, and in 1890 the restless Edwin D. Mead called into question the city's collective intelligence since it had thus far failed to memorialize Phillips.[59]

Within a few years the Wendell Phillips Hall Association had morphed into the Wendell Phillips Memorial Association (WPMA), until 1904 led by the irascible Rev. Jesse H. Jones. The Canadian-born Jones had graduated from Harvard University and the Andover Theological Seminary, served as a captain of a New York regiment during the Civil War and fought at Gettysburg, filled several Congregational pulpits in eastern Massachusetts, and gained a well-earned reputation as a fiery radical labor reformer and advocate of women's suffrage. He shocked many with his assertion that "Jesus Christ lived on the earth and died on the cross to give woman the ballot." Representing the WPMA, Jones took every opportunity to lobby for the statue and promote the memory of Phillips's career, especially to the young. When busts of Phillips were dedicated at the Boston Public Library and Faneuil Hall, Jones figured prominently in the ceremonies. The lobbying finally produced results with the centennial celebration, and in November 1911, Mayor "Honey Fitz" Fitzgerald asked the Boston City Council to create a permanent monument to Phillips of "heroic size." Before the end of the year, the city had placed WPMA secretary William D. Brigham in charge of the committee to erect the statue, and by early spring of 1912 had appropriated $20,000 (over $400,000 in current value) for it.

Additionally, at the suggestion of Brigham's WPMA, the mayor agreed to have the school committee set aside one hour each year on Phillips's birthday to discuss the abolitionist's life and career in every city school. Phillips, uncompromising radical and advocate of the Irish, African Americans, Russians, immigrants of all backgrounds, workers, and of women's rights, proved an irresistible figure, able to draw together city officials, middle-class Protestants and Catholics, and the city's major ethnic groups.[60]

Brigham and the WPMA committee considered the Phillips statue as the central part of a broader civil rights agenda. A member of John Brown's "Secret Six," Franklin B. Sanborn held the honorary position of president; editor and peace advocate Edwin D. Mead filled one of the vice-presidential positions; and NAACP lawyer Moorfield Storey, suffragist Alice Stone Blackwell, and the mercurial William Monroe Trotter (who also sat on the city's committee for the Phillips statue) served among the directors. NAACP member William D. Brigham was secretary and effective head of the association. The mutton-chopped Brigham, a retired businessman, dedicated Congregational churchman, and tireless opponent of racism, had met Phillips just before his death and considered him to be more responsible than anyone for the demise of slavery. He had organized his own centennial celebration of Phillips's birth at his beloved Second Congregational Church in Dorchester, and held up Phillips as a model for the younger generation. Clearly, Brigham considered Phillips's legacy as his most effective weapon against racial prejudice.[61]

In 1913, the WPMA had organized Boston's fiftieth anniversary of the Emancipation Proclamation, and the next year Brigham joined with Moorfield Storey and Francis J. Garrison to protest the city's use of racist songbooks in its schools. Then on April 18, 1915, the WPMA led the protest at Faneuil Hall against the Boston premiere of the bitterly racist film *Birth of a Nation.* Brigham, although an NAACP member, was proud of the WPMA's activism and briefly tangled with Du Bois over his erroneous assertion in *The Crisis* that the NAACP had led the protest. Although Mayor Michael Curley and Gov. David Walsh both claimed to sympathize with the protesters, they still came under intense pressure from the WPMA and Trotter's National Equal Rights League to suppress the film. In fact, Brigham joined a protest of four to five thousand black activists on the State House steps—a group that also included Elizabeth Putnam, a Phillips niece. While they failed in their bid to bar the film—which bothered elected officials and others as an unacceptable act of censorship—the

WPMA's efforts reaffirmed Wendell Phillips as the model advocate of justice and equality.[62]

By the fall of 1912, the Boston Art Commission had selected Daniel Chester French to execute the statue of Phillips. Impressed with French's "Minute Man" statue at Concord Bridge and his other memorial work, the commission never seriously considered another artist. French's assurance that he would avoid the "conventional portrait statue" gave the commission hope for a memorable work of art. French admired Phillips, his stand against slavery, and his willingness to risk death for his principles. In a letter to the former Harvard president Charles W. Eliot—who still smarted from Phillips's 1881 Sanders Theater attack on Harvard intellectuals—French insisted that the man he wished to commemorate "stood out against slavery in a manner to merit the admiration of anyone who loves a hero." He expressed no interest in Phillips the radical, the labor advocate, and feminist, or his censures of the commonwealth's social elite. "I should like it to represent what he stood for in the zenith of his power and usefulness. . . . At any rate, I am going to make my anti-slavery hero as inspiring as I know how."[63]

If St. Gaudens's Shaw Memorial, directly across from the State House, stood as much as a tribute to Boston's Protestant elite as to the Fifty-fourth Massachusetts's martyred colonel and rank and file, then French's grandiloquent Phillips statue on the far side of the Public Garden on Boylston Street recognized the city's growing middle class as much as the admired orator and reformer. While city officials, the Art Commission, and the WPMA argued for almost a year over where to place the statue—at one point trying to force the artist to select a location—at the last minute contending factions compromised on the Boylston Street pedestrian-mall area of the Public Garden, facing south in the direction of the Ball statue of Lincoln and a kneeling slave in Park Square. A short walk from Channing's old Arlington Street Unitarian Church and across from the city's booming business and retail sector, the location fortified the statue's uplifting and accessible message of heroism, oratory, democratic faith, and Christian sacrifice. It carefully and skillfully avoided the historical Phillips, a disturbing challenger to the social order.[64] In fact, the *Boston Globe*'s initial viewing of the statue prior to its installation confirmed its more conventional appeal—French's assurances to the contrary—that it captured truthfully Phillips's appearance and his role as the "conscience of a Nation."[65]

Five to six thousand attended the dedication of the statue on July 5, 1915, an

Figures 11.3 and 11.4. Speakers and ceremony. *Exercises at the Dedication of the Statue of Wendell Phillips*, 1916.

event covered as far away as California and Arizona.[66] The young John C. Phillips, Jr., a great grandnephew of the reformer, performed the unveiling, while a black women's chorus sang out "Glory, Glory Hallelujah!" Three of Phillips's German bodyguards from the 1860s laid a wreath, as did representatives of the labor movement and women suffragists. Thomas P. Taylor, perhaps the last living black Phillips bodyguard, was given a seat of honor. While the event acknowledged Phillips's wide-ranging reform career, even his labor activism, the orators of the day focused on his heroic sacrifice for others and his stand for equal rights. Reflecting the narrowing focus of the city's collective memory, only the aging abolitionist Franklin B. Sanborn, Irish attorney Michael J. Jordan, African American William Monroe Trotter, and committee head William D. Brigham received keynote speaking roles, setting aside women, socialists, workers, and other ethnic groups that were equally important to Phillips. The monument became, in the words of Amherst lawyer Samuel Worcester Dana, an opportunity for the "bitterest foe" and the "warmest friend" to clasp hands. That is not, however, to diminish the significance of the event—or the statue. With African Americans and Irish suffering relentless discrimination and with lynching becoming commonplace throughout the nation, reaffirming an emancipationist interpretation of the Civil War and the need for full civil rights represented essential business for the country's collective memory of Wendell Phillips. He "believed with us," Trotter explained at the ceremony, "that there can be no freedom without equality and no equality without the ballot." Speaking directly to the meaning of Daniel Chester French's creation, the *Boston Globe*'s long-running "Uncle Dudley" column explained: "Today there is a monument in Boston to Wendell Phillips. It is not a statue in the Public Garden. It is a memory and a hope in the hearts of living women and men."[67]

NATIONAL HISTORICAL MEMORY, RADICALISM, AND DECLINE

How Phillips was remembered also resulted from the efforts of his early biographers, essayists, lecturers, and a younger generation of reformers and radicals eager to exploit Phillips's persistent popularity. Phillips's first major biography, which appeared the same year as the subject's death, set the tone for the public's understanding of the great reformer and for nearly all succeeding biographers. George Lowell Austin, the popular regional historian, had known Phillips and crafted his 1884 biography to present a heroic image of the aboli-

Figure 11.5. Elizabeth Glendower Evans, *right,* and striking textile workers from Manchester, New Hampshire, and Lawrence, Massachusetts, May 3, 1922. Evans, a wealthy reformer like Phillips, also became an ardent socialist and often walked picket lines with strikers and headed the American Civil Liberties Union. She compared northern textile workers to southern slaves. Original photograph owned by author.

tionist and reformer. Austin acknowledged the broad range of Phillips's reform efforts, even on behalf of women and labor, but ignored reforms that didn't fit his liberal model, like Indian rights, and especially Phillips's radical critique of capitalism. Instead, Austin focused on his antislavery career. He characterized Phillips as the "friend of mankind," and borrowing from Frederick Douglass's 1884 memorial address, described him as "primarily and pre-eminently the colored man's friend. . . . The cause of the slave was his first love, and from it he never wavered, but was true and steadfast through life." Others, like Elbert Hubbard—founder of the Roycrofters craftsmen movement in upstate New York—sold beautifully designed pamphlets entitled "Little Journeys" to display his colleagues' talent and make key figures of the past accessible to a general audience. Hubbard assured his readers that Phillips was no different from anyone else; he just heard the cry of the oppressed. Collectively, these kinds of works made Phillips the ideal abolitionist, the benchmark of what it was to be a reformer—any kind of reformer. From coast to coast, the popular press during the 1890s made Phillips the standard in achieving success in reform.[68]

Indeed, whenever one gained renown in some area of social reform or oratory, one immediately became known as: the Wendell Phillips of Prohibition, the Wendell Phillips of the pulpit, or like the famed Kansas agitator Mary Lease, the Wendell Phillips of the populists. In 1920, when officers of the Kansas United Mine Workers received jail sentences for their union activities, they claimed status as modern-day Wendell Phillipses. So wide had Phillips's reputation grown that the Japanese orator, politician, and advocate of the League of Nations Saburo Shimada had earned the reputation as the "Wendell Phillips of Japan."[69]

Oratory, in fact, played a critical role in the persistence of Phillips's influence. In his 1912 study of Phillips, John Haynes Holmes, NAACP founder, pacifist, and Unitarian minister, observed that the Boston abolitionist had taken oratory to its highest form as an art, becoming "the supreme orator of the English-speaking world." He was a "must" for every lyceum and attracted enormous crowds—even of those who hated him. Phillips's speeches left one former colleague thunderstruck by the "shock of armies," making the earth throb and the very air alive "with the inspiration fires of noble conflict." To the *Christian Recorder*, "Eloquence with him is nature, not art: it is a part of himself." His memorializer George William Curtis reminded readers of *Harper's* that Phillips kept his audiences in raptures, completely unaware of the passage of time. "He spoke perhaps for two hours, perhaps for half an hour. . . . [T]here was no sense of the lapse of time." Key to Phillips's appeal was the informality, the sense he gave to each member of the audience, as the Biloxi, Mississippi, *Daily Herald* observed in 1900, that he was speaking directly to him or her. He appeared to be improvising on the spot, as Charles Dudley Warner wrote in 1893, as if "golden words" dropped "freshly coined from the brilliant mint of his mind." "He was in constant action," Curtis remarked, "never vehement, never declamatory in tone, walking often to and fro, every gesture expressive, art perfectly concealing art. It was all melody and grace and magic, all wit and paradox and power. . . . It was consummate art, and as noble a display of high oratory as any hearer or spectator had known."[70]

Emphasizing the power of Phillips's oratory, Warner confessed that after one of his speeches on American Indians he had, for a brief moment, come completely under the orator's spell and felt "almost ashamed of himself for being white instead of copper-colored." A month after Phillips's death, the former Speaker of the House and vice-president Schuyler Colfax published his recollections of Phillips. He recalled that the great orator could face a hostile crowd with "the heart of a lion . . . and denounced them to their teeth." Most amazingly, he remembered Phillips's March 18, 1862, speech in Washington, D.C., on Toussaint L'Ouverture. In the event at the Smithsonian Institution, which Colfax recalled included President Lincoln and several members of his cabinet and the Supreme Court, Phillips captivated his audience with his dramatic defense of the Haitian leader, making the hall ring with applause. But after the audience exited, the "witchery of the speaker's voice" had evaporated, and Colfax could hear stunned audience members regain their senses and then fill the air "blue with the indignant oaths" of those who could not believe that Phillips had the temerity to put "'a nigger above [George] Washington!'"[71]

Not surprisingly, Phillips became essential material for the national lecture circuit. Well into the twentieth century, Chautauqua events represented prime methods of public education and entertainment, and beginning in the 1890s, Phillips became an extremely appealing subject for countless regional lectures. Across the country and into the 1920s, reformers, ministers, and educators roamed the land to satisfy the demand for stories about Wendell Phillips. In Chicago, a high-school principal's lecture declared that the Boston abolitionist was greater than Caesar, Napoleon, and Daniel Webster; in Minneapolis and in Indianapolis a Rev. H. A. Cleveland delivered his "celebrated lecture on Wendell Phillips," and in Kalamazoo, Michigan, one lecturer spoke for two hours to the "Ladies literary Club," championing Phillips as the voice of the future and asserting that the "world has been coming to his ideal ever since." Archibald Grimké repeated his Boston lecture many times and took it to Washington, D.C., where he gave it over the course of eight years. Perhaps most astonishing of all was a Mrs. Louis T. Bradfield's lecture on Phillips and William Lloyd Garrison delivered at the Edgewood Literary Club in Birmingham, Alabama.[72]

The most prolific Phillips lecturer proved to be the temperance and women's rights advocate Mary Livermore. Renowned as the "queen of the platform," Livermore gave as many as 150 speeches a year, and in one stretch spoke five nights a week, every week for five months, marking her as one of the most successful—and hardest working—popular lecturers in the country. While her pace declined during the 1890s, Livermore's lectures on temperance, women's rights, and Wendell Phillips carried her from Massachusetts to California and made her a one-person university with a concentration in temperance, suffrage, poverty, abolitionism, and class conflict. While she had met Phillips late in his life when they both had shared a lecture platform, they had no personal relationship. Nevertheless, his eloquence and support for women's rights left her in awe. "He was rich, a natural-born aristocrat, refined in his tastes, the idol of society, handsome as an Apollo." She also found his critique of capitalism appealing and regularly denounced greedy business interests, rejecting the avarice of the rich, but in un-Phillips-like fashion also condemned the slack morals of workers.[73]

In Cleveland, she delivered her Phillips lecture at a meeting of the Women's Christian Temperance Union. In the Boston region, she lectured at Tremont Temple, and after she spoke on Phillips in Melrose, Massachusetts, residents in Haverhill (the former home of John Greenleaf Whittier) insisted that she come to their town to speak. "[W]hat theme, or what speaker, could draw a larger crowd?" the local paper asked. Her Phillips lecture, preserved in her papers at Princeton University, is less a formal address than a precisely arranged series of reminiscences and stories clipped from a variety of newspapers, with special sections highlighted, allowing her to vary her presentation. Despite familiarity with the breadth of Phillips's career, for Livermore, the story she wished to tell—and audiences apparently demanded—was the rise and fall of slavery, with Phillips as the representative figure.[74]

Memory of Wendell Phillips suffused the culture in a variety of other ways. Many towns in and out of Massachusetts formed "Wendell Phillips Clubs" or literary societies. One in Medford, Massachusetts, organized shortly after the reformer's death in 1884, became the Wendell Phillips Literary Association, and for the next twelve years organized local events, with their annual meetings drawing at least three hundred men and women, some former abolitionists or veterans of the Civil War. At least two Phillips organizations had been formed in Benjamin F. Butler's home of Lowell, Massachusetts, with separate African American clubs—news that made headlines as far away as Kansas City. Other clubs rose up in New York City and Chillicothe, Ohio, and fraternal organizations began renaming themselves for the reformer or organizing "Wendell Phillips Councils." Union activists in Trenton, New Jersey, organized a "Wendell Phillips Knights of Labor," and their brethren's newspaper in Greely, Colorado, the *Howitzer*, hawked images of Phillips for fifty cents, advising members that the "elegant" portrait should "adorn the walls of every meeting-room of the K[nights] of L[abor] and the home of every friend of justice." Most surprising, in 1921 the "Wendell Phillips branch of the American Association for Recognition of the Irish Republic" was founded in Anaconda, Montana.[75]

Phillips's presence also grew in public education. In 1881, the reformer had established a competitive prize to be given every four years for the best student orator. Managed by the London Lyceum of New York and the City Lyceum of Boston, the national competition gave the selected student a "Wendell Phillips Medal," with one black student from New Haven, Connecticut, receiving the prize and another student-winner from Philadelphia. In Chicago, the public schools in Oak Park incorporated Phillips into their curriculum, and in 1916 one school celebrated Phillips's birthday, complete with an oration, "Wendell Phillips, My Ideal," by a speaker with the improbable name of George B. McClelland. In Worcester, Massachusetts, high-school graduation took place under the gaze of a Phillips bust, with a special oration given on his antislavery career. In Corvallis, Oregon, the state intercollegiate gold medal was awarded to a student oration on "Wendell Phillips, the Agitator," and the entire speech appeared in the city's newspaper.[76]

Shortly after his death, public schools around the country were named for Phillips. While Boston already possessed one at the crest of Beacon Hill, Kansas City, Indianapolis, Minneapolis, Georgetown in Washington, D.C., and most famously Chicago also established schools in his memory. Chicago's Wendell Phillips High School, opened in 1904 as a predominately white facility, permitting only thirty-seven African American students to attend. One of those, the enterprising and athletic Henry Foster, made national headlines for himself and his school by walking from Chicago to Portland, Maine, in a bid to gain entrance into Harvard University. During its first decades, the school remained the pride of African American residents who, like the activist Ida B. Wells-Barnett, closely monitored the school's largely white administration and led protests whenever its conduct smacked of racism. In 1919, three thousand residents jammed into the school to hear an address by W. E. B. Du Bois, just back to the States to report on the Paris Peace Conference and the following Pan African Conference. By 1918, 56 percent of the student population was black, a direct result of the Great Migration, which sent white politicians into a frenzy to rezone the neighborhood to protect white interests and increase segregation. Nevertheless, the school played a central role in the community, and over the course of its history the likes of Sam Cooke, Nat King Cole, Gwendolyn Brooks, and members of the Harlem Globetrotters passed through its halls.[77]

With labor protests beginning in the 1880s and 1890s, and especially well-publicized ones like the Lawrence, Massachusetts, "Bread and Roses" strike of 1912 and the populist revolt in the South and West, Wendell Phillips became a central figure in the nation's labor movement. At a time when labor unrest was virtually endemic to every city of any size and schemes for "social renovation" became as common as a daily newspaper, even moderate social reformers found in Phillips's postwar career authority, wisdom, and hope. He lived long enough to exert enormous influence on the next generation of radicals, men like Eugene Debs, Ezra Heywood, Henry George—and his disciple the author Hamlin Garland—Henry Demarest Lloyd and beyond to the Presbyterian socialist Norman Thomas. In part, Phillips's radicalism was grounded in a nostalgia for the early days of New England, when the region's distribution of wealth likely reached its most equitable levels. He had hoped for a return to a time—even if imagined—when in most towns there was "no rich man and no poor man in it, all mingling in the same society, every child at the same school, no poorhouse, no beggar." Yet, Wendell Phillips also looked to the future, and that is what labor radicals found so inspiring. "I hail the labor movement," he exclaimed, "it is my only hope for democracy."[78]

When members of the Boston elite like Charles Francis Adams, the stalwart Republican Hoars, or even more sympathetic figures like Thomas Wentworth Higginson heard Phillips expound on the terrors of poverty, labor exploitation, and the injustices of capitalism, they all instinctively grabbed their wallets.

And when they recalled that in 1871 he had declared his support for the Paris Commune by exclaiming: "There is no hope for France but in the Reds," they recoiled in horror. The hate for Phillips after the Civil War certainly matched or exceeded the animosity that Phillips had stirred up during the antebellum era. After one Phillips outburst in 1870, Boston's mainstream Republican journal *Commonwealth* wrote him off: "His influence is gone. No gentleman desires to be in intimate personal relationship with him. . . . The community turns with averted face from him."[79]

Phillips's stand on labor and the power of corporations, however, made him a hero to the labor movement and to a generation of radicals, socialists, and reformers. His blend of Jacksonian rhetoric against the "money power" with modern socialism offered a clear and concise diagnosis of the nation's social ills, ones which only grew worse in the first decades of the twentieth century. For Phillips, the issue became a question of who should rule. Soft money, hard money, silver or gold, it didn't matter. To Phillips, the problem pivoted on control, who should control the nation's wealth, "the *money-kings* or the *people?*" If corruption posed a threat, if it appeared to "roll over us," it did not come from the "humbler classes," Phillips asserted, but from "millionaires who steal banks, mills, and railways; it is defaulters who live in palaces, and make way with millions, it is money-kings who buy up Congress; it is demagogues and editors, in purple and fine linen, who bid fifty thousand dollars for the Presidency itself." To combat the "great money power," Phillips offered a stark solution and one that could not be clearer: "An equalization of property! . . . [W]ell, we do mean it: we do mean just that. That's the meaning of the labor movement,—an equalization of property." Moreover, he blasted the Republican Party as "the tool of capital," determined to rid the nation of "universal suffrage, and enslave the masses to the Money Kings."[80]

Phillips's controversial relationship with Benjamin F. Butler cost him support from moderates, but proved key to his continued importance to the labor movement. Historians remain convinced that Butler was an untrustworthy spoilsman, a rapacious opportunist, a "Caesar" and "demagogue," and that Phillips's relationship with him was as mysterious as it was unfortunate, an unseemly collaboration of "the patrician and the politico." Few have budged from Frank Stearns's view in the 1890s that it represented an "unholy alliance" that only damaged Phillips's reputation, perhaps an indication of his declining "melancholic" mind obsessed with "the ambition of becoming a world reformer."[81]

Yet Butler, a favorite among labor activists, proved devoted to Phillips and considered him a lifelong friend. He dedicated his final public address in December 1890 entirely to Phillips's memory and fascinated the throngs that filled Tremont Temple to hear him praise the reformer as "the statesman who reached beyond his generation." The church shook with laughter when Butler described their friendship and exclaimed that "I don't think he could have treated me better if I had been black." Indeed, he explained that after the start of the Civil War "there was no difference between Phillips and me on any question." Phillips, who had mentored him before he started college, knew Butler well: "Oh, I know what kind of man he is! I am not at all deceived in him," Phillips once remarked. And that man was just what the movement needed, he asserted. As he had written in his popular and incendiary pamphlet *Who Shall Rule US?* Phillips declared, "I shall vote for Gen. Butler because he represents the determination of the PEOPLE TO TAKE THE CURRENCY OUT OF THE CONTROL OF MONEY KINGS,—'the cannibals of Change Alley,' as Lord Chatham called them." He declared that the press had treated the former general in a foul, disgraceful manner, a man whom he considered the commonwealth's "most distinguished political servant." Butler, even after Phillips's death, remained true to his friend's views on labor and on race. In the fall 1884 campaign, the Workingman's Party again rallied behind Butler and appealed directly to African Americans for their support. "Phillips is dead, but Butler Lives," they cried. "A vote for Butler is a vote for justice to all men," and the party promised blacks the same rights as whites. "We call upon you, who count the ballot as a freeman's bullet, to work and vote for Butler and yourself." The lure of Phillips's memory tempted many African Americans in the state, but most could not, as with the activist Amos Webber, abandon the party of Lincoln—whatever Butler's merits—especially as the Democratic Party in the South remained committed to destroying black freedom.[82]

When Edwin D. Mead, editor and peace advocate, had argued for a memorial to Phillips in 1890 he had far more on his mind than Phillips the abolitionist. In his remarkable essay, Mead saw Phillips as inspiring a new "Anti-Slavery movement. For slavery is not something which has to do simply with negroes and plantations. Slavery is whatever chains the soul and hinders the true, full life and growth of any man or woman. . . . [E]ven the slave Uncle Tom, was less a slave than many a woman who to-day makes shirts in Boston, than many a man perhaps who sells wheat in Chicago." Phillips was essential to the 1890s, and Mead warned that the next threat came from the "slavery of poverty, the slavery of our social and industrial inequality. It was this clear vision that made Phillips's last days so prophetic and so great."[83]

A few years after Mead's call for justice, the Boston painter, labor organizer, and Greenback candidate for lieutenant governor William Murray reaffirmed the call for a Wendell Phillips of the 1890s. He published his recollections of Phillips, emphasizing his bravery and commitment to abolitionism. But he focused on Phillips's labor activism and gave him full credit for passage of the 1874 law limiting factory labor to ten hours, for the establishment of the state Bureau of Statistics of Labor, and for helping to organize the Labor Reform Party. He had cooperated with labor leaders to compel the state to adopt the secret ballot, even wrote petitions for union leaders, but economic conditions had only worsened and overwhelmed such efforts. By the 1890s, Murray despaired that without a Wendell Phillips the government was "fast becoming a huge investment shop and collecting agency for the money power."[84]

With protests roiling the country, Phillips's call for economic democracy found willing ears among radicals, labor, and middle-class reformers. He inspired Henry George's popular 1879 *Progress and Poverty*, which remained a force throughout the era and connected the Old South's slavery with its modern industrial equivalent. Henry Demarest Lloyd, progressive journalist and famed author of the 1894 *Wealth Against Commonwealth*, had met Phillips, read his speeches, considered him to be the greatest of the abolitionists, and determined to follow his lead in preserving democracy by attacking monopoly and political corruption. He would finish the job that Phillips and his colleagues had begun. "Wendell Phillips almost alone," Lloyd exclaimed, "was great enough to comprehend that black slavery was only an extreme instance of capitalism." Before a crowd of 2,000 at Chicago's Second Regiment Armory, Lloyd denounced as criminals politicians and especially the police who attacked law-abiding union men. "They destroyed their property, outraged their persons and robbed them of their right of assemblage. . . . The men of the Union attacked had the legal right to resist by force, even unto death. . . . The people who mean to hold their liberties must make their own the motto of Wendell Phillips who said: 'Justice with peace if possible, but at any rate justice.'"[85]

Eugene Debs, the nation's best-known socialist, had met Phillips in 1878 when the great orator lectured at Debs's Occidental Literary Club in Terra Haute, Indiana, on the dangers of monopoly power. Debs admired Phillips enormously: he was "erect as a pine, and the handsomest figure of a courtly gentleman I had ever seen." Even at age sixty-seven, Phillips appeared as a "tower of strength." Seeing the way he had stood up to persecution became a model for Debs. Phillips had thrown "down the gauntlet to the heartless power that held a race in chains. . . . The example was inspiring, the spectacle sublime." When Debs opposed the accommodationist policies of Booker T. Washington as "not at all compatible with organized labor," he turned to the great Boston reformer for support. "Would Wendell Phillips tolerate this scheme of saving the Negro through the charity of his master?" Moreover, Debs believed that Phillips had a "prophetic eye" and understood that the end of slavery "was but the prelude to the infinitely greater struggle for the emancipation of the working class of all races and colors on the face of the earth." He had read Phillips's works, knew thoroughly his career, and concluded that he had dedicated his life to helping ordinary people just like Debs, so that they "might live and enjoy, aspire and fulfill" their lives. To the inspired socialist, Phillips had "challenged the whole wicked, malevolent power of human slavery . . . and demanded the unconditional surrender of the robber systems of chattel and wage slavery."[86]

Farmers in Illinois, outraged that 40 percent of their earnings went into the hands of monopolists, turned to Wendell Phillips, hoping for one so eloquent to speak for them. In Kansas, the anarchist Voltàirine de Cleyre, who went by the name of Flora W. Fox, found inspiration in Phillips's career and denounced economic and gender exploitation as nothing but slavery, "for we are held as white slaves," she exclaimed. Socialists in Baltimore cried out "Socialism or Barbarism" and pointed to Phillips and Garrison as their heroes, while Nebraska reformers reprinted Phillips's 1878 pamphlet *Who Shall Rule US?* seeing in Phillips a statesman who fought against "financial bondage as he did against human slavery." Feminists, free thinkers, anarchists, even Bryan Democrats of the 1890s all found Phillips the model of "moral courage." The Great Commoner himself, William Jennings Bryan, in his relentless attacks on the gold standard, quoted extensively from Phillips's 1878 pamphlet to condemn private control of the nation's money supply, asking, "In whose hands can this almost omnipotent power be trusted?" Bryan, with a deep measure of satisfaction, could cite the easterner's most caustic condemnation of capitalism in defense of the West's populist challenge.[87]

Phillips's attacks on monopoly, corporate capitalism, and economic inequality had reached deep in the culture of the Progressive Era. In 1904, the *Boston*

Globe published an astonishing about-face, entitled "Phillips Vindicated." The paper looked to Phillips's radical 1871 Worcester address to warn against the current dangers of "corporate capital." The paper reminded its readers that Phillips's warnings remained as true as when he spoke them thirty-three years earlier: "corporations of America mean to rule the land." Phillips, the paper asserted, "had the boldness to call attention to the tendency of corporate capital to monopolize the national government, as well as unduly influence state legislation." Indeed, the paper found Phillips's words even more relevant in 1904. "Is not the 'great moneyed force,' which Phillips foresaw looming upon the land, wielding too much power in the government today—in nation, state and city?"[88]

Socialists took advantage of Phillips's continued appeal, reprinting his radical essays and distributing them in cheap pamphlet form alongside reprints of the Communist Manifesto. A Salem, Massachusetts–born devotee of Eugene Debs, Franklin Harcourt Wentworth, traveled throughout the eastern portion of the state, lecturing on socialism and Phillips. At a time when one could hold down a middle-class profession as secretary of the National Fire Protective Association and edit a socialist newspaper, Wentworth could speak at a Faneuil Hall or a GAR hall and attract concerned audiences. Like the *Boston Globe*, Wentworth argued that the economic conditions of Phillips's times bore a striking resemblance to those of 1906. The southern slaveholder could "no more hear the agonizing cries of the shackled millions than they to-day, hear the wails of the little children as they are rudely shaken from their warm beds and driven in the gray dawn into the Southern cotton mills." Critics denounced socialism as a dangerous European import, but Wentworth argued that Phillips had shown its distinctly American roots. He praised Phillips's work on behalf of women and the Irish, but his labor activism rose above all and, to Wentworth, made him "more than the voice of yesterday; which makes him the voice of to-morrow." Everyone understood Phillips as a hero in the antislavery movement, Wentworth reminded his audiences, but it was his purpose to "give him a new, a larger, and more significant setting." If Phillips were alive today, Wentworth declared, "his white plume would be waving upon the barricades of the working-class revolution."[89]

The high point of Phillips's usefulness to the socialist movement may have come on the cusp of the First World War, when the NAACP founder and socialist Charles Edward Russell published his biography of the Boston reformer.

Born in Davenport, Iowa, to a newspaper family, Russell had grown up on the writings of Henry George, Wendell Phillips Stafford, and Phillips: "the god of my idolatry." Russell committed portions of Phillips's speeches to memory and venerated the reformer for overcoming his birth to a class accustomed to "parasitic sloth." Growing up secure in middle-class comfort, Russell suffered a searing shock when a local bank forced his father's newspaper into bankruptcy, thrusting the family out into the street. He fled to New York, where he found the answers he had been searching for in the Socialist Party. For Russell, Phillips represented the essential hero, a man who gave up every advantage in life afforded by his station at birth in order to help others. He had made his life "one long sacrifice on the altars of righteousness. No man ever gave up more for the sake of his faith." He represented, to Russell, the perfect model for the young and saw himself and fellow socialists as the twentieth-century version of the abolitionists. They challenged the "whole force of commerce" arrayed in "defense of the profits arising from the wage system," just as Phillips had attacked the forces that protected "chattel slavery." Russell found in Phillips's career a complete repudiation of the modern "wage system."[90]

After the Russian Revolution of 1917, however, critiques of capitalism took on a new and, for most Americans, sinister context. No more did condemnations of banks and corporations appear as just one more utopian scheme in a nation familiar with visionary quests for a bold new future. By 1920, the Progressive Era had ended and Phillips began to drop out of the nation's popular culture. The ubiquitous biographical sketches, lectures, reprints of his speeches, quotations, or aphorisms related to his life began to disappear from the nation's newspapers. A few mentions persisted in the early 1920s, but even African American newspapers contained few references to him. In his native Boston, only sporadic allusions to him appeared in the city's shrinking periodical press, with brief coverage in 1929 of the 118th anniversary of his birth, organized by the NAACP. Despite fifty years of intense interest and at times near-deification, by the mid-1920s Wendell Phillips had all but vanished from American popular culture.[91]

Even in the academy and among public intellectuals, Phillips's reputation had been transformed and diminished. By the 1920s, the Civil War and the abolitionists' connection to it had become dominated by Lost Cause ideology. Abolitionist memoirs and histories had fallen into neglect, and by 1900 public reaction to the antislavery tradition had soured, and it began viewing their relentless agitation as a cause of the Civil War. Southerners relentlessly disparaged "Yankee history" that insisted on calling southerners "rebels" and peddling histories that were "utterly untruthful," replete with "prejudices and stupendous ignorance." They argued for a new "abolitionism," one that would eliminate "Yankee school histories from our schools." Even the nation's only academic who also became a president, Woodrow Wilson, who welcomed the demise of slavery as a boon to the "New South," could not tolerate abolitionists. They "repelled the mass of the people" and destroyed any possibility of sectional compromise. His predecessor in office, Theodore Roosevelt, sympathized with the antislavery cause, but found its advocates to be fanatics and Garrisonian disunionism "absolutely senseless." He considered Phillips "a very good type of the whole," but he failed to "advance the cause of human freedom." Roosevelt depicted his postwar career as "either mischievous or ridiculous, and usually both." Roosevelt admirer Herbert Croly, in his blockbuster study *The Promise of American Life,* dismissed the abolitionists as "misguided fanatics" who had "lost all sense of proportion, all balance of judgment, and all justice of perception." Their relentless persecution of southerners, whom Croly claimed "did much to mitigate the evils of negro servitude," put the nation on the road to war. Moreover, their misguided agitation clouded the "fact" of inherent black inferiority.[92]

Texts that came to dominate the teaching of the Civil War and Reconstruction eras by Claude Bowers, George Fort Milton, James Truslow Adams, and Arthur Charles Cole depicted a South saddled with negroes who would not work unless compelled, and beset by northern zealots, a group that James Truslow Adams described as "fanaticism akin to insanity, as extreme fanaticism always is." Their Reconstruction policies, especially their interest in black suffrage, amounted to nothing more than the Radicals' attempt to maintain subjugation of the South. Wendell Phillips, according to Adams, led the northern effort to keep the former Confederate states out of the Union until they "had been able to make over the South in its own likeness." One 1921 study of Lincoln and the war predictably characterized the abolitionists as vexing agitators and Wendell Phillips, "[t]heir most gifted orator," as possessing a "fury that might be called malevolent." Frank Owsley, Vanderbilt historian and president of the Southern Historical Association, wrote off abolitionism as "a crusade against the southern people." In the most incendiary assessment of the antislavery movement ever penned, Owsley declared that "neither Dr. Goebbels nor Virginio Gayda nor Stalin's propaganda agents have as yet been able to plumb the depths of vulgarity and obscenity reached and maintained by George Bourne, Stephen Foster, Wendell Phillips, Charles Sumner, and other abolitionists of note."[93]

Amid the deluge of scholarship that excoriated Phillips and his colleagues as insane agitators, a differing interpretative strain persisted. In what southerners discounted as "Yankee history," James Schouler's six-volume United States history, while dismissing most abolitionists as an annoyance, found Phillips "much wiser and more comprehensive in action." Others preferred moderate opposition to slavery as one could find in a Daniel Webster, a Lincoln, a Seward, or perhaps a Benjamin Lundy. Although the great Harvard historian Samuel Eliot Morison generally found abolitionists a troubling element in American history and Garrison's fanaticism as helping to bring on the Civil War, when he approached Phillips his tone changed. Undoubtedly growing up hearing stories about Phillips, the Boston-born Morison could not help but view Phillips as a "gentleman" who suffered social ostracism for the sake of his beliefs. When he considered Phillips, Morison began seeing the antislavery movement as a formidable and noble force for social reform, confessing that so long as slavery existed even white labor was jeopardized. As if befuddled by Wendell Phillips, in his influential *Oxford History of the United States*, Morison asked "How, then shall we estimate the abolitionists?" He concluded that their "sincerity and courage is no longer denied," but that the death of slavery came in spite of them, rather than because of them, and they had left the nation with a "race and color problem" that still roiled the land.[94]

More progressive forces resisted even the ambivalence of a Morison and maintained the emancipationist and socialist traditions that honored a reformer like Phillips. While antislavery memoirs had fallen from favor, small-print-run studies continued to pour from the presses, especially on the Underground Railroad. Popular biographies persisted, such as those by the New York lawyer, author, and essayist John Jay Chapman; NAACP founder Oswald Garrison Villard; and others promoted by the Socialist Party of America. None, however, achieved a greater long-term impact than the work of the Pulitzer Prize–winning scholar Vernon L. Parrington.[95]

The Aurora, Illinois–born Parrington resented his years at Brahmin Harvard University and cultivated scholarship informed by an aggressive agrarian-populist progressivism, born from firsthand experience with the exploitation of poor farmers by rapacious bankers on the Kansas frontier. He despised the powerful and the hypocrite and delighted in Phillips's repudiation of the Harvard intellectual class in his 1881 oration. His award-winning 1927 *Main Currents in American Thought* cast Phillips and his antislavery allies in an entirely new light, designed specifically to answer the new questions raised by the economic inequality of the late 1920s.[96]

Earning the attention of new generations of scholars, Parrington rejected the dominant view of abolitionists as diseased, dishonest fanatics. "Yet as a matter of sober historical fact," he asserted with unequaled authority, "they were the kindest of men, with generous sympathies and disinterested motives. No blackguard was ever an abolitionist—no ward-heeler, or mob-inciter, or purse-patriot. . . . There was no money to be made, no place of honor or power to be got by espousing Abolitionism, but only self-sacrifice and social ostracism."[97] He did not deal with Phillips until he began writing the third volume of his study—dying before any part of it saw print—but there Phillips emerged as the major force of the mid-nineteenth century, "a soldier of the Puritan soul." He rejected the Phillips-as-Christ interpretation, however, and instead viewed him a glorious class traitor and a "child of '76."

Parrington shifted attention away from Phillips the abolitionist, and instead focused on his postwar career as an economic critic, marking him as "more provocative . . . and more dangerous—[espousing] causes that touched the northern pocketbook." He celebrated a Marxist Phillips, one who preferred "cooperation," not competition, and had learned from his abolitionism that all labor had become fundamentally unfair and "unfree, held in the grip of a master, bought and sold in the market." Moreover, he did not risk his fortune and position, Parrington asserted, to turn the chattel slave into a wage slave. His plans for labor, currency reform, banking, and taxation may have incited State Street into howling rage, but "it was rather the talk of an honest equalitarian who understood how incompatible was property rule and the idea of equality." His study slowly and methodically built the case for seeing Phillips as an essential social critic, if not a Marxist, and laying the foundation for Parrington's own progressive ideals. To Parrington's mind, Phillips would tolerate "no half-way measures, but goes straight to the economic core of the problem. Pretty much all of Marxism is there, even to the class war. The capitalists had whetted their swords and he would have labor put its sword likewise to the grindstone. If the war were cruel, where did labor learn it—'learned it of capital, learned it of our enemies.' In a world of economic concentration where caste follows property accumulation he had come to rest his hopes on the international solidarity of labor." To Parrington, Phillips "had taken the measure of existing law and order and was casting about for a juster [*sic*] law and a more generous order." This is a view of Wendell Phillips grounded in the desperation of midwestern farmers, the arrogance of the East, and memory's heartfelt "needs of the moment."[98]

With time, Parrington's reconsideration of Phillips and the abolitionists became increasingly rooted in the academy. Scholars proved slow to give up inherited views of antislavery fanaticism, but the number of sympathetic studies began to build.[99] The prolific team of Charles and Mary Beard, writing between 1933 and 1942, at first saw abolitionism as "relentless and virulent" and, amusingly, asserted that the antislavery movement diverted women's attention away from feminism. By 1939, however, the Beards no longer viewed the abolitionists as fanatics, but as "the humanistic wing of American democracy." They delighted in Phillips's feminism and cherished his postwar career, clearly relishing the opportunity to reprint Phillip's fiery 1871 Worcester, Massachusetts, speech in which he advocated "the overthrow of the whole profit-making system." To the Beards, as with Parrington, Phillips had become a hero for the working class.[100]

By the time Columbia University's Richard Hofstadter published his 1948 landmark reassessment of Phillips in the *American Political Tradition*, the terrain of abolitionist studies had begun to change. In both historical memory and among scholars, the growing civil rights movement had compelled a reassessment. As the *Boston Globe* observed in 1940, Wendell Phillips had become the archetype for the antislavery movement, the Mugwumps, and anti-imperialists, and "kept a fire under the social conscience of the community."[101] As Hofstadter admitted, Wendell Phillips also had been fortunate in attracting a set of sympathetic if not admiring biographers who never accepted the Lost Cause interpretation of American history. Hofstadter, however, went further, not only assessing Phillips's entire career, including his postwar radicalism, but ranking him in importance to American history alongside Thomas Jefferson, Andrew Jackson, John C. Calhoun, William Jennings Bryan, Theodore Roosevelt, Woodrow Wilson, Herbert Hoover, and Franklin Delano Roosevelt. After Hofstadter, a trickle turned into a stream, and a stream into a river of reassessments of Phillips and the antislavery movement, clearly in answer to the needs of the new national interest in civil rights. The reinterpretation of abolitionism, seeing it as humanistic, democratic, and equalitarian, gave the postwar effort to win civil rights a foundation that stretched back into the nineteenth century. When the Baltimore *Afro-American* reviewed Louis Filler's collection of Phillips writings, *Wendell Phillips on Civil Rights*, in the fall of 1965, it could with justice assert that "Wendell Phillips' name has been all but forgotten." The reviewer, however, wisely cited Filler's estimation of what the old Boston reformer could say to another generation of Americans: "[He] was an arrow to the future which extends its flight into our very own era."[102]

CONCLUSION

Americans of the 1960s found a new role for Wendell Phillips, seeing in him the necessary force to resist racial oppression and dangerous social conformity in a nuclear age. Liberal academics and social critics appealed to his role as an abolitionist to help lay a foundation for the modern civil rights movement. But, as the *Afro-American* had observed in 1965, his name meant—and means—little or nothing to most of the country.[103] As those who had known him passed away, turning collective memory into historical memory, Wendell Phillips's legacy quickly vanished from popular culture, surviving mostly in the academy's ivy-covered halls. As the majority of Americans have rejected the antidemocratic era of Jim Crow and twice elected an African American president, both the antislavery movement and the Civil War have begun to loosen the iron grip they once held over the nation's imagination, making the need for Phillips as promoter of racial equality increasingly unnecessary. Clearly, there is no lack of more contemporary figures to fill that role. Thus, he has become largely anonymous. Most of the public schools that still bear his name, if still in use, have little or nothing to say at their websites about his extraordinary career in helping to forge modern America. Although his legacy dominated discussions of freedom, democracy, and economic equality for over fifty years after his death, one would be hard-pressed today to walk by his monument in Boston's Public Garden and find anyone familiar with the orator so elegantly posed on his pedestal. Moreover, our era's disturbing levels of wealth disparities, which rivals the Gilded Age, and which has produced its share of contemporary critics, has found no role for Phillips. The modern "Occupy Movement" and its populist counterparts, whatever the merits of their critiques—and they are considerable—lack historical memory of a central historical figure who could take up the cause of the powerless against the powerful. In that role, Wendell Phillips still has much to offer.[104]

NOTES

1. Phillips was buried next to his father, but after his wife's death his body was exhumed and moved to the Milton cemetery, where both were permanently interred in a Greene family plot. *Washington Post*, April 29, 1886.

2. *Congregationalist*, February 7, 1884; Boston *Daily Advertiser*, February 11, 1884; Arthur Mann, *Yankee Reformers in the Urban Age* (Cambridge: Harvard University Press, 1954), 19.

3. Boston *Daily Advertiser*, February 11, 1884.

4. David Blight, "If You Don't Tell It Like It Was, It Can Never Be as It Ought to Be," in *Slavery and Public History: The Tough Stuff of American Memory*, ed. James Oliver Horton and Lois E. Horton (New York: New Press, 2006), 23–24; Blight, *Beyond the Battlefield: Race, Memory, and the American Civil War* (Amherst: University of Massachusetts Press, 2002), 2–3, 120–21; Blight, "William Lloyd Garrison at Two Hundred: His Radicalism and His Legacy for Our Time," in *William Lloyd Garrison at Two Hundred: History, Legacy, and Memory*, ed. James Brewer Stewart (New Haven: Yale University Press, 2008), 3. Also see Blight's remarkable *Race and Reunion: The Civil War in American Memory* (Cambridge: Harvard University Press, 2001); Pierre Nora, "Between Memory and History: Les Lieux de Mémarre," in *History and Memory in African-American Culture*, ed. Geneviève Fabre and Robert O'Meally (New York: Oxford University Press, 1994), 285; Maurice Halbwachs, *On Collective Memory*, trans. Lewis A. Coger (Chicago: University of Chicago Press, 1992), 49; Yannis Hamilakis and Jo Labanyi, "Time, Materiality, and the Work of Memory," *History & Memory* 20 (Fall–Winter 2008): 8, 12.

5. John Lukacs, *Historical Consciousness or the Remembered Past* (1968; New York: Schocken Books, 1985), 33; Roy Rosenzweig and David Thelen, *The Presence of the Past: Popular Uses of History in American Life* (New York: Columbia University Press, 1998), 15–18, 92–93; Louis Menand, "Seeing It Now," *New Yorker* (July 9, 16, 2012): 94.

6. Halbwachs, *On Collective Memory*, 40, 166, 182–83, quoted.

7. George Lipsitz, *Time Passages: Collective Memory and American Popular Culture* (Minneapolis: University of Minnesota Press, 1990), 5; Alison Landsberg, *Prosthetic Memory: The Transformation of American Remembrance in the Age of Mass Culture* (New York: Columbia University Press, 2004), 8–9; Greg Dickinson, Carole Blair, and Brian L. Oft, eds., *Places of Public Memory: The Rhetoric of Museums and Memorials* (Tuscaloosa: University of Alabama Press, 2010), 6; Fabre and O'Meally, eds., *History and Memory in African-American Culture*, 52; David Blight, "W. E. B. Du Bois and the Struggle for American Historical Memory," in *History and Memory in African-American Culture*, ed. Fabre and O'Meally, 45–71.

8. Carlos Martyn, *Wendell Phillips: The Agitator* (New York: Funk & Wagnalls, 1890), 479–85; New York *Tribune*, February 7, 1884; Boston *Daily Advertiser*, February 6–7, 1884; Philadelphia *Inquirer*, February 6, 1884; Boston *Journal*, February 5, 1884.

9. New York *Tribune*, February 7, 1884; Boston *Daily Advertiser*, February 7, 1884; *Congregationalist*, February 14, 1884; Boston *Journal*, February 9, 1884, quoted; George Lowell Austin, *Life and Times of Wendell Phillips* (Boston: B. B. Russell & Co., 1884), 361–69.

10. *A Memorial of Wendell Phillips* (Boston: City of, 1884), 11; Joan Waugh, *Unsentimental Reformer: The Life of Josephine Shaw Lowell* (Cambridge: Harvard University Press, 1997), 37–40, 45–46, 157; George William Curtis, "Editor's Easy Chair," *Harper's New Monthly Magazine* (April 1884): 804–5; Mark A. Peterson, "Stone Witnesses, Dumb Pictures, and Voices from the Grave: Objects, Images, and Collective Memory in Early Boston," in *Commemoration in America: Essays on Monuments, Memorialization, and Memory*, ed. David Gobel and Daves Rossell (Charlottesville: University of Virginia Press, 2013), 60–67. I thank the cataloger of the Massachusetts Historical Society, Mary E. Yacovone, for tallying the number of published memorials produced by the city of Boston. My own copy of the 1884 *Memorial of Wendell Phillips* originally was given to a teenage boy by a local lawyer.

11. For example, see the Dallas *Weekly Herald*, April 24, 1884; Boston *Daily Advertiser*, April 19, 1884; *Memorial of Wendell Phillips*, 35–38, 45, 47–50.

12. Boston *Daily Advertiser*, February 6, 1884.

13. *Liberator*, January 21, 1837; December 28, 1838.

14. *North Star*, December 3, 1847; William C. Nell, *Services of Colored Americans, in the Wars of 1776 and 1812* (Boston: Robert F. Wallcut, 1852), and *Colored Patriots of the American Revolution* (Boston: Robert F. Wallcut, 1855).

15. I am much indebted to Lewis scholar Marilyn Richardson for alerting me to the existence of the medallion of Phillips by Lewis, which is—instead of a bust—likely the work of art referred to by the *Christian Recorder*: "The Colored Genius at Rome," *Christian Recorder*, March 31, 1866, www.invaluable.com/auction-lot/edmonia-lewis-american,-1845-1907-portrait-medall-1127-c-28aae049ed; Greener could have owned the original marble version or a plaster or metal copy. John A. Hewitt, "A Black New York Newspaperman's Impressions of Boston, 1883," *Massachusetts Review* 32 (Autumn 1991): 446; David Levering Lewis, *W. E. B. Du Bois: Biography of a Race, 1868–1919* (New York: Henry Holt, 1993), 50–51; W. E. B. Du Bois, *Autobiography*, ed. Werner Sollors (New York: Oxford University Press, 2007), 63.

16. "Wendell Phillips Memorial," *Christian Recorder*, February 28, 1884. Eric R. Jackson, "Wendell Phillips Dabney," in *The African American National Biography*, ed. Henry Louis Gates, Jr., and Evelyn Brooks Higginbotham, 8 vols. (New York: Oxford University Press, 2008), vol. 2: 528–29. Boston *Journal*, April 15, 1886; May 23, 1895.

17. New York *Freeman*, November 21, 1885; New York *Age*, January 21, 1888. On black laborers, see New York *Herald-Tribune*, September 2, 1884; Macon *Telegraph*, September 2, 1884. For the labor quote see, New York *Tribune*, February 11, 1884.

18. *People's Advocate*, March 8, 1884; *Washington Post*, February 23, 1884; Boston *Daily Advertiser*, February 23, 1884. For other events and commentary, see Huntsville, Ala., *Gazette*, February, 9, 1884; New York *Globe*, February 9, March 1, May 17, 1884; for one at Wilberforce University, see "Wendell Phillips Memorial Meeting," *Christian Recorder*, April 17, 1884.

19. Boston *Daily Advertiser*, April 10, 1884; Dickson D. Bruce, Jr., *Archibald Grimké: Portrait of a Black Independent* (Baton Rouge: Louisiana State University Press, 1993), 28–31, 34, 50; Archibald H.

Grimké, *A Eulogy on Wendell Phillips* (Boston: Rockwell and Church, 1884), 7–8, 27–29, 32, 34. On antislavery friendships, see my "Abolitionists and the Language of Fraternal Love," in *Meanings for Manhood: Constructions of Masculinity in Victorian America*, ed. Mark C. Carnes and Clyde Griffen (Chicago: University of Chicago Press, 1990), 85–95.

20. Galveston *Daily News*, February 3, 1884; St. Louis *Globe-Democrat*, February 3, 1884; *Congregationalist*, February 7, 1884; *Southwestern Christian Advocate* (New Orleans), February 7, 1884; *Rocky Mountain News* (Denver), February 7, 1884; Cincinnati *Commercial Tribune*, February 7, 1884; New York *Freeman*, February 6, 1884; New York *Tribune*, February 11, 1884.

21. New York *Tribune*, February 11, 1884; *New York Times*, February 11, 1884; John Henry Barrows, *Services in Honor of Wendell Phillips* (Chicago: Jameson & Morse, 1884); New Haven *Register*, February 2, 1884; New Orleans *Times-Picayune*, February 17, 1884.

22. The only readable poem today remains that penned by the Boston activist and journalist John Boyle O'Reilly. *Christian Recorder*, February 28, March 27, June 19, 1884; Thomas Bailey Aldrich, "Monody on the Death of Wendell Phillips," *Century Magazine* 41 (February 1891): 578–79; George Clinton Rowe, "Wendell Phillips," in *Thoughts in Verse* (Charleston, S.C.: Kahrs, Stolze & Welch, 1887), 42–44; Barrows, *Services in Honor of Wendell Phillips*, 8 quoted.

23. Henry Adams to Charles Francis Adams, June 22, 1869, in *The Letters of Henry Adams, vol. 2, 1868–1885*, ed. J. C. Levenson, Ernest Samuels, Charles Vandersee, and Viola Hopkins Winner (Cambridge: Harvard University Press, 1982), 39; Henry Adams, *The Education of Henry Adams: A Centennial Version* (Boston: Massachusetts Historical Society, 2007), 33; George F. Hoar, *Autobiography of Seventy Years*, 2 vols. (New York: Charles Scribner's Sons, 1903), vol. 2: 361–62; *Washington Post*, May 30, 1913, for the Lodge story about Hoar.

24. Nora Perry, "Wendell Phillips," *Christian Recorder*, June 19, 1884, originally from the *Congregationalist*. On Perry, see www.bostonathenaeum.org/library/book-recommendations/athenaeum-authors/nora-perry; Thomas Wentworth Higginson, *Wendell Phillips* (Boston: Lee & Shepard, 1884), v, vi–vii, xv–xviii, xix, originally an essay in *The Nation*; *Christian Recorder*, February 14, 1884; *Frank Leslie's Sunday Magazine* 23 (June 1888): 471.

25. James Freeman Clark, "His Virtues and Defects," Boston *Daily Advertiser*, February 11, 1884; Higginson, *Wendell Phillips*, v, vi–vii, xv–xvi.

26. Chicago *Daily Tribune*, February 20, 1884; *Congressional Record*, February 25, 1884, 1351–52; Rockford *Daily Register*, February 9, 1884; Boston *Daily Journal*, February 9, 1884; *New York Times*, February 9, 1884. Edwin M. Irish, the Maine-born Michigan lawyer and Republican politician, remained deeply ambivalent over Phillips, seeing him both as a heroic reformer and an impractical visionary, whose refusal to accept compensated emancipation and his opposition to Lincoln helped bring on the Civil War. Edwin M. Irish, *Abraham Lincoln–Wendell Phillips: Addresses* (Kalamazoo, Mich.: privately printed, 1910), 34–35, 55–58.

27. Baltimore *Sun*, February 4, 1884; St. Louis *Globe-Democrat*, February 3, 1884.

28. Macon *Weekly Telegraph*, February 22, 1884; New Orleans *Times Picayune*, February 8, 1884; Dallas *Weekly Herald*, February 14, 1884.

29. New Orleans *Times Picayune*, February 8, 1884, reporting on the Memphis paper. Wheeling (W. Va.) *Register*, February 28, 1884.

30. Blight, *Race and Reunion*, 123, Godkin quoted, 138; Blight, "'For Something beyond the

Battlefield': Frederick Douglass and the Struggle for the Memory of the Civil War," *Journal of American History* 75 (March 1989): 1162–63, 1169, Douglass quoted; Blight, "The Shaw Memorial in the Landscape of Civil War Memory," in *Hope & Glory: Essays on the Legacy of the 54th Massachusetts Regiment*, ed. Martin H. Blatt, Thomas J. Brown, and Donald Yacovone (Amherst: University of Massachusetts Press, 2001), 81, Tourgée quoted.

31. Wolfgang Schivelbusch, *The Culture of Defeat: On National Trauma, Mourning, and Recovery* (New York: Henry Holt and Co., 2003), 20–21, quoted; Martin Griffin, *Ashes of the Mind: War and Memory in Northern Literature, 1865–1900* (Amherst: University of Massachusetts Press, 2009), 2, 7, 15–17; Blight, "For Something beyond the Battlefield," 1159; Blight, *Beyond the Battlefield*, 111; Hilary A. Herbert, *Why the Solid South? or, Reconstruction and Its Results* (Baltimore: R. H. Woodward & Co., 1890), 1–28; Bruce E. Baker, *What Reconstruction Meant: Historical Memory in the American South* (Charlottesville: University of Virginia Press, 2007), 23–25, 69–75.

32. Blight, *Race and Reunion, Afro-American* quoted 390; Julie Roy Jeffrey, *Abolitionists Remember: Antislavery Autobiographies and the Unfinished Work of Emancipation* (Chapel Hill: University of North Carolina Press, 2008), 157–59 for the Warner quote.

33. Albion W. Tourgée, *A Fool's Errand, By One of the Fools*, illus. ed., 2 parts (New York: Fords, Howard, & Hulbert, 1880), 167–70.

34. Blight, *Beyond the Battlefield*, 97; Blight, *Race and Reunion*, 2–3, 193–94, 303–7; Blight, "The Shaw Memorial in the Landscape of the Civil War," 89, quoted.

35. William Sumner Crosby and Theodore Dwight Weld, *Memorial Services Upon the Seventy-fourth Birthday of Wendell Phillips* (Boston: J. Cooper, 1886), 1–6. Undoubtedly, Phillips knew the merchant and city official Sumner Crosby, William's father. Perhaps more important, however, William's wife, Eleanor Frances Davis, was a blood relation of Phillips's, and he gave Eleanor away at her marriage to William Sumner Crosby in 1877. *One Line of Descendants from Dolar Davis and Richard Everett* (Boston: George H. Ellis, 1911), 18; Boston *Journal*, May 31, 1887; Boston *Daily Advertiser*, May 31, 1887.

36. Spaulding, who possessed forty-three patents related to conducting electricity underground and underwater, worked with a number of Boston business interests to promote the subway. His insistence that the subway would improve the morals of its users would amuse any modern denizen of the MBTA. Boston *Journal*, October 6, November 5, 1891; Boston *Herald*, September 3, 1885, February 20, 1891; *Boston Globe*, February 13, 1888; New York *Tribune*, April 17, 1893.

37. Much of the story of the Wendell Phillips Union is in David A. Zonderman, *Uneasy Allies: Working for Labor Reform in Nineteenth-Century Boston* (Amherst: University of Massachusetts Press, 2011), 219–23; Boston *Journal*, October 3, October 6, December 19, 1891; Boston *Advertiser*, October 3, 1891. The Wendell Phillips Women's Club was led by Martha M. Avery, a Christian socialist; see Boston *Journal*, January 14, 1892.

38. Boston *Daily Advertiser*, November 2, 1887; Boston *Journal*, February 23, 1888; "Reunion of Abolitionists," September 23, 1889[?], in Wendell Phillips Hall Association Papers, Box 1889, Massachusetts Historical Society.

39. Wendell Phillips Hall Association, misc. printing [1889?], printed letters, October 1889, November 29, 1889, *The Freedom of Speech of Wendell Phillips* (Boston: WPHA, 1890), Wendell

Phillips Hall Association, Box 1889, Massachusetts Historical Society; Boston *Journal*, June 2, 1890.

40. Boston *Journal*, June 2, October 11, November 28, 30, December 9, 1890; William C. Nell, "Wendell Phillips's Speech," New York *Age*, December 20, 1890. Williams would go on to a career in Congress and in the diplomatic corps.

41. Edwin D. Mead, "A Monument to Wendell Phillips," *New England Magazine* 9 (December 1890): 536; Boston *Daily Advertiser*, October 8, 1890; Springfield *Republican*, June 14, 1890; New York *Age*, December 19, 1891; Detroit *Plain Dealer*, July 11, 1890.

42. The actual funds raised went to the creation of a Phillips scholarship at Harvard and Tufts University for promising students in oratory. Until 1904, the scholarship fund was managed by Rev. Jesse H. Jones. Both are still active. *Exercises at the Dedication of the Statue of Wendell Phillips, July 5, 1915* (Boston: City of, 1916), 11; *Harvard Crimson*, January 8, 1897. I thank Joice Himawan, director of the Dyer Memorial Library, for alerting me to the *Crimson* piece.

43. Boston *Journal*, October 18, 1890; December 1, 9, 10, 1891. Boston *Advertiser*, June 17, 1891. Before disappearing, the association closed its Tremont Street offices and moved to Chinatown. In 1921, a building named for Phillips was erected on Boston's Essex Street. It became an apartment building and later lost the Phillips name. *Monument Magazine* 69 (September 29, 1921): 790.

44. In addition to recognizing his home, the four-by-six-foot tablet proclaimed: "He Lived to See Justice Triumphant, Freedom Universal." *Boston Globe*, November 26, 1894; William Lloyd Garrison, Jr., and the irrepressible Dr. Samuel Abbott Green addressed the crowd. Boston *Journal*, November 23, 26 1894.

45. Adelaide Cromwell, *The Other Brahmins: Boston's Black Upper Class, 1750–1950* (Fayetteville: University of Arkansas Press, 1994), 75–78. Boston *Journal*, November 7, 1890; January 3, 1891; May 31, November 29, 1895. New Haven *Register*, June 6, 1887. New York *Freeman*, July 16, 1887. Records of the Wendell Phillips Club, 1893–1898, Harvard University Archives. A "Wendell Phillips Club" reemerged about 1900 and participated in debates on campus into the 1920s. As late as 1943, another "Wendell Phillips Club" was founded under the direction of the American Youth for Democracy, an antifascist organization, and drew students from Harvard, Radcliffe, MIT, and Northeastern. *Harvard Crimson*, December 22, 1922; December 7, 1943.

46. Philadelphia *Inquirer*, December 1, 1911; also see Horace H. Hagan, "Wendell Phillips," *Sewanee Review* 21 (July 1913): 324–40. Hagan, a Georgetown-trained attorney, became an assistant attorney general in Tulsa, Oklahoma. In 1923, he authored a series of portraits of nineteenth-century lawyers, clearly preferring the careers of Judah P. Benjamin and Rufus Choate to Phillips, whom he disdained as responsible for helping to bring on the Civil War.

47. George Edward Woodberry, *Wendell Phillips: Faith of an American* (Boston: Woodberry Society, 1912), quoted 26, 29–30.

48. Chicago *Broad Axe*, March 11, December 2, 1911; Baltimore *Afro-American*, December 2, 16, 1911; N. Barnett Dodson, "Generous Appreciation for Wendell Phillips," Baltimore *Afro-American*, December 16, 1911.

49. David Wills, "Reverdy C. Ransom: The Making of an A.M.E. Bishop," in *Black Apostles: Afro-American Clergy Confront the Twentieth Century*, ed. Randall Burkett and Richard Newman

(Boston: G. K. Hall, 1978), 181–212; Reverdy C. Ransom, "Wendell Phillips: Centennial Oration," in *Making the Gospel Plain: The Writings of Bishop Reverdy C. Ransom*, ed. Anthony B. Pinn (Harrisburg, Pa.: Trinity Press International, 1999), 123–34.

50. Charles Edward Russell, "Wendell Phillips," *The Crisis* 3 (December 1911): 66–67. Oddly, Russell made no mention of the celebrations in New York and Boston.

51. Boston *Journal*, November 30, 1911.

52. *Boston Globe*, November 29, 1911.

53. Wendell Phillips Stafford, *Wendell Phillips: A Centennial Oration* (New York: NAACP, 1911); Wendell Phillips Stafford, *Speeches* (St. Johnsbury, Vt.: Arthur F. Stone, 1913); Boston *Journal*, November 30, 1911; Washington *Bee*, December 24, 1910.

54. Wendell Phillips Stafford, "The Negro and the Nation," in Stafford, *Speeches*, 264–70; William H. Jeffrey, *Successful Vermonters* (E. Burke, Vt.: Historical Publishing Co., 1904), 52; *Liberator*, February 2, 1855; *Washington Post*, June 8, 1904; Washington *Bee*, December 24, 1910; Chicago *Broad Axe*, June 5, 1909; Fort Worth *Star*, June 4, 1909; Paul S. Gillies, "The Style of Wendell Phillips Stafford," *Vermont Bar Journal* 39 (Spring 2013): 9, quoted.

55. Washington *Bee*, December 9, 1911. The reference in the event's proceedings to a "full-length" portrait of Phillips behind the speaker's podium may refer to a three-quarter-view oil portrait by Frederic P. Vinton, who had died the previous May. It might also refer to Charles Bond's 1849 oil portrait of a seated Phillips, one that for many years hung over my desk at the Massachusetts Historical Society. Several other artists of the region, such as Darius Cobb and E. T. Billings, also executed portraits of Phillips. The life-size (head and chest) oil portrait of Phillips (now lost) by the African American artist Cloyd Lee Boykin was not unveiled until the following spring. Stafford, *Centennial Oration*, 5–9; *Boston Globe*, March 6, 1912; *Christian Science Monitor*, March 6, 1912.

56. Stafford, *Centennial Oration*, 16–18, 25–26.

57. Ibid., 25–26, 33–35. Stafford went on to repeat his performance at the Metropolitan AME Church in Washington, D.C., evoking five minutes of rapturous applause. Washington *Post*, November 30, 1911; Washington *Bee*, December 9, 1911. For Zachariah Walker, see Dennis B. Downey and Raymond M. Hyser, *No Crooked Death: Coatesville, Pennsylvania, and the Lynching of Zachariah Walker* (Urbana: University of Illinois Press, 1991).

58. Dell Upton, "Why Do Monuments Talk So Much?" in *Commemoration in America*, ed. Gobel and Rossell, 19–20; Thomas J. Brown, "Reconstructing Boston: Civic Monuments of the Civil War," in *Hope & Glory*, ed. Blatt, Brown, and Yacovone, 138–45; Kirk Savage, *Standing Soldiers, Kneeling Slaves: Race, War, and Monument in Nineteenth-Century America* (Princeton: Princeton University Press, 1979), 120–22; New York *Age*, March 23, 1889, July 25, 1891, quoted; San Francisco *Bulletin*, May 20, 1886.

59. Boston *Daily Advertiser*, February 9, 1884; Mead, "A Monument to Wendell Phillips," 535.

60. Jones died unexpectedly in 1904; see Boston *Herald*, April 21, 1904; Boston *Journal*, March 27, 1900, November 30, 1912; *Boston Globe*, July 31, 1903; *New Englander and Yale Review* 30 (April 1871): 350, Jones quoted; *Exercises at the Dedication of the Statue of Wendell Phillips*, 54–57. According to the city's official account, the association lay dormant until revived in 1911 by Dr. A. N. Abbott, the association treasurer, which ignores the work of Rev. Jesse Jones. The city

actually spent $20,189 on the statue, with $4,000 going to artist Daniel Chester French. *Annual Report—Auditing Department* (Boston: City of, 1915), 59. The WPMA's activities were covered by the black press; see: Baltimore *Afro-American*, December 7, 1912.

61. William D. Brigham to W. E. B. Du Bois, May 26, 1915, Du Bois Papers, University of Massachusetts, Amherst, microfilm edition, reel 5: #287; Boston *Herald*, November 27, 1912; *Boston Globe*, November 27, 1911; Boston *Herald*, July 8, 1922; W. I. Brigham, *The History of the Brigham Family . . .* (New York: Grafton Press, 1907), 465.

62. William D. Brigham to W. E. B. Du Bois, May 26, 1915, Du Bois Papers, University of Massachusetts, Amherst, microfilm edition, reel 5: #287; Boston *Herald*, November 27, 1912; *Boston Globe*, November 13, 1914; Springfield *Republican*, April 20, 1915; Stephen Fox, *The Guardian of Boston: William Monroe Trotter* (New York: Atheneum, 1970), 189–97; Mark R. Schneider, *Boston Confronts Jim Crow, 1890–1920* (Boston: Northeastern University Press, 1997), 147–52; Paul Polgar, "Fighting Lightning with Fire: Black Boston's Battle against 'The Birth of a Nation,'" *Massachusetts Historical Review* 10 (2008): 84–113.

63. Daniel Chester French to Thomas Allen, November 9, 1912; Daniel Chester French to Charles W. Eliot, January 28, 1914, Daniel Chester French Papers, Library of Congress; *Exercises at the Dedication of the Statue of Wendell Phillips*, 13.

64. Boston *Journal*, October 17, December 12, 1914; *Exercises at the Dedication of the Statue of Wendell Phillips*, 11–12; Daniel Chester French to Charles Gibson, August 5, 1914, Daniel Chester French Papers; *Granite, Marble & Bronze* 25 (January 1915): 138.

65. *Boston Globe*, October 17, 1914.

66. Baltimore *Afro-American*, July 24, 1915; Oakland (Calif.) *Sunshine*, July 31, August 21, 1915; *Western Outlook*, July 31, 1915; Tucson *Citizen*, July 5, 1915.

67. The German bodyguards were George Gramlich, Henry Foss, and John Koch; *Exercises at the Dedication of the Statue of Wendell Phillips*, 13–14, 36, 39 Trotter quoted, 42–51, 56. Boston *Herald*, July 6, 1915. Samuel Worcester Dana, *Law and Letters: Essays and Addresses* (Boston: Gorham Press, 1915), 21, 35–36. *Boston Globe*, July 5, 1915.

68. Austin, *The Life and Times of Wendell Phillips*, Douglass quoted, 416; In an essay copyrighted by the muckraking publishing baron S. S. McClure, and reprinted across the country, James R. Gilmore (alias Edmund Kirke) briefly sketched Phillips's career, following closely the format begun by Austin. *Oregonian*, March 31, 1895; Elbert Hubbard, *Little Journeys to the Homes of Eminent Orators: Phillips* (East Aurora, N.Y.: Roycrofters, 1903), 161, 169, passim.

69. Baltimore *Sun*, October 12, 1895; November 21, 1906, Mark Twain, *Autobiography*, ed., Benjamin Griffin, Harriet Elinor Smith, Victor Fischer, Michael B. Frank (Berkeley: University of California Press, 2013), vol. 2: 282; Sioux City *Journal*, September 16, 1895; mine workers reported in the Portland *Morning Oregonian*, May 16, 1920; Idaho *Statesman*, July 13, 1915; *Japan Review* 4 (1919): 47–48.

70. John Haynes Holmes, *Wendell Phillips, Champion of the Oppressed* (New York: Church of the Messiah, 1912), 16; *Christian Recorder*, March 29, 1862; Richard J. Hinton, "Wendell Phillips: A Character Study," *The Arena* 13 (1895): 227; George William Curtis, "Editor's Easy Chair," *Harper's New Monthly Magazine* (April 1887): 625, 804–5; Charles Dudley Warner, *Harper's New Monthly Magazine* (June 1893): 152–53; Frank P. Stearns, *Sketches from Concord and Appledore.*

Concord Thirty Years Ago (New York: G. P. Putnam's Sons, 1895), 197–98; Biloxi (Miss.) *Daily Herald*, September 19, 1900; Higginson, *Wendell Phillips*, xi; especially see James Brewer Stewart, *Wendell Phillips: Liberty's Hero* (Baton Rouge: Louisiana State University Press, 1986), 177–208.

71. Warner, *Harper's New Monthly Magazine*, 152–53; Schuyler Colfax, "Wendell Phillips: A Reminiscence," *The Congregationalist*, March 27, 1884. Colfax's memory is confirmed by a journalist who also attended the Phillips lecture on L'Ouverture; see William A. Croffut, *An American Procession, 1855–1914: A Personal Chronicle of Famous Men* (Boston: Little, Brown, and Co., 1931), 68. In the 1920s and 1930s, Phillips remained the standard of oratorical excellence and became the subject of academic study; see Mildred Pomeroy, "The Imagery of Wendell Phillips," MA thesis, Northwestern University, 1925; Edgar DeWitt Jones, *Lords of Speech: Portraits of Fifteen American Orators* (1937; Freeport, N.Y.: Books for Libraries Press, 1969), 65–77; Raymond H. Barnard, "An Objective Study of the Speeches of Wendell Phillips," *Quarterly Journal of Speech* 18 (November 1932): 571–84; and Barnard, "The Freedom Speeches of Wendell Phillips," *Quarterly Journal of Speech* 25 (December 1939): 596–611.

72. Chicago *Inter Ocean*, February 24, 1892; Minneapolis *Journal*, September 30, 1895; Kalamazoo *Gazette*, April 7, 1896; *Colored American*, December 10, 1898; *Washington Post*, April 13, 1906; Birmingham *Age*, November 17, 1895; Chicago *Broad Axe*, February 26, 1921.

73. Wendy Hamand Venet, *A Strong-minded Woman: The Life of Mary Livermore* (Amherst: University of Massachusetts Press, 2005), 1–4, 7, 161, 195–97, 199, 229; Lillie Buffum Chace Wyman, *American Chivalry* (Boston: W. B. Clarke Co., 1913), 14–15; Livermore is quoted in the *Washington Post*, February 10, 1884, a reprinted column from the Cleveland *Herald*.

74. Boston *Daily Advertiser*, May 19, 1885; Cleveland *Plain Dealer*, November 10, 1885; Haverhill *Bulletin*, December 30, 1884, quoted; "Wendell Phillips and His Times," Livermore Collection, box 5, Princeton University.

75. Boston *Journal*, February 2, 1893; April 9, 1896. *New York Times*, October 24, 1886. Kansas City *Times*, October 12, 1890. Indianapolis *Freeman*, August 6, 1892. Worcester *Daily Spy*, May 21, 1894; August 13, 1895. Trenton *Evening Times*, October 10, 1886. *Howitzer*, December 12, 1886. Anaconda *Standard*, January 17, 1921.

76. New York *Herald*, July 20, 1885; *Daily Inter Ocean*, June 7, 1895; Worcester *Daily Spy*, June 1, 1895; *Sunday Oregonian*, March 10, 1901; Chicago *Broad Axe*, December 9, 1916. At Howard University, President Jeremiah E. Rankin delivered an oration on Phillips as the nation's "greatest orator, humanitarian, and noted apostle of abolition." *Colored American*, January 20, 1900.

77. Kansas City *Star*, July 3, 1885. *Washington Post*, November 13, 1910. Philip T. K. Daniel, "A History of Discrimination Against Black Students in Chicago Secondary Schools," *History of Education Quarterly* 20 (Summer 1980): 151–52. Brooks did not, however, graduate from the school. George E. Kent, "Gwendolyn Brooks—Portrait, in Part, of the Artist as Young Girl and Apprentice Writer," *Callaloo* 7 (October 1979): 82. Chicago *Broad Axe*, February 27, 1915, May 24, 1919.

78. Mann, *Yankee Reformers*, 16, quoted, 126–39; Brian Greenberg, "Wendell Phillips and the Idea of Industrial Democracy in Early Postbellum America," in *The Struggle for Equality: Essays on Sectional Conflict, the Civil War, and the Long Reconstruction*, ed. Orville Vernon Burton, Jerald Podair, and Jennifer L. Weber (Charlottesville: University of Virginia Press, 2011), 138; John L. Thomas, *Alternative America: Henry George, Edward Bellamy, Henry Demarest Lloyd and the Adver-*

sary Tradition (Cambridge: Harvard University Press, 1983), 2; Keith Newland, *Hamlin Garland: A Life* (Lincoln: University of Nebraska Press, 2008), 62–67, 83–85, 102–4; Wendell Phillips, *The Labor Question* (Boston: Lee and Shepard, 1884), 3 quoted; Norman Thomas, *Great Dissenters* (New York: W. W. Norton, 1961).

79. Timothy Messer-Kruse, *The Yankee International: Marxism and the American Reform Tradition, 1848–1876* (Chapel Hill: University of North Carolina Press, 1998), 103 quoted; *Commonwealth* quoted in Greenberg, "Wendell Phillips and the Idea of Industrial Democracy," 147.

80. Wendell Phillips, *Who Shall Rule US? Money, or the People?* (Boston: Franklin Press, Rand, Avery & Co., 1878), 3, 5, 8, emphasis in original; Phillips, *The Labor Question*, 13–14, 19–21, which reprints his two 1871 speeches.

81. David Montgomery, *Beyond Equality: Labor and the Radical Republicans, 1862–1872* (Urbana: University of Illinois Press, 1981, 1967), 265–66, 367, 369–70; Greenberg, "Wendell Phillips and the Idea of Industrial Democracy," 146; Stearns, *Sketches from Concord and Appledore*, 214–17.

82. *Boston Globe*, December 14, 1890. Butler even printed wartime correspondence with Phillips in the article. Wyman, *American Chivalry*, 24–25; Phillips, *Who Shall Rule US?* 4–5, 7; Worcester *Daily Spy*, August 18, 30, 1884; Nick Salvatore, *We All Got History: The Memory Books of Amos Webber* (New York: Random House, 1996), 244–45.

83. Mead, "A Monument to Wendell Phillips," 537–39.

84. William Murray, "Reminiscences of Wendell Phillips: An Address Delivered before the Wendell Phillips Club in Paine Hall," Boston *Investigator*, September 4, 11, 1897. Just before Phillips's death, Murray named one of his sons after the reformer. The Boston Athenaeum's clipping may be the only surviving copy of the two-part article. *Boston Globe*, December 1, 1886.

85. Thomas, *Alternative America*, 24–25, 62–63, 319; Greenberg, "Wendell Phillips and the Idea of Industrial Democracy," 138; Henry George, *Poverty and Progress* (1879; New York: Walter J. Black, 1942), especially 295–96; Chester McArthur Destler, *Henry Demarest Lloyd and the Empire of Reform* (Philadelphia: University of Pennsylvania Press, 1963), 37, 39, 44–70; Henry Demarest Lloyd, *Mazzini and Other Essays* (New York: G. P. Putnam's Sons, 1910), 10; Henry Demarest Lloyd, "The New Conscience" (1888), "The Labor Movement" (1889), "The Scholar in Contemporary Practical Questions" (1895), in *Henry Demarest Lloyd's Critiques of American Capitalism, 1881–1903*, ed. Alun Munslow and Owen R. Ashton (Lewiston, N.Y.: Edwin Mellen Press, 1995), 50, 94–95, 158; Chicago *Herald*, December 28, 1891.

86. J. Robert Constantine, ed., *The Letters of Eugene V. Debs*, 3 vols. (Urbana: University of Illinois Press, 1990), vol. 1: li, lxxvii; vol. 3: 459. Eugene V. Debs, *Pastels of Men* (New York: Pearson's Library, 1919), 21–31. Max Eastman, *The Trial of Eugene Debs* (New York: Liberator Pub., 1918?), 18; Cleveland *Gazette*, September 12, 1903, on Booker T. Washington.

87. Chicago *Herald*, March 20, 1890. Baltimore *Sun*, July 5, 1895. *Lucifer, the Light-Bearer*, May 22, 1896; January 21, 1899. Omaha *World Herald*, March 9, July 18, 1896. Chicago *Broad Axe*, November 11, 1899, Bryan quoted.

88. "Phillips Vindicated," *Boston Globe*, June 29, 1904. Also see the work of the NAACP founder, Unitarian minister, and pacifist, John Haynes Holmes, *Wendell Phillips: Champion of the Oppressed*.

89. *Daily People*, March 26, 1911; March 23, 1913. Constantine, ed., *Letters of Eugene V. Debs*,

vol. 1: 261. Cambridge *Tribune*, June 4, 1910. *Boston Globe*, November 1, 1908. *Worker*, December 8, 16, 29, 1906; February 2, 1907. Franklin H. Wentworth, *Wendell Phillips: An Address . . . Delivered in Faneuil Hall, Boston . . . Dec. 4, 1906* (New York: Socialist Literature Co., 1906?).

90. Charles Edward Russell, *Bare Hands and Stone Walls: Some Recollections of a Side-Line Reformer* (New York: Charles Scribner's Sons, 1933), 24–25, 38, 196–97; the autobiography's frontispiece is a portrait of Wendell Phillips. Charles Edward Russell, *The Story of Wendell Phillips: Soldier of the Common Good* (Chicago: C. H. Kerr & Co., 1914), 8, 10, 12, 19–22.

91. Chicago *Daily Tribune*, September 22, 1920. "The Whatnot Column," Baltimore *Afro-American*, February 1, 1924. *Boston Globe*, March 30, September 8, 1928; November 30, 1929, February 15, 1934. Because many electronic newspaper databases grow sparse after 1920, I did an individual search of papers in Boston, New York, Baltimore, Atlanta, Cleveland, Chicago, San Francisco, and Los Angeles, which confirmed the virtual disappearance of Phillips from the popular press. He does appear in book reviews, but virtually nowhere else.

92. Jeffrey, *Abolitionists Remember*, 164–65; James M. McPherson, "Long-Legged Yankee Lies: The Southern Textbook Crusade," in *The Memory of the Civil War in American Culture*, ed. Alice Fahs and Joan Waugh (Chapel Hill: University of North Carolina Press, 2004), 68–69; Charles Regan Wilson, *Baptized in Blood: The Religion of the Lost Cause, 1865–1920* (Athens: University of Georgia Press, 2009, 1980), 125; Woodrow Wilson, *Division and Reunion, 1829–1889* (New York: Longman's, Green, 1926), 125–26; Daniel Ruddy, ed., *Theodore Roosevelt's History of the United States* (New York: HarperCollins, Smithsonian, 2010), 173; Herbert Croly, *The Promise of American Life* (New York: Macmillan Co., 1909), 80–81.

93. Although a progressive Democrat, Claude Bowers disdained the move for racial justice and considered the KKK a legitimate force to protect the South from Yankee carpetbaggers. Peter J. Schlinger and Holman Hamilton, *Spokesman for Democracy, 1878–1958* (Indianapolis: Indiana Historical Society, 2000). Claude Bowers, *The Tragic Era: The Revolution After Lincoln* (Cambridge: Riverside Press, 1929), vii, 60, passim. George Fort Milton, *The Age of Hate: Andrew Johnson and the Radicals* (New York: Coward-McCain, 1930), 20–35, 59–73, 139–40. James Truslow Adams, *The March of Democracy: A History of the United States*, 3 vols. (New York: Charles Scribner's Sons, 1965, 1932), vol. 2: 232–33 quoted, vol. 3: 179–80, quoted. Arthur Charles Cole, *The Irrepressible Conflict, 1850–1865* (New York: Macmillan Co., 1938), 275, 335. Nathaniel W. Stephenson, *Abraham Lincoln and the Union: A Chronicle of the Embattled North* (New Haven: Yale University Press, 1921), 187 quoted. Frank L. Owsley, "The Fundamental Cause of the Civil War: Egocentric Sectionalism," *Journal of Southern History* 7 (February 1941): 3–18. I thank John Stauffer for alerting me to Owsley's remarks.

94. James Schouler, *History of the United States of America under the Constitution*, 6 vols. (Washington, D.C.: Morrison, 1882), vol. 6: 227; David Saville Muzzey, *An American History* (Boston: Ginn and Co., 1917), 319–20, 308; Arthur Meier Schlesinger, *New Viewpoints in American History* (New York: Macmillan Co., 1922), 118–19; Samuel Eliot Morison, *The Oxford History of the United States, 1783–1917*, 2 vols. (London: Oxford University Press, 1927), vol. 1: 452–53, 454–57, 460.

95. Jeffrey, *Abolitionists Remember*, 226–27; Jacques Barzun, ed., *The Selected Writings of John Jay Chapman* (Garden City, N.Y.: Doubleday, 1959), 3–152, especially 148; Oswald Garrison Villard, "Wendell Phillips, After Fifty Years,"' *American Mercury* 34 (January 1935): 93–99; Alistair Coleman, *Pioneers of Freedom* (1929; Freeport, N.Y.: Books for Libraries Press, 1968,), v–vi, 77.

96. Richard Hofstadter, *The Progressive Historians: Turner, Beard, Parrington* (New York: Vintage, 1970), 350–51, 368–71; Vernon L. Parrington, *Main Currents in American Thought*, 2 vols. (1927; New York: Harcourt, Brace & World, 1954), and vol. 3: *Beginnings of Critical Realism in America: 1860–1920* (1930; New York: Harcourt, Brace & World, 1958).

97. Parrington, *Main Currents* 2: 343.

98. Ibid., 3: 140–46.

99. Especially see John Jay Chapman's *William Lloyd Garrison* (New York: Moffat, Yard and Co., 1913); Mary Stoughton Locke, *Anti-Slavery in America (1619–1808)* (Cambridge: Radcliffe College, 1901); Alice Dana Adams, *The Neglected Period of Anti-Slavery in America (1808–1831)* (Cambridge: Radcliffe College, 1908); Gilbert Hobbs Barnes, *The Anti-Slavery Impulse, 1830–1844* (Washington, D.C.: American Historical Association, 1933). Barnes, a student of U. B. Phillips, disdained New England abolitionists and preferred their midwestern brethren; Henry Steele Commager, *Theodore Parker* (1936; Boston: Beacon Press, 1960); W. E. B. Du Bois, *Black Reconstruction in America, 1860–1880* (1935; Cleveland: World Publishing Co., 1962); and Dwight Lowell Dumond, *Antislavery Origins of the Civil War in the United States* (1939; Ann Arbor: University of Michigan Press, 1958).

100. Charles A. Beard and Mary R. Beard, *The Rise of American Civilization* (1927; New York: Macmillan Co., 1933), 696–99, 759; Beard and Beard, *America in Midpassage*, 2 vols. (New York: Macmillan Co., 1939), vol. 2: 507; Beard and Beard, *The American Spirit* (New York: Macmillan, 1942), 189–91. Also see the publication of the American Communist Party, James J. Green, *Wendell Phillips* (New York: International Publishers, 1943), which argued that Parrington's and Phillips's analysis fell short of real Marxism.

101. Richard Hofstadter, "Wendell Phillips: The Patrician as Agitator," *The American Political Tradition: And the Men Who Made It* (New York: Vintage Books, 1948), chapter 6, 137–63, remains a penetrating assessment of the Bostonian. Austin, *The Life and Times of Wendell Phillips*; Martyn, *Wendell Phillips: The Agitator*; Lorenzo Sears, *Wendell Phillips: Orator and Agitator* (1909; New York: Benjamin Blom, 1967); Russell, *The Story of Wendell Phillips*; Hofstadter also had read the earlier dissertation version of Oscar Sherwin's *The Prophet of Liberty: The Life and Times of Wendell Phillips* (New York: Bookman Associates, 1958). Charles A. Madison's *Critics & Crusaders* (New York: Henry Holt & Co., 1947–48), iii, claimed that Phillips was the wellspring of the modern movement for social, political, and economic justice, an enemy of "rampant and rapacious capitalism." A year earlier, Earl Conrad published *Jim Crow America*, which credited Phillips, Garrison, and Douglass as having given birth to the modern civil rights movement; see *New York Times*, April 6, 1947; Louis M. Lyons, "Keeping a Fire Under the Social Conscience," *Boston Globe*, September 18, 1940.

102. For the change in attitude, both in popular culture and in the academy, see Edwin T. Buehrer, "Eugene V. Debs: Prophetic Voice of Labor," 1949, and his "Wendell Phillips: Exemplar of American Liberalism," 1949, transcripts, Andover Harvard Divinity School, Harvard University; Ralph Korngold, *Two Friends of Man: The Story of William Lloyd Garrison and Wendell Phillips and Their Relationship with Abraham Lincoln* (Boston: Little, Brown and Co., 1950); *New York Times*, January 22, 1950; and *Boston Globe*, January 22, 1950, for reviews of Korngold's book which clearly placed the work in the context of the civil rights movement. Uncle Dudley's "Improper Bostonians," *Boston Globe*, June 29, 1958; Arkansas *State Press*, March 27, 1959. Among the other books

representing a new and dramatically different view of the antislavery movement are Russell B. Nye, *Fettered Freedom: Civil Liberties and the Slavery Controversy, 1830–1860* (1949; East Lansing: Michigan State University Press, 1963), and Nye, *William Lloyd Garrison and the Humanitarian Reformers* (Boston: Little, Brown, 1955); Hazel Catherine Wolf, *On Freedom's Altar: The Martyr Complex in the Abolition Movement* (Madison: University of Wisconsin Press, 1952); Irving Bartlett, *Wendell Phillips: Brahmin Radical* (Boston: Beacon Press, 1961); Louis Filler, *The Crusade Against Slavery, 1830–1860* (New York: Harper's, 1960); Louis Filler, ed., *Wendell Phillips on Civil Rights and Freedom* (New York: Hill and Wang, 1965); Martin Duberman, ed., *The Antislavery Vanguard: New Essays on the Abolitionists* (Princeton: Princeton University Press, 1965); Baltimore *Afro-American*, October 30, 1965.

103. Even the Presbyterian socialist and perennial presidential candidate Norman Thomas—who ranked Phillips alongside Socrates, Galileo, Thomas Paine, and Gandhi—confessed that few Americans had heard of Wendell Phillips. Thomas, *Great Dissenters*, 11–18, 129–68.

104. Thomas J. Brown, ed., *Remixing the Civil War: Meditations on the Sesquicentennial* (Baltimore: Johns Hopkins University Press, 2011), 11; Michael Kazin, *The Populist Persuasion: An American History* (New York: Basic Books, 1995), 1–2, passim. Phillips appears nowhere in Kazin's book; Susan Van Gelder, *This Changes Everything: Occupy Wall Street and the 99% Movement* (San Francisco: Berrett-Koehler Publishers, 2011), 1–12, 23, passim; Eli Zaretsky, *Why America Needs a Left* (Cambridge, U.K.: Polity Press, 2012), 1–15, 158–59.

12

THE PHILLIPS COMMUNITY OF MINNEAPOLIS

Historical Memory and the Quest for Social Justice

DAVID MOORE, HARVEY M. WINJE, AND SUSAN ANN GUST
IN CONSULTATION WITH JAMES BREWER STEWART

Why, in 2008, would someone publish a political cartoon like the one below (fig. 12.1), foregrounding a vivid likeness of Wendell Phillips together with that of U.S. Senator Paul Wellstone, who was killed in an airplane crash in 2002? There are in fact as many as eighty other cartoons that feature Phillips in one way or another, published over a twenty-seven-year span and still counting. What motivates this prolific cartoonist and his publisher? Whom did they intend these cartoons to speak to and with what expectations in mind? What historical circumstances explain all this? How can it be that the "spirit" of Wendell Phillips seems to be living on well into the twenty-first century?

The cartoon surely does suggest that memories of Wendell Phillips continue "living," but not as one might expect, solely among civic-minded Bostonians. Long-sustained political identification with Phillips is actually the hallmark of people who reside in an economically marginalized community in central Minneapolis. Known to everyone as the Phillips Community, it is served by *The Alley Newspaper*, a small local publication founded in 1976 that publishes the cartoons along with a wealth of local news. One of the authors of this essay, Harvey Winje, edits the paper. Another, Dave Moore (in close collaboration with Linnea Hadaway), composes the cartoons. The third, Susan Gust, is a local activist and volunteer with *The Alley*. Why does the memory of Wendell Phillips hold such a powerful political meaning for us personally and for our community—in many ways the polar opposite of the opulent Beacon Hill neighborhood once so familiar to Wendell Phillips?

We chose this first cartoon because it provides an easy way to begin explaining why we identify Wendell Phillips with our own politics, our community,

Figure 12.1. The "Spirit of Phillips": I Have Mountains of Ice Before Me to Melt. *The Alley Newspaper*, December 2007.

its history, and with its ongoing struggles to better itself. Under the banner of "THE SPIRIT OF PHILLIPS," this cartoon presents two charismatic figures united in one full-throated affirmation of their shared commitment to battle for social justice. Wendell Phillips *is* "Our Neighborhood Namesake," the cartoon insists, and Paul Wellstone *is* "*our Senator!*" (Not the State of Minnesota's, mind you—but OURS!). The quotation attributed to Phillips—although actually from his antislavery contemporary William Lloyd Garrison—is equally Wellstone's because, as the cartoon makes clear, the senator actually used it, especially in his 2002 memoir, *Conscience of a Liberal*. We also heard Wellstone say it plainly in 1998 when he told us that the quote, which he attributed to Phillips, was his favorite. Thus, the two speak with one voice and, as only popular historical memory can do, Phillips and Wellstone together declare that they are "*On* FIRE *because I have Mountains of Ice Before me to Melt!*"

A bit more attention to the cartoon helps to pin down these observations. By picturing Phillips as living on through our former U.S. senator Paul Wellstone our aim (whenever we get the chance) is to make the name of our neighborhood synonymous in the minds of its residents with a deeply rooted and empowering tradition of democratic activism. Wellstone's zestful "thumbs up" gives immediate currency to the sober image of the historical Phillips. Through Wellstone, as in all of the cartoons, the underlying message is consistent—Wendell Phillips should be remembered, celebrated, admired, and emulated for his convictions and the eloquence with which he expressed them. Phillips is our local champion, our condemner of corruption, our denouncer of economic exploitation, our opponent of racism and sexism, our educator, and speaker of truth to power. The "Spirit of Phillips" sustains our impulse to battle injustice and work for local betterment. The memory of Wendell Phillips challenges our thoughts, deepens our resolve, and enriches our political imaginations as we engage a neighborhood that is Minneapolis's poorest, most multiethnic, least well-educated, most politically ill-served, most transient, and most heavily exploited by outside interests.

Located in the heart of this city of 393,000 and founded before the Civil War, the Phillips Community is home to about 20,000 people. In 1926, city officials named a new neighborhood junior high school after Wendell Phillips, who had lectured in downtown Minneapolis at the city's opera house in March 1868. During the early decades of the twentieth century, other Minneapolis school districts and parks were also graced with prominent names from the nineteenth century, such as Seward, Whittier, Longfellow, Cooper, Loring, and Bancroft. In 1967, as the result of a federal "Model Cities" grant, the city of Minneapolis drew official neighborhood boundaries and named each after a particular luminary. The Phillips name and what is contained within its boundaries, however, carry special significance.[1]

We have resided in the neighborhood on and off for decades, and one of us has lived here since 1940. During this time, Phillips Community residents have sustained noteworthy resistance against racism, poverty, and economic exploitation. During these same decades, beyond the headlines, inventive neighborhood groups have incrementally developed many cultural resources and social services that combat poverty and offer substantial hope. For all its serious challenges, the Phillips Community we live in is, beyond all dispute, dynamic, creative, self-starting, and accomplished. However, much to our deep frustration, the region's mainstream media and the larger political culture for which they speak have persisted in portraying our neighborhood as entirely swallowed by crime, poverty, blight, drugs, gangs, racial strife, and hopelessness. These ugly stereotypes, by focusing solely on the challenges our community faces, only magnify the anger and deepen the alienation of those they marginalize. Whatever else we can accomplish, inspiration and resistance are what our newspaper and our cartoons are about.

In 1972, we discovered Oscar Sherwin's 1958 biography, *Wendell Phillips: Prophet of Liberty*, and it revolutionized our understanding of our own community, inspiring us with the name of one of history's most distinguished advocates of racial and gender equality and working peoples' rights. With that book, we felt the weight of history shifting in our favor. We found ourselves directly connected to a formidable hero of yesteryear, who, over a lifetime, had devoted his enormous talents to causes much like those with which our neighborhood has always contended. We dug into his speeches and turned up a wealth of political slogans and aphorisms, some deeply inspirational, others bitterly critical, all highly arresting and enormously quotable. They struck us as forceful provocations from the past and spurs to the future that are directly applicable to us and our neighborhood. Phillips's words from so long ago expressed far better than we could state what angers us, what sustains our resolve, and what gives us hope.

There are, as Wendell Phillips would have thoroughly understood, enormous challenges before us, ones similar to those he discovered in his own city. Median Phillips household income in 1999 was $28,700, but by 2009, in constant dollars, that number had fallen to $27,374. Citywide 2009 median income, however, reached $46,700. In 2010, renters outnumbered homeowners five to one, with a quarter of the residents born in another state and half of the population having moved into the neighborhood since 2005, and with at least 35 percent of all residents foreign born. Currently, 37.9 percent of Phillips's residents live in poverty, another 15 percent live with income between 100 and 150 percent of poverty levels, and just over 25 percent of adults are unemployed. Close to 75 percent of its population are forty-four years of age or younger, and nearly eight out of ten are people of color: 33 percent African American, 30.5

percent Latino or Hispanic, 7.7 percent Native American, 2.6 percent Asian, and 2.5 percent African born. More recent data reveal burgeoning Hispanic and Somali populations. The Phillips Community struggles against a high incidence of crime, as well as all the other predictable consequences of poverty and dislocation—lowered life expectancy, heightened infant mortality rates, and disturbingly elevated statistics measuring drug addiction, alcohol abuse, and homelessness.[2]

Since well before World War II, one large immigrant group after another has chosen the low-rent Phillips neighborhood as their initial staging area in a quest for opportunity and equal rights: Finlanders, Swedes, and Norwegians fleeing agricultural collapse at the close of the nineteenth century; African Americans during the second "great migration" in the 1940s and 1950s; immigrants from Mexico and Central America beginning in the 1970s and continuing still; Hmong refugees from postwar Vietnam and Cambodia; Somalis and West Africans in the 1990s and 2000s, fleeing terrorism and civil war; and for at least the past century, significant numbers of Chippewa, Lakota, Dakota, and Ojibwe, who migrate back and forth between our neighborhood and the upper Midwest's numerous Indian reservations. From across the Twin Cities of St. Paul and Minneapolis, these groups comprise one of the largest urban Native American populations in the United States. A second cartoon (fig. 12.2) attempts to capture the tight connections we feel between the rich diversity that history has bequeathed us and our belief in the abiding presence of the "Spirit of Phillips" within our community.

Considering these enormous challenges and complexities, the inspiration we draw from how the "real" Wendell Phillips might have responded sustains us. Would the many varieties of immigrants he found in Boston—Irish, Russian, German, and others—have moved him to speak out in their defense? Would the close correspondence between his lifelong demands for racial equality and his quest for economic and political justice have moved him to defend all nonwhite populations? Would he have found in the unemployment, poverty, and social distress on our streets today a parallel to the needs of lower-class workers during the 1870s and 1880s? Would his denunciations of "liquor dealers" find resonance in our dealers of drugs, and would not his condemnation of the "barons of businesses and banks" find a receptive audience in our own new Gilded Age? Imagining "abolition's golden trumpet" as vividly as we do, our answer is *Of course he would!*

In the face of uncertainty, what sustains our faith as publishers of *The Alley*

Figure 12.2. The "Spirit of Phillips": We Welcome Every One of Every Race to Our Soil. *The Alley Newspaper*, August 2006.

is the reliable level of public interest in each monthly issue and at least one hundred financial benefactors who choose to support us through our annual fund-raising. The amazing support of our advertisers over the decades, in particular, represents an enormous vote of confidence. But whether or not one believes in the "Spirit of Phillips" or in the influence of *The Alley*, one basic fact remains clear. It is evident over the decades that a deep democratic ideological impulse has repeatedly inspired our community to face up to its internal challenges and resist those outside its borders who seek to exploit it. One of Wendell Phillips's pungent aphorisms in the third cartoon (fig. 12.3) captures the fullest sense of this impulse—a pointed reminder that unrestrained power inevitably undermines democracy.

The unvarnished truth of Phillips's dictum is illustrated by a decades-long struggle begun in the late 1960s when, without public discussion, major health complexes began aggressively expanding within our neighborhood. In the late 1960s, four hospitals along Chicago Avenue, a major Phillips traffic artery, formed the Minneapolis Medical Center, Inc. Their intent, they announced, was to "increase the quality of patient care in a cost-effective manner." Thus was formed the nucleus of what eventually became a health-care colossus that would expand exponentially over the objections of the citizens of Phillips.

Figure 12.3. The "Spirit of Phillips": Power is ever stealing from the many to the few. *The Alley Newspaper*, April 1989.

The Phillips Community had been home to numerous hospitals, and by the early 1970s the list included Northwestern Hospital, Children's Hospital, Mount Sinai Hospital, Deaconess Hospital, and the Sister Kenney Institute—a formidable consortium. Until the mid-1960s, however, few regarded these hospitals as threats to the community. But at that time independent brokers covertly began buying owner-occupied homes and rental properties. They then secretly sold them all to the newly established Children's Hospital, which promptly demolished nearly a full residential block in order to clear space for its own new facility. Soon enough, additional houses vanished as the hospital added square footage and constructed parking ramps. Anticipating further expansion, ever more numerous real-estate speculators plunged into the Phillips housing market. Precisely as Wendell Phillips had cautioned, power quite openly had begun "stealing from the many to the few." Facing an urgent crisis, residents organized in earnest to defend the fabric of their community. Some of us had been veterans of labor-union struggles, while others were seasoned civil rights and anti–Vietnam War activists. In challenging the destruction of our neighborhood, we also aimed to build a permanent force that would speak for us.

Three circumstances worked in our favor. First, the state of Minnesota required that hospitals submit a "Certificate of Need" statement to prove the necessity for facility expansion and that it would have no negative impact on other local health-care institutions. Second, applications for tax-free bonding stood a far better chance of success if accompanied by documentation of community support. Third, we benefited from the vision and political acumen of the health-care leaders charged by the president of Abbot Northwestern Hospital to develop a Community Advisory Committee (CAC). When Phillips Community representatives offered the CAC creative solutions, insisted on tough negotiations, and mobilized public opinion against them, the committee was compelled to listen. In response, the CAC in some significant instances offered viable alternatives and workable compromises. Although we were unaware of it at the time, Phillips neighborhood representatives had broken significant new ground as urban planners and local advocates.

Only in retrospect could we appreciate the extent of our gains, even as we acknowledged our losses. We held firm, demanding limits on land consumption, housing loss, and increases in vehicle traffic. We insisted on what became known as the Six Block Agreement, intended to limit the height of new buildings and the number of blocks to be consumed by health-care expansion. As negotiations continued, the area covered eventually doubled to become the Twelve Block Agreement and succeeded in preventing the worst abuses. But it failed to stop expansion by nonparticipating health-care enterprises. In 2004, in blatant defiance of the Twelve Block Agreement, a major health-care complex tracked its oversized footprints into an entire city block. Children's Hospital surreptitiously bought twenty-eight homes, along with a former church building and a gas station. It rapidly leveled all, save two that were moved elsewhere, scarring our neighborhood permanently and inflicting deep trauma and distrust which, to this day, many of our residents deeply resent. In place of the demolished buildings went a huge new clinic and a seven-hundred-plus car parking garage. Children's Hospital then added its own heliport. The racket of helicopters ferrying patients in and out at all hours adds mightily to the pollution and cacophony of street traffic, sirens, generators, air-conditioning units, and a hospital waste incinerator.

While lamenting the trauma wrought by the Children's Hospital experience, we believe that our negotiations restrained further developmental "sprawl" and saved housing stock. Additionally, we bargained successfully for new employment opportunities for residents, and for enhanced communication between neighborhood activists, elected officials, and the public at large. We are proud to have established, among other hard-won gains, several collaborations between the community, Allina Health, Abbot Northwestern Hospital, and city and county agencies designed to benefit the people of the Phillips Community. Gordon Sprenger, retired president of Abbot-Northwestern Hospital and CEO of Allina Health, attests that our engagement is responsible for significant joint ventures, such as the Phillips Partnership, involving an extensive job-training program, a housing stabilization initiative, and the periodic infusion of developmental dollars. Another success is the "Backyard Initiative," involving a major public-health campaign directly aimed at our community and four adjoining neighborhoods. Developed in collaboration with Allina, this program promotes a highly expanded definition of "wellness" and is governed almost entirely by local residents. A third successful collaboration resulted in the Midtown Greenway Project, involving the conversion of an abandoned railroad trench into an attractive pedestrian and cycling thoroughfare that now traverses the city.

From 1987 through 2007, our community followed Wendell Phillips's exhortation to shame greedy men into humanity, creating unprecedented solidarity

Figure 12.4. The "Spirit of Phillips": Shame Greedy Men into Humanity! *The Alley Newspaper*, April 2004.

to oppose mounting injustices. Throughout these struggles we surely did "Call Things by Their Right Names." Thanks to twelve years of uninterrupted protest, our own research, and attracting the attention of the media, we achieved a clear-cut environmental victory, not only for the neighborhood, but for the entire city. None of this would have come to pass unless, as Phillips advised, we had done everything possible to "shame greedy men into humanity."

In 1987, the Hennepin County Department of Environmental Management, the duly appointed manager of waste for Minnesota's most populous county, attempted to saddle us with a ten-acre trash and garbage transfer station. Over ten million dollars had been appropriated by the county commissioners to consolidate and transport waste from every part of Minneapolis, using city compactor garbage trucks making approximately 750 trips per day to the proposed transfer facility. From there, the garbage would be loaded into semitrailer trucks and delivered to the county's existing garbage incinerator in downtown Minneapolis. After *thirty-five houses and eight businesses were summarily demolished* by eminent domain, the neighborhood rose up, unified by deep indignation and driven by an imperative to resist. We demanded that the statute-required public hearings be held in the Phillips Community, something that city officials had never done. We felt united to battle for the future of *our* children, and we knew that our chances of success would be greatest if the city came to our own turf to defend their plans. We sought much more than a political victory; we were determined to prove that our children deserved better than a garbage-transfer station in their backyard. They most certainly deserved better than increased truck traffic and an endless succession of rank-smelling garbage trucks rumbling through our streets and permanently demeaning our home. Thus began years of uninterrupted agitation and protest.

For the first time in the recent history of the Phillips Community, homeowners and renters joined in common cause. We coalesced into a truly multicultural protest movement with people from every ethnic group "blending with one another like the colors on a pigeon's neck" (this simile was a Wendell Phillips favorite). Native Americans, many of them women, played a prominent role as frontline resisters. Little Earth of United Tribes of Minnesota, the nation's largest American Indian public-housing complex, sat three blocks from the proposed transfer-station location. We forced the authorities to hold the public hearings required for the permitting process in the Little Earth gymnasium. At the meetings, Indian children waved hand-lettered signs and banners they had made proclaiming: "We may be poor but we are not stupid" and "We are worth more than garbage." Mothers and grandmothers who had never attended or spoken at a public meeting testified forcefully, condemning the increased truck-traffic dangers faced by them and their children. What deeper motives drove those in authority, these women asked, when they grievously threatened the children of our nation's First People?

The combined impact of incessant protesting, media attention, and political arm-twisting kept the transfer station at bay for more than a decade.

The conflict turned decisively in our favor once we proposed a solution to the waste-management problem that was simply too intelligent and practical for those with authority to turn down. After analyzing the same statistics and technical information cited by the "experts" in defense of the transfer station, as well as garbage-truck routes and recycling statistics, we proved definitively that Hennepin County's current recycling efforts made the proposed project completely unnecessary. Instead of wasting 10 million dollars, Hennepin County could, at minimal cost, position itself as a national leader in the "greening" of American cities—*and the people of Phillips showed them how to do it.*

Our initial struggles against the transfer station had required several of us to immerse ourselves in the theories and practices of developing a "green economy" and the realities of what we termed "environmental racism." We sought additional knowledge and advice from experts in other environmentally distressed, racially polarized cities, such as Los Angeles. These environmental-justice activists challenged us to consider what we would do next, now that the building of the garbage-transfer station had been defeated. Some of us who had worked on this struggle knew there was gold in the garbage. Around 33 percent of the solid-waste stream in Minneapolis was made up of construction materials, much of it reusable. Instead of paying to get rid of refuse, we could be generating serious income!

Thus was born the Green Institute, which in 1995 opened the Re-Use Center, a twenty-six-thousand-square-foot facility set in a low-end, 1950s-style shopping center located at one of the key commercial edges of the Phillips Community. The enterprise brought many benefits to our neighborhood that went far beyond generating profits from discarded building materials. The Re-Use Center created jobs for about a dozen local residents, offered home-improvement classes, conducted environmental education workshops for local elementary schools, mimicked the organization of a Home Depot store, and sold an amazing range and quantity of recycled building materials. In all these creative endeavors, as Wendell Phillips might well have pointed out, power itself was now being recycled from "the few"—who had attempted to victimize our neighborhood—back into the hands of "the many," where it surely belongs and where, as the Phillips residents have shown, it does the most good.

Had the people of the Phillips Community achieved environmental justice? Not yet. In 2003, a few years after our battle against the transfer station, we learned of a soil-sample study demonstrating that our neighborhood was awash in arsenic poison emanating from an abandoned industrial site. The neighborhood promptly labeled the site "Arsenic Triangle," which describes the geometry of its borders. Right away, *The Alley* opened an all-out campaign to educate its readers and to mobilize them around demands that the powers that be deliver effective solutions. Wendell Phillips captured perfectly our journalistic motivations when reflecting on his own distinguished career: "*We came into the world to give truth a little jog onward and help our neighbors' rights.*" (We display this quotation on our newspaper's masthead.)

Buoyed by this historical connection, we filled *The Alley* with a volley of in-depth pieces explaining the problem and spotlighting the government agencies responsible for solving it. Between January 2005 and November 2007, we published nine articles about arsenic contamination that demanded action by those in charge. We publicized each and every community meeting (of which there were dozens), printed letters from residents expressing anger and concern, and composed pungent editorials criticizing government bureaucrats for inadequate responses. In 1852, Wendell Phillips had delivered a compelling speech, "Public Opinion," in which he stressed that agitators who expose corruption and denounce its practitioners are, in truth, democracy's most vital defenders. Our actions throughout the struggle to clean up "Arsenic Triangle" followed his example.

The resolution of this crisis confirmed the truth of Phillips's insight. A passionate local activist and parent, H. Lynn Adelsman, researched and laid out the problem with such exceptional clarity that neighborhoods beyond the borders of Phillips suddenly realized that our cause was also theirs. Additionally, our state representative, Karen Clark, pushed for intervention by higher levels of government, resulting in 2007 with a broad area of the "Arsenic Triangle" declared a federal Superfund project. Two years later, the Environmental Protection Agency appropriated up to twenty-five million dollars to remediate and restore not only the site, but also approximately five hundred adjoining arsenic-affected residential properties. The work on the arsenic-tainted land followed a ten-year collaboration to reduce childhood lead-poisoning in Phillips. Our partners included five University of Minnesota medical and science departments, the Minneapolis and Minnesota health departments, the office of Karen Clark, the Sustainable Resources Center, and the Honeywell Foundation. These combined efforts resulted in three federally funded, multimillion-dollar, community-governed research grants based on the expectation of designing improved intervention programs. The research was co-conducted with neighborhood members employed at living wages as peer educators, data-entry specialists, and translators. Although we did not know it at the time, we had designed a community-based participatory research model of shared power and decision-making that worked to the benefit of all involved. All information and analysis developed through this research needed first to be shared with the community before being published in specialized academic journals. As a consequence, in 2000, local residents and academic researchers co-produced a twelve-page insert in *The Alley* that summarized for everyone what our research had revealed about the dangers of lead poisoning as well as cost-effective prevention strategies. Exactly as Wendell Phillips had recommended, we chose to "Call Things by Their Right Names."

When the American Indian Movement (AIM) exploded into the headlines in the summer of 1968, the Phillips Community became one of its primary hubs. Initially, many of the movement's leaders were Phillips residents, and the one paired with Wendell Phillips in this cartoon, Clyde Bellecourt (fig 12.5), today lives in South Minneapolis and directs the Native American Interpretive Center, an activist museum that promotes Native American language revitalization, social justice, and history. We know that our neighborhood namesake would endorse AIM in a heartbeat, just as he advanced Indian rights in his own day. AIM's beginnings in the Phillips neighborhood was no accident. In fact, about 1,600 of Minnesota's roughly 61,000 Native Americans reside in our community, forming a tightly knit, highly visible presence. For American Indians living throughout Minnesota, the Dakotas, Iowa, western Wisconsin, and the southern regions of central Canada, this portion of our population functions as the political and cultural capital of "Urban Indian America" and as the epicenter of Native American activism.

Back in 1968, when AIM first went public, the area they occupied on Franklin Avenue, a major local thoroughfare, had been a grievously blighted ghetto, poverty-stricken, rigidly segregated, saturated with bars, liquor stores, flophouses, and marked by homelessness, drug dealing, muggings, and prostitution. Little wonder that AIM's initial appeal focused on anger and invited confrontation. Fast-forward more than four decades, however, and the profound transformation wrought by the Native American community is manifest along Franklin Avenue. While poverty persists, the bars, flophouses, and liquor peddlers have vanished, replaced by an impressive succession of substantial,

Figure 12.5. The "Spirit of Phillips": Phillips and the Native American Community. *The Alley Newspaper,* March 2013.

eye-catching buildings that fill several blocks. Each incorporates a distinctive Indian architectural motif, and with still other buildings south and east of Franklin Avenue, they house organizations with names such as the Little Earth Neighborhood Early Learning Center, the Nawayee-Naaway'll-Cokatawaenter School, Phillips Indian Educators, the Minneapolis American Indian Center, the Native American Community Clinic, the Indian Health Board, the Native Community Development Institute, Many Rivers Housing, the New Native Theater, the Minnesota Indian Women's Resource Center, All My Relations Art Gallery, the Little Earth of United Tribes Housing Corporation, Bii Di Gain

Dash Anwebi (in Ojibwe) Elder Housing, and others. Several major midwestern tribes also maintain local offices here, and because the Native American presence had become so significant, the city of Minneapolis designated the area as the Native American Cultural Corridor. It provides an impressive and unmatched array of essential services to Native Americans not only in Phillips but throughout Minnesota.

But why and how did all this develop in the Phillips Community? In large measure, credit goes to AIM. Best known for its violent 1973 confrontation with the FBI at Wounded Knee, AIM also waged many campaigns in defense of treaty rights, and against the racism inherent in the names of professional sports teams that adopted identities demeaning to Native Americans, such as the Cleveland Indians, the Atlanta Braves, the Kansas City Chiefs, and most egregiously, the Washington Redskins. AIM's work on Franklin Avenue, however, never made national headlines. The goals within the Phillips Community were defined by Native American traditions that place the highest premium on nurturing the young and honoring the old, which meant developing affordable housing and health care, along with schools committed to educating Native children.

Unlike AIM leadership during the 1970s and 1980s—almost exclusively male—on Franklin Avenue, Native American women assumed leadership. While the national media continued to focus on male leaders, in our community Native American women exerted decisive leadership and innovation while organizing, developing, and managing a four-block retail and business incubator strip of properties along Franklin Avenue under the auspices of a new nonprofit they formed called the American Indian Business Development Corporation. Many individuals and new groups have been responsible for continuing that remarkable initiative, extending Indian ownership and architectural influence six more blocks along Franklin Avenue and establishing that portion of the avenue as the American Indian Cultural Corridor south to Twenty-sixth Street. Little Earth of United Tribes is especially noteworthy because its residents withstood extreme adversity and consistently strove for their rights by lobbying, demonstrating, and negotiating with politicians, business leaders, and foundation officials until they delivered the funding and political support required to realize the Native American community's most important priority: safe, affordable housing. The results of a four-decade struggle can be seen today in the 9.4-acre Little Earth of United Tribes Housing Complex that anchors the far end of Twenty-fourth Street, along Hiawatha and Cedar avenues, two other major Phillips thoroughfares. It is home to a majority of Phillips's Native American population, a thousand residents living in 212 HUD-subsidized units. It offers rent-controlled housing in dwellings acquired beyond Phillips and makes special provisions for retirees and those with serious health problems. Additionally, it administers a home-ownership program that offers financial counseling and low-interest home loans for first-time purchasers.

Founded in 1973 with a HUD grant transferred from a foreclosed housing project, Little Earth initially faced enormous challenges: poor site preparation, low-grade building design and materials, unlivable conditions, police brutality, erratic city services, poor management, and financial instability. Throughout the 1980s and 1990s, the project struggled with crime and gang violence, elevated school dropout rates, and chronic marginalization. The entire neighborhood at times felt under siege, but tireless efforts by ordinary people helped stabilize and improve the livability of the complex, even as the authorities let the project deteriorate. Conditions began to change only when the residents of Little Earth began to believe in their own power to make substantial change. Project directors brought the residents together for extensive interviews to assess circumstances from the residents' perspective, the starting point for developing a community-based, consensus-driven planning process. Residents stressed the importance of opening access to services that promoted self-sufficiency, employability, youth education, and enhanced public safety, themes that became the cornerstones of a ten-year revitalization plan.

At present, project goals are closer to realization, with unemployment and school-dropout rates diminishing and an increasing number of families no longer in need of government-subsidized housing. When Wendell Phillips insisted that "America should do Justice to the Indians: It costs too much to wrong them," he voiced an enduring truth, confirmed by the residents of the Little Earth of United Tribes and by the entrepreneurs, educators, and activists whose ambitions and imaginations have created the Cultural Corridor and adjacent facilities and programs.

This final cartoon (fig. 12.6) depicts our "Spirit of Phillips" avatar, symbolizing how we define his mission, and how we have responded to his challenge. Although he calls to mind the image of Superman, we know him as "THE AGITATOR," a larger-than-life hero who appears whenever needed and inspires us to battle our enemies and develop effective strategies and plans for the

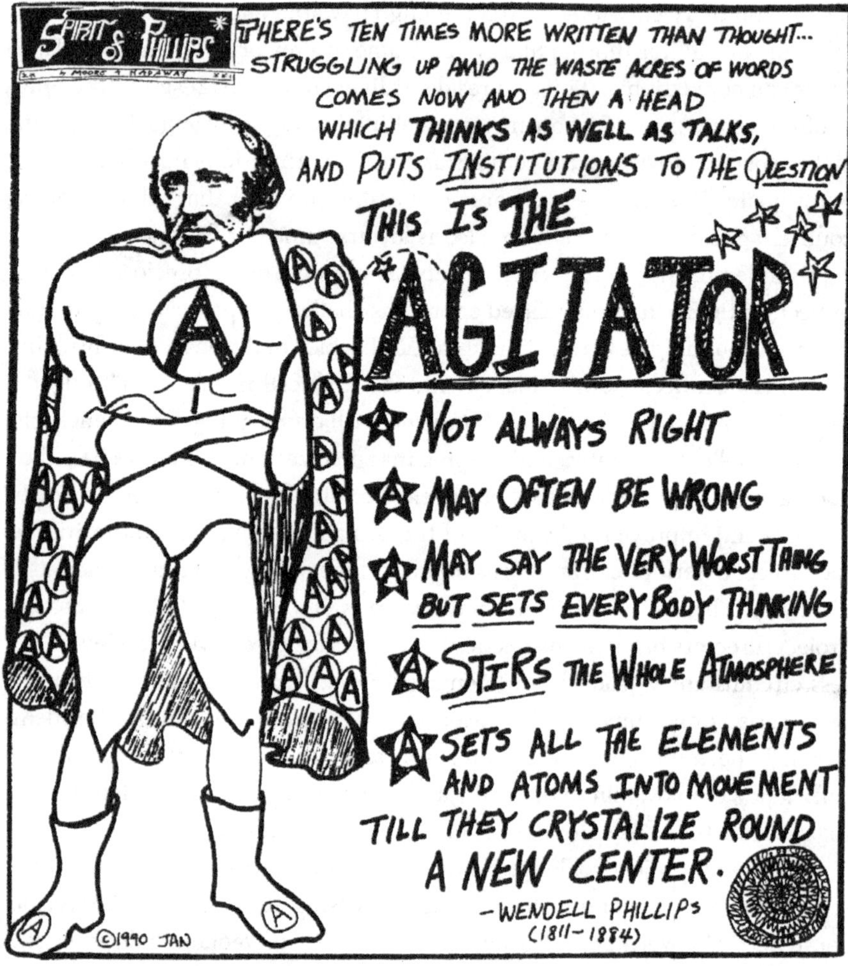

Figure 12.6. The "Spirit of Phillips": This Is the Agitator. *The Alley Newspaper,* January 1990.

neighborhood's greater good. Whenever we find ourselves provoked to organize protests, issue condemnatory press releases, and demand accountability from the powers that be, we channel the "Spirit of Phillips." As he once said, we "may not always be right, may often be wrong and may say the very worst things," but we surely do "put institutions to the question." We celebrate our right to resist, and find in Wendell Phillips a model for community action. But we also cherish our ability to creatively solve problems that, as the "Spirit of

Phillips" exclaims, "sets all the elements and atoms into movement till they crystallize around a new center." With Wendell Phillips as our inspiration, we are proud to catalog even more of our achievements:

(1) We forced the closing of three X-rated movie houses and saw them reopened as community theaters and cultural centers. One, In The Heart of the Beast Puppet Theater, produces original plays and tour productions, creates specially commissioned pageants throughout Minnesota, and teaches puppetry and pageantry through residencies and workshops for students, teachers, and communities. It also sponsors a hugely popular May Day Parade and Pageant that each year gives voice to the creative "Spirit of Phillips" as it wends its way through our neighborhood.

(2) After much petitioning, political pressuring, and organizing led by Phillips activists, a coalition of many neighborhoods prevailed on Hennepin County to purchase a 5.7-mile unused railroad right-of-way to repurpose as a beautiful greenway for the exclusive use of pedestrians and cyclists. The trail itself is owned and maintained by the city of Minneapolis and now spans the entire city. The sustainable gardens and three thousand trees along its route are but another example of the creative "Spirit of Phillips."

(3) We forced the state's largest electricity provider, Xcel Energy, to abandon its environmentally degrading project of stringing new transmission cables on massive ugly metal towers across the neighborhood, menacing our homes and the greenway. Instead, we compelled Xcel to adhere to its agreement to place all new transmission cables underground. After Phillips Community activists pressed this issue at the state legislature, before regulatory bodies, and in the courts, Xcel Energy agreed to spread the cost statewide, not solely burdening the residents of Phillips.

(4) We attacked drugs on the streets by demanding that the police remove the dealers and by insisting that the authorities partner with us in a number of ambitious initiatives designed to revitalize chronically distressed areas. The construction of new housing, the repurposing of decrepit structures, and the establishment of community gardens on previously abandoned lots are the best ways we know of removing eyesores, neutralizing magnets for crime, and infusing

healthy energy into our neighborhood. These activities also provide the most obvious strategy for minimizing the traumas inflicted on us by hospital expansion. Additionally, through sustained petitioning and agitation, the neighborhood has been able to purchase and close down a lucrative liquor store located disturbingly close to a public park. What was once a hub of illicit activities is today the Touchstone Plaza and Amen Corner, a welcoming venue for music, political demonstrating, picnicking, and conversation.

(5) One of our most ambitious and successful approaches to rooting out crime and building stability is Hope Community. Begun in 1999, Hope Community acquires abandoned structures, rehabilitates them, and then rents and manages them. It also builds hundreds of new single-family dwellings, turning them into permanent homes. One of its projects in particular has repurposed a once-condemned 1920s apartment building as very-low-rent "second chance" housing for people who otherwise would be homeless. Another high-ambition project involves construction of large three-story apartment buildings with retail space on the ground floors, each on a corner of a previously ruined intersection. So far, this project has created 225 units for both rental and purchase, and another corner has just been cleared for new construction. Still another Hope Community project turns abandoned houses into single-family homes and duplexes, currently totaling fifty rental units.

If Wendell Phillips could visit the projects undertaken by our community, he might well see them as twenty-first-century incarnations of Radical Reconstruction. As with his goals for the freedpeople in the post–Civil War South, we aim to overcome powerlessness, exploitation, and homelessness by mobilizing law, politics, economic clout, agitation, and community organizing to empower ordinary citizens to create their own truly democratic social and political order. Our Phillips neighborhood is dynamic, creative, democratic, and accomplished. In it, the "Spirit of Phillips" lives on, embodying his answer to the question, "What is defeat? Nothing but education. Nothing but the first step to something better."

NOTES

1. Minneapolis *Tribune*, March 13, 14, 15, 1868. Phillips spoke as part of a "Union" series of lectures and, according to the *Tribune*, delivered "decidedly the best of the season, and was attended by one of the finest audiences that ever graced the Opera House with their presence." The following day he and the mayor "drove through our city, and visited the Falls of St. Anthony, and the famed Minne-ha-ha. He expressed himself as delighted with our city and its surroundings." We wish to thank Sue Hunter Weir for documenting Wendell Phillips's visit to the Twin Cities and for explaining when and how the Phillips neighborhood was given its official boundaries and political status.

2. The demographic information on the Phillips neighborhood cited here and elsewhere in the essay is taken from the 2010 U.S. Census; www.mncompass.org/profiles/neighborhoods/minneapolis/midtown-phillips; www.city-data.com/neighborhood/Phillips-Minneapolis-MN.html; and www.metrocouncil.org/METC/files/35/35358ee4–7976–42e6–999d-9e54790d45fe.pdf. Also see the Minneapolis City Survey, www.city-data.com/neighborhood/Phillips-Minneapolis-MN.html.

CONTRIBUTORS

A J AISÉIRITHE is Consulting Editor of the *Frederick Douglass Papers* and was the Director of the Wendell Phillips Bicentennial Project. She has taught at the State University of New York, Binghamton, and the University of Chicago, and previously served as Assistant Editor for the Papers of Abraham Lincoln. A historian of the nineteenth-century United States, she has delivered numerous scholarly papers and public talks on abolitionism, Abraham Lincoln, and the Civil War to audiences in the United States and Europe. She is completing a history of abolitionism during the Civil War and Reconstruction.

MICHAEL LES BENEDICT, Professor Emeritus in History from Ohio State University, is an authority on Anglo-American constitutional and legal history, the history of civil rights and liberties, the federal system, and the Civil War and Reconstruction. His *The Impeachment and Trial of Andrew Johnson* and *A Compromise of Principle: Congressional Republicans and Reconstruction* are required reading for all students of the Civil War and Reconstruction. He has authored widely used textbooks and readers and penned over forty essays in American constitutional and legal history. He also prepared the American Historical Association's bicentennial essay on the history of American civil liberty, *Civil Rights and Liberties*, and coedited *The History of Ohio Law.*

MILLINGTON W. BERGESON-LOCKWOOD specializes in the history of nineteenth-century race, politics, and law in the United States. He received his PhD in history from the University of Michigan and has taught at George Mason University and the University of Maryland. In 2012 and 2013, he was the postdoctoral fellow in the Center for African American Urban Studies and the Economy (CAUSE) at Carnegie Mellon University. He is completing a book-length study of African American politics in Boston at the end of the nineteenth century and most recently published "'We Do Not Care Particularly About the Skating Rinks': African American Challenges to Racial Discrimination in Places of Public Amusement in Nineteenth-Century Boston, Massachusetts," in the *Journal of the Civil War Era.*

DEAN GRODZINS is a Visiting Scholar at the Massachusetts Historical Society and Research Associate on the History of American Democracy at the Harvard Business School. He received his PhD in history from Harvard University and has served as Lecturer in History and Literature at Harvard and Associate Professor of History at Meadville Lombard Theological School. For fifteen years, he edited *The Journal of Unitarian Universalist History.* He is the author of *American Heretic: Theodore Parker and Transcendentalism* and is currently writing a book about runaway slaves in Boston.

W. CALEB MCDANIEL is Associate Professor of History at Rice University. He is the author of *The Problem of Democracy in the Age of Slavery: Garrisonian Abolitionists and Transatlantic Reform* (Louisiana State University Press), which received the Merle Curti Award from the Organization of American Historians and the James Broussard First Book Prize from the Society for Historians of the Early American Republic.

DAN MCKANAN is Ralph Waldo Emerson Unitarian Universalist Association Senior Lecturer at Harvard Divinity School, where he has taught since 2008. Previously he chaired the Theology Department at the College of Saint Benedict / Saint John's University in Minnesota. A scholar of religion and social change in the United States, he is the author of four books, the most recent of which is *Prophetic Encounters: Religion and the American Radical Tradition.*

ANGELA F. MURPHY, Associate Professor of History at Texas State University in San Marcos, is an expert on the antebellum era, with a particular interest in the relationship of abolitionism to other reform movements. She published *American Slavery, Irish Freedom: Abolition, Immigrant Citizenship, and the Transatlantic Movement for Irish Repeal,* in Louisiana State University Press's Antislavery, Abolition and the Atlantic World series in 2010. Her most recent book is *The Jerry Rescue: The Fugitive Slave Law, Northern Rights, and the American Sectional Crisis,* published in 2015 as part of Oxford University Press's Critical Historical Encounters Series.

HÉLÈNE QUANQUIN is Associate Professor of American Civilization at Sorbonne Nouvelle–Paris 3 University, France. She has published three books, the most recent of which is *Refaire l'Amérique: Imaginaire et histoire aux États-Unis* (Presses de la Sorbonne Nouvelle), coedited with Didier Aubert. She is currently working on a book on men active in the American nineteenth-century women's rights movement. She has been the recipient of fellowships from the Radcliffe Institute's Schlesinger Library, Massachusetts Historical Society, Smith College's Sophia Smith Collection, and the American Antiquarian Society.

JAMES BREWER STEWART is the former James Wallace Professor of History at Macalester College and the nation's leading expert on the pre–Civil War abolitionist movement. For more than thirty years he taught courses about the Western Hemisphere and the United States prior to the twentieth century, emphasizing the topics of race, politics, law, and social movements. He has published biographies of Joshua R. Giddings, Wendell Phillips, William Lloyd Garrison, and Hosea Easton. His most recent books include *Abolitionist Politics and the Coming of the Civil War* and *Venture Smith and the Business of Slavery and Freedom*. He also founded Historians Against Slavery, an international group of scholars who actively oppose slavery today.

HARVEY WINJE is a first-generation American, born in 1940 in the community named in the 1960s for the abolitionist Wendell Phillips, and serves as the volunteer editor of *The Alley*, a monthly newspaper. He is a carpenter, small-business owner, great-grandfather, and an inveterate keeper of history and building parts. SUSAN ANN GUST, who first moved to the Phillips Community in 1973, is a local development consultant and co-owner of a small business with Harvey Winje. She is currently involved in several local and national initiatives working on research equity, valuing cultural knowledge, and building models of shared governance in community-academic partnerships. DAVE MOORE, who moved into Phillips in 1983, and partner Linnea Hadaway have observed waves of change in the Phillips neighborhood for over thirty years, while working in medicine, literature, and education. Encouraged by former *Alley* editor Steve Compton, they began the "Spirit of Phillips" cartoon series in 1987. Enthralled by the Wendell Phillips presented in the Sherwin biography that Harvey lent them, they still have not yet returned the book.

PETER WIRZBICKI is finishing his dissertation at New York University, "Black Intellectuals, White Abolitionists, and Revolutionary Transcendentalists: Creating the Radical Intellectual Tradition in Antebellum Boston." It focuses on the impact of transcendentalism, African American intellectual traditions, and European radicals. He is the recipient of an ACLS/Mellon Dissertation Completion Fellowship as well as the Suzanne and Caleb Loring Fellowship on the Civil War, Its Origins, and Consequences.

DONALD YACOVONE, former Manager of Research and Program Development at the Hutchins Center's W. E. B. Du Bois Institute at Harvard University, has taught at Pitzer College, the University of Arizona, and Millersville University of Pennsylvania and was an Editor at the Black Abolitionist Papers project. He also served as the Senior Associate Editor at the Massachusetts Historical Society, where he founded and edited the *Massachusetts Historical Review.* An expert in Victorian manhood, the antislavery movement, and the Fifty-fourth Massachusetts Regiment, he has published seven other books, including *The African Americans: Many Rivers to Cross* with Henry Louis Gates, Jr.

INDEX